COUNTING NEW BEANS

intrinsic impact and the value of art

featuring

MEASURING THE INTRINSIC IMPACT OF LIVE THEATRE

the final report on the landmark two-year intrinsic impact theatre study from research firm **WOLFBROWN** and authors **ALAN BROWN** and **REBECCA RATZKIN**

essays by
ARLENE GOLDBARD, CLAYTON LORD, REBECCA NOVICK and **DIANE RAGSDALE**

and interviews with
Susan Atkinson ~ Keith Baker ~ Anne Bogart ~ Dudley Cocke ~ David Dower
Oskar Eustis ~ Steven Glaudini ~ Taylor Greenthal ~ Rachel Grossman ~ Todd Haimes
David Kilpatrick ~ Jessica Kubzansky ~ Martha Lavey ~ Barry Levine ~ Rob Melrose
Bonnie Metzgar ~ Michael Michetti ~ Terrence Nolen ~ Diane Paulus ~ Jill Rafson
Bill Rauch ~ Jack Reuler ~ Michael Rohd ~ Howard Shalwitz ~ Tony Taccone
Sarah Taines ~ Sydni Taines ~ Sixto Wagan

with a foreword by **BEN CAMERON** *and introduction by* **BRAD ERICKSON**

edited by **CLAYTON LORD**

theatre Published by Theatre Bay Area
1663 Mission Street, Suite 525, San Francisco, CA 94103

COUNTING NEW BEANS: INTRINSIC IMPACT AND THE VALUE OF ART.
Copyright © 2012 by Theatre Bay Area and the various authors.

Design by Clayton Lord

Cover image: "Bean Farmer" by bahuvrihi from Flickr, used under Creative Commons license.
http://www.flickr.com/photos/bahuvrihi/1658718613/

Visit www.theatrebayarea.org or www.intrinsicimpact.org

Printed in the United States of America

First Printing: March 2012

ISBN 978-0-9851452-0-0

Theatre Bay Area's mission is to unite, strengthen, promote and advance the theatre community in the San Francisco Bay Area, working on behalf of our conviction that theatre and all the arts are an essential public good, critical to a healthy and truly democratic society, and invaluable as a source of personal enrichment and growth.

To find out more about intrinsic impact, or to start conducting intrinsic impact surveys for your own organization, please visit:

www.theatrebayarea.org/intrinsicimpact

or

www.intrinsicimpact.org

Table of Contents

8   Acknowledgements

13   Introduction
by Brad Erickson

17   Foreword
by Ben Cameron

21   **CHAPTER 1: CHANGING THE CONVERSATION**

  23   Sowing New Beans: The Making of Memory
and the Measuring of Impact
by Clayton Lord

  55   Creative Destruction
a conversation with Diane Ragsdale

65   **CHAPTER 2: QUANTIFYING ARTISTIC IMPACT**

  67   Understanding the Intrinsic Impact of Live Theatre: Patterns
of Audience Feedback across 18 Theatres and 58 Productions
by Alan Brown and Rebecca Ratzkin, WolfBrown

    69 Overview of the Study
    71 Key Themes and Findings
    76 Methodology & Response Rates
    84 Motivations for Attending
    93 Demographic Results (Age and Gender)
  100 Decision Role and Ticket Type
  105 Annual Frequency of Attendance
  108 Comparisons of Impact and Readiness Results for Different Types
of Theatrical Productions
  119 Illustrative Results for Select Productions
  126 Illustrative Results for Select Theatres
  131 Who Leaves with Unanswered Questions?
  136 Pre- and Post-Performance Engagement
  151 Summative Impact
  155 Discussion of Qualitative Data
     155 Unanswered Questions
     158 Emotions
  161 The Appendix: Categorization of Productions by Attribute

165 CHAPTER 3: ASKING ARTISTIC LEADERS ABOUT AUDIENCES

169 The Importance of Beginning: The Changing Relationships of Artists, Organizations and Communities
by Rebecca Novick

189 Visualizing the Artist-Audience Relationship
Word clouds

211 Artistic Leaders in Conversation

213 Anne Bogart   *SITI Company*
219 Howard Shalwitz & Rachel Grossman   *Woolly Mammoth Theatre Company*
231 David Kilpatrick   *La Crosse Community Theatre*
239 Bill Rauch   *Oregon Shakespeare Festival*
251 Steven Glaudini   *Musical Theatre West*
257 Martha Lavey   *Steppenwolf Theatre Company*
262 Rob Melrose   *The Cutting Ball Theater*
267 Sixto Wagan   *DiverseWorks*
272 Todd Haimes & Jill Rafson   *Roundabout Theatre Company*
279 Oskar Eustis   *Public Theater*
283 Jessica Kubzansky & Michael Michetti   *The Theatre @ Boston Court*
291 Susan Atkinson & Keith Baker   *Bristol Riverside Theatre*
300 Tony Taccone   *Berkeley Repertory Theatre*
308 Michael Rohd   *Sojourn Theatre*
316 Jack Reuler   *Mixed Blood Theatre*
323 Dudley Cocke   *Roadside Theater*
333 Terrence Nolen   *Arden Theatre Company*
339 David Dower   *Arena Stage*
347 Bonnie Metzgar   *About Face Theatre*
357 Diane Paulus   *American Repertory Theatre*

367 CHAPTER 4: THE VALUE OF ART

371 Symposium: Seven Characters in Search of an Audience (with apologies to Plato)
by Arlene Goldbard

407 The Patrons Speak

408 Taylor Greenthal
417 Barry Levine
425 Sydni and Sarah Taines
439 Sean McKenna

447 CHAPTER 5: GLOSSARY

457 BIOGRAPHIES OF CONTRIBUTING AUTHORS

Acknowledgements

This research, commissioned by Theatre Bay Area, was conducted by Alan Brown and Rebecca Ratzkin of the research firm WolfBrown, by independent arts consultants Rebecca Novick and Erin Gilley and by Theatre Bay Area's Clayton Lord. The project manager was Clayton Lord. The research was generously supported by The Doris Duke Charitable Foundation, The Andrew W. Mellon Foundation, The National Endowment for the Arts, The Pew Center for Arts & Heritage, The San Francisco Arts Commission Cultural Equity Grants, The City of San Jose Office of Cultural Affairs, Theatre Development Fund, Arts Midwest, The LA Stage Alliance and the Helen Hayes Awards/theatreWashington.

ART SERVICES ORGANIZATION PARTNERS
Theatre Bay Area, *San Francisco Bay Area, CA*
LA Stage Alliance, *Los Angeles, CA*
Arts Midwest, *Minneapolis/St. Paul, MN*
A.R.T./New York, *New York, NY*
Theatre Alliance of Greater Philadelphia, *Philadelphia, PA*
Helen Hayes Awards/theatreWashington, *Washington, DC*

THEATRE COMPANY RESEARCH PARTICIPANTS
Arden Theatre Company, *Philadelphia, PA*
Arena Stage, *Washington, DC*
Berkeley Repertory Theatre, *Berkeley, CA*
Bristol Riverside Theatre Company, *Bristol, PA*
City Lights Theater Company, *San Jose, CA*
La Crosse Community Theatre, *La Crosse, WI*
MetroStage, *Alexandria, VA*
Mixed Blood Theatre, *St. Paul, MN*
Musical Theatre West, *Los Angeles, CA*
Park Square Theatre, *St. Paul, MN*
People's Light & Theatre, *Malvern, PA*
Public Theater, *New York, NY*
Roundabout Theatre Company, *New York, NY*
South Coast Repertory, *Costa Mesa, CA*
The Cutting Ball Theater, *San Francisco, CA*
The Pearl Theatre Company, *New York, NY*
The Theatre @ Boston Court, *Pasadena, CA*
Woolly Mammoth Theatre Company, *Washington, DC*

ARTISTIC LEADER INTERVIEWEES

Susan Atkinson and Keith Baker, Bristol Riverside Theatre Company
Anne Bogart, SITI Company
Dudley Cocke, Roadside Theater
David Dower, Arena Stage
Oskar Eustis, Public Theater
Steven Glaudini, Musical Theatre West
Todd Haimes and Jill Rafson, Roundabout Theatre Company
David Kilpatrick, La Crosse Community Theatre
Jessica Kubzansky and Michael Michetti, The Theatre @ Boston Court
Martha Lavey, Steppenwolf Theatre Company
Rob Melrose, The Cutting Ball Theater
Bonnie Metzgar, About Face Theatre
Terrence Nolan, Arden Theatre Company
Diane Paulus, American Repertory Theatre
Bill Rauch, Oregon Shakespeare Festival
Jack Reuler, Mixed Blood Theatre
Michael Rohd, Sojourn Theatre
Howard Shalwitz and Rachel Grossman, Woolly Mammoth Theatre Company
Tony Taccone, Berkeley Repertory Theatre
Sixto Wagan, DiverseWorks

PATRON INTERVIEWEES

Taylor Greenthal
Barry Levine
Sean McKenna
Sydni and Sarah Taines

SPECIAL THANKS

We would like to thank the following people for their support of and engagement with this work. Emika Abe, Ellys Abrams, Victoria Bailey, Timothy Baker, Chad Bauman, John Beck, Shira Beckerman, Susan Berdahl, Ben Cameron, Polly Carl, Susan Chandler, Deb Clapp, Douglas Clayton, Brett Conner, Leah Cooper, Stephanie Deras, Pj Doyle, Ron Evans, Susan Feder, Rachel Fink, Amanda Folena, Adam Frank, Alison French, Claudine Gawin, Erin Gilley, Taylor Gramps, Carolyn Griffin, Kerry Hapner-Adams, Jeffrey Hermann, Tom Holm, Alli Houseworth, Sunil Iyengar, Tom Kaiden, Fran Kumin, Michael Kyrioglou, Gigi Lamm, Karen Lane, Carol Lanoux Lee, Kendra Lawton, Linda Levy Grossman, Julia C. Levy, Ginny Louloudes, Lisa Mallette, Shannon Marcotte, Terence McFarland, Susan Medak, Seth Miller, Ian David Moss, Michael-jon Pease, Catherine Peterson, Frances Phillips, Brian Polak, Sam Read, Debbie Richards, Beth Richardson, Beth Richardson, Margie Salvante, Bil Schroeder, Kary Schulman, Aaron Schwartzbord, Yelena Seyko, Holly Sidford, Molly Smith, David Steffen, Katie Turick-Steger, Shawn Stone, Robert Sweibel, Amy Clare Tasker, Christine Taylor, Andrew Taylor, Ben Thiem, Daniel Thomas, Nella Vera, Emily Wilhoit and San San Wong.

"We try to measure what we value.
We come to value what we measure."

- Donella Meadows

Introduction

by **Brad Erickson**
Executive Director, Theatre Bay Area

I first encountered the tenets behind this study as I was breakout surfing at the 2007 National Arts Marketing Project (NAMP) Conference in Miami. I was leaning against a room divider at the back of a session, trying to assess the merits of staying here or moving on. At the front, on a large screen, flashed multi-color charts—the kind of charts one expects to see at a national conference—and at the podium stood a man I would learn was Alan Brown. Alan was reporting on the findings from his recently completed national study commissioned by a cohort of university presenters. Through a mix of factors—aesthetic growth, social bonding, intellectual and emotional engagement—Brown was describing how he assessed the effect of the various productions on their audiences. He was purporting to have measured, to have quantified, the intrinsic impact of the art. I stared at the screen. I double-checked my conference program. I stared back at the screen, looked at Alan, and thought, "You're measuring what?"

I had been introduced to this phrase, "the intrinsic impact of the arts experience," just that previous spring, lying by a pool in Palm Springs, reading the then-newly released RAND study Gifts of the Muse. Poring through it, I came upon a passage that described how for years, advocates trying to describe the value of the arts had "borrowed language from the social sciences" and focused on what they hoped everyone could agree had value.

"The arts," the authors asserted, "are said to improve test scores... to be good for business and a stimulus to the tourist industry... They are even said to be a mechanism for urban revitalization." The arguments of the day sought to justify the arts through their worthy, but ultimately secondary, instrumental benefits. But, the authors emphasized, "people are not drawn to the arts for their instrumental effects, but because the arts can provide them with meaning and with a distinctive type of pleasure and emotional stimulation." What we needed to be studying and talking about were the deep intrinsic impact of the arts.

I slammed the book down on the patio tile and reflexively cried, "Yes!" Which drew glances from the other hotel guests. And which also left me immediately wondering how was I going to stand before lawmakers in Sacramento or San Francisco's City Hall and cite, with a straight face, what the authors claimed were the arts' truest benefits: "captivation" and "pleasure."

Just a few years earlier, California had slashed funding for the arts by 97%. Around the country, we were watching the arts lose support from government and private sources alike—and many of us surmised that the traditional arguments were not making the case. We had been trying to describe the sun and could speak only of the corona—the halo of test scores and economic activity that surround the bright center of the arts. We had no means to assess the thing itself. And there was Alan, standing at a podium, telling us that it was, in fact, possible to measure—not just wax poetical about—the glowing orb of the arts experience. This was exciting.

After the NAMP session, I pressed my way over to Brown, pumped his hand and got his card. A year later, with support from the Doris Duke Charitable Foundation, Theatre Bay Area commissioned WolfBrown to conduct a pilot study looking into the intrinsic impact Free Night of Theater performances on audiences here in the Bay Area, and the intriguing results and the enthusiasm of our region's theatre community (80 companies volunteered to participate in the study) made us eager to pursue this line of inquiry more deeply. As a service organization, we value research of all kinds, but we are especially drawn to studies that can demonstrably advance the work of our members, to inquiries that can empower artists and administrators to move the field forward. By measuring the intrinsic impact of their work on their audiences, theatres were finding a new way to ask, and answer, a fundamental question, "What are we trying to do with this play, with this production, and are we doing it?"

We were eager to take the inquiry deeper, to push it further. What if we sat down with a theatre's leaders before a production, talked about their thoughts around intrinsic impact, asked them to set goals, measured the results, and returned to reflect on the findings? What if we did this over an entire season? What if we conducted a national study, with 18 diverse theatres, in six major theatre centers across the country? What would we find?

You have in your hands what we found after two years of planning, research and analysis—the culmination of the largest research project we've ever overseen. We could not have done it alone.

In making this study possible, we are enormously grateful for the early and continued support of the Doris Duke Charitable Foundation and the leadership of Ben Cameron. We are humbled by a cohort of renowned funders who have joined together to back this work. And we are indebted to our fellow service organizations for their enthusiastic participation in the project.

We are amazed by the vision and intellectual rigor of Alan Brown, Rebecca Ratzkin and the whole research team of WolfBrown. We are enriched by the contributions of thinkers like Diane Ragsdale, Rebecca Novick and Arlene Goldbard. And we are inspired by the 18 theatres that dived into this work so enthusiastically (and the many more who contributed interviews), to their artistic directors and managing directors, the marketers and all the staff who executed the various parts of this research over many months.

Personally, I want to acknowledge the extraordinary commitment, tenacity and keen insight of Clay Lord, who has shepherded this sprawling project from its start through the publication of this report and beyond.

We hope to contribute to the national conversation on the meaning and value of the arts. We hope theatres across the country will find in this research a powerful tool for deepening the impact of their work on their audiences. And we hope that someday soon measuring the intrinsic impact of the art experience on the audience will become as commonplace—and as crucial—as counting box office receipts.

Because it's true what they say: what we measure is what we value.

Foreword

by **Ben Cameron**
Program Officer for the Arts, Doris Duke Charitable Foundation

As someone long engaged in arts advocacy, I've always been a bit uneasy about how we talk about our value to legislators and policymakers. While yes, absolutely, I do believe the arts have enormous economic and educational impact and that these are powerful arguments, do artists really create work to leverage additional dollars for the local economy? Do audiences really go to the theatre to drive local SAT scores higher? And are we setting ourselves up for disaster if we discover other economic drivers or educational enhancements are more powerful in these goals than the arts?

In 2004, Kevin McCarthy and the RAND Corporation published *Gifts of the Muse*, a report that distinguished the arts' "extrinsic" values—the above mentioned collective benefits of economic impact or enhanced educational performance or even neighborhood safety that accrue to a community through the presence of the arts—from the "intrinsic" values—that landscape of emotional and intellectual, transformative experiences that impact an individual engaging with the arts. Here were values to claim, not *instead* of the extrinsic, but *in addition* to them—values that seemed more authentic and critical to artmaking. But recognizing the value of the quantifiable in advancing any cause, how could such experiences—experiences like captivation or empathy—actually be measured?

Alan Brown has been one of the great leaders in stepping up to this challenge, working with artists, arts organizations and audiences to define more precisely the intrinsic value of the work they offer. As his studies have grown in number and embraced different disciplines, the excitement from organizations with whom he has worked—organizations who have found his work revelatory, realistic and actionable—has grown.

In 2010, he and Theatre Bay Area approached the Doris Duke Charitable Foundation (where we had helped fund research efforts in theatre, jazz, presenting and dance) to seek funding for the creation of an "artistic dashboard," a low-cost audience research method that would enable individual arts organizations to measure and understand the intrinsic impact of their work on their audiences and would offer additional support to train people in how to use it.

All of our grants are decided by peer panels, rather than by Foundation staff, and this proposal initially set off some alarms. How would artistic directors respond to their work being measured in such a way? Would this information drive the choice of repertoire in a way that would subvert the role of the artistic leader? Would it become a bludgeon of sorts for boards to use in dismissing artistic leaders at theatres where intrinsic impact in some dimensions was low? Would this compound what some saw as an already troubling trend toward audience pandering?

Other panelists argued passionately for this work, noting the steady erosion of audiences as TCG's annual report, *Theatre Facts*—which shows rising aggregate earned revenue through escalating ticket prices while the actual body count dwindles—attest. In a time when audiences are overwhelmed with choices, how do we compete for their leisure time? Do we even really know why they come—and (conversely) why they stay away? If we listened more carefully to what our audiences *do* value—instead of to what we *think* they value—what would we do with that information? What if we find that what drives them to our theatres is more the social experience than the aesthetic? What if we find that the impact of our work is not as deep as we had thought? Or what if we find that there is more hunger for a kind of experimentation and risk than we had anticipated? That our impact is even deeper? Could this become transferable to other fields? Could what we learn change, not only our marketing, but our approach in advocacy as well? And might it even be possible that understanding our audiences could somehow make our work better?

There was no question from any panelist that the work Alan and Theatre Bay Area were proposing was doable, thoughtful and thorough. There was no question that it addressed real and urgent needs. There was no question that Theatre Bay Area, under the extraordinary leadership of Brad Erickson, was fully equipped and logically positioned to be the organizational harbor and coordinator of this effort. The final comment that provoked one of those bell-like moments of clarity came from an initially skeptical panelist, who said quietly, "This is smart. Rigorous, but realist, intellectually generous, passionate and compelling."

Needless to say, they got the grant. And the pages that follow are the fruits of that labor—the results of hard work and changes in direction at times and evolving formats, but true to the original spirit.

The collection you hold is a rich and juicy read. The data is impressive in its scope and precision: there are more than a few light bulb moments, some confirming what we may have been groping towards but unable to express, others challenging some of our most sacred assumptions. The interviews that accompany the data—interviews with artists and arts leaders who share their impressions of this information for us—remind us of how complex this work can be. Read Diane Paulus and Michael Rohd and Tony Taccone and Martha Lavey, about how the audience factors into choice of productions and into shaping the work itself, and you'll begin to appreciate how differently this data can resonate. Indeed, their interviews are a prelude to the debate and discussion that we hope will happen with colleagues and staffs and, yes, boards of directors about what these studies mean for us and our audiences, wherever we are and whoever we may be.

I've never forgotten a story told to me by Cornerstone Theater founder (and now Oregon Shakespeare Festival artistic director) Bill Rauch. He recounted an early residency undertaken by the company in a small Kansas community of less than a thousand people (I think), where they were mounting *Tartuffe*, a production in which (as is Cornerstone's practice) the leading roles were undertaken by local citizens while the professional artists played secondary roles. Bill and his colleagues were especially excited by the timeliness of this production, coming at the same time that the Jim and Tammy Faye Baker scandals were rocking the country: what a wonderful opportunity to skewer religious fundamental hypocrisy.

And yet as rehearsals progressed, the play never seemed to "catch fire." The actors all knew their lines, they clearly were doing their best to please Bill, there was a sense of collegiality in the room, yet that elusive spark that makes a play combust rather than merely consume time had yet to appear. And then

Bill began talking less and listening more to the way, not that *he* talked about the play, but that the local *citizens* talked about the play. Their conversation kept returning again and again to Act IV, when Tartuffe, confronted with his own misdeeds, storms out of the house, vowing revenge, threatening to return with officers to drive the family out of house and home, and to Act V when he returns, eviction letter in hand.

And Bill realized that, for these struggling farmers in rural Kansas, *Tartuffe* was not about religious hypocrisy. It was about federal farm foreclosure. And as he surrendered control of the play to the community and to what they valued, the play came alive.

It changed the way that Bill worked—and works. It transformed the audience connection to the play. And it made the work better.

I thought about that story often as I read this report. Just as Bill's community told him what they valued, our audiences will tell us what they value. If only we will listen.

This study reminds us in a measurable and concrete way that what we often suppose our audiences experience and what they themselves experience are often not synonymous. It reminds us that the social dimension of our work is, in some cases and for some groups, as important—or even more important—than the aesthetic dimension. It reminds us that our "audience" is really many audiences, plural, and that an overwhelming number of them are open and eager to tell us generously, passionately, insightfully what they do value and what our work means to them.

Knowledge is power, and knowing what our audiences value does not dictate what we must do. Rather it opens the door for us to confirm, to distill, to imagine, to change, depending on who we are and what we hear.

On behalf of all of us at the Doris Duke Charitable Foundation, our deepest thanks to Alan Brown, Brad Erickson, Theatre Bay Area and the 18 theatres that have been brave enough to undertake this work. It has been our true honor and privilege to support your efforts.

Keep listening. And happy reading.

1 CHANGING THE CONVERSATION

Sowing New Beans
The Making of Memory and the Measuring of Impact

by **Clayton Lord**

When she was eleven months old, my infant daughter, Cici, learned how to ride a rocking horse. Her grandmother taught her. Cici was scared of the rocking horse at first, but eventually got over that fear, and then she rocked it back and forth gently, then more forcefully, and then like a little tiny madwoman racing away from a burning barn. Once she had learned it, she loved it. She did it often; she did it well. Whenever we went over to Grandma's house, she made a beeline for the horse, petted its mane, climbed up, with some help, and pressed the little button secreted in the tip of the horse's floppy ear that made it neigh and whinny. Then she'd smile and giggle and launch herself forward and back, precarious, uncaring, happy with this new trick and enjoying it with abandon.

About a month later, Cici received a large plastic dump truck for her birthday. We showed her how to put stuff in the back and then flip it up, and she laughed whenever the various odds and ends spilled out onto the floor. But when we left her to her own devices, she mostly ignored the truck, and when she did play with it, she would—instead of filling up the back—simply flip up the bright yellow bed, revealing the black undercarriage, straddle the middle of the truck and begin to bounce back and forth. Cici, it turns out, was interacting with the dump truck in the best way she knew how—by treating it as a rocking horse. A month in, she'd become comfortable with the idioms of riding the rocking horse—she made a "click-click-click" sound with her mouth

23

to imitate a horse's hooves, she petted the mane (even when the only mane was plastic and red and sat behind the driver's seat) and held onto the doors like reins. When presented with a changed situation, she simply transferred the old idioms to the new obstacle.

That's, I think, where we are in terms of valuing and evaluating the impact of art. As an industry, the arts suffer from a value problem, because we keep trying to ride a rocking horse even when it has turned into something else.

All over the country, arts organizations attempt to justify their existence by talking about two things: anecdote and economics. That's our rocking horse. We learned it thirty or forty years ago, after the great enlightenment of the Kennedy years gave way to the darkness after, when we were told that talking about feeding the soul wasn't going to get us the bucks unless it came with some easy-to-digest numbers and graphics attached. As much as it might have once been the case that the leaders of our world truly believed, as Kennedy did, that "this country cannot be materially rich and spiritually poor," it seems increasingly that the material aspect of what we do, troublesome and relatively secondary as it might be, is trooped out on demand and modeled as the way we ought to best show ourselves.

For nonprofits, whose true essence sits at zero dollars, artistry is justified in terms of money in and money out. This is a problem—especially now. Because it's one thing to make economic arguments when everyone is flush, but it's another thing to make them when things with "true" economic value (that is to say, economic impact on a much larger scale) are also suffering and seeking support.

Simon Brault, Vice-Chair of the Canada Council for the Arts, argues in his book *No Culture, No Future* that "culture constitutes a dimension of life that precedes and surpasses sectoral and economic concerns." He goes on to articulate that by not considering all of the stuff that sits outside of those sectoral and economic concerns—by not addressing the value conversation holistically—we are disadvantaging ourselves, reducing our own standing within our ranks and forgetting how to speak about the fact that art is, in fact, essential.

But explicating that non-sectoral, non-economic value is difficult, especially for something as impermanent and subjective as art. Incredibly smart, articulate people—people whose livelihoods are based on their ability to be eloquent and linguistically facile—have terrific difficulty succinctly explaining that particular, peculiar power that sits inside our work. But we all

24

know what that value is: we're artists, we believe strongly in the ability of art to stretch across divides, to instill empathy, to educate about new experiences, to encourage creative and critical thought, to transform relationships. More than that, we believe in something even more primal to what we do, pre-language, pre-thought: an *ur*-impulse in art that, upon contact, rearranges something within us when we interact with it, changes our emotional and intellectual make-up in some fundamental way and leaves us different.

So let's talk about that. And let's talk about that in a way that makes sense to people seeking the "certainty" of numbers and graphs.

Alan Brown, the lead researcher for "Measuring the Intrinsic Impact of Live Theatre," the six-city, 18-theatre, 2-year study that has sought to further define a way forward between anecdote and numbers, tells the story of sitting in a presentation by Kevin McCarthy, the lead investigator in the *Gifts of the Muse* study, at the Wallace Foundation offices in New York. *Gifts of the Muse*, about which more later, was the first articulate argument for shifting the conversation away from the "extrinsic" impact of art and toward the "intrinsic" impact. This was prior to the public release, and McCarthy gave a full presentation of the findings and then opened up the floor for questions.

As Brown says, "It was one of those funny moments in a meeting where the floor is opened up for questions, and you have a room full of people and no one is saying anything. So I raised my hand and I said, 'After ten years of heavy emphasis on measurable outcomes, isn't it funny that you're telling us that the real benefits of the arts are intrinsic and can't be measured.'"

And there was more silence in the room. And then Ed Pauly, the evaluation director of the Wallace Foundation, turned his head around and said to Brown, "Alan, if you can describe something you can measure it."

This caught Brown off-guard, and it took him two years of close reading of the report to tease out what might be a manageable way to move forward with Pauly's admonition. Many iterations of that effort later, we have come to this work, the most comprehensive analysis of the actual true intrinsic impact of live theatre ever conducted.

***

David Kilpatrick, the executive director of the La Crosse Community Theatre in La Crosse, Wisconsin, when asked about the surveying and other measurement that he has done with his audience, mentions all the usual suspects—basic demographics, frequency of attendance, relative income. Kilpatrick, who is deeply academic and holds a Ph.D., finds it abhorrent to have to make his measurements in that way, and yet admits that when, as he often does, he has to argue for his community theatre's worth to the community, he mostly does it economically.

Kilpatrick shrugs this off as the simple reality of the day.

"As artists and arts administrators," he says, "we've turned ourselves into bean counters because the people we deal with, what they count is beans."

The truth of this drives me mad.

We make art because we believe it makes better human beings. We make art because we believe it makes being human better. And yet we spend all of our time talking about the fact that one dollar into the arts generates eighteen dollars out. And this line of argument, dangling so much of our own self-perceived value on the numbers we already know how to talk about, has been getting us into trouble.

We talk about economic impact on our communities, about percentage of house sold and number of people served. We are asked to focus on building the largest, most inclusive tent possible for our work, and to ensure a diversity of audience almost without regard for those for whom the work was actually created. We are pressed and pressed to explain economic failure, and at the same time we often understand deep down that the work itself was spectacular. We talk about butts in seats, and dollars per head, and return on dollar-for-dollar investment. We talk about side impacts to restaurants, businesses, parking garages, coffee shops. We count the beans we know how to count, and then present them to other people who know how to count them, and declare ourselves valuable.

But the truth is that we, none of us, got into this work to give more business to the restaurant down the street. We know, deep down, what is valuable in what we do—whether artists, or artistic directors or administrative staff, we strive forward from a place of purpose, driven either abstractly or specifically by a true belief that what we are doing is changing lives.

Per the NEA research note *Time and Money*, the cultural industries contribute $70.9 billion to the U.S. annual GDP—an impressive sum, but the total U.S. annual GDP is $14 trillion, which basically means the entire cultural sector contributes .51% of the entire GDP in any given year. On any given day, 1.5 million people partake in our performing arts events, which sounds impressive—but in any given *year*, per the Survey on Public Participation in the Arts (SPPA), only 34% of the whole US population, or about 78 million people, go to any performing arts at all—and many of those people go only once. Nothing to sneeze at but still, we're relatively tiny—important, but tiny.

In the southern rainforests of India, a sect of Brahmins, or priests, has been singing the same songs for thousands and thousands of years. They pass the songs downward through the generations, taking care that the exact length, intonation, order and speed are maintained. It's a very, very careful process, painstaking and inefficient, but it's also absolutely necessary, because the songs they sing are so old that they're in a language that no one understands anymore. The music has literally outlived the knowledge of the words, making the singing a true act of faith and the passing down of its non-literal attributes fervent and difficult.

I like that story both because it speaks to the ongoing power of art—the transcendence of it beyond the particular meaning, the continuation of its force even after the literal part of you ceases to be able to understand it—and also because it mirrors some of where we are as a field. We seem to have lost our way back to the bridge that will allow us to take our stories and translate them back into the language of numbers without stripping them of their real power. We need a new vocabulary—we need to come up with some new beans that people will be able to count—that speaks more specifically about the parts of art that aren't related to the economic argument. Because it is frustrating, although also fantastic, that we have gotten so good at measuring "things financial" without truly understanding how lacking we are in measuring the stuff that's left when financial things are removed from the table.

***

Noam Chomsky, a linguist and political theorist now known more for the second appellation than the first, outlined a concept in the late 1960's that he called "universal grammar." He was investigating how languages are created and acquired, and he settled on this idea that all of us, from the moment we're born, carry in us common, innate, fundamental rules of grammar and we use that inherent understanding to gradually build up our language comprehension and production.

I often think of art in this way—as the manifestation of something fundamental and internal, built from blocks we all carry with us even if we don't know it. The experience is held within us and activated when we attend

27

a performance or see a painting, and it transforms us into something we were not before.

What we're really talking about here, whether we use the terms "impact," "memory," or "meaning" is the framing that art places on a life. Theologist and author Karen Armstrong has yet another word for it: *myth*. In her book, *A Short History of Myth*, Armstrong argues that myth was in many ways the ordering impulse in human existence for most of time until the dawn of the so-called Age of Reason, when mythological explanations were supplanted by data-based efforts to explain every aspect of the universe. This adoption of science and analytics as the whole basis for explanation of the universe (for many in the population) has led to much uncertainty and a lack of hope and harmony. In the modern context, Armstrong argues, the creation and consumption of art has essentially rushed in to fill that void.

As Armstrong says:

> Today the word "myth" is often used to describe something that is simply not true…When we hear of gods walking the earth, of dead men striding out of tombs, or of seas miraculously parting to let a favored people escape from their enemies, we dismiss these stories as incredible and demonstrably untrue…We have developed a scientific view of history; we are concerned above all with what actually happened…but mythology is an art form that points beyond history to what is timeless in human existence, helping us get beyond the chaotic flux of random events, and glimpse the core of reality.

Elsewhere, she puts it more bluntly: "Myth shows us how we should behave."

Myth, or in our particular context, art, also shows us how we *have* behaved. Myths can elicit change by revealing our follies or successes, our foibles. Myth is uncertain, and can waiver and change as our needs and fears as a society waiver and change. It reflects and distills the best advice, the most aspirational hope, that we as a society have to offer in the face of shame and fear and anger. And if we've truly lost our mythology, as Karen Armstrong suggests, then we really are in need of a strong dose of art.

As she closes the book, Armstrong notes that art, "like a myth, teaches us to see the world differently; it shows us how to look into our own hearts and to see our world from a perspective that goes beyond our own self-interest." What makes art so powerful is its ability to show us, in those narrowly personal moments, something so incredibly universal.

In her last line, Armstrong gives a (soft, academic) call to arms. She says, "If professional religious leaders can [no longer] instruct us in mythical lore, our artists and creative writers can perhaps step into this priestly role and bring fresh insight to our lost and damaged world."

It's a problem when we're being called upon to give humanity a new frame in which to function—to cushion the reality of our world, to teach the mistakes of the past, to inspire the future—and then we have to get down to brass tacks to get any money to make that happen. But the truth is, much as we may all love extemporizing about the value of our work, conversations tend to shift back to specifics somewhere between the dream and the dollar. And when you're dealing with people who don't actually work in the arts (and speaking here not just of external interested parties but, for example, board members), who often inherently approach value and evaluation from a financial perspective, there is an expectation that that articulation will occur with graphs and numbers.

The gap between data and anecdote is profound and frustrating, so wide as to make them seem at times like two separate languages—one the common tongue of our boards and legislators and funders, the other the natural way we speak to each other as artistic souls thinking about ourselves and our value. But if we are to carry forward new arguments about arts and arts education that veer less from our natural inclinations as storytellers, we need to construct a bridge between data and story and use it to take skeptics along with us.

We must turn an analytical eye on the previously "unmeasurable" parts of art, to fill the sling with a new set of arrows that might be better received by those we're looking to woo. Incidentally, those are also a better set of measurements for those we seek to serve, whether we're talking about the artists whose generative impulse is interior, amorphous and truly ethereal, or the audience member whose reason for being in your theatre may be anything from a need for a transformative experience to a need not to annoy one's partner by staying home.

Measuring economic indicators as stand-ins for value forces arts organizations to shift away from their core missions. It leads to the problem, highlighted by NEA Chairman Rocco Landesman, of regional theatres shifting away from their founding principles as incubators for emergent local work in favor of the same slate of 15 plays seen everywhere else in the country that happen to be more economically viable. And, perhaps more dangerous, it starts framing what we do economically to government officials, which moves art from "essential public good" to "esoteric luxury."

The author Barbara Kingsolver, in her book *High Tide in Tucson*, writes about wants and needs, and the difference. She says, "Want is a thing that unfurls unbidden like fungus, opening large upon itself, stopless, filling the sky. But needs, from one day to the next, are few enough to fit in a bucket, with room enough left to rattle like brittle brush in a dry wind."

Art, and the expression of empathy, emotion and connectedness that goes along with art, is as fundamental a need as anything else that would rattle around in that bucket, but it's clear to me that not many others think that way. Under the auspices of personal freedom and lack of government interference, the fringe right is attacking the very existence of government-subsidized culture in the United States as an affront to their right to hold only their own point of view. Sarah Palin and her ilk have advocated for the dissolution of the National Endowment for the Arts, essentially saying that the agency's already miniscule annual budget (equivalent to one-half of one day of war expenses for the United States) should be re-appropriated. Arts education continues to disappear from schools, as it has for the last three decades—it's not even really a part of the conversation anymore, as much as some of our best and brightest try to shift STEM to STEAM.

We find ourselves pressed against a mightily fractured world being run by a series of generations who have, by and large, had little or no sustained education in (or using) the arts, and who consequently are acting like people that don't care about a looming loss simply because that loss has never been personally felt. As Diane Ragsdale says in her interview later in this book, "We have ignored the larger part of society for so long that they no longer think that we're important—*and* they have evidence that we're not important in their lives because they haven't been going, nobody that they know has been going, and they're all doing fine."

We have accidentally convinced people that art is primarily a transactional good: a luxury, not a necessity. We may have even convinced ourselves to a degree. We have encouraged ourselves, our organizations, our funders, to lose focus, to miss the true impact of art: empathy, intellectual stimulation, artistic growth, emotional resonance, social connection, escape.

Of course, the argument goes, none of those things can only be achieved through art. And even if that were true, are those things really *necessary* in society, or just nice?

How can that be a valid point of view? How can we have so marginalized ourselves that people can legitimately believe that a world that doesn't teach its children empathy, doesn't allow them to understand their emotions, doesn't provide them tools to bond with people like and not like themselves, doesn't allow them a break from reality every once in a while, is going to be okay?

We have encouraged a mindset in which a world without art is "not as good" as one with it, yes, but we have equally encouraged a mindset in which a world without art is still a functional alternative. Sure, if that theatre shuts its doors, those other businesses are going to lose some traffic, but, when you're counting the beans we count, the loss of this art or that art, seen in purely economic terms, is manageable. By not formulating and disseminating a vocabulary about the arts that includes terms for explaining the intrinsic impacts of the work we do on the people who watch us do it, we're turning off the part of the conversation that is about what a world without art would do to the people living in it.

It's a hard place to find ourselves in, a shrinking minority in a country with very little love for something that has been framed (by both them and us) as a luxury, a "want" instead of a "need." It is even harder when we find ourselves grasping for the tools necessary to bridge what is a difficult gap, between those who, at this point, inherently care because they have experienced the power of art, and those that simply don't.

For years, our visualizations of our value have been filled with things that are only a small part of what we believe make art vital. But by the metrics we've spent all our time measuring, we're really not that successful. Where we are successful, and wildly so, is in manufacturing moments that transform individuals, make better human beings, and create transcendent memories that inform the way people live their lives. We need to start valuing ourselves in this way, understanding our impacts beyond economics for ourselves, and then we can start explaining our case to our government representatives, our funders, and the 305.5 million U.S. citizens who don't participate in our arts activities on any given day.

Arts advocate and theorist Arlene Goldbard, whose essay, "Symposium," occurs later in this book, put our conundrum eloquently in a speech she gave at the 2011 Association of Performing Arts Service Organizations conference in Austin, Texas:

> The best argument for arts education is that children today practice endlessly interacting with machines, developing a certain type of cognitive facility. But without the opportunity that arts education affords to face human stories in all their diversity and particularity, to experience emotional responses in a safe space and rehearse one's reactions, to feel compassion and imagine alternative worlds, their emotional and moral development will never keep pace.

We know all of this. We know the conundrums, maybe not coherently, but in some sense. And yet, in almost everything we do to advocate for the arts, to even discuss the arts simply among ourselves, we place financial worth front and center, and in so doing we allow, even encourage, the people we're trying to convince of art's value to forget that that value is much more than economic.

We are able to fairly easily express our value and impact in terms of sales numbers, butts in seats, community economic impact. We love our anecdotes, but they're non-specific (or perhaps too specific), easily dismissed in a way because they're *that* guy's experience, not mine. For better or worse, many of the arbiters of our financial fate trust numbers to tell the story of the masses, and so without a common language and a common set of metrics that allow us to really bridge the gap between the anecdote and the data, we're kind of at a loss.

We are very comfortable talking with audience members about their experience of the art, but are, by and large, deeply uncomfortable with the idea of translating that experience into something numeric. There's a fear that by tracking some amount of the artistic experience an individual has through graphs and charts, we are somehow reducing that experience to something "less than." And what's important to be said here is that, while it's unfortunate that it's a fear, that sentiment is true: asking people questions that can be answered on scales will never really give a complete, round view of the entire experience of an artistic piece. And yet.

Intrinsic impact measurement, or impact assessment, is based in the tenet that anything is measurable if you can only learn to accurately describe what you're looking to measure. It rests in the belief that the intangible aspect of the art, while never knowable in a complete way, is more knowable than it has been, and that by learning to measure and talk about the intellectual, emotional, social and empathetic impact of art on an individual using *standard metrics* and a *common vocabulary*, we can move the conversation forward in a dynamic and new way.

The way Alan Brown puts this is: envision the artistic process as a beautiful, elusive wild animal, walking down a riverbed, stalking through the land so quickly that it's impossible to catch a glimpse of the real thing. Brown notes, "You can never see the animal itself, it's gone. But you sure as hell can see its footprint, and you can measure the footprint, and you can infer from the footprint about the animal itself."

Brown continues: "We can either throw our hands in the air and say, 'Art is too complex, too complicated, and the way it works on people is unknowable so we're not going to even try.' Or you can say, 'We'll never fully understand how art works on people, but we can describe its effects, and we can ask people about them, and we might learn something.'"

***

One Saturday in 2011, I took a drive through a ferocious late spring rainstorm to the house of an eleven-year-old theatregoer named Sydni. I was interviewing Sydni and her mother, Sarah—you can read the resulting transcript deeper inside—as part of an effort to gather a set of interviews from a small group of everyday theatre patrons, which in turn was a way of trying to understand why they go to theatre, why they value it and what it means to them.

We were videotaping the interviews in hopes of crafting advocacy materials, so when we arrived I chitchatted with Sydni and her mother, Sarah, while the video and lights got set up. Sydni was shy, talking into the chicken soup she was eating for breakfast, refusing to look at me, deflecting by talking about and chasing her cats. We sat down once everything was set, Sydni snuggled with Sarah, and began.

The question set eases interviewees in with basic questions about themselves, who they are, what they like doing with their spare time. The interviewee catalogs her life in terms of the things that make her feel fulfilled—in other words, she is asked to strip away everything and only focus on the things that hold (and make) meaning within her life. And then she's asked to think about all of those activities and to try to connect the dots. What are the common threads, what do those specific activities say about you? Why are those activities the things that come up? What themes emerge, and what do they mean? Only then do any questions about the arts come into it at all.

This gradual peeling of the individual, taking her by the hand and encouraging her to draw conclusions about her experiences and choices, allows interviewees to be surprisingly eloquent about how the various parts of their lives are connected and, when primed with those connections, to speak coherently and forcefully about how the arts, and particularly theatre, fit into the schema.

Eventually, the interviewee is asked to think hard and discuss a specific, memorable theatre experience in extreme detail. When asked to delve into a specific memorable theatre experience, eyes tear up, voices get breathless and excited, bodies become frenetic, bouncing around the frame and then sitting stock still, gesticulating to make sure the magnitude of the memory is apparent. When, in turn, asked why theatre matters, the big core question, and why they're passionate about the arts, and what a world without theatre would be like, the interviewees speak with a vociferous forcefulness that is a dream for the interviewer.

Well, usually. It turns out that with an introverted, artistic, awkward eleven-year-old girl, words seem to fail—though I can vouch, Sydni does love theatre, that's clear. She has seen *Wicked* eight times in her short life, starting right after the show opened in 2003 (when, incidentally, she was four years old). On the wall of her bedroom hangs what can only be described as a small shrine to the show, centered on an autographed posterette of the original New York cast and surrounded by ticket stubs, buttons, a raffle card from the *Wicked* lottery and, most touchingly, a single green feather that escaped a costume and floated into Sydni's lap during one of the shows, gently pasted to the bottom left corner of the frame.

This is a girl who not only saw her own middle school's play this year, for which she was the spotlight operator, but who also went to see the local high school's play and not one but two of the local elementary school plays. When asked directly, she says she likes theatre, plans on seeing more theatre as she grows up, plans on being in more productions (though only backstage).

And yet for all that, her shyness forces short answers, monosyllables spoken into her chest as she nervously plays with her hair or follows one or the other of her cats with her eyes as they dart around the room. When I ask her to talk to me about *Wicked*, she summarizes the show very literally, listing out the characters one by one and then briefly summarizing the scene chronology in the play. She says, "It's about things that happen before Dorothy. And so it kind of, like, gives explanation about the Tin Man and the Lion and the Scarecrow. And then it shows how the Wicked Witch of the West became wicked. And then it showed how Galinda and the Wicked Witch of the West were like friends but then…it just showed that. And then it showed how the monkey became flying."

When I ask her why she likes going to theatre, she says that she likes musicals because of the music, and that she thinks that *Wicked* is "cool" and "neat." She often checks in with her mother, their eyes locking as Sarah encourages Sydni to continue. Sydni says seeing the show with a good friend who now lives in Belgium made her "happy," but when I ask her to elaborate her face furrows as she tries to formulate the beginning of the words to describe what she felt and then just as quickly loses the thought to adolescent awkwardness and a lack of confidence. The forming sentence collapses into a quietly mumbled trail, and then silence. Her eyes dart at the bright lights we're using to film and she goes silent and her mother takes over.

Sarah, her mother, is as blunt as, if more articulate than, her daughter. She's the type of woman who, when asked if she's "passionate" about theatre quickly weighs the significance of that word and discards it with a, "No, I'm not passionate," before carrying on to explain that she appreciates the arts, finds them "very important." Sarah and her husband take their two children to as much theatre, of as many types, as possible.

"It opens your mind to other things that are out there, versus just being in your own little cocoon," Sarah says. "I think without the artistic outlets, Sydni wouldn't have an outlet for herself, to express herself."

Sarah goes on: "She's shy, so having the opportunity…does help express who she is and be who she is."

I read all of this in hindsight, in the transcript, and can see a lot of deeply moving water—a mother fighting a shyness in her daughter, seeking out moments in the world where her daughter can relax and be herself and escape—but in the moment, I find myself going off script to throw out obviously leading questions, which Sydni dutifully answers with relatively unusable monosyllabic Yeses and Noes. What was meant to be an hour-long interview is done in half that, and we shut down the cameras. I am at a loss as we begin to pack up, and then her stepfather suggests that Sydni show us some of her artwork.

She perks up, bringing out first a large paint cutout of Minnie Mouse that she proudly says she did at home just because she was bored one day. Sydni, it turns out, loves Disney. She wants to work at Disneyland when she grows up, as a cast member or ride operator. In free moments, when she's not drawing scenes involving the characters from *Wicked*, Sydni draws surprisingly spot-on drawings of other Disney characters, detailed geometric abstractions in marker and colored pencil, forced-perspective drawings of cities and towns, and beautiful, bold color-block drawings of her cats that are as strangely vibrant as they are accurate. Her mom says that the art allows her to let out her feelings, to express what she's not able to say. She says they make her feel like part of something, and it's easy to see in the way Sydni talks about things and draws the world that the art she makes and sees allows her to overlay parameters on her life, make meaning and memory out of the chaotic world.

As we prepared to depart, Sydni went back into her room and returned with one final drawing, this one of the Yellow Brick Road, with Dorothy, the Scarecrow, the Lion, the Tin Man, all of them, arms linked, marching into the distance like the famous scene in the movie. Except the Road had been transplanted into a large and threatening-looking city, each building labeled for what is was used as, all in blues and blacks and grays. At the left, a tall skyscraper, labeled "Jail," stretched from the bottom to almost the top of the page. And sitting on top of it, sketched tinily enough that I missed it until Sydni proudly pointed it out, was the Wicked Witch, escaped from the confines of the jail, green and black, about to launch into the blue, blue sky, watching the heroes dance their way to Oz. It was a psychologist's dream, the artistic translation of so many different threads of adolescent isolation paired with the clearly structured narrative of the *Wicked* story, cold skies, gray buildings and a little witch freed.

When I told Sydni how talented she was, she beamed into her chest, turned and disappeared, not to be seen again. I ducked back out into the rain, shouting goodbyes and driving away.

So. What does that series of experiences mean to Sydni? How much weight can I throw behind her tossing off short statements on camera like, "It's fun to see a new play or whatever I see. I enjoy it?" And how frustrating is it that, after a lot of hard work trying to get her to verbally articulate the kind of person she is—the kind of person who goes to student theatre shows at other schools in the school system without knowing anyone in them—that her most meaningful expressions were silent, articulated on paper with paint and crayons and markers: a giant Minnie Mouse, a drawing of four misfits marching through a grayed-out city and a lovingly-framed set of autographs off-set by a single green feather?

The research Theatre Bay Area commissioned from WolfBrown is both wrapped around and entirely too rudimentary for experiences like Sydni's. And there have been many times along the way when I've been unsure whether we'd really be able to pull this off—in particular whether the "specialness" of the arts is really something that can fit inside a box: standard size, standard packaging, able to be measured against others' experiences, talked about in a vocabulary we all shared.

The measurement of things-beyond-economics is like taking a step into Plato's cave, where all we're viewing is shadows and light, all we're measuring is afterimages of something so unknowable and individual that we can never really get close enough to wrap a measuring tape around its form and write it down. We don't have the animal. We have the footprint. So. Is measuring the footprint enough? In essence, we are trying to understand the way art transforms humanity and, at a micro level, the way it changes a mind, at once and over time. What is the meaning made? What is the role of that memory in a life?

It's good, I think, as part of documenting this project—a project about creating a vocabulary and a measurement system to talk about the intangible power of theatre and art—to be reminded that some things just sit inside us, ours and ours alone. I hope that, when she's older, Sydni is able to articulate what those eight trips to Oz meant to her, how they molded her, what memories they made. But maybe she won't be able to. At any rate, she will always hold those theatrical experiences inside of her, part of her, linking one aspect of her personality to another.

***

What we traffic in is memories. Theatre, particularly, but all the arts, are representations of abstracted or concrete parts of this world, pushed out from artists to audience with the goal of sticking in the head. We are memory makers, and it's important that we try not to forget that when we're building out experience packages and talking about the value we have to audiences in our materials. Daniel Kahneman, a Nobel laureate and founder of behavioral economics, has spoken eloquently about the importance of memory in terms of future experience. Kahneman, who among many other things has deeply researched the phenomena of memory and experience, speaks of two selves: the "remembering self" and the "experiencing self."

Most current measurements of audience satisfaction focus on aspects of the *experience*: were the seats comfortable, was traffic bad, how were the bathroom lines, etc. These are the realm of the experiencing self, and they are all very valuable markers to understand, but ultimately they and a thousand other things swirl together in the mind to create the *memory* of the experience. Memory is what is held onto by the remembering self, and while it's a subtle difference, psychologically it's very important: people choose or don't choose to repeat an activity based on the abstract feelings and impressions that are packaged together in a memory. This is part of why you can have a delicious dinner at a beautiful restaurant, but if the waiter is rude, the entire experience is tainted.

Essentially, in terms of decision-making, the remembering self is the one and only. As Kahneman puts it, "The remembering self [is]...the one that makes decisions...the experiencing self has no voice in this choice. We actually don't choose between experiences, we choose between memories of experiences. And even when we think about the future, we don't think of the future as experiences, we think of the future as anticipated memories."

Memories don't tag every aspect of an experience with equal significance; some things are deemed more important by the brain than others, and often those things are almost entirely unrelated to the central component of the experience (like, say, a child continuously kicking the back of your seat during a play). The memory makes the meaning—it provides you a lens on the world, it triggers empathetic and emotional cues that shift a person back to an earlier state, sometimes just for a flash, sometimes for quite a while and over and over. We, as artists, make memories for people, powerful, complete memories, and in so doing, we traffic in the making of meaning: the translation of the cacophony of life into understandable, memorable moments and the passing on of one person's transformative life experience to another person's narrative, forever.

From researching intrinsic impact, we now know that we can affect the level of impact a production has, and from there, can affect how sticky a performance is—how strong the memory is. One of the findings of WolfBrown's research, written up deeper inside this work, for example, is that anticipation, one of the lead indicators of impact, increases the more familiar a person is with the work they're about to see. In other words, increasing the more a person knows going in (the more prepared they are), the more they anticipate the work, and the more they anticipate the work, the higher the ultimate impacts are. Preparing your patrons for their experience actually sets them up for a better, stronger future memory of the show.

By the same token, patrons who engaged with the performance afterwards—whether through structured post-performance events like talkbacks or through vigorous discussion on their own—reported more intellectual stimulation. Our work primes people's brains more when they engage with it before and after.

Finally, the more impact a patron said a production had on them, the higher they ranked the likelihood of remembering that production a year in the future. This is intuitive, but it's also important: when a production hits you, and hits you hard, that's a strong "anticipated memory," as Kahneman calls it. That's a win.

Barry Levine is a retired finance guy who lives with his wife of forty years in a nice neighborhood in Oakland and an extraordinarily active theatre consumer—he and his wife attend more than 100 arts events *per year*. Barry, who grew up going to see theatre in New York with his father, has strong memories of those special times. For him, as he says, "Art is a human expression. It's a way for people to express themselves to others. We need that. We need those kinds of vehicles."

Later, he continues, "We support the theatre and we're passionate about it because we're always open to surprise, and we just don't know what the next adventure will be. Sometimes there's nothing, but you never know, it could be that one that sticks in your mind forever. That's what theatre is all about, at least as far as we're concerned."

For Barry and his wife, finding those memories is essentially a quest, the ultimate fulfillment of which is a lingering wonderful taste, visceral and able to be lustily, robustly recounted. When I ask him about one such memory, he speaks mesmerizingly and at great length about seeing *Journey's End* in London. This play, about a group of doomed soldiers in World War I heading off to their deaths, ended (in this production) with what the *New York Times* called "one of the most chilling curtain calls ever appended to a commercial drama," in which the actors stood silently in front of a brilliant white wall covered with names of the dead. As Barry described it (with his eyes visibly welling up at the memory):

> So at the end of the play, the guys go over the top. The end of the play. And you hear some gunshots...and that's it. And after the end of the play, after this is all done...the play is over and then, all of a sudden, down from the proscenium arch, there's this big, grayish-white scrim. It comes down and it's got names on it, names of hundreds and hundreds of people who died, British.
>
> In front of that are the members of the cast standing at attention. This thing comes down, they're standing at attention, it's a bright light—and not one person in the audience applauds. Not one. Because of the emotional impact... and I had tears in my eyes. Everybody had tears in their eyes. You could drop a pin and there was no... You couldn't applaud because it was...so emotionally wrenching—and you couldn't applaud because it would seem to be improper that you would do that.
>
> The experience was just amazing. The emotional impact of the stupidity, particularly World War I, the stupidity of it... I mean, it's bringing tears to my eyes right now. It was just an overwhelming experience. You would just walk out of there like, "Wow." You got...*bam.* You got hit like that.
>
> It's one of those things that, when you go to theatre, if something like that happens—it doesn't happen all the time, but when it does happen, it's *live*. It's there in front of you like that. It's just... You have to experience it. It's tough to talk about it. But that's what it felt like. *Boom!* And I'll never forget it, ever.
>
> That's what theatre can do for you. Because it's live; it's right in front of you. There's no distractions, you're just there.

There are a lot of different underlying concepts wrapped up in that recounting. There's the access to history—to the common shared human experience—in this case in the form of the experience of soldiers in World War I. There's the reference to the artistry, the pure stagecraft of the moment. There's the circumvention of expectation—a curtain call without sound, a celebratory moment turned to a solemn one, which seems especially appropriate for a play about death. There's what Barry calls the "emotional impact," both in the moment and, as the tears in Barry's eyes indicate, years later, sitting on his couch in his living room. There's this repeated inarticulate effect, which occurs over and over in interviews, "*Bam!*" and "*Boom!*" – the wallop of an artistic experience smacking into your brain forever. And there's the liveness of it all, the connectedness, the lack of distraction, the singularity, the fragility.

As written about by Diane Ragsdale on her ArtsJournal blog, *Jumper* (and echoed, recently, from a variety of foundations who all seem to be shifting their guidelines to take mission fulfillment more centrally into account), we're heading quickly towards a moment where being able to clearly and concisely discuss the memory impact of a program (as an extension of mission fulfillment) is going to move from a rare desirable to a necessity. As Ragsdale says in her speech/essay, *The Excellence Barrier*: "Success is measured not when the ticket gets sold at the box office, but thirty minutes after the show when everyone is still lingering, buzzing and talking with one another and the artists."

Later in his interview, the text of which has been published as part of this work, Barry says, "Theatre is talking about ideas. And ideas might change your thinking; they might change your viewpoint. I think, just by virtue of getting ideas and listening and seeing different perspectives and things, I think that can change your approach, your life, to some extent. But you don't know it. It's like when you read something. An idea sticks in your head and you change your view on something. It shifts your perspective."

Daniel Kahneman talks about how the life we lead as we move forward in time is dictated by the memories that fill our minds. Like good Pavlovian subjects, we make our decisions about how to move forward based on how we've come—an experience that anyone who still feels queasy at the sight of a food that previously made you sick can understand. In an artistic context, that means that we are, in some small or large way, the sum of the artistic experiences that have stayed with us—the stickiest, the most captivating.

We need to embrace that, to preach the message, and we need to do it differently than we have been. It is time to start trying to sow some new beans, to start quantifying, as best we can, the formerly unquantifiable, most-important-part-of, art. And that's what this book is about. It's about an incredibly exciting, hopefully revolutionary, study that was conducted in 2010 and 2011 throughout the country—the first ever national study of the intrinsic impact of live theatre. In 18 theatres in six cities across the country, almost 19,000 people took the time to complete a survey designed by the research firm WolfBrown, the questions of which made the audacious attempt to quantify the intellectual, social, emotional and empathic impacts of the art we do.

In addition, we interviewed some of the most prominent (and not-so-prominent) artistic directors in the United States to try and understand the complex and thorny relationship of the artist and the audience, and what the role of the organization should be in that relationship. We spoke to major thinkers, funders, audience members and more about how and why we value the arts the way that we do, and what it means that we've gotten ourselves to this place. And we have sifted through all of that in an attempt to develop a new coherent argument for our value—a new vocabulary that will allow us to more accurately express why art matters.

The centerpiece of the book is the full final report of "Measuring the Intrinsic Impact of Live Theatre," a landmark study commissioned by Theatre Bay Area from research firm WolfBrown and researchers Alan Brown and Rebecca Ratzkin. This work, rooted in the concept of measuring intrinsic impact, is the latest step in a long journey for this research. Impact assessment was pioneered in 2006 by WolfBrown following the publication of the RAND Corporation study *Gifts of the Muse*. This study, commissioned and published by the RAND Corporation in 2004, forcefully made the argument that many major organizations were essentially encouraging research and measurement into all the wrong things. In terms of advocacy and research, the report went, organizations were spending a lot of time measuring and figuring out how to talk about what are called the "extrinsic impacts" of art instead of talking about the stuff that was sitting inside of the artistic process—the stuff that makes the arts unique and which allows the arts to impact such a variety of people so profoundly.

Alan Brown, in grappling with *Gifts of the Muse*, developed this graphic (see figure at right), which articulates the impact of an arts experience temporally and from individual to society, and forms the basis for the underlying work that has become the impact assessment constructs. He called this the "Value System for Arts Experience."

42

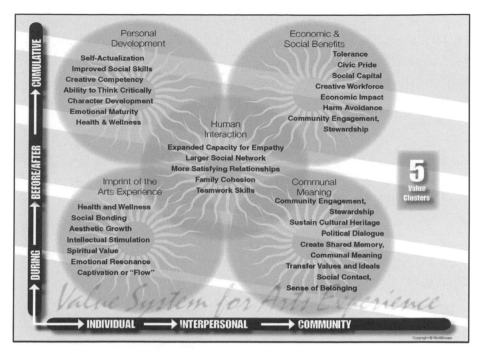

Orienting to this graph, there are five basic "value clusters" for how to talk about the arts, arrayed on two axes—the horizontal axis starts at the individual and moves to the community, and the vertical axis starts at the immediate (i.e. during the performance) and then moves outward to the cumulative (i.e. the overall effect of art over time). Where we, as advocates, spend most of our time is out in the top right cluster, "Economic and Social Benefit"—things like money for the community, supporting artists through wages, increasing tolerance, engaging in civic pride, encouraging people to participate in art so that they aren't, instead, participating in gangs.

In the next layer inward, "Personal Development," "Human Interaction" and "Communal Meaning," you see impacts that are transitioning between the individual and the community, that are happening on different time scales, but are still essentially extrinsic. In fact, of these five clusters, the only one that really focuses on the intrinsic benefit of art is the bottom left cluster: the impacts that occur on an individual during a performance. This cluster is crucial because if you don't have the imprint of an arts experience on an individual in the moment—if that transformative input doesn't occur—then nothing subsequent can occur: no societal growth, no communal pride. If the viewer doesn't experience the art in a way that is "sticky," if they don't move back out into the world after the experience having been changed in some way

43

large or small, then they can't redistribute that change outward, and aren't engaging in any of those other extrinsic benefits that we spend so much time talking about.

Since the publication of the original intrinsic impact study, commissioned by the Major University Presenters in 2006, Alan Brown and his team have conducted various versions of this research here in the US as well as in Australia and the United Kingdom. Our interest, at Theatre Bay Area, got piqued because we found ourselves repeatedly confronted with a particular challenge: we kept coming up against this very limited and inaccurate vocabulary to describe the impact of art, a vocabulary that mostly centered around economics. And among those who were attempting to move away from centering their language around economics, everyone was saying different things—essentially speaking in their own variations of the language: anecdote, impacts on artists, community equity, social engagement, reduced recidivism. Worse, people were using the same terms to mean different things, and were watering down the real value of the conversation by sticking with abstractions, at least until it became a conversation about money, numbers, people who attended, etc, at which point a common vocabulary was achieved, with a lot of negative consequences both internally and externally.

Within organizations, we heard a lot of stories about how hard it was to discuss the actual product across departments without either feeling confused or having one department or another feel disadvantaged or encroached upon. In general, there is an unease, or at least a feeling of complexity, between the artistic staff and the audience—an impulse that informed the second part of this research, conducted by independent consultant Rebecca Novick in the form of 20 interviews with artistic leaders of organizations both inside and outside the WolfBrown study. We felt that, in conjunction with this new level of quantitative work, it was important to also provide a qualitative context for where the artist/audience relationship was starting.

What is the role of the audience in the artistic product? What is the role of the organization in transferring the artistic product's impact to the audience? When does the audience begin to be considered? The answers varied, strongly and powerfully: Diane Paulus, the controversial new artistic director at American Repertory Theatre in Boston, focuses her attention on the audience over the artist almost from the very first conversation about a piece. Martha Lavey, the artistic director of Steppenwolf Theatre in Chicago, looks in the other direction, focusing all of her attention on nurturing projects of, by and for her ensemble to the point of completion before then (thoughtfully) considering how to make sure the audience that comes is along for the ride. There's a lot of room to be responsive to audiences without compromising artistic ideals, and there are many organizations that feel that they are responsive to audiences in a completely healthy way that still allows them to maintain artistic integrity.

That said, most of that responsiveness is based on gut—the so called "feeling of the room." There was not a real viable, standard way to evaluate the artistic product that was being created, in part because the only metrics available answered questions that were different than the ones being asked by the work—questions like how many people came, how much did they pay, how many people stuck around afterwards, how many people came back. Externally, within the field as well as to special interests outside the field (both those seeking information to try and support the arts and, more often, those looking for ways to defund and de-emphasize the role of arts even further in American culture), similar problems existed. Boards, stakeholders, interested parties, funders were, for comfort or ease of comparison, looking for standard metrics to evaluate work, which meant the same beans again and again.

We set out to find those beans.

This study, "Measuring the Intrinsic Impact of Live Theatre," was developed, conducted and analyzed over the course of two years by research firm WolfBrown and primary researchers Alan Brown and Rebecca Ratzkin. The actual research phase covered 10 months from December 2010 to September 2011. It involved 18 theatres in 6 cities across the country, each one surveying three or four productions, for a total of 58 productions. We distributed over 60,000 surveys and received nearly 19,000 surveys back, an amazing number of responses. In the final research report, included in this book, WolfBrown notes that this high response rate is indicative of a hunger on the part of audiences to engage with the work they're seeing in this way. In the other direction, the authors of the study also point out that encouraging this kind of "audience feedback loop," where staff is checking actual audience impact against the assumptions they made about what the work would do, also enriches the audience's experience in a variety of ways.

Put bluntly, asking these questions, in a way, educates the audience about how to engage with the art, because the questions being asked within the research are the questions one would hope an audience member were engaging with in some way without you there—but which they likely are not. Providing these questions, directing the conversation, allows a deeper engagement that may make the experience more lasting and the memory more powerful. The act of providing feedback is in itself a form of aesthetic development in the audience, and allows people to feel like they've had a more direct interaction with the piece over time. It also allows for an important milestone in the customer relationship.

In the course of developing the research methodology that formed the backbone of this study, WolfBrown has identified five constructs of intrinsic impact that interact to create the particular impression, memory or meaning of an artistic event: captivation, aesthetic growth, intellectual stimulation, social bridging and bonding and emotional resonance.

As you'll see as you take a look at the research report from WolfBrown, the particular mix of impacts among these constructs for a particular piece of art can vary. What's important to remember is that any set of scores is completely valid, and success is based more on whether the impacts align with expectations about the work than how they compared to a different show next door. For example, Roundabout Theatre Company's production of *Anything Goes*, the frothy tap musical from Cole Porter, was surely not meant to have the same impact on an audience as Arena Stage's production of the drama *Ruined*. Both productions were deemed "successful" by their producing organizations based on the fact that the expectations and reality for each show (as measured by staff scores versus audience scores for what the impacts were supposed to be and what they were) were relatively aligned. One of the basic tenets of this work is that impact assessment has to happen on the terms of the particular piece of art—it's not about whose work was *more* impactful, it's about how well those impact scores matched with the goals of the artistic staff who slotted in that production.

The alchemy of how these five aspects of impact combine to create a memorable, meaningful, sticky experience is in part the subject of this work, but in a way this research was also as much about technique, uptake and general understanding of the field. Research into intrinsic impact is young and evolving. The nature of the work, the possible uses for such data in terms of articulating value and evaluating success internally and externally, are very much still being investigated. Regardless of that ongoing progress, however, it is clear that by examining these five constructs we can understand more about the nature of the work, the experience that was had and the memory that remains after.

Joseph Stiglitz, the famous economist, said, "What you measure affects what you do. If you measure the right thing, you do the right thing." Part of the problem here, of course, is that we are often not measuring the right thing, and so, in turn, we are not doing the right thing. The conversations we have are built around numbers that put us at a disadvantage externally, and can lead to odd imbalances and unfortunate resentments and siloing of work internally.

We have heard from some of our interviews during this process that there is often a tension between marketing impulses (and departments) and the artistic staff—a feeling that the marketing staff can fall back on reams of data (sales records, audience satisfaction reports, etc) in order to infringe, in a way, on the artistic selection process. This either can manifest as resentment within an organization, if the system functions this way, or as an equally detrimental policy of departmental isolation for fear that the system *will* function this way, in which the marketing staff is kept out of conversations about the upcoming art and is, essentially, presented with a finished palette and told to "figure it out"—and in which, on the other side, marketing materials and strategy are developed without substantial involvement from the artistic staff.

That type of relationship is not wonderful, and those organizations that are excelling at audience engagement and impact have figured out how to harness the inherent tension between artistic and marketing staff and transform it into something that allows each staff more information before, during and after a work (including better methods of assessing whether a piece of art was a success in the context of what it was supposed to do for the organization or audience).

To give all staff members a better context for engaging with the intrinsic impact results, members of the staff are asked to take the survey themselves, prior to opening, with an eye towards what they *think* an audience member's experience of the show will be. By asking staff members in various departments to assess their expectations for a work (based on their experience and conversations internally in their role at the organization), we are able to provide a frame for understanding the ultimate audience response that goes beyond "this production 'did better' than that production," which in this case isn't useful.

Ultimately, the goal is to instigate conversations internally, as staff members attempt to understand what areas are not matching expectations and how they might improve that accuracy going forward. This can allow staff of all types, but particularly artistic staff who had previously lacked much data-based response, to pair anecdotal/qualitative response with more data-driven/

quantitative response to see a fuller picture with more specificity.

Looking at the intrinsic impact of a piece of work also allows staff members to examine all the things that go on around a piece of work. Marketing, artistic and audience development staff can delve into the effectiveness of pre- and post-engagement materials, dramaturgical writing, creative conversation-building activities etc, all with an eye towards better understanding both what people are actually using to augment their core artistic experience and, within that set of activities, which ones seem most able to move the dial on ultimate impact of the work. Even as we complete this work, we have already seen organizations utilizing the early results of their surveying to adjust (both nominally and drastically) the engagement efforts they are doing to more effectively meet the newly understood needs of the patron.

And of course impact assessment allows for many new conversations with funders and government officials, both for the individual organization and for the artistic community as a whole, in particular because it provides a third alternative to the two ways that most organizations currently demonstrate their value to the community when asked: economic data and production reviews.

In her application to participate in this work, one artistic director wrote movingly about how, as a very small organization, she often was unable to secure reviewers to attend her work. Setting aside the unfortunate implications for ticket sales, this also left this artistic director without the generally-requested "support materials" to demonstrate her organization's value and impact on the community to grantmakers and other funders. Lacking in those clippings, the artistic director instead often substituted a heartfelt personal artistic statement interspersed with quotes from patrons and artists about how the company had affected them, with mixed success.

This artistic director wrote about the hope she had that this work—doing this type of research on her audiences, being able to showcase these types of results—might revolutionize her ability to demonstrate her organization's value specifically and realistically. While continuing to carry the testimonials into her writing, she envisioned a day where she could also pull a graph, for example for the question "How much were your eyes opened to an idea or point of view you hadn't considered before?" and show that X% of her audience significantly had their worldview expanded by seeing this show. That's a new conversation, for her, and it does a variety of things.

First, of course, it takes what was previously an esoteric, even touchy-feeling concept—empathy—and specifies it down to a particular question, a particular scale, a particular result. Second, it turns the conversation from one about how many people were served into a conversation about how deeply those that came were affected. Finally, framing up the conversation in this way allows the artistic director to intelligently and specifically discuss the value of her organization on its own terms. Is your organization, like The Cutting Ball Theater in San Francisco, a specialist in *avant garde* work: work that is cerebral, heavy on aesthetic growth potential, but probably isn't going to encourage a lot of social or even emotional engagement? Then own that, and speak about your impact from your strengths. If, instead, your organization is like Musical Theatre West in Los Angeles and is dedicated to producing great musicals (many of them giant, frothy, glossy pieces), then talking about intellectual engagement probably needs to take a backseat to talking about the extraordinary social bonding that goes on at your work.

In a way, then, we've been using a one-size-fits-all frame in a conversation that really deserves to be custom made, and our hope is that working from a place of assessing the impact of the artistic product itself, we can get away from the generalist mentality.

We're trying to more deeply understand intrinsic impact because, as earlier research from WolfBrown and Theatre Bay Area shows, increasing intrinsic impact can demonstrably increase the likelihood of audience members returning to a company, a form or a piece of work. In addition, a deeply impactful experience is also one that will remain in the memory more vividly and for longer. And since memory is the core of future decision-making, as well as one of the driving forces for all sorts of day-to-day actions within society, it is by increasing these impacts, and therefore increasing the resonance of the memories of that experience, that we can increase frequency of attendance, perceived value of the particular experience and of the arts in general, and most grandly, affect change in society in terms of the more extrinsic benefits that we all spend so much time trying to discuss now anyway.

And so, we're doing this work. It's a giant project—19,000 survey responses, 24 interviews, hundreds of hours of analysis. We want to take this work from abstract to specific. We want to integrate it into the conversation as strongly as we currently have integrated butts in seats, financial impact on community and star ratings for shows. Through a new online resource, available right now at www.intrinsicimpact.org, we hope to take this work from a $600,000 sprawling study down to a quick, easy and cheap, self-contained survey engine that any company anywhere could use to instantly gain better understanding of their impact on audiences.

All of this serves an effort that we articulated from the beginning, which is to change the conversation about the value of the arts. Our goal with all of this work comes down to five words. We want to make research into intrinsic impact—measurement of the whole experience of a patron in an artistic situation:

- **Accessible.** Intrinsic impact assessment used to be hard to do unless you managed to get into one of the studies being conducted by WolfBrown and its partner organizations. In the run-up to this study alone we had requests from nearly 100 companies wanting to participate which, for lack of funds, we had to narrow down to the present cohort of 18. Theatre Bay Area and WolfBrown want impact assessment to be accessible by everyone, quickly and easily.

- **Affordable.** This research study had an overall price tag of nearly $600,000—a giant amount of money that was only possible thanks to generous funding from the Doris Duke Charitable Foundation, National Endowment for the Arts, Mellon Foundation, Pew Center for Arts & Heritage and other local funders around the country. That's not sustainable if the goal is to get the research into the hands of as many people and organizations as possible. As part of this work, therefore, we have developed, with WolfBrown, the US firm Jacobson Consulting Applications and the UK firm Baker Richards Consulting, an online interface, available for all genres at www.intrinsicimpact.org, that will allow for anyone with an internet connection, patron emails and as little as $1,000 (or less) to get easy, instant impact assessment feedback from their audiences.

- **Standardized.** We have to stop talking past each other, both inside organizations and when talking as a community outward. Part of this dissemination effort is to insert a set of important new words into the lexicon, and to give artists, arts administrators, stakeholders and funders a good understanding of what those terms might mean. As part of that, included in the back of this report is a glossary of the impact assessment terms used throughout the book—including both WolfBrown's core impact constructs as well as other terms drawn from many different sources including psychological literature, popular books and the day-to-day.

- **Understood.** People like graphs and numbers for a reason. Where there may be fewer nuances, there is more easy comprehension. Working with WolfBrown, Theatre Bay Area is creating a series of documents and trainings to allow companies that are doing impact assessment to more deeply understand the results. We hope to link what might seem esoteric with concrete actionable change items within an organization.

- **Routine.** Everyone knows how to talk about profit and loss. Everyone knows to count ticket stubs and to occasionally survey basic demographics. We want impact assessment to enter the lexicon of "the things you just always do" to keep tabs on your organization's health. By removing the cost and opportunity barriers to this type of assessment work—making it cheap, quick and painless—we hope to also make it ubiquitous. If you are in a position where measuring impact becomes as day-to-day as counting how many people come to your show, how much money you make, then you'll suddenly be in a much richer position when you have to go talk to someone about the work that you're doing. It's a different conversation to have.

***

Impact assessment contrasts impact against the promise of what the organization is saying the impact is going to be and, whether you ever share the results or not, measuring intrinsic impact allows you to understand how close you're getting to your mission fulfillment goals. It is both a benchmarking tool for organizations to share with external stakeholders, and a diagnostic tool for use inside the organization to evaluate the work the organization is producing, and to make sure that one set of artistic responsibilities isn't overtaking another one. And, in general, it's a way of developing a more sophisticated and well-rounded understanding of how the work is being received, and to continuously improve the impact, stickiness and engagement of the art with the audience.

Intrinsic impact is mission fulfillment, and mission fulfillment is increasingly core to the assessment of success. Mission fulfillment is about changing lives, creating memories, transforming people. It's about providing the stepping stones through an artistic life, the touch points that bring us back to the world when we get caught up in things that don't really matter.

We all have an artistic lifecycle—a series of artistic events that have mattered, that have made, in a way, your life.

This ticker tape of a life, running out behind all of us, pointing the way, is the making of meaning in this world. And it has been equally the making of each of us, just as, I think, it has been the making of Barry and will continue to be the making of Sydni. And in the end, those lingering moments, those strong, thin strings that connect a heart today to the heart of younger you in some past artistic experience, are the manifestation of all the power that is tied up in the making and seeing of art.

And when I find myself caught in such a memory tornado, as past artistic experiences flicker like friendly ghosts into my day-to-day, I'm reminding of something that Alan Brown has taken to saying lately: "The true value of an artistic experience is that it pays out dividends." It's an investment, and the return is every moment for the rest of your life that you catch on something and are suddenly reminded of some part, large or small, from that experience.

My favorite poem is "Postscript" by Seamus Heaney. It is ostensibly a recommendation to a traveler to stop and watch some swans, but it has always seemed to me to be equally about the consuming of art, ethereal, stunning, confusing and capable of complete transformation. It ends with these five lines:

> Useless to think you'll park or capture it
> More thoroughly. You are neither here nor there,
> A hurry through which known and strange things pass
> As big soft buffetings come at the car sideways
> And catch the heart off guard and blow it open

Often, we don't choose to analyze our life in general, let alone the artistic experiences large and small that filter through it. Tied up in memory, or myth, or impact, or meaning—tied up in the framing of our lives through the music we listen to, the theatre we see, the dancing we do, the art that bombards our eyes, the crafts and sounds and sights and smells that feed the part of our brain that numbers and figures and facts don't—there is a powerful, strident, necessary truth about the wayfinding power of art. It points you where you want to go even when you don't know where that is, it nudges you this way and that as you make yourself, it blinds you with its simplicity and comedic beauty while teaching you a little something profound. It catches your heart off-guard and blows it open.

We can know more about that power. We can know more about the consequences of what we do, the impact of what we do, the changes we make in the fabric of lives. We can measure transformation.

For the sake of the field, and the betterment of the people we serve, we need to get started counting some new beans, and we need to teach the people who control our funding how to understand the worth of those new beans. The drums are beating, our time may be short. There are many different contingents looking to see us eviscerated, blotted from the landscape. But art is not optional. Art is life. It changes our rhythms, connects us to our humanity, teaches us to live and love. It makes us smarter, stronger, more coherent. It makes us care, and think, and innovate. It can, indeed, transform the way we think and act and live our lives.

So let's put that center stage, and see where it gets us.

Creative Destruction

a conversation with **Diane Ragsdale**
Ph.D. candidate, University of Rotterdam
blogger at ArtsJournal.com/Jumper

The core question for a lot of this intrinsic impact research is, "What is the role of the audience in the artistic process, here particularly talking about art that is made for audience consumption?" Where does mission fall into that question, do you think?

In his book *Integrating Mission and Strategy for Nonprofit Organizations*, Jim Phills at Stanford University describes "mission" as the "social value" of the organization. He says that, while a nonprofit organization might have economic value, its social value should transcend that economic value. But how do we define "social value?" Often terms like "artist-focused" or "audience-focused" are used to describe the value that organizations see themselves providing to society. And often we present these terms as dichotomous, which can be problematic.

It is important to distinguish between the role of a nonprofit arts institution in society and the role of an artist; they are different. I tend to think that the most dynamic role an arts organization can play is enabling a connection between artists and a community at the appropriate time in the artistic process (which will differ per artist or project). The organization exists, in large part, to support artists and artmaking and the artistic process, but decisions made about which shows to produce and present, and how, and in what context, are ideally made with the needs of the local community at top of mind.

But what do we mean by "the audience?" Do we mean the people that are already attending, whom we desperately want to retain? Or the people who are demographically similar to those that already attend, but don't, that we expect would be inclined to like what we do? Or instead do we mean the community-at-large?

To what degree should the perceived tastes of current subscribers and attendees influence programming? If you read historical accounts of the American theatre, you begin to notice, relatively early in the movement's history, references to programming becoming "cookie-cutter," homogenous, formulaic, safe, aimed at the conservative tastes of subscribers. Based on such observations one could argue that the American theatre has done a pretty good job of being "audience"-focused (in the sense of becoming rather adept at programming a season of work that will appeal to the tastes of a base of subscribers). It's worth asking, however, whether this focus has come at the expense of broader relevance (on the one hand) or artistic risk-taking (on the other).

Just to point it out, if you were talking about any other business in the world, catering to the tastes of the people who support you would be an incredibly smart thing to do.

That's right, that's exactly right. For a market-driven rather than mission-driven organization it would be a very smart thing to do.

Of course it's not surprising that many organizations, as they grow, orient their programming to aging, upper-middle-class, educated people, since that is the demographic that still subscribes out of habit, can give donations, and that we assume has the capacity to understand the work. But this rather myopic focus on current subscribers has meant that arts organizations often fail to look past them, to the community-at-large—though of course it's not one community, it's many communities—and ask: "What does this *community* value? Is there some part of this community that is clearly being overlooked by the arts? What's *not* being done here? Where's the *gap*? What is *missing*?"

Rather than doing what's popular with subscribers, organizations might then do what's *missing* in the community. Doing so might have negative financial consequences in the short term but it could create greater social value and, equally as important, it could reduce the competition among organizations for audiences and resources.

What you're bringing up is a very interesting dichotomy: mission versus financial stability. How do you navigate that dichotomy between a socially-directed mission, which I think is dead-on for nonprofits, and financially viability?

I think it's tough. We may need to question the viability of the infrastructure that we have built in support of the ideal of "professional, nonprofit theatre" in America—or at least of so *many* "professional, nonprofit theatres" in America. There's an inherent tension between those words. If we define "professional" to mean that this endeavor is no longer a labor of love and everybody is paid a stable, middle class wage—if that's the ideal that we're aiming for—then it would seem that, at its current size, our field cannot sustain that ideal, at least not continuing to be "nonprofit." There are not enough people in the U.S. willing to pay (or donate) for that idea to be manifested thousands of times over.

Moreover, it seems that wealthy people, by and large, want to associate with a *certain* type of organization. It would be quite convenient if wealthy arts patrons were equally passionate about supporting the small Hispanic theatre in town as the leading established regional theatre. Evidently, they're not. We've seen how this American model plays out: we've seen where people with significant capacity to give like to give their money, and who gets it and who doesn't, and we've seen that this results in a certain kind of theatre that appeals to a certain demographic.

And so this is where the whole idea of supply/demand comes up: nonprofit social welfare ideals coming up against financial realities necessary for long-term sustainability in the sector. Ironically, by catering to the people we have, we're sort of slowly strangling the whole sector with an ever-smaller group of fans dictating ever-more-homogenous work— but by thinking about expanding to a larger "community" we might be jeopardizing ourselves as well.

That's right—if you define the "sector" as "nonprofit professional resident theatres." But what about alternative, grassroots, community, and popular theatres? How do they fit into this equation? There was "community" theatre before there was "nonprofit professional resident theatre" (and before "community" got the "less than" connotation it has now). So who are you trying to save? What is it that you're trying to fix? Which practices and forms of theatre in this system need to be encouraged with incentives, and which need to be discouraged by removing incentives or even implementing disincentives?

Are you primarily concerned with the perpetuation of the existing leading nonprofit institutions, those that are the largest (and, thus, we often presume "the best")? TCG ranks its members in the categories 6, 5, 4 (largest to smallest). Is it the number 6's you're worried about? The number 1's? Or is it those that don't even show up in the TCG membership because they're too small, or too lightly institutionalized, or they're community theatres or loose collectives of artists? Which part of this bigger system of nonprofit theatre are you concerned about?

You've written about "creative destruction," this idea that we either need to take control of our growth and make decisions about what survives, or natural forces will do it for us. But what is the rubric for understanding where the culling of the herd needs to happen, and who does the culling? Foundations? Market forces? Attendance figures? What are the evaluative terms? If the art isn't going to stop, then how do the organizational structures decrease? Who decides? Who are the arbiters of which organizations are "valuable," and what are the terms?

Artists and communities make up a constantly evolving and changing environment. It's the *institutions* that are stuck, holding onto beliefs and practices about what is or is not "legitimate theatre" and denying the changing tastes, habits and demographics of their communities. Perhaps the impulse should be to destroy, not necessarily the institutions themselves, but the need that those institutions have to hold onto the power, to control the conversation. What if, instead, arts institutions evolved in response to the evolution of artists and their communities?

Now, is that more viable from a business model standpoint? I don't know. But consider someone like Diane Paulus at American Repertory Theatre. I know some theatre practitioners (at least at the time of this interview) are still quite on the fence about, or even opposed to, what she's doing there. She reinvented her second stage and endeavored to create something that would be more dynamically responsive to what she thought today's twenty-year-olds would find engaging. And she was successful: they showed up in droves, repeatedly, and brought friends. She doubled her attendance in a year, as I understand it.

I look at that box office success and think, "That's interesting. Clearly, there's some latent demand there." Rather than being curious about this latent demand and what it might say about changing tastes and the changing nature of theatre, however, some in the field started to question the legitimacy of what she was doing: "Well, is that *art* what she's doing in her second stage nightclub? Is burlesque art? Is *The Donkey Show* art?"

Until the mid-twentieth century, for the most part, theatres existed only on box office receipts. Before the creation of "nonprofit professional resident theatres"' there was summer stock, there was "the road" (commercial touring) and there were community (aka "little") theatres and other grassroots theatres. They existed on box office, and so the programming, by necessity, was intended to have broad (or at least broader) appeal. Many of these theatres were able to operate with what they could earn at the box office because they were small and (in the case of community theatres) because the people associated with the theatres were volunteers or paid modest wages. The same is true today when you look at the majority of small theatres. They operate out of what they make at the box office and the people working at these theatres are paid very little or nothing.

In the resident theatre movement, the "professional nonprofit theatre" movement, there was an intentional move away from the more populist and commercial theatre forms that existed and an attempt to carve out, rather artificially, a *certain* kind of theatre for a *certain* kind of audience. It was an artificial intervention into a market that existed before that moment.

When we say we need to try to find a way to make things "more sustainable," what are we talking about? Sustaining middle class livings for those salaried professional administrators that have them? Sustaining the capacity for artistic risk-taking? Sustaining broad and deep community engagement with the theatre? The "what" is really important. And if we're talking about nonprofit, mission-driven organizations, then we need to be able to answer the "what" with regard to the social value we are trying to sustain or create. A half-century ago, a group of people intervened and articulated a very particular value for the resident theatre movement—but that doesn't mean that the same value logic holds today.

We keep saying we want to see the next thing arrive, but at the same time desperately try to preserve what we've already created. It's very difficult to do both; most often, you need to destroy the old in order to allow for the emergence of the new. This is the idea behind "creative destruction."

In my research, I'm trying to understand how the theatre has evolved in the last 25 years or so in response to various forces. I want to know what that evolution tells us about the American nonprofit model. I think you're grappling with some of the most important questions that we can be grappling with at the moment. But I also think the "impact" question makes the field a little nervous—and so does the supply/demand conversation—because we sense that we've arrived at a day of reckoning. The money is tight and the environment is hyper-competitive. The conversation has been controlled for a long time by a small group of people. For years we've had a field-wide understanding of who were the field leaders, and there was no displacing them.

To some degree we've gamed and worked the system to maximum output of whatever could be derived from it, and now we have come to the end of the line. It's time to start asking ourselves the disruptive questions. Does it make sense to subsidize large resident theatres and not commercial theatres? Does it make sense to subsidize professional theatres and not amateur theatres performing in churches or high school gymnasiums? Does it make sense to subsidize those that are most able to garner patronage from wealthy, culturally elite audiences? Should those organizations that primarily serve upper middle class audiences be eligible for government and foundation grants?

We're rather protectionist in the U.S. nonprofit arts sector because we know, or at least suspect in our gut, that if we start measuring intrinsic impact—testing our assumptions about the impact of the art we make— we might find out that there is greater intrinsic impact from watching an episode of *The Wire* than going to any kind of live theatre. Or we may find that small-scale productions in churches or coffee shops are just as impactful (or more so) than large-scale professional productions in traditional theatre spaces. Are we prepared, if we find this sort of evidence, to change the way we behave in light of it?

Even prior to these studies on intrinsic impact, when we had a lack of real data on these points, we certainly did *not* lack for anecdotal evidence that much of what is happening in the unprofessional, mostly unsubsidized part of the sector—and/or in the commercial part of the sector—is dramatically impactful. Many people, for example, if asked, would probably say that their most transformative arts experience was seeing a musical on Broadway. And Broadway producers have been saying since 1979, "We deserve subsidy as much as these nonprofit theatres. Not only do we provide great artistic experiences, we provide enormous economic value to the city of New York; but it's getting harder and harder to produce work because costs keep rising."

Lately, I find myself scratching my head and saying, "You know, it's a fair point. Why *is* it that we don't subsidize the commercial theatres if we subsidize large regional theatres?" If, out of this type of research, we discovered hard data that that work is, indeed, intrinsically impactful—has great social value—would we act on that discovery?

Can we somehow use these new metrics to help us see the world in a different space? Can they give us better arguments for going to state, city, maybe even federal governments and saying, "Look, this is how you're currently distributing your money. If you instead distributed it this other way, you would reach many more constituents and have a greater social impact with your money?"

Because right now it appears we have a winner-take-all system in the arts. The few at the top continue to grow while the rest of the sector is forced to divide a shrinking pie among an increasing number of organizations. Assuming we're not going to have significantly more resources coming into the sector, can we talk about redistribution from large organizations to smaller ones? Can we allow for a different idea to emerge about which are the most important organizations to fund?

Who's at the top? Who's at the bottom? Who's considered leading? These are rankings that were established decades ago and it's nearly impossible for even an incredibly worthy and high-performing entrant to displace one of the 'pioneering' incumbent organizations at the top of the pyramid.

We need data that can help us see the field differently. Sure, if you rank theatres by budget, if you rank them by how many thousands of people they perform to in a year, then you will continue to rank them 1, 2, 3, as they are currently ranked. But if you were to rank theatres according to who reaches the immigrant communities in their cities best, for instance, you'd probably rank the list differently. Which theatres best reach "the rest" of the community? Which theatres generate community-wide discourse or help the community tell its stories? Which theatres are artistic innovators? Which theatres would community members say "changed their lives?"

I imagine if you asked these questions you'd get different rankings each time.

We need new ways of ordering the sector, and understanding what contributes to a healthy arts ecosystem. A lot of money has come into the sector, but it hasn't been distributed very well. The ecology is out of balance.

Arlene Goldbard speaks about how extraordinary it is that people in government can get away with saying that, by defunding the NEA and saving $160 million, they're making a significant impact on the budget, while at the same time they're spending twice that every single day that they're at war. She says that that phenomenon is essentially our fault—that due in large part to the way we have valued and talked about ourselves, we now find ourselves in a situation where the general population just doesn't really think about us very much. Do you have any thoughts about how we can start creating a language that engages the general population? Are there examples of how arts sectors have fought the perception that art is optional, and expensive, and not necessarily the government's obligation to foster?

What does it mean when government cuts support for the arts? In a democracy, the government represents the people. My sense is that the government cut the arts when it perceives that it will not encounter a huge political backlash for doing so. The government doesn't value the arts because it perceives that the *people* don't value the arts.

It's always interesting to see in which countries and in which places people do rally and fight, when governments attempt to make cuts to the arts, and in which places they don't. It says something about the value of culture in that particular society, and who it reaches, and how much they're willing to advocate for it, and how much they're willing to sacrifice in order to have it.

Ultimately, we have a real image problem in the arts. In the U.S., most people perceive "subsidies for the arts" to mean subsidies for the SOB's (symphony, opera, and ballet)—the organizations that are perceived to serve this very narrow, upper-middle-class demographic. It's no wonder, then, that the common man doesn't stomp up and down when arts subsidies are being threatened. It shouldn't surprise anyone that the rhetoric ("The arts are important to a thriving society," etc.) hasn't worked in a long time. Most people simply don't have a relationship to the arts, or don't perceive that they have one–meaning they are pretty sure that whatever they consider to be "art" would not be considered "art" by the "art world."

Right now, we not only don't have the words to compel people to see the importance of the art, we have ignored the larger part of society for so long that they no longer think that we're important—*and* they have evidence that we're not important in their lives because they haven't been going, nobody that they know has been going, and they're all doing fine.

Who gets to decide which theatres stay and which go? Well, we have a decentralized, indirect subsidy system, meaning, in theory, "everybody" could get to decide. But in reality don't we see that those with money get to decide? And by extension, then, friends of those with money are the winners and everyone else loses. And then some say, "No one should decide; we should let nature take its course." But what do we mean by "nature?" Do we mean that we should let "the market" decide?

That's not valid. You can't, on the one hand, say "We have to subsidize this particular form of art ('serious theatre') in order to compensate for market failure," and then on the other hand say you're going to let "the market" decide.

But it would seem that the market is not able to tell us who to keep and who to lose because we've put interventions in place that enable organizations to exist for a ridiculously long time even if they're *not* particularly relevant, or doing particularly good work. By intervening in the system and subsidizing it in the first place, as the Ford Foundation and others did in the 60's and 70's when they selected certain types of theatres for subsidies and not others, we've basically said, "We don't trust the marketplace to decide." Many organizations exist today because someone saw them as meriting support 40 or 50 years ago. Why do we resist the idea that some entity or entities should be able to intervene now and discontinue funding for certain organizations (that seem less worthy or relevant now) and encourage or enable funding for others?

The system does not seem to deal with underperforming organizations proficiently or effectively. And if you can't eliminate underperforming organizations, over time, they compete with other, more worthy organizations for resources. If they have built up a larger development staff over time (because they have been around longer), these underperforming organizations sometimes even do a better job of capturing those resources.

Of course somebody has to decide. A *bunch* of 'somebodies' has to decide. But how do you coordinate that? This is the challenge with our decentralized, indirect subsidy system.

I'm a big believer in Alan Brown's work, and what you are doing, and I'm hopeful that it can help reframe the conversation about social value and about what it means to be a "leading organization." Right now, though, what we know is that major foundations provide an imprimatur; they are able to change the perceptions of organizations as they give money and take it away. The press matters. Service organizations matter. And there are others. Any of these can stand on a bully pulpit and say, "Here are the organizations that we perceive to be leaders." And if it's a very different list from the list that we've had in our minds for a long time, if the names are not simply those that we've historically perceived to be leading, it will begin to shift our understanding of what we mean when we say "leading" (i.e., not just oldest and largest). It also provides leverage to the new leaders, increase their ability to fundraise, and change the way others perceive them.

The formation of the nonprofit arts sector was essentially an effort to create exclusive organizations to serve wealthy people – that was the goal; that was the idea at the outset. We have reached a logical result of having created such a system. Arts organizations are sleeping in beds they made. People have been talking about this for twenty or thirty years. To some degree, it's ridiculous that the sector doesn't understand how it ended up in this situation.

There are consequences for catering to subscribers.

There are consequences for turning these organizations into places that cater to wealthy people.

Of course the rest of society is not rallying on our behalf.

And the idea that we need to keep sustaining it—well, I'm not convinced that this particular thing we've created, this current model, needs to be sustained. It is proving to be unsustainable perhaps *because* it caters to a few rather than serving the many. The next generation, if they're excited about anything, it's going to be a very different kind of organization, a very different type of place, a very different type of experience. Maybe it's time to blow things up, rather than sustain the *status quo*.

2 QUANTIFYING ARTISTIC IMPACT

Understanding the Intrinsic Impact of Live Theatre:

Patterns of Audience Feedback across 18 Theatres and 58 Productions

 commissioned by **Theatre Bay Area**
report by **Alan Brown and Rebecca Ratzkin, WolfBrown**

Overview of the Study

- With funding from the Doris Duke Charitable Foundation, the Andrew W. Mellon Foundation, the National Endowment for the Arts and other funders, Theatre Bay Area set out in 2010 to support a cohort of 18 diverse theatres in assessing the impacts of their productions on audiences. To facilitate this assessment, Theatre Bay Area commissioned the research firm WolfBrown to develop a survey methodology based on their extensive experience with impact assessment.

    - **A summary of previous research on audience impact by WolfBrown and other researchers can be found at www.intrinsicimpact.org. A description of the constructs of "readiness to receive" and "intrinsic impact" may be found on pages 80-81.**

- Theatres were selected through a competitive application process, in partnership with local agencies or funders in each of the six regions covered by the study: The San Francisco Bay Area, Greater Los Angeles, Minneapolis/St. Paul, New York City, Washington DC, and Philadelphia.

- The project represents a critical step forward in the theatre field towards encouraging audiences to provide meaningful feedback on the art itself, and towards providing the 18 theatres and the theatre community more generally with new tools to gather and interpret feedback on their creative output.

- Following a planning phase from May to November 2010, data was collected between November 2010 and September 2011, and analyzed between September 2011 and January 2012.

- Individual theatres were provided with proprietary access to their own survey results through an online dashboard reporting tool co-developed by WolfBrown and Theatre Bay Area, with the assistance of Baker Richards Consulting in the UK and Jacobson Consulting Applications in the US.

- Engaging the individual theatres in a meaningful discussion of their impact results was the primary goal of the study. This report captures cross-site learnings and larger patterns of results, in order for the field to benefit from the study.

- Analysis cohorts covered in this report include:
  - SELF-REPORTED VARIABLES: age, gender, ticket type, role in the decision process, annual frequency of attendance at the host theatre, motivations for attending, and pre- and post-performance engagement
  - ADMINISTRATIVE VARIABLES: size of house, percentage of house sold, and production attributes (e.g., plays vs. musicals, family-friendly, classic vs. contemporary, etc.)
- This report was prepared to complement a larger report prepared by Theatre Bay Area on the intrinsic impact project.
  - This report includes only a minor focus on comparing results across the 18 theatres or 58 specific productions, in order to avoid making inappropriate comparisons between theatres with different audiences, different venues, and different markets. Results from this study should not be extrapolated to represent all audiences for plays and musicals, since the samples of theatres and productions were not designed to be representative of the entire theatre field.
- Working with the 18 theatres was a truly rewarding experience. They were invested and dedicated to the success of this project, and it is through their good efforts that this report is available for the field.

Key Themes and Observations

- **High response rates** (45%, on average) suggest that theatre patrons are willing, able and ready to provide meaningful feedback on their artistic experiences. The quality of responses to open-ended questions was high. The investment of time and psychic energy on the part of patrons in completing almost 19,000 surveys was staggering.

- While the purpose of the study was to engage theatres around impact assessment, patrons also benefit from the **process of providing feedback**, since, in taking the survey, they are forced to articulate a critical reaction to the art.

  - In future efforts it will be important to provide respondents with immediate feedback on how their results compare to those of other patrons, in order to complete the circle of learning and encourage future cooperation with surveys of a similar nature. This feedback might take the form of online graphs and charts, dynamic word clouds projected onto a wall in the lobby, or re-publishing selected audience comments on the theatre's website (e.g., "here's what people are saying about last night's performance").

- Results bring to light what might be considered the **central riddle of impact**: On average, single-ticket buyers report significantly higher impacts than subscribers.

  - Is there a sense of "novelty" or "newness" that increases impact for low-frequency attenders?

  - Why are more frequent theatregoers less satisfied, on average? Are they more sophisticated, and therefore harder to please? Certainly they are much more familiar with theatre in general.

  - If first-timers and low-frequency attenders are more satisfied than high-frequency attenders, on average, why are they not attending more frequently? This seems counter-intuitive, and might speak to an underlying driver of the "churn" phenomenon. It seems to suggest that satisfaction with the artistic experience, alone, is not enough to drive repeat purchase. If excellent artistic work is not enough to retain satisfied patrons, what is?

- Respondents were asked to choose three from a list of 11 reasons why people attend theatre performances. The top three **motivations** are "to relax and escape," "to be emotionally moved," and "to discover something new." Younger respondents are more socially motivated, and are more likely to attend "for educational purposes" suggesting a personal connection to the art form. High frequency patrons (89% of whom are subscribers) are much more likely to cite emotional and intellectual reasons for attending, whereas low frequency attenders

(87% of whom are single-ticket buyers) are motivated by production-specific factors (e.g., "to see the work of a specific artist"). Although many low-frequency attenders are regular theatregoers, they are "picking and choosing" the programs they want to see at the host theatre. Among the least frequent attenders (i.e., those attending the host theatre for the first time in a year or more), 35% came "because someone else invited me," illustrating **the power of social context** to drive attendance among infrequent attenders.

- Overall, motivations can vary dramatically from production to production, suggesting a need to carefully align marketing messages with motivations on a production-by-production basis.

- Younger respondents (age 15-24) reported lower levels of familiarity with theatre in general, but higher levels of familiarity with the playwright and the cast. Overall, these and other survey results suggest that young theatregoers are more likely than older theatregoers to be personally involved in theatre through acting, writing, etc., and are prime candidates for engagement.

- Women reported higher impacts than men across all 58 productions, in particular feeling "emotionally charged" after a performance, and "reflecting on one's opinions." Some of this difference may be explained by the fact that women were more likely than men to be sole decision-makers (see next point).

- Decision makers (i.e., those who say that "I made the decision to attend") reported higher levels of context and familiarity, and are more likely to prepare. All of this ties into generally **higher levels of anticipation and impacts among decision-makers** (presumably ticket buyers) compared to those who attend with them.

- In some ways, decision-makers act as cultural guides to others. How might theatres help reinforce and reward this nurturing behavior?

- These findings also suggest a problem with surveys that only reach ticket buyers, which bias results in favor of the more knowledgeable and engaged audience members.

- Results were analyzed across different types of productions, with intuitive results. **Plays** generated higher levels of intellectual stimulation and social bridging outcomes, while **musicals** generated higher captivation levels, higher levels of feeling "emotional charged," higher levels of aesthetic validation and social connectedness with others in the audience. Productions with a **comedic element** tended to precipitate higher social outcomes, suggesting that laughing together creates a social bond that is less prevalent in more serious work. As would be expected, productions involving **challenging material** elicited stronger intellectual impacts.

- Several theatres within the sample presented the same, or similar, productions. Both Arena Stage and Berkeley Repertory Theatre surveyed audiences at *Ruined* (different productions of the same play), yielding strikingly similar results. The same two theatres presented the same production of Anna Deavere Smith's *Let Me Down Easy*, with similar patterns of results, but a much higher magnitude of impacts reported by single-ticket buyers at surveyed performances late in the Berkeley run. Comparison of results between two plays by Tennessee Williams (*The Milk Train Doesn't Stop Here Anymore* and *Camino Real*) point to the diversity of impacts within one playwright's body of work.

- One of the key questions used in the protocol asks respondents, "Did you leave the performance with questions you would have liked to have asked the actors, director or playwright?" Overall, 35% of respondents left the performance with unanswered questions, and 98% of these people responded to a follow-up open-ended question, "What were one or two of your questions?", resulting in an enormous body of qualitative data about what was on their minds. Respondents who reported having questions tended to have higher levels of familiarity with the playwright/composer or with the cast, but lower levels of familiarity with the story of the play. In other words, unfamiliar work generates more questions, which stands to reason.

  - **Being able to formulate questions about a theatre production you've attended is a form of critical thinking, and relates to positive impacts. Patrons who are not able to articulate their questions or seek answers miss an important opportunity to make meaning from their experience. Analysis of open-ended responses suggests groupings of questions - some around the "why" of the production, some around the "how" of the production. Helping patrons achieve the "moment of curatorial insight" (i.e., the "aha" moment when understanding dawns) should be the focus of pre- and post-performance engagement efforts.**

- Reading previews, reviews and social media comments prior to attending has a small but significant effect on increasing anticipation levels, but does not correlate with higher impacts. A much stronger relationship was found between anticipation and respondents' levels of familiarity with the story, cast, and playwright. All three of these familiarities contribute significantly to anticipation. In other words, as familiarity rises, so do anticipation levels. Familiarity with the story of the production contributes twice the predictive value compared to familiarity with the cast or the playwright.

- This suggests something intuitive about theatre participation: as theatregoers advance along their arc of involvement with the art form, their levels of anticipation and involvement rise.

- It also suggests that marketing efforts focusing on building familiarity with the story are more likely to build anticipation levels, as opposed to marketing efforts that focus on the playwright or cast (except in the case of stars).

- A strong predictive relationship was found between the intensity of discussion that patrons have with each other and the main indicator of intellectual stimulation ("To what extent did you gain new insight or learning?"). Respondents who reported having an "intense exchange" after the performance reported an average score of 3.7 on the "insight or learning" indicator, compared to an average score of 3.2 for those who reported a "casual exchange." An even stronger relationship was observed between the intensity of discussion and the indicator of self-reflection, "To what extent did the performance cause you to reflect on your own opinions or beliefs?" Similarly, structured post-performance engagement activities such as talkbacks were found to have significant predictive power over "insight or learning" outcomes, although it is impossible to prove a causal relationship.

  - Results clearly indicate the benefits of post-performance engagement in terms of increased intellectual outcomes.

- An open-ended question asking respondents to articulate in their own words the emotions they were feeling as they left the theatre provides a nuanced view of the complexity of emotions that a theatre performance can have on an individual and on an audience. Several word clouds included in the report illustrate how different performances take audiences on unique emotional journeys. For example, respondents to Woolly Mammoth's production of *Booty Candy* were predominantly happy, sad, confused, entertained and dissatisfied. From an impact perspective, being *"affected"* is what matters (i.e., deeper-felt emotion leads to deeper impact, even if that emotion is anger or sadness). Individual theatres, however, can use this open-ended question to compare their own suppositions about what emotions their audience members are feeling with the reality, and to make judgments about the prevalence of one emotion or another in the context of the artistic work.

- Overall the most helpful summative indicator of impact is: "When you look back at this performance a year from now, how much of an impression do you think will be left?" because it tracks most closely with the range of impacts. The two productions that garnered the very highest levels of summative impact could not be more different: *Avenue Q* (a raunchy adults-only musical with puppets) and *Ruined* (a dark, wrenching drama about female genital mutilation in the Congo).

74

- The following diagram illustrates key relationships between readiness, impact and loyalty, based on the totality of the data set. In general, these results corroborate and expand upon the original impact assessment work from 2006.

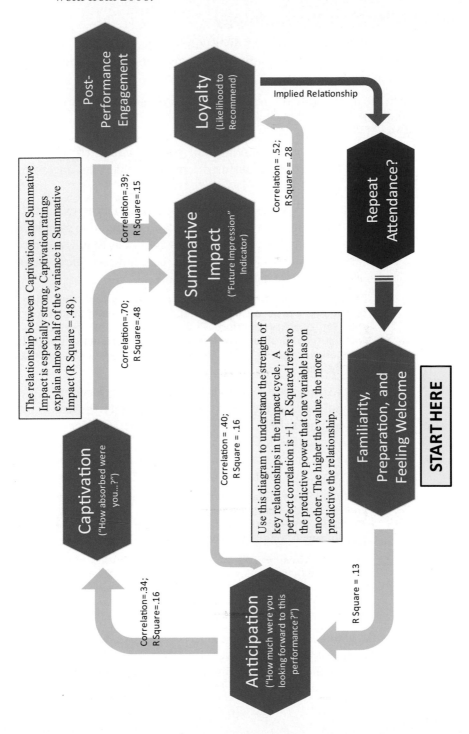

Methodology and Response Rates

Data Collection Methodology

- Data collection consisted of distributing survey packets in-venue at a select number of performances during the run of three different productions.

- Each theatre identified three productions which would be the focus of data collection. They were instructed to distribute 900 mail packets per production, with the goal of generating a sample of 300 completed surveys per production. Survey mail packets consisted of a cover letter, survey and pre-paid business reply envelope – all enclosed in an outer envelope.

- In general, three to six was the number of performances identified as optimal for surveying in order to provide a representative sample and a good cross-section of performance days and times (e.g., so as not to over-represent matinees, opening nights, etc, and to achieve a good mix of subscribers and single-ticket buyers).

  - **The number of performances surveyed varied from theatre to theatre based on overall capacity and estimated capacity sold for each production. This meant that all performances were surveyed in smaller theatres, or in productions with low estimated capacity sold, in order to generate an adequate sample size.**

- There were two options for distributing surveys: 1) pre-setting surveys on every "Nth" seat in the theatre prior to opening the house ("N" stands for the number by which you count patrons in order to identify those who receive the survey (e.g. every 3rd person get a survey packet), thereby ensuring random selection); or 2) handing out survey packets to every "Nth" audience member as audience exit the theatre.

  - **Methodology was determined in coordination with the theatre, and depended upon venue logistics, size of house and capacity of staff (smaller sized staff for some theatres meant that distributing at exits was more feasible).**

  - **As many theatres utilize smaller size houses (i.e., 250 or fewer seats), surveys were placed on all seats at the majority of performances during the run. For example, The Cutting Ball Theater in San Francisco (capacity of 60 seats) canvassed their house at every performance.**

- Survey workers counted the number of surveys remaining in the theatre at the end of every surveyed performance in order to report the number of pick-ups (to calculate pick-up and response rates as described in the following section), and to re-use them for another performance. Many theatres were able to "recycle" surveys, thereby enhancing the probability of response as one survey might be distributed at three different performances until it is picked up, taken home and completed.

- **Those who were successful in recycling surveys tended to achieve higher response rates, as they effectually distributed anywhere between 900 and about 2,000 surveys.**

- Patrons were instructed to take the survey mail packet home, complete the survey within 24 hours and then mail it back in the postage-paid business reply envelope addressed to the WolfBrown office.

Response Rates

- Overall, 65,738 surveys were distributed. Out of the 42,402 audience members who left the venue with a survey, 18,973 completed it, yielding an average response rate of 45% across all 18 theatres (note this does not include online administration for Berkeley Repertory Theatre's *Let Me Down Easy*).

  - **Response rates range from a high of 61% (La Crosse Community Theatre's *Doubt*) to a low of 22% (Arena Stage's *Ruined*).**

  - **These rates are calculated by dividing the number of completed surveys received out of the total number picked up.**

- Another important figure to take note of is the pick-up rate. This is the number of surveys picked up and taken home out of the total number distributed. The overall average pick-up rate was 65%, with a high of 100% (for those companies that distributed surveys by hand like MetroStage), and a low of 43% (for City Lights Theater Company's production of *Equus*).

- Response enhancement methods were encouraged, including lobby signage, curtain speeches, announcements in general e-newsletters or advance notice emails to ticket buyers.

- It is hard to pinpoint what exactly influences the response rate, although a few factors to consider include:

  - **In general, theatres who achieved higher pick-up rates achieved higher response rates. Most of the theatres who achieved a pick-up rate greater than 70% had response rates between 38% and 50%.**

- The implementation of response enhancements, such as curtain speeches, has a significant impact on pick-up rates. At least one of the theatres that was unable to do curtain speeches also had difficulty in generating the target sample per production. On the flip side, one of the smallest theatres in the study made a significant effort with curtain announcements and lobby signage, and succeeded far beyond expectations given the limitations of its size.

- Not surprisingly, we observed a difference between urban and suburban markets, and by location. In general, theatres in more suburban and small city markets had higher response rates than theatres in large urban markets, with some major exceptions. For example, La Crosse Community Theatre had an average pick-up rate of 78% compared to Woolly Mammoth's 83%, but La Crosse's overall response rate was 50% compared to a lower 38% for Woolly Mammoth.

- Overall, response rates seem to correlate with the level of effort in terms of response enhancement and diligence in distributing surveys according to procedures.

Questionnaire Design

- Protocols were customized by artistic, managing and marketing staff at each theatre based upon a master template. The template included a wide range of questions covering buyer behavior (e.g., frequency of attendance, motivations), "readiness to receive," intrinsic impact, summative impact, post-performance engagement, loyalty and artistic quality.

  - Great effort was made to ensure that both marketing and artistic staff were involved in shaping the protocol for each theatre, in order to maximize engagement with the results.

- There were 19 mandatory questions (listed on the next page) in order to allow for analysis by certain subgroups of respondents (e.g., by age, by ticket type), as well as to ensure adequate data for measuring readiness and impact. The staff at each theatre was allowed to choose an additional three to five questions based on their own interests and goals. All surveys were vetted and approved by both Theatre Bay Area and the individual theatre companies.

  - Some theatres wanted to know about audiences' perceptions of artistic quality and/or loyalty to the organization. Others who either had no interest in that line of questioning or had previously done surveys around those topics opted to include questions around audience engagement, motivations and impact.

- For example, three theatres (Berkeley Repertory Theatre, Woolly Mammoth, and Mixed Blood Theatre Company) whose work aims to move audiences to action opted for an indicator of emotional resonance: "To what extent did the performance spur you to take some action or make a change?"

- The master template was improved and adjusted during induction meetings with the 18 theatres, most notably with the addition of a question specifically about reading reviews before the performance (an indicator of context). Several theatres required further customization based on special circumstances (e.g., The Public Theater's Shakespeare in the Park respondents could not be classified by ticket type given that all tickets were free. Rather, they were classified by mode of ticket acquisition).

- The key limitations on design were: 1) the inclusion of mandatory questions, 2) the standardization of questions analysis across theatres, to preserve consistency in interpretation and allow for aggregate analyses), and 3) survey length (no more than three pages of questions).

- To help catalyze conversation within each theatre, staff were surveyed as to the impacts they expected for each show, and these figures were reported in the company dashboards for context.

List of Mandatory Survey Questions

Annual frequency of attendance
- "In a typical year, approximately how many times do you attend [Theatre Company's] productions?

Role in decision-making
- "Whose decision was it to attend this performance?"

Ticket type
- "What type of ticket did you hold?"

Context
- "Did you do anything to prepare yourself for the performance and understand what to expect?"

Relevance
- "Apart from this performance, I am likely to attend professional theatre productions."

Anticipation
- "Overall, how much were you looking forward to this performance?"

Captivation
- "Overall, to what degree were you absorbed in the performance?"

Emotional Resonance
- "Overall, how strong was your emotional response to the performance?"

- "To what degree did you feel a connection with one or more of the characters?" (empathy)

Intellectual Stimulation
- "To what degree did you gain new insight and learning?"
- "Did you leave with any unanswered questions you would have liked to ask the actor, director or playwright?"
- "If yes, what were one or two of your questions?"

Aesthetic Enrichment
- "To what extent were you exposed to a style or type of theatre or a playwright that you didn't know about previously?"

Social Bridging and Bonding
- "How much did you feel a sense of connection to others in the audience?"

Post-performance Engagement
- "Afterwards, did you discuss the performance with others who attended?"
- "Are there any of the scenes or lines [or music] from the performance still bouncing around in your head?"

Summative Impact
- "Overall, at what level were your expectations fulfilled for this performance?"

Demographics
- Gender
- Age

Constructs of "Readiness to Receive" and Intrinsic Impact

- The theoretical basis for this study grows out of WolfBrown's work for the Major University Presenters consortium in the U.S. in 2006, and has been further developed through work commissioned by the Australia Council for the Arts (2009) and the Liverpool Arts Regency Consortium (2010). Additional context for the study was gained from a 2008 Theatre Bay Area pilot study of Bay Area audiences associated with Free Night of Theater, a national program sponsored by Theatre Communications Group. All final reports from these studies may be accessed at www.intrinsicimpact.org. In the original MUP study, audience members were surveyed both before performances, to assess their "readiness to receive" the art, and after performances, to assess the impacts they derived from the experience. In the Theatre Bay Area study, the methodology was streamlined so that only one survey had to be administered after the experience. The design of the survey focused on the three constructs of "readiness to receive" and five constructs of intrinsic impact.

- **Readiness to Receive:** In a given audience, some people have a lot of knowledge about what they are about to see, while others may be attending for the first time. Arts and cultural groups can use this information to gauge their success at attracting first-timers, and to assess the need for educational work and interpretive assistance. There are three constructs of readiness investigated in this study:

- **CONTEXT:** The overall level of preparedness an audience member has for the experience, including prior knowledge of the art form and familiarity with the specific work(s) to be presented. Example: "Before the performance, how familiar were you with the playwright/composer/lyricist?"

- **RELEVANCE:** The extent to which the arts activity in question is relevant to the participant; primarily to identify individuals who do not normally attend the arts (not investigated in this study, but included here for definitional purposes). Example: "How much do you agree with the statement 'Apart from this performance, I am likely to attend professional theatre performances'?"

- **ANTICIPATION:** An audience member's psychological state prior to the experience, especially the degree to which they are looking forward to the event. Example: "Overall, how much were you looking forward to this performance?"

- **Intrinsic Impact** describes the core benefits that can accrue to individuals by virtue of attending a performance. The five impacts explored in the study are:

  - **CAPTIVATION:** The extent to which the audience member was absorbed in the performance or exhibition; captivation is the lynchpin of impact—if you are captivated, other impacts are likely to happen, whereas if you are not captivated (or, worse, if you sleep through a concert), other impacts are less likely to happen. Example: "How absorbed were you in the performance?"

  - **INTELLECTUAL STIMULATION:** The degree to which the performance or exhibition triggered thinking about the art, issues or topics, or caused critical reflection. Example: "Afterwards, did you discuss the performance with others who attended?"

  - **EMOTIONAL RESONANCE:** The extent to which the audience member experienced a heightened emotional state during or after the performance or exhibition. Example: "How strong was your emotional response to the performance?"

  - **AESTHETIC ENRICHMENT:** The extent to which the audience member was exposed to a new style or type of art or a new artist (aesthetic growth), and also the extent to which the experience served to validate and celebrate art that is familiar (aesthetic validation). Example: "Did this performance expose you to a style or type of theatre with which you were unfamiliar?"

- ▪ SOCIAL BRIDGING AND BONDING: Connectedness with the rest of the audience, new insight on one's own culture or a culture outside of one's life experience, or new perspective on human relationships or social issues. Example: "Did you feel a sense of connectedness with the rest of the audience?"

- It is important to remember that different works of art produce different impacts, often by design. Do not assume that all impacts could or should be associated with any given work of art. For example, one would not expect audiences at *The Wedding Singer* and *Equus* to report the same impacts. Often, different works of art are presented for different reasons, such as when a new play about a challenging topic is produced as part of a season with more popular fare. **It is essential not to make value judgments about the worth of different works of art based solely on impact indicators, or to prioritize certain impacts (e.g., intellectual stimulation) over others (e.g., aesthetic validation).**

Overview of Statistical Approaches

- A number of statistical tools were used in the analysis of data for this report. Given the substantial size of the overall sample (almost 19,000 cases), we wanted to use the opportunity to explore relationships between variables (e.g., post-performance engagement and impact), as the large sample size ensures statistical stability and that many of relationships observed will be statistically significant.

- Multiple types of relational statistical approaches, as follows:
  - ▪ CROSSTAB COMPARISON: In many ways, this is the simplest approach to investigating relationships between variables. A crosstab comparison describes how many respondents of one group exhibits a certain behavior or preference. For example, 8,000 respondents reported on whether or not they read a review by a professional critic. Of those 8,000, 2,833 said yes, they did read a review, or 35% of the sample.

  - ▪ COMPARISON OF MEANS: This approach calculates the average rating for a certain group of respondents in comparison with that of another group (e.g., subscribers have a higher average rating (mean) for familiarity with theatre in general in comparison with single ticket buyers).

- **BIVARIATE CORRELATION (PEARSON'S R CORRELATION):** Correlation is a measurement of the association between two variables. The Pearson's r is a number that represents that relationship on a scale from -1 to +1, with +1 representing a perfectly positive relationship, and -1 a perfectly negative relationship. For example, the Pearson correlation coefficient of .34 between levels of anticipation and captivation suggests a moderately strong relationship between these variables. Note that there is no proof of causality in this analysis as the direction of influence may occur in either way (i.e., greater anticipation may yield higher levels of captivation and vice versa).

- **LINEAR REGRESSION (REGRESSION COEFFICIENT):** Regression is an analysis in which the amount of variance in a dependent variable is explained by the amount of variance in a set of independent variables. The regression coefficient (R-squared) defines the actual amount of variance. For example, the R-squared for how captivation levels affect summative impact is .48. Therefore, we can deduce that 48% of the variance for summative impact is explained by the variance in captivation. Causality is suggested. However, it is important to note that there are a number of other factors that may influence the variation observed in both captivation, and, subsequently, summative impact.

- Because of the large sample size, many multivariate analyses produce statistically significant differences, even though the differences are small in size. In other words, they are significant in a statistical sense, but not always meaningful. Therefore, we focus instead on reporting 'effect sizes' – the amount of variation explained by a given relationship (e.g., R-squared in a regression analysis), rather than the statistical significance.

Motivations for Attending

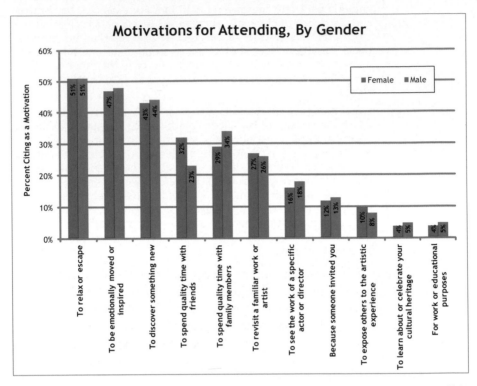

Motivations for Attending, By Gender

- Respondents were asked to choose three from a list of 11 possible motivations for attending, covering a wide range of both internally-motivated and externally-motivated reasons.

- The top three motivations reported were: 1) "to relax or escape," 2) "to be emotionally moved or inspired," and 3) "to discover something new."

- A factor analysis suggests several weak correlations between these 11 items. For example, "to expose others to the artistic experience" tends to group with "to learn about or celebrate your cultural heritage." None of these relationships is strong enough to warrant deleting items based on redundancy.

- Females were significantly more likely than males to cite "friendship" social motivations (32% vs. 23%, respectively), while males were more likely than females to cite "family member" social motivations (34% vs. 29%, respectively).

Motivations by Age Cohort

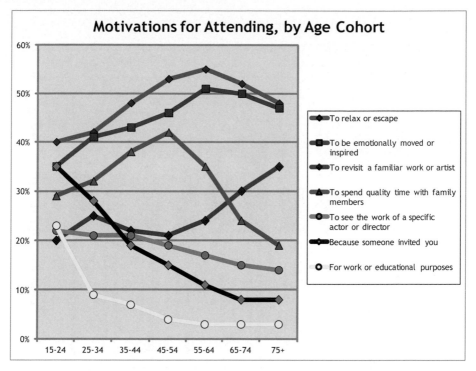

Motivations for Attending, by Age Cohort

Legend:
- To relax or escape
- To be emotionally moved or inspired
- To revisit a familiar work or artist
- To spend quality time with family members
- To see the work of a specific actor or director
- Because someone invited you
- For work or educational purposes

- Several interesting patterns are observed across age cohorts. The desire to be emotionally moved (red line), for example, rises dramatically with age, and then levels off after age 55.

- The desire to revisit familiar works (purple line) rises dramatically with age, as might be expected.

- The desire to spend time with family members (green line) rises through the child-rearing age cohorts, and then declines sharply.

- As might be expected, younger theatregoers are more likely to attend "for work or educational purposes" (yellow line), especially those in the youngest age cohort (15-24). This is consistent with other research suggesting that many of the young adults who attend theatre are personally involved in some fashion.

- As would be expected, the prevalence of an external stimulus ("because someone else invited you" – the black line) drops sharply with age, underscoring the importance of external social context in driving attendance amongst young adults.

Motivations by Annual Frequency of Attendance

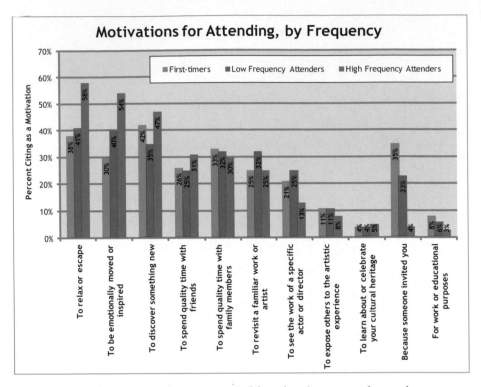

- High-frequency theatregoers (blue bars) reported much stronger emotional ("To be emotionally moved") and intellectual ("To discover something new") motivations, while first-time attendees relied on external stimuli more often ("Because someone else invited you").

- Recall that "first-timers" (green bars) in this case refers to patrons who were at their first production at the participating theatre in the past year. They may attend other arts programs at a higher frequency, and may have a high level of knowledge about theatre.

- The variation in salience of emotional motivations is particularly striking. Low-frequency patrons (orange bars) are more likely to cite artist-specific motivations, which makes sense: they are picking and choosing specific programs.

- It is also interesting that high-frequency patrons (presumably subscribers) are far more likely than low-frequency patrons to cite "to relax or escape."

Motivations for Three Arena Stage Productions Compared

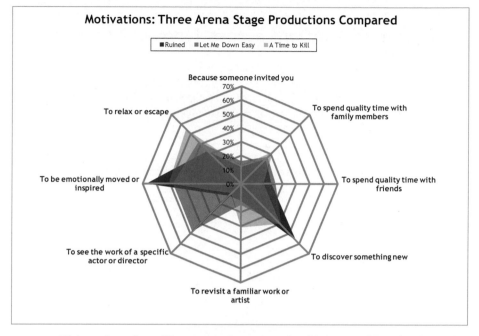

Motivations: Three Arena Stage Productions Compared

■ Ruined ■ Let Me Down Easy ■ A Time to Kill

- This radar chart illustrates the mix of self-reported motivations for the three surveyed productions at Arena Stage, and provides a good example of how motivations can vary depending on the nature of the production.

- Recall that patrons were reporting motivations retrospectively on a post-performance questionnaire. Since we did not survey patrons prior to performance, we cannot know how they might have reported motivations differently.

- For example, *Ruined* patrons reported much stronger emotional motivations ("to be emotionally moved or inspired") than patrons at the two other productions.

- Similarly, patrons at *Let Me Down Easy*, starring Anna Deavere Smith, reported much stronger motivations "to see the work of a specific actor or director."

- In contrast, patrons at *A Time to Kill* (a stage adaptation of John Grisham's novel of the same name) reported motivations more consistent with that production – "to revisit a familiar work or artist" and "to relax or escape."

- The larger discussion relates to how these self-reported motivations align with marketing messages, and how this information might be used to fine-tune marketing messages in the future.

Patterns in Motivations across Types of Theatrical Productions

The radar charts on this page and the following three pages illustrate differences in motivations across various types of theatrical productions. Note that several motivations are left off of these charts because of low prevalence and lack of variation. Lists of productions included in the various categories may be found in The Appendix.

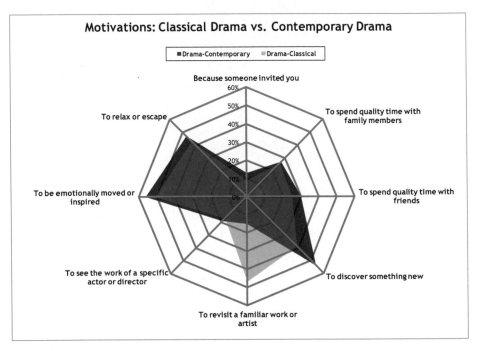

- The chart on this page summarizes the differences between classical drama and contemporary drama.

- One of the dominant motivations for attending classical drama is "to revisit a familiar work or artist" which is much less of a factor for contemporary drama audiences.

- Conversely, "to discover something new" is much greater a factor for contemporary drama audiences.

- Both classical and contemporary drama audiences are motivated by the promise of emotional, relaxation, and social impacts.

Motivations for Comedy versus "Challenging Material"

- We thought it might be interesting to look at differences in motivations for comedy vs. plays considered by the theatres to be "challenging material."

- As might be expected, patrons at comedic productions reported greater relaxation motivations, while patrons at "challenging material" productions reported higher emotional motivations.

- Social motivations were similar, except that comedy patrons were more likely to report social motivations within the family, perhaps suggesting the greater appropriateness of comedies for families, as opposed to friends.

Motivations for Contemporary Drama vs. Contemporary Musicals

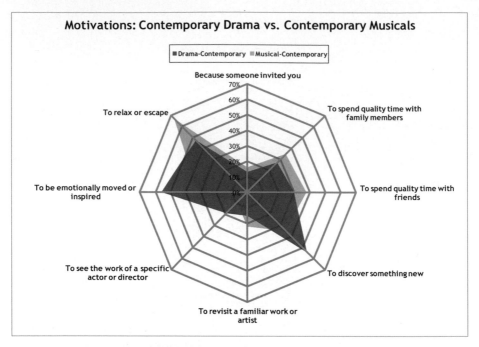

- Looking at contemporary drama vs. contemporary musicals, a clear pattern emerges.

- Audiences for contemporary musicals are more socially motivated, and more likely to seek out relaxation and escape, while audiences for contemporary drama are more likely to seek out emotional, aesthetic and intellectual stimulation.

Motivations for Classic vs. Contemporary Musicals

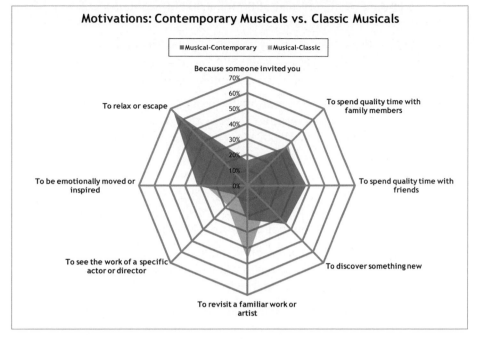

- As would be expected, patrons attending classic musicals like *Anything Goes* and *Cats* were more likely to be motivated by a desire "to revisit a familiar work or artist" while patrons at contemporary musicals like *Avenue Q* were more likely to be motivated by a desire "to discover something new."

- Respondents at contemporary musicals were also more likely to attach more importance to socializing with friends.

- The larger observation here is the predominance of relaxation as a motivation for attending musicals in general.

Motivations as Predictors of Anticipation and Impact

- Are certain motivations associated with higher levels of anticipation? Overall, the highest anticipation levels were associated with two motivations related to seeing specific works: "to revisit a familiar work or artist" and "to see the work of a specific actor or director." Patrons who seek "to expose others to the artistic experience" also experience higher levels of anticipation themselves.

- With respect to impact, several pairs of motivations and impacts were analyzed to explore the hypothesis that motivation leads to fulfillment (a finding of the original 2006 impact study commissioned by Major University Presenters).

- Does a desire "to discover something new" lead to higher levels of "gaining new insight or learning?" Yes, the relationship is statistically significant (R-squared = .01), but not necessarily causal.

- Does a desire "to be emotionally moved or inspired" lead to higher levels of feeling "inspired?" Yes, the relationship is statistically significant (R-squared = .02), but not necessarily causal.

- Did patrons who wanted "to learn about or celebrate your cultural heritage" report higher levels of social bonding (i.e., To what extent did the performance celebrate your cultural heritage or express a part of your identity")? Yes, the relationship is statistically significant (R-squared = .01), but not necessarily causal.

- Similarly, some inverse relationships were found with respect to negative correlations between relaxation and escape motivations and intellectual stimulation outcomes.

- While we cannot conclude anything about causality, there do appear to be intuitive relationships between motivations and impacts. In other words, people tend to report that the outcomes they derive from attending are the same ones that they were seeking on the way in to the theatre (i.e., as a general rule, outcomes relate to intentions and motivations). As with so many other things in life, clarity of intentions is often rewarded with the desired outcome.
  - **This points to the importance of accurate messaging during the marketing cycle, so as to build "attainable expectations" that can be fulfilled. It also suggests that patrons who arrive without some sense of what they want to get out of the experience are less likely to report intrinsic outcomes.**

Demographic Results (Age and Gender)

Age Patterns by Ticket Type

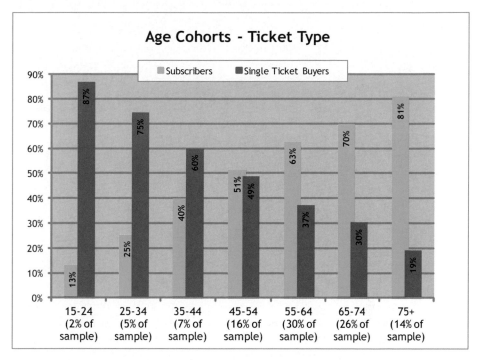

- To facilitate analysis, survey respondents across all 18 theatres were asked several questions relating to their ticket type, role in the decision process, and frequency of attendance.

  - **In total, 49% of all subscribers who responded to the survey are age 65 or over, compared to 27% of single-ticket buyers (STB).**

- In considering age patterns, the most striking relationship is a positive correlation between age and subscriber status, illustrated in the chart above. Over three-quarters (78%) of respondents under age 35 are single-ticket buyers (STB).

- Conversely, older respondents are much more likely to be subscribers (74% of respondents over age 65 are subscribers), as they typically have greater means and greater inclination and ability to make advance commitments.

Age Patterns by Annual Frequency of Attendance

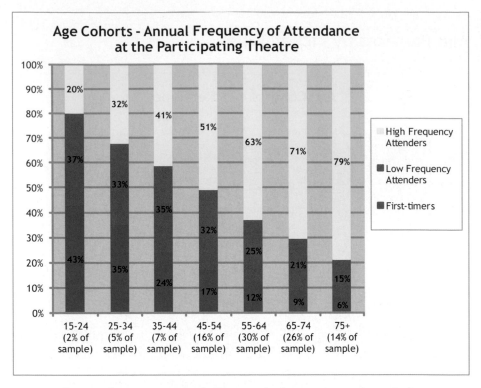

- Respondents were asked, "In a typical year, approximately how many times have you attended [name of theatre company]?" Responses allow for comparison of results by frequency of annual attendance:
  - **High frequency attenders are defined as those who have attended three or more times over the past year;**
  - **Low frequency attenders are defined as those who've attended one or two times over the last year;**
  - **First-timers are defined as respondents who are at their first production offer by the host theatre in a year or more.**

- Overall, 60% of all respondents self-defined as high frequency attenders, 25% as low frequency attenders (two or fewer times a year), and only 14% as first-timers.
  - **In all likelihood, this reflects a form of response bias (i.e., more frequent attenders are more likely to respond to a survey).**
  - **Recall that 89% of high-frequency attenders are subscribers.**

- As would be expected, younger buyers (under 35) are much more likely to be first-timers (35% between 25 and 34, and 43% under 25), while frequency rises dramatically by age cohort.

Indicators of "Readiness to Receive" by Age Cohort

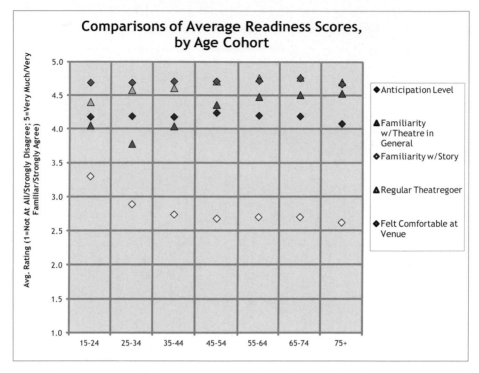

Comparisons of Average Readiness Scores, by Age Cohort

Avg. Rating (1=Not At All/Strongly Disagree; 5=Very Much/Very Familiar/Strongly Agree)

Legend:
- ◆ Anticipation Level
- ▲ Familiarity w/Theatre in General
- ◆ Familiarity w/Story
- ▲ Regular Theatregoer
- ◆ Felt Comfortable at Venue

Age cohorts: 15-24, 25-34, 35-44, 45-54, 55-64, 65-74, 75+

- This chart displays average ratings figures for five indicators of "readiness to receive."

- Ratings are high across all age cohorts for all except "familiarity with the story of the play." Some patterns by age include:

  - Anticipation levels are relatively consistent across the age cohorts.

  - Familiarity with theatre in general drops from the first to the second age cohort, suggesting that the youngest patrons in the audience, then steadily and significantly increases with age (4.0 for those under 25 years old up to 4.5 for respondents age 65+).

  - By and large, a large majority of all respondents claim to be regular theatregoers (i.e., "apart from this performance, I am likely to attend a theatre performance"), although the average figures rise somewhat with age, from 4.4 for 15 to 24 year olds to 4.7 for respondents age 65+.

  - One of the more interesting results is how "familiarity with the story of the play or musical" decreases with age, from 3.3 for respondents age 15-24 to 2.6 for those age 65+). Again, this suggests that younger patrons are more likely to have a personal connection to the theatre.

Key Indicators of Intrinsic Impact by Age

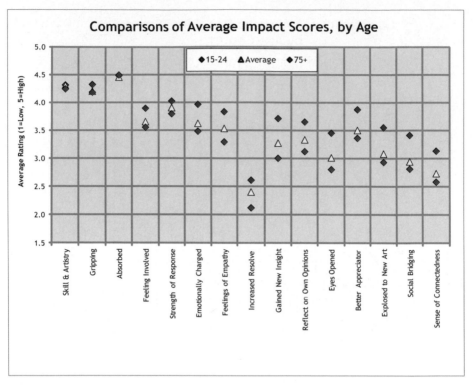

Comparisons of Average Impact Scores, by Age

- This chart shows average ratings for a select group of impact indicators by for respondents in the youngest and oldest age cohorts, along with the average figures for all respondents.

- Captivation is high across all age cohorts.

- Respondents in the youngest age cohort (15-24, red dots) reported systematically higher impacts across a range of impact indicators, especially those related to aesthetic enrichment (exposed to new work, better appreciating theatre) and social bonding (being connected to others in the audience and gaining an appreciation of other cultures).

- Younger respondents also reported higher impacts for several of the emotional resonance indicators, including "feeling emotionally charged," "connected to characters on stage," and encouraged to take action (increased resolve).

  - **This corroborates other findings suggesting that younger theatregoers (presumably students) have a personal connection to the art form.**

- Conversely, respondents in the oldest age cohort reported somewhat lower impact scores across a range of indicators. Results for the other age cohorts follow a similar pattern between these two extremes.

Gender Patterns in Decision-Making and Ticket Type

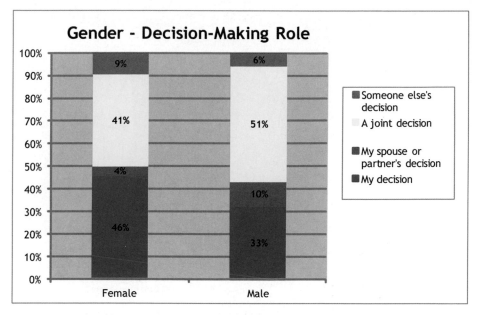

- Subtle differences regarding decision-making were observed between men and women. Most notably, women were more likely to have solely made the decision of whether or not attend (46% compared to 33% for men), whereas men were more likely to have been part of a joint decision, most likely with their partner.

- Women were just slightly more likely than men to be subscribers (62% vs. 59%, respectively).

Gender Differences with Respect to Readiness and Impact

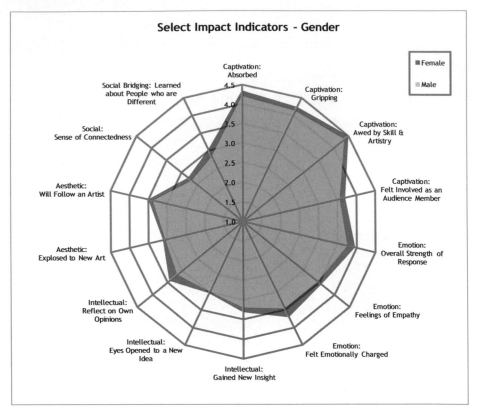

Select Impact Indicators - Gender

- Women and men reported similar levels of readiness, except that women reported higher levels of anticipation, on average, compared to men. This undoubtedly relates more to their role in the decision process (see next section) rather than their gender.

- In terms of impact (see chart this page), women reported generally higher impacts across the board, especially for feeling "emotionally charged" after the production.

  - Are there different patterns when viewed on a production by production basis? To some extent, but the pattern still holds overall.

  - Of course the extent of the difference between men and women will change by production. For example, overall, women rated their degree of empathy with characters .12 points higher than men across all productions. Men who attended *Equus* (a play where the lead character is a young man), on the other hand, reported higher levels of empathy than women, by .04 points.

- No significant difference was observed in the proportion of men and women who reported leaving with unanswered questions (35%, not shown).

Decision Role and Ticket Type

Variations in Readiness by Decision Role

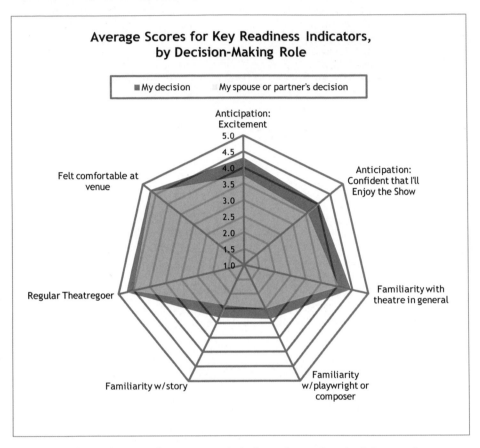

Average Scores for Key Readiness Indicators, by Decision-Making Role

■ My decision　　■ My spouse or partner's decision

- Respondents who reported being the sole decision-maker were significantly more likely to report higher anticipation levels, and were more likely to report familiarity with the playwright/composer and story.

- Decision-makers are also more likely to be regular theatregoers and to be familiar with theatre in general, as would be expected.

- Respondents whose spouse or partner made the decision reported lower levels of relevance, context and anticipation overall, as did respondents who said that someone else (not a spouse or partner) made the decision.

- Respondents who reported making a "joint decision" fall in between

100

these extremes (not shown).

- Decision-makers were also much more likely than those whose spouse or partner made the decision to report having done any preparation (27% vs. 18%, respectively).

  ▪ This illustrates one of the key differences between decision-makers and non-decision-makers, and suggests why surveys of ticket buyers do not always paint an accurate picture of the total audience. Decision-makers (who, presumably, are most often the ticket purchaser) have more information about what they are about to see, and have a higher emotional investment in the outing, as evidenced by higher anticipation levels.

Variations in Impact by Decision Role

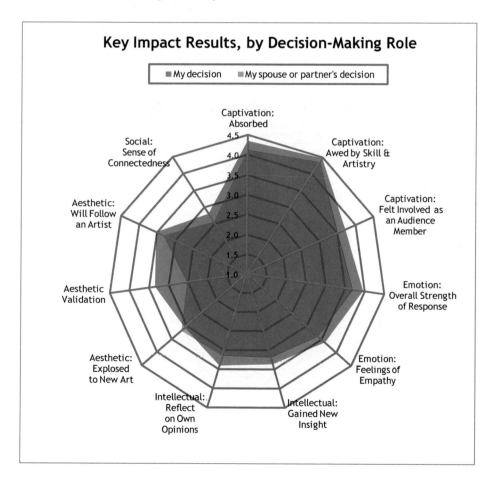

101

- As was the case with key indicators of readiness, decision-makers also reported higher levels of intrinsic impact on a small but significant margin.

- As might be expected, non-decision makers reported higher aesthetic growth impacts ("being exposed to something new").

- Conversely, decision-makers were substantially more likely than non-decision makers to report aesthetic validation outcomes ("How much did the performance remind you how much you love [the featured work on the program]?")

  - **Results suggest that ticket buyers are, in a sense, cultural guides or docents for the people they attend with. They are more knowledgeable, and better able to derive or extract impacts from a theatre experience. What might theatres do to reinforce this self-perception amongst ticket buyers?**

Variations in Readiness by Ticket Type

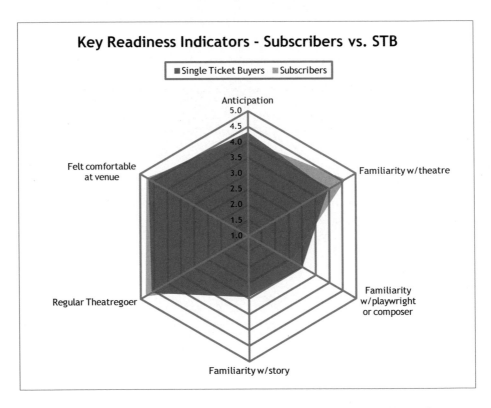

- There are notable and interesting differences in readiness between subscribers and single-ticket buyers (STB).

- Anticipation is higher for STB compared to subscribers. This is likely due, in part, to the fact that STB are significantly more likely than subscribers to be sole decision-makers (49% vs. 35%, respectively).

- Subscribers are more likely to be familiar with theatre in general, and, of course, more likely to attend more frequently, although STB are almost as likely as subscribers to say that they regularly attend the theatre.

- Levels of familiarity with the playwright/composer and with the story are higher for STB, as would be expected, since more STB are selecting shows based on the attributes of the individual show, while subscribers are more likely to attend shows that they did not specifically select, except as part of a package.

- Subscribers and STB feel equally comfortable and welcome at the theatre.

- In terms of motivations for attending (not shown), STB were more likely than subscribers to cite "to see the work of a specific artist or director" and "to revisit a familiar work or artist." In other words, their motivations correspond more directly to their level of context around a specific production.

  - These results may be interpreted in several ways. One implication is that a focus on educating subscribers about the art form will result in higher levels of intentionality, appreciation and impact for these key customers. Another implication is that education efforts should focus on opening up STB to new experiences that they would not necessarily choose for themselves.

Variations in Impact by Ticket Type

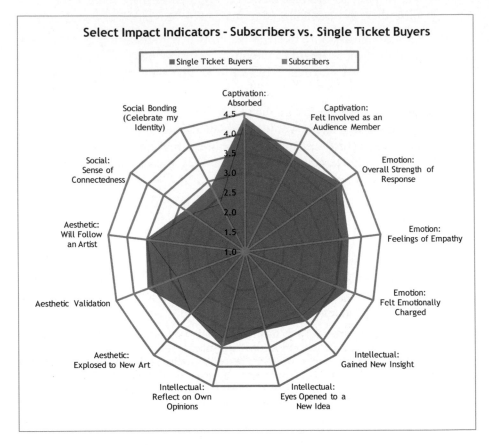

Select Impact Indicators - Subscribers vs. Single Ticket Buyers

■ Single Ticket Buyers   ■ Subscribers

- This chart tells a compelling and paradoxical story about impact. On average, single-ticket buyers reported higher impacts across all 58 productions.

- These findings correspond with patterns observed by age: younger respondents are more likely to be STB and more likely to be sole decision-makers. However, when this analysis is repeated for sole decision-makers only, the differences persevere.

- The paradox is this: The best customers (subscribers) have less impactful experiences, on average, compared to more infrequent buyers, most of whom are STB. Perhaps this helps to explain the slow erosion in subscription patterns industry-wide. Infrequent buyers, contrariwise, have more impactful experiences, but do not return at a frequency that will sustain the theatre.

  - **This raises all sorts of questions about why STB buyers do not return more frequently, if their experience is so satisfying.**

Annual Frequency of Attendance at the Host Theatre

Variations in Readiness by Frequency of Attendance

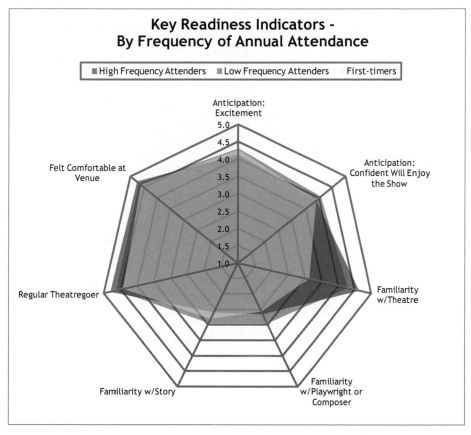

Key Readiness Indicators - By Frequency of Annual Attendance

- ■ High Frequency Attenders ■ Low Frequency Attenders First-timers

- Analysis of key readiness indicators by frequency of annual attendance at the host theatre yields intuitive patterns.

- As would be expected, first-timers (i.e., those who are at their first production at the host theatre company in the past 12 months) are less familiar with theatre in general (3.1 vs. 4.6 for high frequency respondents), and less likely to be a regular theatregoer relative to high frequency attenders (4.4 vs. 4.8, respectively). With an average score of 4.4 out of 5, however, 'first-timers' are, on average, regular theatregoers – they are just less familiar with theatre (self-reported).

- Low frequency attenders are most likely to be familiar with the playwright or composer/lyricist and with the story. This pattern corresponds with that observed by ticket type (single ticket buyers are more likely to be familiar with playwright/composer and story than subscribers).

- Anticipations levels are comparable for all three frequency cohorts, and all three report feeling welcome at the theatre.

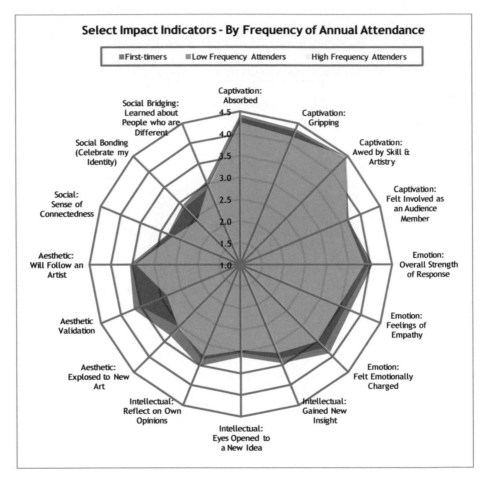

- First-timers (the blue area in the above radar chart) reported somewhat higher impacts across all indicators shown in chart above save for their sense of awe for the 'skill and artistry' of the performers, which is high for everyone.

- In particular, first-timers reported higher aesthetic enrichment impacts ('exposed to a style or type of theatre that you didn't know about') and intellectual stimulation impacts ('eyes opened to an idea or point of view...' and '...reflect on your own opinions or beliefs').

106

- High frequency attenders (89% of whom are subscribers) reported lower levels of impact on most indicators, especially aesthetic validation (i.e., revisiting familiar works), and lower levels of social bonding (i.e., works that "celebrate your cultural heritage or express a part of your identity," typified by *Avenue Q*).

  - Are high frequency attenders "used to" the performance experience? Or simply used to that particular theatre company's productions? Is there an element of 'newness' or 'surprise' that increases impact? For example, were first-timers less clear on what to expect and therefore more strongly affected? Like other pleasures in life, is less frequent indulgence more pleasurable? Does the wonder of theatre wear off if you see too much of it?

Comparisons of Impact and Readiness Results for Different Types of Theatrical Productions

Production Attributes

- To facilitate analysis across all 58 productions, the 18 participating theatres were asked to categorize their productions using a common set of attributes or categories. While every production is unique, it is useful to aggregate them on common dimensions in order to investigate commonalities and differences. For example, do respondents at comedic productions report different impacts than respondents at plays with challenging themes? How do plays and musicals compare in terms of reported impacts?

- Production attributes explored in this report include:

  - **Plays vs. musicals**

  - **Productions with Comedic Qualities (e.g., *Hatchetman*, *Abraham Lincoln's Big Gay Dance Party*) vs. productions with challenging material (e.g., *Ruined*, *Doubt*)**

  - **Shakespeare productions (e.g., *Measure for Measure*) vs. other dramas**

  - **Classic dramas (e.g., *Rosmersholm*) vs. contemporary dramas (*Three Days of Rain*)**

  - **Classic musicals (e.g., *Chicago*) vs. contemporary musicals (e.g., *Avenue Q*)**

  - **Star-driven (e.g., *Compulsion*, with Mandy Patinkin) vs. non star-driven**

  - **Family-friendly (e.g., *Little Women*) vs. non family-friendly**

- The goal here was to explore contrasts (e.g., funny versus serious work), although these classifications are sometimes ambiguous and overlapping.

- A complete listing of the individual productions associated with each attribute may be found in The Appendix.

Variations in Readiness: Plays vs. Musicals

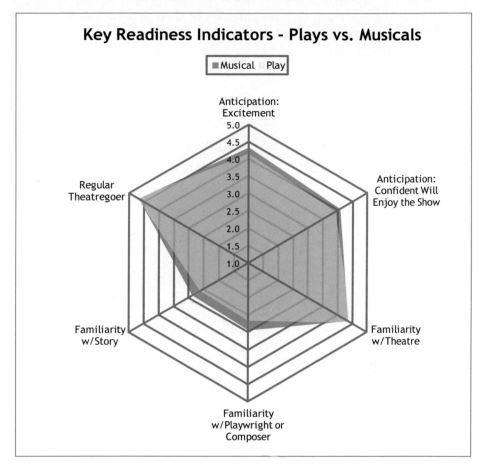

- Respondents who attended musicals reported slightly higher levels of anticipation (4.3 vs. 4.2, respectively), were more confident that they'd enjoy the performance, and reported higher levels of familiarity with the story, and with the playwright or composer/lyricist. This is intuitive given the higher popularity levels associated with musicals like *Cats*, *Chicago* and *Avenue Q*.

- Respondents who attended plays were slight more likely than those who attended musicals to report higher familiarity with theatre in general, and to be a regular theatregoer, although the difference is not significant.

Variations in Impact: Plays vs. Musicals

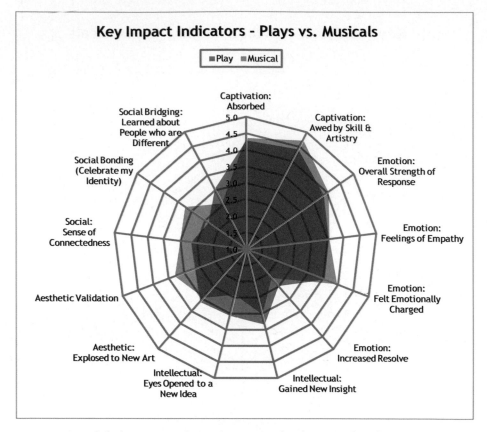

- As might be expected, results comparing impacts for plays vs. musicals reveal intuitive differences.

- While both plays and musicals generated similar captivation levels in terms of absorption, musicals generated substantially higher levels of captivation in terms of appreciation for the skill and artistry of the performers. Musical also generated higher levels of emotional charge, aesthetic validation ("How much did the performance remind you how much you love [the featured work on the program]?"), and social bonding ("To what extent did the performance celebrate your cultural heritage or express a part of your identity?"), which was especially high for *Avenue Q* and *A Broadway Christmas Carol*.

- Plays, on the other hand, achieved higher intellectual stimulation impacts, and higher impacts for social bridging ("To what extent did you gain a new appreciation for a culture other than your own?"), especially for The Public Theater's *Urge for Going* (the story of Palestinian girl growing up in a Lebanese refugee camp), Mixed Blood's *The House of Spirits* (the story of a Chilean family), and Arena's *Ruined*.

  - Of course many of these results are a function of the storyline of each production. For example, none of the musicals that were part of the study included topics relating to other cultures (such as *Miss Saigon* might have). So, we must be careful here not to generalize about all plays and all musicals.

Variations in Impact: Comedic Productions vs. Plays with Challenging Material

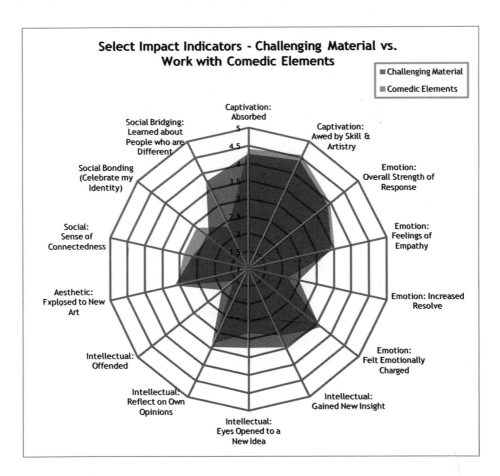

- A number of productions included in the study dealt with challenging issues (e.g., war, sexuality, rape, health care, death). The chart on the previous page compares impacts for these types of productions with impacts for productions involving comedic elements.
    - **Note that a few productions were coded for both comedic elements and challenging material, such as Woolly Mammoth's production of *Booty Candy*.**

- As might be expected, challenging works generated stronger intellectual stimulation impacts, including gaining new insight or learning and having one's eyes opened to a new idea or point of view that you hadn't fully considered.

- On the other hand, productions with comedic elements generated stronger social connectedness and social bonding impacts.
    - **When audiences laugh together, they form a social bond.**

Variations in Readiness:
Shakespearean vs. Other Plays

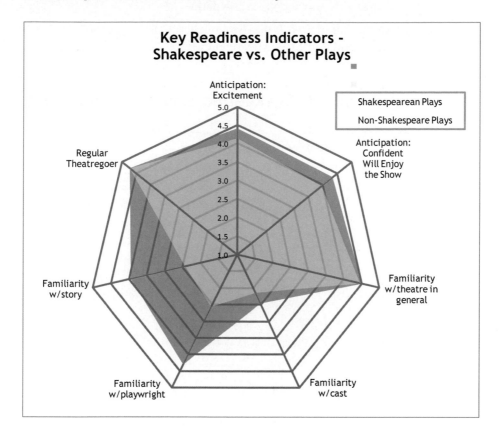

- Four of the 58 productions were plays by Shakespeare: *The Tempest* (a highly experimental production by The Cutting Ball Theater), *A Midsummer Night's Dream*, *Measure for Measure* and *All's Well That Ends Well*, the last two being The Public Theater's summertime productions in Central Park. We must be careful not to generalize about all Shakespearean work based on this limited cross-section of work. Even so, there are some interesting and intuitive patterns.

- In comparison with non-Shakespearean plays, respondents who attended Shakespearean productions were vastly more familiar with the story and with the playwright. They also reported higher levels of anticipation as well as confidence that they would enjoy the performance.

- These findings are intuitive given the general popularity and knowledge of Shakespeare's work amongst frequent theatregoers, particularly the Shakespeare enthusiasts who attend The Public Theater's productions in the park.

- Note that "familiarity with theatre in general" is comparable between Shakespeare and non-Shakespeare audiences.

Variations in Impact: Shakespearean vs. Other Plays

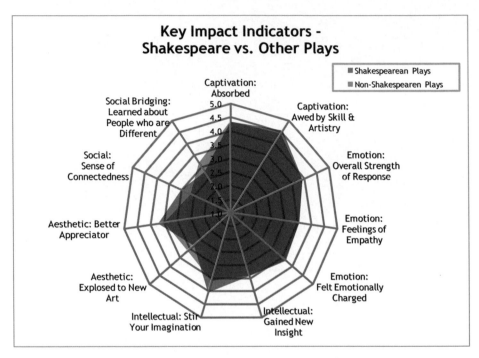

- Similar impacts are reported between Shakespearean and non-Shakespearean plays, with some interesting exceptions.

- The four Shakespearean productions were significantly more likely to "stir the imagination," (score of 4.0 vs. 3.6, respectively), although we cannot say if this was a function of the work itself, the director's interpretation, or some other factor.

- The Shakespearean productions were also more likely to generate a sense of "social connectedness" (score of 3.0 vs. 2.6, respectively).

  - This might be explained in part by the enhanced social setting offered at the two Shakespeare in the Park productions.

114

- Non-Shakespearean dramas generated higher impact scores for social bridging, which is most likely a function of subject matter (e.g., *Ruined* is more likely to generate higher social bridging scores than a Shakespeare play).

Variations in Impact: Star vs. Non-Star

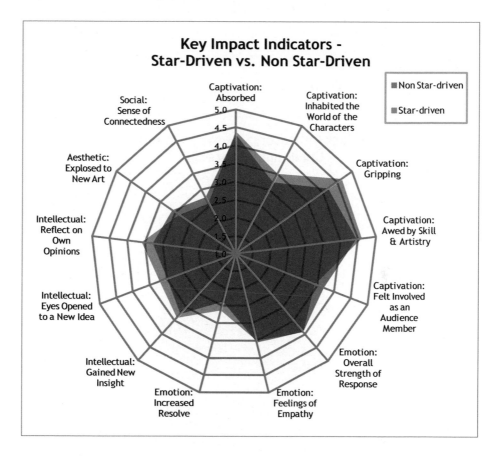

- The productions coded for "star" included *Compulsion* with Mandy Patinkin (The Public Theater), *The Milk Train Doesn't Stop Here Anymore* with Olympia Dukakis, two productions of *Let Me Down Easy*, a one-woman show with Anna Deavere Smith (Arena Stage and Berkeley Rep), and several others.

  - **It is difficult to conclude anything about the impact of star-driven productions without looking at a larger cross-section of productions.**

- Most interestingly, captivation levels were found to be higher for productions with star performers, which might reflect a sort of fascination with star performers, or might reflect the forcefulness of Anna Deavere Smith's performance, which weighed heavily in this category.

- Several intellectual stimulation impacts were also found to be higher among respondents at star-driven productions, which undoubtedly relates to the nature of those productions and not to the star power.

Variations in Impact: Family-Friendly Fare vs. Challenging Material

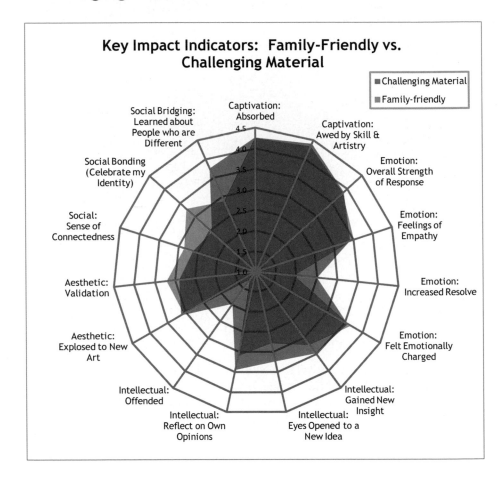

- Family-friendly productions (15 of the 58 productions surveyed) generated quite a different impact profile compared to productions with challenging material (18 out of 58), as illustrated in the chart at left. While these were family-friendly productions, note that surveys were filled out by adults, not children.

- Family-friendly productions were more likely to generate social impacts like feelings of connectedness and social bonding (i.e., celebrating one's own culture or identity), and were also more likely to generate aesthetic validation outcomes (i.e., revisiting familiar work), as would be expected with productions like *The Little Prince* (Bristol Riverside Theatre).

  - **The primary difference between family-friendly work and non-family friendly work (i.e., everything else) is just the increased social impacts.**

- In contrast, productions with challenging material were more likely to generate intellectual stimulation impacts (including being offended), increased resolve to make a change in your life (an emotional outcome) and social bridging impacts.

- It is interesting to note that both of these categories invoked the same levels of captivation and emotional response.

Anticipation Levels and Percent Capacity Sold

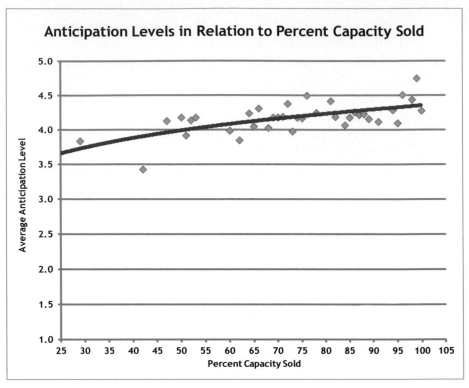

- The 18 participating theatres were required to report the seating capacity of the theatre and the percent of capacity sold for each sampled performance, allowing for analysis of readiness and impact results by house size and by percent capacity sold.

- No significant results were found between house size and indicators of readiness or impact.

- However, regression analysis reveals a significant relationship between percent capacity sold and anticipation levels, as illustrated in the chart above (R-squared = .02). As houses fill up, anticipation levels rise by a statistically significant level, though the effect size is not very large.

    - Other factors may play into this relationship, such as the popularity of the production or the presence of a star performer. Nevertheless, there appears to be a statistical relationship between fuller houses and a heightened sense of anticipation. This might be interpreted as rationale for using pricing tactics and other methods of "dressing the house" on slower nights.

Illustrative Results for Selected Productions

Impact Comparisons for Two Different Productions of *Ruined*

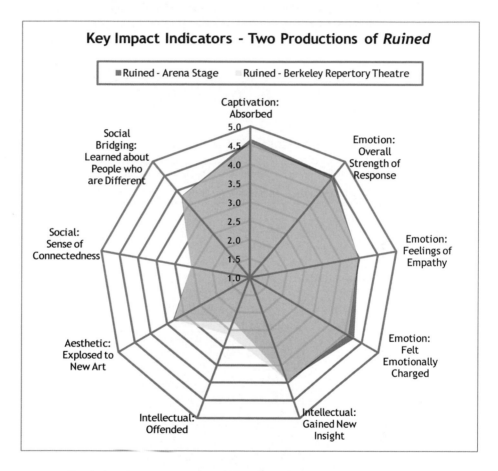

- Berkeley Repertory Theatre and Arena Stage presented two different productions of the same Pulitzer-Prize winning play, *Ruined*, by Lynn Nottage. The play is about women in the war-torn Republic of Congo, and addresses challenging topics such as rape and racial discrimination.

- Berkeley audiences were more likely than Arena Stage audiences to report being offended (scores of 2.7 vs. 2.3, respectively).

- Was this more about being outraged or truly about being uncomfortable with subject matter?

- Arena Stage audiences were just slightly more captivated, and reported slightly higher levels of emotional response, although the impact profile of these two productions is remarkably similar.

- On another indicator of intellectual stimulation, 51% of Arena Stage respondents reported leaving *Ruined* with unanswered questions, compared to 31% of Berkeley Rep audiences.

  - What might explain this difference? Something about the two different productions? The levels of audience engagement?

Impact Comparisons for the Same Production in Two Different Markets – *Let Me Down Easy*

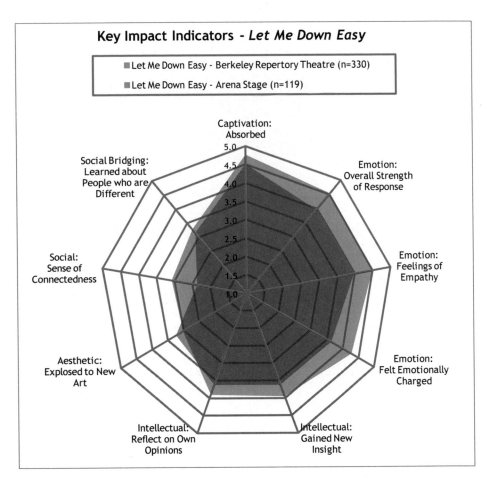

- Berkeley Repertory Theatre and Arena Stage also presented the same production of the same play - Anna Deavere Smith's *Let Me Down Easy*. (Note that data collection for Berkeley's production occurred online during an extension of the run, and that nearly all respondents were single-ticket buyers), while Arena Stage's data collection occurred in-venue using paper questionnaires, and included a mix of 60% subscribers and 40% STB. Only single-ticket buyers were included in this analysis, to increase comparability.

  - **Given the different data collection methodologies, comparison of results is not conclusive and should be considered experimental only.**

- Berkeley respondents reported higher impacts for all indicators except for aesthetic growth, suggest that Arena's STB for this production were relatively less familiar with Anna Deavere Smith's work, or the type of work.

- A separate analysis was run only on Arena Stage's audience for this production, comparing subscribers and STB. The only interesting difference is that subscribers reported higher levels of aesthetic growth (i.e., more of them were introduced to something new).

Impact Comparisons of Student and Adult Audiences - *The Odyssey*

Park Square Theatre Company in St. Paul mounted a production of The Odyssey. *As part of their sampling efforts, they coordinated with teachers during an educational student matinee event to distribute a modified version of the impact survey to students back in the classroom after the performance.*

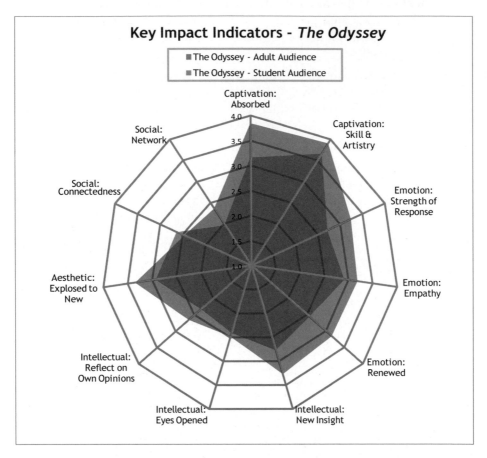

- Adult audiences reported higher impacts overall, with the exception of social connectedness. For example, adult audiences reported much higher levels of captivation (absorption) compared to students (3.9 vs. 3.2, respectively).

- Given that students attended with classmates with whom they already have a relationship (i.e., they already know and have a connection with many people in the audience), it makes sense that they would report higher social connectedness scores.

- Unlike adults, the students did not choose to attend this performance, but rather it was part of their regular classroom activities (i.e., classroom field trip). Does this help to explain the lower impact results?

- This was a pilot study, and we are grateful to staff members of Park Square Theatre and the teachers who cooperated with the study. Many of the students were impacted by the production, and it is not really reasonable to compare them to adults to opted to attend. Additionally, some of the students may have had issues with comprehending the questions on the survey.

- It would be interesting to compare different groups of students (by grade level, etc.) on their reactions to the same production. Are there other survey questions that would help younger audiences to better communicate about, or "unpack," their experience?

As part of the experiment-within-the-experiment of looking at student and adult audiences at Park Square's production of The Odyssey, *we encouraged the teachers in two classes that participated in the study to work with their students to see what they thought of the survey, what the questions were able to spark in terms of classroom conversation, etc.* **Christine Taylor**, *the director of operations at Arts Midwest, our Minneapolis/St. Paul partner in this work, observed two of those classes, and this is her report back. - CL*

I observed two classes that had seen The Odyssey the previous week and used this Monday's classes to take a modified version of the survey and have a discussion. There was some confusion, as you'll see, about whether the goal was to see if the students understood the survey, or to see how the survey worked – affecting the conversation about the show – both cases provided interesting observations.

The morning class focused mainly on the survey's vocabulary and comprehension of what the question was trying to ask. Discussion revolved around who the term 'cast' referred to—the actors as people or the characters they were playing. Most of the students agreed the survey was easy to follow and answer, the instructions were adequate and they felt comfortable being honest in answering, instead of feeling they should provide a correct answer. The students actually proposed a set of questions that they wanted to answer, but were not included in their particular survey: "Which characters did you agree with?" and "Which characters acted most like how you would have acted in a similar circumstance?"

The afternoon class was much more engaged. These students also agreed the survey was easy to take and asked good questions. They acknowledged that attending the performance brought them closer together as a class and gave them a shared experience, but, as one student said, they "had no interest in making it a *Dr. Phil* episode" and sharing feelings. One student commented that attending a different performance, *Of Mice and Men* for example, would have "related better" to those in the room. When

123

the teacher dug deeper to have the students define what they meant by "relate" and how *The Odyssey* actually related to them, students discussed circumstances such as "a father who was in jail" and "being separated from your parents for many years."

The students then turned the conversation to reflect on general audience reaction during the performance. Most students commented there were times when other audience members were disrespectful, interrupting the students' enjoyment of the performance. Students specifically mentioned using cell phones, crinkling candy wrappers, and talking as interruptions. This class, when pressed, also wondered why there wasn't a question asking, "Which character did you relate to most?"

As I was leaving this second classroom after the conversation ended, as the door was shutting behind me, the students began engaging in deeper conversations about which characters they related to most.

Comparison of Two Tennessee Williams Plays

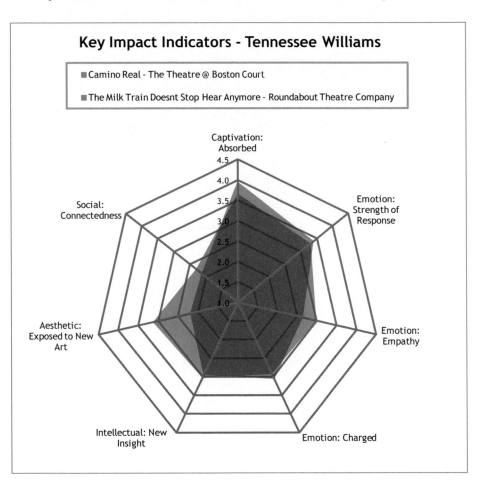

124

- The chart at left compares two different productions of plays by Tennessee Williams: Roundabout Theatre Company's *The Milk Train Doesn't Stop Here Anymore* and The Theatre @ Boston Court's *Camino Real*.

  - **Milk Train is about a woman dying at the end of a long terminal illness, and a conversation she has with a young man who trespasses on her property. Roundabout's production starred Olympia Dukakis. *Camino Real* takes place in a poor border town and is a surreal story that involves several "famous" characters like Don Quixote and Casanova.**

- *Milk Train* respondents reported higher levels of captivation (4.0 vs. 3.7 for absorption), on average. This may have been influenced by the presence of a star actress.

- In contrast, *Camino Real* generated higher rates of empathy (3.0 vs. 2.6) and aesthetic growth (3.1 vs. 2.2). The higher result for aesthetic growth is to be expected given that *Camino Real* is one of the lesser known Williams plays, and, most likely, new material for many in the audience.

- *Camino Real* respondents also reported somewhat higher levels of social connectedness. Could this be a function of the more intimate layout of Boston Court's 99-seat thrust stage theatre, compared to Roundabout's 404-seat venue for *Milk Train*?

  - **The overall learning from this comparison is to consider how plot elements of different plays by the same playwright may impact audiences differently, and how the relative obscurity of a work can drive aesthetic growth outcomes.**

Illustrative Results for Selected Theatres

This section provides results for three randomly-selected theatres, in order to illustrate variations across the three productions surveyed. The purpose here is not to identify 'winners' and 'losers' but to illustrate the range of impacts generated by different productions.

Three Productions Compared: Woolly Mammoth Theatre Company

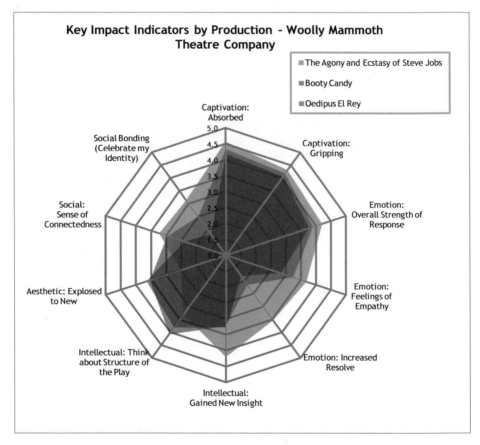

- Woolly Mammoth's three productions included a one-man show (*The Agony and Ecstasy of Steve Jobs*), a "dramedy" dealing with sexuality and race (*Booty Candy*), and a contemporary Chicano interpretation of a classical Greek drama (*Oedipus el Rey*). Overall, Woolly Mammoth's respondents were quite young and inquisitive.

- *Steve Jobs* respondents reported the highest impact ratings for all indicators save for "thinking about structure," and "being exposed to something new."
    - Given that many respondents reported motivations to attend "to see the work of a particular artist," it is not surprising that the performance did not expose them to new work.
- *Booty Candy* generated strong impacts in particular in "thinking about the structure" of the production, and similarly strong results for aesthetic growth. The structure of the play itself called for "breaking the 4th wall" (i.e., directly engaging the audience), and many of the unanswered questions dealt with this element of the performance:
    - "Twice in the play the '4th wall' was broken...I didn't feel the 2nd instance added anything and only left questions."
    - "Why did you opt for the 'play within a play' format?"
- *Oedipus el Rey* elicited lower impacts overall, except for aesthetic growth, which was highest of the three productions.

Three Productions Compared:
Roundabout Theatre Company

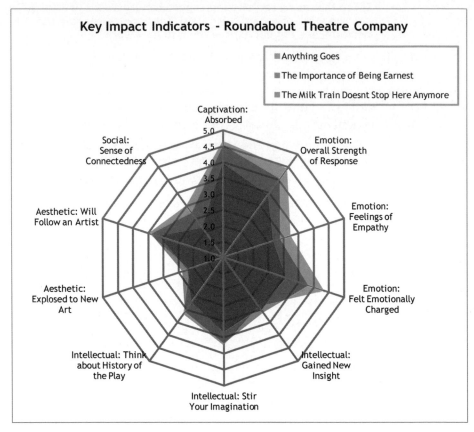

Key Impact Indicators - Roundabout Theatre Company

- Examining results from Roundabout Theatre Company's productions allows for a comparison across three "classic" production attributes: the classic comedy (*The Importance of Being Earnest)*, the classic drama (*The Milk Train...*) and the classic musical (*Anything Goes*).

- Respondents who attended *Earnest* reported highest impacts for "new insight" (3.1 vs. 2.9 for *Milk Train* and *Anything Goes*) and "being exposed to something new." Could these results have been influenced by the fact that Lady Bracknell was portrayed by a male actor (Brian Bedford)? Many of the unanswered questions addressed this:

    - "What was it like for Brian Bedford to play the role of a woman?"

    - "What was it like dressing up as a 19th Century woman?"

    - "What prompted the gender-switching? Brian: Are you looking into other plays where you could play the female's lead? Would you consider Lady Macbeth?"

- Overall, the classic musical *Anything Goes* received higher ratings for captivation, emotional resonance and social connectedness, while *Milk Train* respondents reported lower scores on most indicators.

Three Productions Compared: La Crosse Community Theatre

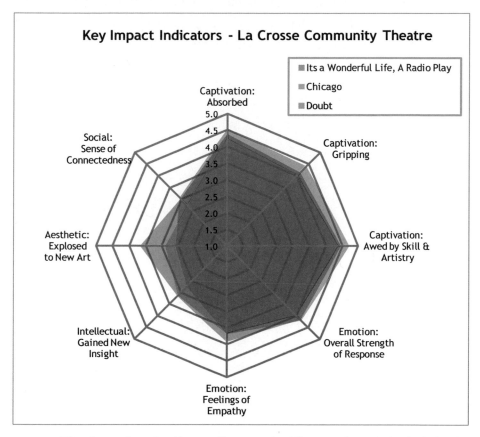

Key Impact Indicators - La Crosse Community Theatre

- The three plays La Crosse Community Theatre chose to include in the study were a holiday play (radio play adaptation of *It's a Wonderful Life*), a contemporary drama (audience choice winner *Doubt*) and a classic musical (*Chicago*).

- The radio play element of *It's a Wonderful Life* most likely led respondents to report higher impacts around aesthetic growth.

  - **Many of the unanswered questions revolved around the traditional radio play task of making staged sound effects using various props ("more information about the sound effects they used").**

- *Doubt* respondents reported somewhat lower impacts, except for around intellectual stimulation – gaining new insight, which were on par with *Wonderful Life*.

- Following similar patterns discussed earlier with respect to musicals vs. plays, *Chicago* respondents reported higher levels of captivation than those at *Doubt* or *Wonderful Life*.

- Overall, La Crosse audiences reported high scores on many of the key indicators, illustrating how community theatres can deliver on impact for their unique audiences.

Who Leaves with Unanswered Questions?

Unanswered Questions by Age Cohort

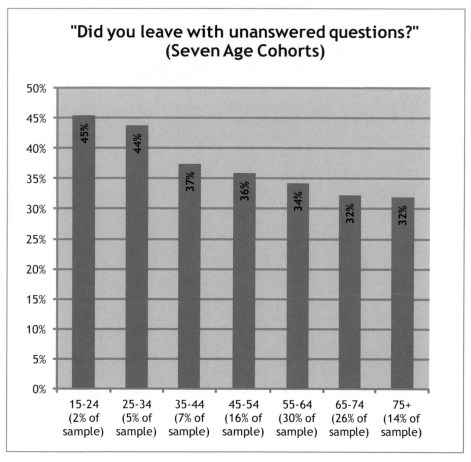

"Did you leave with unanswered questions?"
(Seven Age Cohorts)

- One of the key indicators denoting intellectual stimulation is "Did you leave the performance with questions you would have liked to have asked the actors, director or playwright?"

- Overall, 35% of respondents left the performance with unanswered questions. This figure ranged from a low of 10% for La Crosse Community Theatre's production of *It's a Wonderful Life, a Radio Play* to a high of 67% for The Theatre @ Boston Court's production of *El Camino Real*. If fact, all three of The Theatre @ Boston Court's productions topped the list of unanswered questions.

- In general, younger respondents (under 35) were more likely than older respondents to have unanswered questions (44% vs. 33% for those over 55 years old).

- Single-ticket buyers were slightly more likely than subscribers to leave with questions, while respondents who did anything to prepare for the performance were more likely than those who didn't prepare to generate questions (42% vs. 32%, respectively).

  - **Many factors might explain the variations in this indicator across productions (the nature of the production itself), theatres (the theatre's history of engaging audiences), and marketplaces (underlying demographics).**

- A discussion of the types of questions that audience left with (based on qualitative data from a follow-up open-ended question) can be found later in the report.

132

Unanswered Questions by Production Attribute

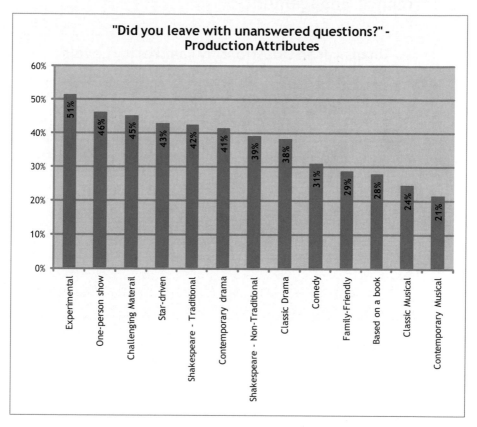

- Experimental productions, as might be expected, generated that highest percentage of unanswered questions, while classical and contemporary musicals generated the lowest percentages of unanswered questions.
  - Clearly, the nature of the production itself plays a large role in determining the likelihood of audiences leaving with unanswered questions.

Unanswered Questions by Familiarity and Post-Performance Engagement

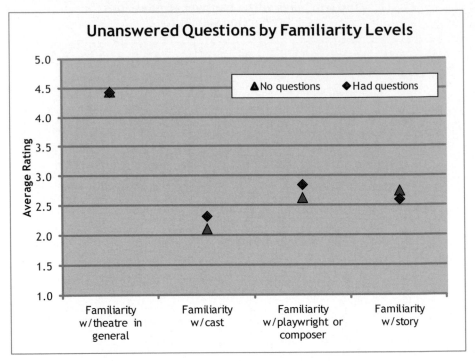

Unanswered Questions by Familiarity Levels

Average Rating

▲ No questions   ◆ Had questions

Familiarity w/theatre in general · Familiarity w/cast · Familiarity w/playwright or composer · Familiarity w/story

- When examining the relationship between familiarity and unanswered questions (above), it is clear that respondents with questions had greater familiarity with the cast and/or playwright/composer than those without questions. Both are positively correlated with whether or not a respondent had questions (Pearson correlation coefficient of .07 for familiarity with cast and .05 for familiarity with playwright/composer).

  - **Does increased familiarity actually inspire curiosity and a deeper desire for insight?**

- However, familiarity with the story is negatively associated with unanswered questions, which is intuitive. People who expressed more familiarity with the story were less likely to have questions about the play.

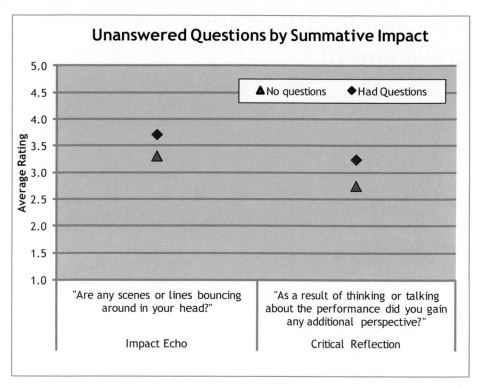

Unanswered Questions by Summative Impact

- This chart describes the strong positive relationship between unanswered questions and indicators of post-performance engagement (i.e., "impact echo" and critical reflection (Pearson correlation of .151 for impact echo and .181 for critical reflection). Simply having questions is associated with critical thinking overall, as well as an increased likelihood of extended impact.

    - This argues for audience education. Having unanswered questions is an indicator of positive impact, although not having an opportunity to discuss those questions is a missed opportunity. Creating ways to help audiences learn critical thinking skills (e.g., now to raise questions and seek answers) may lead to a more lasting impact over time.

Pre- and Post-Performance Engagement

Pre- and Post-Performance Engagement by Gender

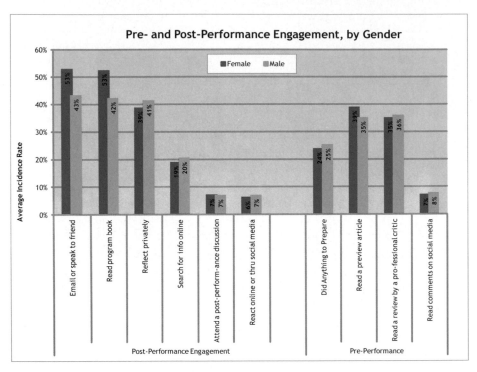

- In regards to post-performance processing, women were more likely than men to engage by emailing or speaking to friends about the performance afterwards, and by reading the printed program.

- Men, on the other hand, were slightly more likely to "reflect privately," and to "search for more information online."

- No significant gender differences were observed with respect to preparation or consumption of previews and reviews.

  - Note that the question about preparation ("Beforehand, did you do anything (apart from reading advertisements or brochures) in order to prepare yourself for the performance and understand what to expect?") was asked independently of the questions about having previews and reviews etc., suggesting that some people consider "reading a preview article" or "reading a review by a professional critic" to be preparation, while others don't.

136

Intensity of Post-Performance Conversation by Age Cohort

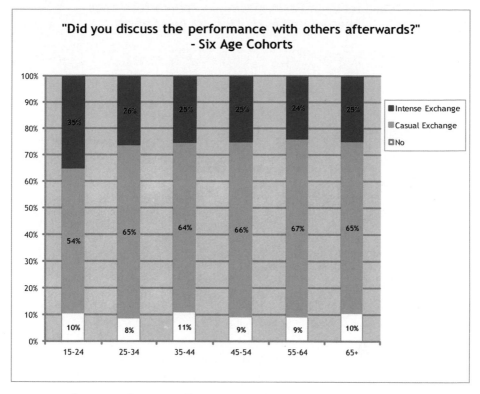

"Did you discuss the performance with others afterwards?"
- Six Age Cohorts

- A key question regarding post-performance engagement is whether or not, and how intensely, respondents discussed the performance with others.

- Overall, about 60% of all respondents reported having a "casual conversation" with others, and another quarter reported having an "intense exchange." In sum, nine out of ten patrons reported some discussion, suggesting that informal conversation is the dominant form of post-performance engagement.

- Note how younger respondents (under 25) are more likely than older cohorts report an intense exchange.

  - This might be due to the higher prevalence of participatory theatre involvement among younger audience members (i.e., more of them are acting students, etc.), which is borne out in other studies, but was not addressed in this one (i.e., none of the theatres elected to ask about current or prior involvement with theatre).

Pre-Performance Engagement by Age Cohort

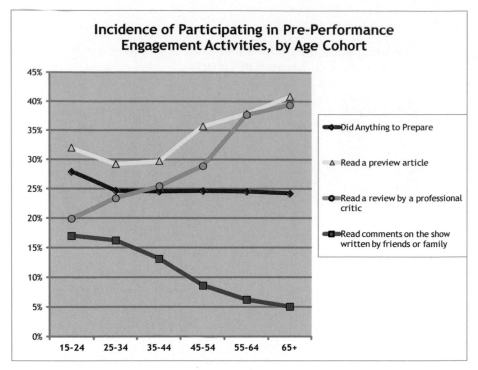

Incidence of Participating in Pre-Performance Engagement Activities, by Age Cohort

Legend:
- ◆ Did Anything to Prepare
- △ Read a preview article
- ● Read a review by a professional critic
- ■ Read comments on the show written by friends or family

- Most of the 18 participating theatres were interested in better understanding patterns of pre- and post-performance engagement.

- On average, 24% of all respondents indicated that they did anything to prepare, as illustrated in the chart above broken down by age cohort. A follow-up open-ended question asked them what, specifically, they did to prepare (see next page).

- The 18 theatres were particularly interested in the extent to which patrons had read previews or reviews in advance of attending, or had read comments about the play "written by friends, family members, or audiences members (e.g., on Facebook)."

- Older respondents were significantly more likely to report reading previews and reviews. In fact, patrons in the 65+ age cohort were twice as likely as patrons in the 15-24 age cohort to report having read a review by a professional critic (39% vs. 20%, respectively). The disparity in age between preview readers is not so extreme, suggesting that advance media coverage reaches a more diverse cross-section of the market with respect to age.

- Younger patrons, however, were significantly more likely than older patrons to "read comments on the show written by friends, family members, or audiences members (e.g., on Facebook)," illustrating the generational shift in what are considered to be credible sources of information about cultural events.

What "Preparation" Means

- As a follow up to "did you do anything to prepare," six theatres opted to include an open-ended question asking respondents to describe what preparatory activities they did: "Please give an example of what you did to prepare specifically for this performance."

- Often, preparatory activities were determined by the nature of the production itself (e.g., reading the book upon which a play is based).

- Open-ended responses were coded into the following seven general categories of responses:

  1. Reading reviews or preview articles (including interviews)
     - **"I read a review in the *Washington Post*."**

  2. Searching for information online (including watching videos on the theatre's website or on YouTube)
     - **"I Googled the background of the story."**

  3. Reviewing collateral material from the theatre (brochure, website, email)
     - **"I read the brochure and website description of the production."**

  4. Reading the printed program

  5. Reading or watching the source material upon which the play is based (e.g., the play itself, a book, a movie)
     - **"Read the play" and "Re-read the play"**

  6. Listening to soundtrack (specific to musicals)

  7. Talking with others beforehand
     - **"Asked someone who was familiar with the drama about it."**
     - **"My wife informed me of the history of the story and its performances."**

- Note that some responses were coded for multiple activities.

- Results for three diverse productions were compared: 1) The Cutting Ball Theater's production of *The Tempest*, Musical Theatre West's production of *Cats*, and Arena Stage's production of *Ruined*.

- Of the193 respondents for *The Tempest*, 73 (or 38%) reported a specific preparatory activity.
- Of the 375 respondents for *Cats*, 52 (or 14%) reported a specific preparatory activity.
- Of the 188 respondents for *Ruined*, 47 (or 25%) reported a specific preparatory activity.

Specific Preparatory Activities for Three Productions

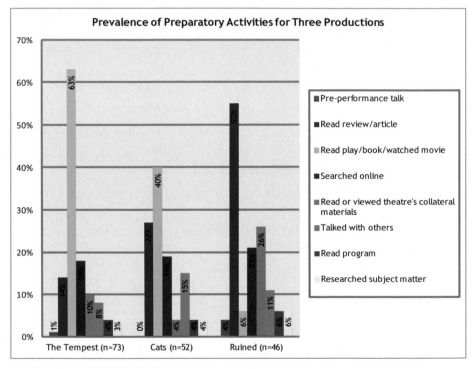

- This chart illustrates the relative proportion of respondents who cited doing specific preparatory activities out of all respondents who answered that question and attended that particular performance.
  - Thus, the percentages in this graph do not represent all patrons at these productions, but only those patrons who reported doing at least one specific preparatory activity. Moreover, the figures may be influenced by the availability of some of these activities (e.g., a production may not have been reviewed).
- Key differences between the three productions:
  - About six in ten respondents who attended *The Tempest* read the play (sometimes for a second or third time), or read a

140

synopsis. Several actually viewed several movie interpretations (e.g., Peter Greenaway).

- A little over half of Arena Stage *Ruined* respondents who answered this question read a review and/or preview article about the play. It is interesting to note that respondents to all of Arena's productions were highly likely to note having read a review or article in advance of any of the three productions included in the survey. One quarter of *Ruined* respondents also read or viewed the theatre's collateral materials, in particular information on the Arena website, and 21% reported online activity.

- *Cats* respondents did a range of different activities, with 40% reading T.S. Eliot's poetry (*Old Possum's Book of Practical Cats*) or watching a movie version of the musical. About one-quarter read a review or article in the local paper, and 19% searched for information online. Note that *Cats* respondents were most likely to have talked with others in advance of the performance. Some noted speaking to their children or grandchildren about the play, helping to prepare them and hopefully instill a greater sense of anticipation.

- The differences observed here are intuitive: those who attended Shakespeare brushed up on their Shakespeare (perhaps anticipating a challenging evening?), and those who reside in a heavily media-influenced metropolitan area (in this instance D.C.) are likely to read critical reviews.

  - It's interesting to note that some respondents reporting re-reading the play, listening to the soundtrack again or re-watching the movie (of *Cats*). There is a sense of revisiting the work that is a form of aesthetic validation in and of itself.

  - Results also underscore the critical role that criticism plays in the arc of engagement, especially in large competitive markets.

141

Post-Performance Engagement by Age Cohort

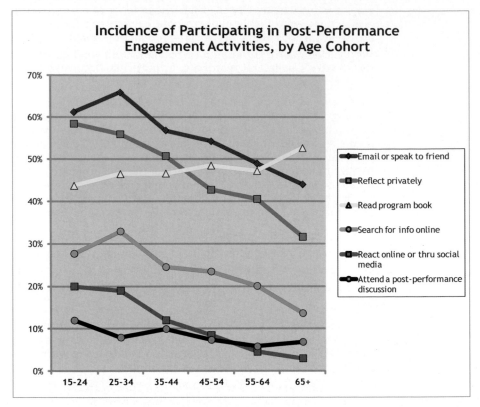

Incidence of Participating in Post-Performance Engagement Activities, by Age Cohort

Legend:
- Email or speak to friend
- Reflect privately
- Read program book
- Search for info online
- React online or thru social media
- Attend a post-performance discussion

- The chart above shows results for six post-performance engagement activities by age cohort. (Note that multiple responses were allowed.)

- In general, informal conversation (i.e., "email or speak to a friend afterwards") and private modes of reflection ("reflect privately," "review the program book") were most prominent across all age cohorts.

- Younger respondents reported generally higher levels of post-performance engagement, with the exception of reading program books. As might be expected, younger respondents (under 35) are far more likely than older respondents to engage in word of mouth ("email or speak to a friend about the performance") and online activities ("search for information online" and "react to the performance online or through social media").

- It is interesting to note that younger respondents were also much more likely to reflect privately.

- ▪ **What might explain this? What can theatre companies do to encourage private reflection?**

- Results point to the value of printed programs as a means of post-performance engagement, especially for older patrons.

  - ▪ **How might printed programs be leveraged to stimulate informal conversation about the production afterwards? What incentives might motivate patrons to share printed programs with friends?**

- Overall, results point to the need to offer multiple channels of post-processing so that regardless of age (and experience levels), all audience members can find the "right" means of making sense of their theatre experiences.

Pre- and Post-Performance Engagement by Ticket Type

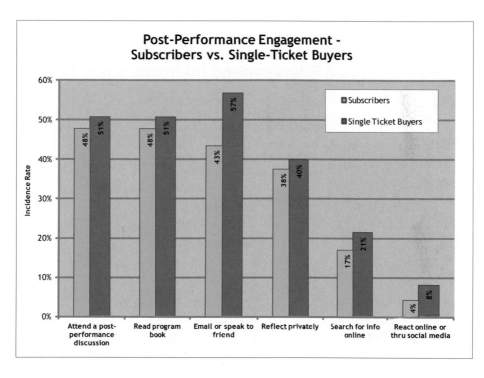

- Single-ticket buyers were more likely than subscribers to report having done something to prepare (27% vs. 22%, respectively). No significant differences were observed by ticket type with respect to reading previews or reviews, although STB were twice as likely as subscribers to have read comments "written by friends, family members, or audiences members (e.g., on Facebook)" (10% vs. 5%, respectively).

- As illustrated in the chart on the previous page, STB reported somewhat higher rates of engagement in all six post-performance activities, which is consistent with their overall higher impacts.

- STB were also six percentage points more likely than subscribers to report an "intense exchange" afterwards (28% vs. 22%, respectively).

- Note the significantly higher rate of engagement in "email or speak to a friend about the performance" (57%) among STB.

  - Results suggest that STB are emissaries for word-of-mouth, and should be encouraged to do what they do naturally—spread the word about where they've been and what they've seen. Over half of them are already doing it.

Pre-Performance Engagement by Production Type

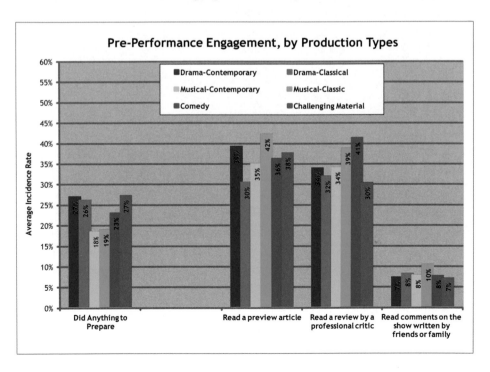

144

- Interesting variations in patterns of pre-performance engagement can be observed across the production types.

- For example, respondents attending dramas were more likely than respondents attending musicals to say that they did anything to prepare (27% vs. 19%, respectively).

- Respondents attending comedic productions were only slightly less likely than respondents attending "challenging material" productions to say that they prepared (23% vs. 27%, respectively).

- Preview articles were more likely to be cited by contemporary drama patrons compared to classic drama patrons (39% vs. 30%, respectively), which may reflect patterns of media coverage or respondents' appetites for reading about classic plays they may have already seen.

- "Reading a review by a professional critic" was most likely to be cited by respondents at comedic productions, although we were unable to track which productions in which markets received reviews.

- Respondents at classic musicals were slightly more likely to report having read comments "written by friends, family members, or audiences members (e.g., on Facebook)."
  - **Overall, results point to the continued importance of media coverage and professional criticism in driving theatre attendance.**

- Also plotted in this chart is the average level of familiarity with theatre in general (the gray line), which rises with age (except for the youngest age cohort, which may be more involved with theatre, and therefore report higher levels of familiarity).

- Are younger theatregoers more "susceptible" to impact because they know less about theatre (i.e., "it's all fabulous because I don't know enough to be critical")? This does not seem to be the case, given the higher familiarity levels associated with the youngest age cohort. Does a lifetime of theatregoing "raise the bar" of impact so high as to temper impact among older, more seasoned theatregoers?

  - **We should be careful to point out that older theatregoers attend much more frequently than younger theatregoers despite the fact that older theatregoers report less fulfilling experiences, on average.**

- A variety of other relationships were observed with respect to summative impact.

- Single-ticket buyers reported systematically higher levels of summative impact, compared to subscribers. This underscores the earlier findings about higher impacts for STB.

  - **On the fulfillment indicator, the average score for STB was 4.1 compared to 3.8 for subscribers (R-squared =.01)**

  - **On the "future impression" indicator, the average score for STB was 3.5 compared to 3.1 for subscribers (R-squared =.02)**

- Similarly, less frequent attenders reported higher summative impacts, ranging from an average score of 3.6 for first-timers to 3.1 for high-frequency attenders (on the fulfillment indicator).

  - **Why are more frequent theatregoers less satisfied, on average? Are they more sophisticated, and therefore harder to please? Given that high-frequency attenders are much more familiar with theatre in general than first-timers and low-frequency attenders, this hypothesis is at least partially supported by the data. However, if first-timers and low-frequency attenders are more satisfied, on average, why are they not attending more frequently? This seems counter-intuitive, and might speak to an underlying driver of the "churn" phenomenon. It seems to suggest that satisfaction with the artistic experience, alone, is not enough to drive repeat purchase. If excellent artistic work is not enough to retain loyal patrons, what is?**

- We did not find significant relationships between summative impact and venue size or percent capacity sold, although subsequent analysis points to a relationship between percent capacity sold and anticipation levels.

Discussion of Qualitative Data

Overview of Qualitative Data Sources

- Theatres were required to include one open-ended question relating to intellectual stimulation: "What questions would you have liked to ask the actor, director or playwright?" (conditional on answering "Yes" to the previous question, "Did you leave with any unanswered questions…").

- A number of other open-ended questions about motivations, preparation, comfort, emotional response and satisfaction were optional:
    - In your own words, what was the main reason you attended this performance?
    - Please give an example of what you did to prepare specifically for this performance.
    - What, if anything, would have made you feel more comfortable or welcome at the theatre?
    - What emotions were you feeling as you left the theatre?
    - Was there anything that made your experience at the performance particularly satisfying or unsatisfying? If so, please share.
    - What would you like for us to know about our work on stage?

- The following pages provide an overview and interpretation of responses to the key questions relating to intrinsic impact in particular: intellectual stimulation and emotional resonance. Examining the richness of response provides insight and nuance to quantitative results.

Questions Patrons Would Have Liked to Ask

- On average, 35% of respondents indicated that they left with unanswered questions for the actors, director or playwright.

- Ninety-eight percent of those respondents took the time to write down one or two of their questions, resulting in a mountain of 6,300 nuanced, qualitative responses about what was on their mind. The majority of the responses were in the form of a question. Many respondents chose to comment on a particular aspect of the performance through praise and/or criticism. Others responded that they had no questions, or that their questions were answered at a post-performance discussion or Q & A session.

- Responses ranged from deep reflections on the subject matter or a question the play invoked to practical questions about costumes and lighting. Most were directed at actors, and were often about character development, preparation and how it felt to portray this character or have to express certain actions and/or feelings.

- We observed five different categories of questions respondents would have liked to have asked. Examples of questions within each category are provided over the following pages. The five categories are (in rough order of prevalence):

  - QUESTIONS ABOUT INSPIRATION AND PERSONAL CONNECTION: These questions were directed at the actors and playwrights primarily. Respondents were interested in how the characters and the story were developed, and in particular the emotional connection the playwright and/or actor had to the characters. Some respondents wanted to know why the theatre company choose to produce the play. Sometimes these questions were a reflection of dislike or dissatisfaction with the experience.

    - How did it feel to be completely naked on stage?

    - Why did Ibsen write a play so negative about progressive politicians when he was often associated with progressive views?

    - Why choose *The Tempest* to produce?

    - Where you emotionally drained playing a *"Ruined"* woman to the extent that your own intimate relationships changed?

  - QUESTIONS ABOUT CHARACTER DEVELOPMENT AND TRAINING/PERFORMING: These questions were a little more practical in nature and focused on the craft of acting. Often they were accompanied by words of praise or derision about actors' performances.

    - How did you prepare for the more awkward scenes (i.e. naked, being a horse)?

    - I would've wanted to discuss why physical violence was the main character's response to his feelings of cowardice.

    - As a director, how did you ensure the actor portrayed the vision comfortably?

    - How did the actors do it nightly and keep it fresh? What was the hardest thing about playing your role?

  - QUESTIONS ABOUT INTERPRETATION AND MEANING: Respondents often had comments and questions around interpretation of characters and the subject matter. These were the types of questions aimed at directors about their choice to include one thing or another. In general, these questions alluded to respondents desire to understand the meaning behind the choices that created that specific performance - why one character did this or that, why the director or actor decided to interpret the character or story in one way or another, etc.

156

- Why did it end as it did?

- Was the playwright trying to explain Sid's pathology as being a result of his Jewish identity?

- What symbolic connection was Anne's presence in bed intended to convey?

- Given the many elements the audience has to take on faith, why did the rain have to be so literal? (I hope it was at least slightly warm.)

- QUESTIONS ABOUT PLOT AND SUBJECT MATTER: **Although questions about plot are scattered throughout other question categories, it seemed clear that some respondents were seeking clarity in regards to plot. Sometimes this line of questioning was directed towards endings, and illustrated a curiosity about "what happens after this?" almost as if the respondent wanted to continue the experience.**

  - Why was Maria in love with Kyneston as opposed to merely adoring him?

  - What is being done to sensitize doctors to patients' feelings and final journey?

  - I'm very interested in the access to unionists in China and wanted to hear more about their struggles.

  - Why did "Pip" inherit the house? Why was the quality of design by the "firm" not good after Theo died if in fact he wasn't the creative one of the pair?

- QUESTIONS ABOUT STRUCTURE AND PRODUCTION DESIGN: **More practically-oriented, these questions were often more prevalent for productions where there was an unusual design element (e.g., the use of puppets) or play structure. *Booty Candy* is an example of this.**

  - Curious about the period setting—looked great, but why this choice?

  - I wanted to ask the sound guy about his process of arriving at his design. I thought it was so well-suited to the show and enhanced it tremendously.

  - Does the order of the play truly change based on audience choice, and what challenges does that present for cast and crew?

  - How did they decide on the stage setup? How did the actors adapt to being in the middle of the audience?

- Overall, all questions point to the fact that many respondents are seeking what we call the "moment of curatorial insight" – that "aha" moment when they understand the motivations and the "why" that helps them to make meaning out of the artistic experience. This is exemplified by the simple question posed by several respondents: *"What's it all about?"*

157

Emotional Response

Word clouds: "What emotions were you feeling as you left the theatre?"

- Impacts around emotional resonance are complex. The strength of emotional response does not communicate what kinds of emotions and the degree to which those emotions were shared amongst audience members. Most artists and arts organizations are seeking an emotional connection, and the study's findings show how the 58 productions elicited strong emotional responses across a range of different types of productions.

- To better understand the range of emotions respondents felt after a performance, some theatres opted to ask respondents to share the specific emotions they were feeling in their own words.

- This open-ended question generated a wide range of responses, depending on the nature of the play. Musicals and family-friendly works mostly elicited responses of happiness, joy, enjoyment, elation, etc.

- The majority of plays at which this question was posed, however, prompted an array of various and often contradictory responses. One play can inspire tremendous sadness and happiness at the same time. Inspiration, admiration for characters, actors, playwrights is often alluded to, reflecting the sense of awe and appreciation many feel after a performance.

- The same performance can produce tremendously different emotional impacts for different audience members. On the next several pages, word clouds based on responses for three different plays communicate the complexity of emotions elicited by each play.

  - *Ruined,* produced by Arena Stage - a contemporary drama about women in war-torn Republic of Congo (physical and emotional violence are plentiful).

  - *Compleat Female Stage Beauty,* produced by City Lights Theater Company - contemporary drama about one actor's struggle in the time when the practice of men portraying women on stage was fading (the main character was a man who was famous for playing female roles).

  - *Booty Candy,* produced by Woolly Mammoth Theatre Company - a 'dramedy' about a gay African-American's experience that explores issues around sexuality and race.

Ruined, Arena Stage

- Note the juxtaposition of "hopeful" and "happy" with "sad" and "anger" – illustrating how the work elicited a wide range of emotions.

Compleat Female Stage Beauty, City Lights Theater Company

- Generally, this production elicited consistently positive emotions.

- Again, note the extreme juxtaposition of emotions associated with this 'dramedy' – capturing the essence of the work.

The Appendix: Categorization of Productions

Production Attributes

Companies were asked to categorize each surveyed production in a variety of ways for comparison.

Experimental theatre

(experimental, perhaps surreal interpretations of either contemporary or classical works)
The Tempest (The Cutting Ball Theater)
Bone to Pick & *Diadem* (The Cutting Ball Theater)
Lady Grey...in Ever Lower Light and Other Plays (The Cutting Ball Theater)

One-Person Shows

(plays written and performed by one actor)
Let Me Down Easy (Arena Stage and Berkeley Repertory Theatre)
The Agony and Ecstasy of Steve Jobs (Woolly Mammoth Theatre Company)
The Eyes of Babylon (Bristol Riverside Theatre Company)

Challenging Material

(plays that address sensitive and/or provocative subject matter)
The Eyes of Babylon (Bristol Riverside Theatre Company)
Ruined (Arena Stage and Berkeley Repertory Theatre)
Oedipus el Rey (Woolly Mammoth Theatre Company)
The Agony and Ecstasy of Steve Jobs (Woolly Mammoth Theatre Company)
Booty Candy (Woolly Mammoth Theatre Company)
The Tempest (The Cutting Ball Theater)
Bone to Pick & *Diadem* (The Cutting Ball Theater)
Lady Grey...in Ever Lower Light and Other Plays (The Cutting Ball Theater)
Camino Real (The Theatre @ Boston Court)
How to Disappear Completely and Never Be Found (The Theatre @ Boston Court)
Completeness (South Coast Repertory)
Three Days of Rain (South Coast Repertory)
The House of Spirits (Mixed Blood Theatre Company)
Agnes Under the Big Top (Mixed Blood Theatre Company)
Doubt (La Crosse Community Theatre)
Opus (Park Square Theatre)
Rosmersholm (The Pearl Theatre Company)
The Milk Train Doesn't Stop Here Anymore (Roundabout Theatre Company)
Urge for Going (The Public Theater)

Shakespeare – Non-Traditional Interpretation

The Tempest (The Cutting Ball Theater)
A Midsummer Night's Dream (South Coast Repertory)

Shakespeare –Traditional Interpretation
All's Well That Ends Well (The Public Theater)
Measure for Measure (The Public Theater)

Star-Driven
(Productions that included a mainstream star actor)
Let Me Down Easy (Arena Stage and Berkeley Repertory Theatre)
A Time to Kill (Arena Stage)
The Importance of Being Earnest (Roundabout Theatre Company)
The Milk Train Doesn't Stop Here Anymore (Roundabout Theatre Company)
Compulsion (The Public Theater)

Comedy
Superior Donuts (Arden Theatre Company)
Hatchetman (The People's Light & Theatre Company)
A Broadway Christmas Carol (MetroStage)
The Real Inspector Hound (MetroStage)
Booty Candy (Woolly Mammoth Theatre Company)
Lemony Snicket's The Composer is Dead (Berkeley Repertory Theatre)
Abraham Lincoln's Big Gay Dance Party (City Lights Theater Company)
Distracted (City Lights Theater Company)
A Midsummer Night's Dream (South Coast Repertory)
Completeness (South Coast Repertory)
Avenue Q (Mixed Blood Theatre Company)
It's a Wonderful Life, A Radio Play (La Crosse Community Theatre)
Chicago (La Crosse Community Theatre)
The Misanthrope (The Pearl Theatre Company)
Wittenburg (The Pearl Theatre Company)
The Importance of Being Earnest (Roundabout Theatre Company)
Anything Goes (Roundabout Theatre Company)

Classic Musical
Chicago (La Crosse Community Theatre)
Anything Goes (Roundabout Theatre Company)
Cats (Musical Theatre West)
His Eye Is on the Sparrow (MetroStage)

Contemporary Musical
A Broadway Christmas Carol (MetroStage)
Avenue Q (Mixed Blood Theatre Company)
Lemony Snicket's The Composer is Dead (Berkeley Repertory Theatre)
Summer of Love (Musical Theatre West)
The Wedding Singer (Musical Theatre West)
Little Women (Bristol Riverside Theatre Company)

Family-Friendly
The Little Prince (Bristol Riverside Theatre Company)
Little Women (Bristol Riverside Theatre Company)
The Adventures of Tom Sawyer (The People's Light & Theatre Company)
Lemony Snicket's The Composer is Dead (Berkeley Repertory Theatre)
The Arabian Nights (Berkeley Repertory Theatre)
A Broadway Christmas Carol (MetroStage)

Cats (Musical Theatre West)
It's a Wonderful Life, A Radio Play (La Crosse Community Theatre)
The Odyssey (Park Square Theatre)
To Kill a Mockingbird (Park Square Theatre)
The Importance of Being Earnest (Roundabout Theatre Company)
Anything Goes (Roundabout Theatre Company)
Urge for Going (The Public Theater)
All's Well That Ends Well (The Public Theater)
Measure for Measure (The Public Theater)

Contemporary Drama
Superior Donuts (Arden Theatre Company)
Wanamaker's Pursuit (Arden Theatre Company)
Completeness (South Coast Repertory)
Let Me Down Easy (Arena Stage and Berkeley Repertory Theatre)
A Time to Kill (Arena Stage)
Ruined (Arena Stage and Berkeley Repertory Theatre)
Oedipus el Rey (Woolly Mammoth Theatre Company)
The Agony and Ecstasy of Steve Jobs (Woolly Mammoth Theatre Company)
Booty Candy (Woolly Mammoth Theatre Company)
The Arabian Nights (Berkeley Repertory Theatre)
Bone to Pick & *Diadem* (The Cutting Ball Theater)
Lady Grey...in Ever Lower Light and Other Plays (The Cutting Ball Theater)
Compulsion (The Public Theater)
Compleat Female Stage Beauty (City Lights Theater Company)
Equus (City Lights Theater Company)
Camino Real (The Theatre @ Boston Court)
How to Disappear Completely and Never Be Found (The Theatre @ Boston Court)
Heavier Than... (The Theatre @ Boston Court)
Completeness (South Coast Repertory)
Three Days of Rain (South Coast Repertory)
The House of Spirits (Mixed Blood Theatre Company)
Agnes Under the Big Top (Mixed Blood Theatre Company)
Doubt (La Crosse Community Theatre)
Opus (Park Square Theatre)
Wittenburg (The Pearl Theatre Company)
Compulsion (The Public Theater)
Urge for Going (The Public Theater)

Classic Drama
A Moon for the Misbegotten (Arden Theatre Company)
The Tempest (The Cutting Ball Theater)
Bone to Pick & *Diadem* (The Cutting Ball Theater)
The Odyssey (Park Square Theatre)
To Kill a Mockingbird (Park Square Theatre)
Rosmersholm (The Pearl Theatre Company)
The Misanthrope (The Pearl Theatre Company)
The Milk Train Doesn't Stop Here Anymore (Roundabout Theatre Company)

Based on a Book
The Little Prince (Bristol Riverside Theatre Company)
Little Women (Bristol Riverside Theatre Company)
A Time to Kill (Arena Stage)

The Arabian Nights (Berkeley Repertory Theatre)
Lemony Snicket's The Composer is Dead (Berkeley Repertory Theatre)
The House of Spirits (Mixed Blood Theatre Company)
It's a Wonderful Life, A Radio Play (La Crosse Community Theatre)
The Odyssey (Park Square Theatre)
To Kill a Mockingbird (Park Square Theatre)

3 ASKING ARTISTIC LEADERS ABOUT AUDIENCES

At the core of this research is an attempt to understand the impact that art is having on an individual audience member. Equally important, however, is understanding further what impact the audience is having on the artistic leadership of organizations.

In order to pursue that question, we enlisted theatre director and arts consultant Rebecca Novick to conduct twenty interviews with artistic leaders from across the theatre field. The questions are meant to allow for a frank conversation about the role of the audience in the selection, creation and dissemination of work.

This section begins with a thoughtful and thought-provoking essay by Novick, who now heads the Triangle Lab, an experimental collaboration between the California Shakespeare Theater and Intersection for the Arts in San Francisco that is seeking ways to re-fashion the artist-audience relationship.

Following her essay, we have included twenty word clouds that give you a visual representation of the twenty interviews, along with a brief introduction to give some context. These then lead into the interviews themselves, which I hope you will take the time to read. They are provocative, engaging and, above all, very, very thoughtful. Even amidst a terrifically diversified set of "answers" to issues related to audiences, the common, resounding theme is that no one is taking the question of audiences lightly, everyone is trying to negotiate the adjustments that are occurring, and each artistic leader is hyper-aware of the particular needs and peculiarities of the people who fill their houses each night.

Would you like to contribute your thoughts about audiences? We have set up an ongoing survey that asks the same questions Novick did, and will be periodically rolling out more responses through the web. Please visit http://www.theatrebayarea.org/intrinsicimpact for more information. - CL

The Importance of Beginning
The Changing Relationships of Artists, Organizations and Communities

by **Rebecca Novick**

In a recent rehearsal, wrestling through a difficult play on a difficult topic with playwright and cast, one of the actors said that she wished the audience could get to experience the conversation we were having. It was a familiar sentiment, the idea that the most precious part of the theatre can be what we artists get to discover in rehearsal, what actors do on stage, what painters do as they pick up their brushes or potters do at their wheels. It's the *making* that we love as well—or perhaps more—than what we make. I've been a spectator at many extraordinary theatre performances in my life, but the ones that have stayed with me the most, that were truly transformative for me, are the ones that I was part of creating.

Perhaps that's one explanation for the rise in what's been called "active arts participation," even while attendance at traditional arts events is in steep decline. Driven by multiple factors like easy access to online tools for creation and curation (Flickr, YouTube, blogs, etc.), participatory arts traditions in immigrant cultures (social dancing, etc.) and a culture-wide turn towards hands-on, homemade experiences (urban homesteading), there is more art everywhere, but less participation by traditional means. Guitar sales and salsa lessons are up, but ticket sales at theatres nationwide are down.

There seems to be no lack of enthusiasm for making art—or for consuming it digitally in the comfort of your home or the convenience of your mobile device—but it's becoming harder and harder to persuade audiences, especially younger audiences, to attend live performance in traditional venues. We're living through a major shift in the way people make and consume culture, one that we can't yet see the end of. What does seem clear is that theatre institutions must respond to this change—and the field must evolve—or face increasing irrelevance. So, what is essential to theatre-making and what can be discarded? Whose stories get told and how? What is the particular value of live performance? And, if you're an artistic director who wants to shift your relationship with your audience, where should you start?

As part of Theatre Bay Area's intrinsic impact study, we interviewed twenty artistic leaders representing a wide variety of theatres with diverse budget sizes, programming and geographic location. We were interested in learning more about how audience feedback influences artistic leaders, who they mean when they say "our audience" and how they think about the kind of impact they're seeking to have on those audiences. The leaders I spoke with fell across the spectrum of reform, some speaking openly about their distaste for old models of audience engagement and some rejecting the premise that reform is needed. All of them were passionate, smart leaders grappling with how to find relevance and sustainability in the midst of major change. I encourage you to read all of them in the pages that follow.

A small group of the interviewees, however, were particularly interested in discovering a more participatory model for engaging audiences. Two of these theatres (Sojourn and Roadside) were founded with community engagement at the center of their missions. Three more (Mixed Blood, Woolly Mammoth, and the A.R.T,) are engaged in a variety of experiments that are moving them towards a different kind of audience participation.

Most of the artistic directors I interviewed were deep believers in the transformative possibilities of the ordinary theatre experience. In fact, the intrinsic impact study was designed specifically to measure the ways in which watching a live performance can create long-lasting impacts on an audience member. At theatre after theatre participating in the study, audience members reported that they were indeed captivated by watching live theatre, that they went home and talked about it after, that they learned something, felt something, changed their minds about something. But, what if these impacts aren't enough – or aren't unique to live performance? What if the real social impact theatres often claim to be accomplishing is simply not happening in traditional contexts?

It's customary for artistic directors to talk about their work making people "lean forward in their seats." They talk about it "creating community dialogue" or "sparking conversation" and advance those effects as arguments for why theatres should be publicly supported. Perhaps the most frequent claim is that attending live theatre is a social experience, a chance to have a shared experience with the people you came with, as well as the strangers sitting next to you. Some theatres specifically strive to attract extremely diverse audiences, with the explicit goal of bringing together people who might otherwise not encounter each other, using a theatre event to build community. Research like the intrinsic impact report from WolfBrown (in these pages) and other such reports seem to indicate that perhaps sitting in the dark next to strangers while watching the same event does not in fact offer a communal experience.

If simply watching a live event does not build connections or community, then what would? What could we offer as part of the live experience that would make it clearly more valuable than watching the same performance on your laptop?

Recently, the James Irvine Foundation, a major arts funder in California, announced that it would be shifting the majority of their support to projects that expand how Californians engage actively in the arts "by making or practicing art." The foundation made this change after careful study into changing patterns of arts participation revealed increasing hunger for active engagement instead of passive consumption, with tremendous personal and community benefits resulting from that more active kind of engagement. In a report on the subject for the Irvine Foundation, Alan Brown (the same researcher who conducted this intrinsic impact study) writes:

> People are thinking about the experience of culture differently than in the past, placing value on a more immersive and interactive experience than is possible through mere observation. From the resurgence of knitting circles to the growing legions of rusty musicians and aspiring storytellers, Americans are activating their own creativity in new and unusual ways. This phenomenon is not limited to culture, but part of a larger "participation economy" in which social connection eclipses consumption. Increasingly, Americans want to meet the people who make our products, share in the work of the makers and make things ourselves.

He goes on to delineate a spectrum of audience involvement, ranging from receptive activities like spectating or "enhanced engagement" (like talkbacks or panels on the play's topic) on to activities that are actually participatory such as crowd-sourced projects (like an open photo contest that becomes a museum exhibit), co-created projects where audiences contribute to work curated by a professional (like a community mural), all the way to what he calls "audience-as-artist" where audiences participate as equals in the creation of a work or event. (The full report, entitled "Getting in on the Act" is available at www. irvine.org).

Theater professionals' reactions to this report, and to the Irvine Foundation's shift in funding priorities, have been mixed. After all, most plays at most theatres fall into the "passive" category, with little or no opportunity for audiences to participate actively in the experience. Does this signal the beginning of a de-investment by funders in the presentation of conventional plays in conventional venues? Is the implication here that we should never do a conventional production of *Hamlet* again? Is the talkback after the show now more important than the production? Do high school students actually receive more benefit from participating in a production of *Hamlet* than from seeing one?

For Michael Rohd, these questions arise from what he sees as a lack of sophistication in the theatre industry around this topic. Rohd is the artistic director of Sojourn Theater and a founder of the Center for Performance, Public Practice and Civic Innovation at Northwestern University. His career has focused on creating work in deep engagement with communities, from his years as an artist in residence with Hope is Vital creating plays around the country with community groups aimed at addressing particular issues, to his work with Sojourn, an ensemble company focused on creating new work that promotes civic dialogue. Rohd explains, "Everything is changing—all the notions of co-authorship and collaboration and what 'participation' even means."

Rohd was at the 2010 Theatre Communications Group conference taking part in a discussion about audience participation when a person who runs what he called a "traditional regional theatre" in Chicago offered a definition: "What participation means to me is when people lean forward in their chairs."

Rohd's reaction was strong, and expressed his frustration with the topic: "I was like, 'You know what? The rest of the art world—other disciplines—think we're children when we talk like that. We just seem like children.'"

172

Rohd's own work has moved through a variety of ways to engage deep kinds of participation, not just during performances, but by integrating community members deeply into the process of developing the work itself. *The Penelope Project*, a recent Sojourn collaboration with the University of Wisconsin, the Center for Age and Community and Luther Manor, a long-term care facility outside Milwaukee, exemplified some of his methods.

Sojourn ensemble members, over the course of two years and many visits to the Manor, worked with playwright Anne Basting, Luther Manor staff, residents and their families to devise an adaptation of *The Odyssey* that was particularly focused on Penelope's waiting. The work was a multidisciplinary piece that used a variety of different participatory art-making events to gather stories and images from the residents of Luther Manor, particularly those with Alzheimer's or dementia, and their families and caregivers. The piece was set in the Manor itself, and conducted viewers on a half-mile journey around the building and grounds as actors performed the piece for an audience composed of residents and their families, as well as theatregoers who had arrived from Milwaukee.

In his work, Rohd always has both artistic aims for a project and goals around a specific kind of exchange or dialogue that he is trying to create. In talking about how he measured the success of *The Penelope Project*, Rohd describes the relationships that developed among all the participants as they collaborated creatively, as well as the value of the work to others in the field of senior care.

"There were people that came in from around the country to see the show," says Rohd, "to look at it as a potential model for creative work inside care facilities for Alzheimer's and dementia patients."

Referring to the experience of mental health professionals in the audience of *The Penelope Project*, Rohd says they had "an audience experience that allowed them to feel and observe the value of the work as an artistic experience but also, in this particular case, as an applied model."

This project included a host of ways to shift modes of participation, braided together into a complex process that began long before "the curtain" went up and continued long after:

- The investigation of the topic proceeded in concert with the people actually affected by the issue
- Residents were offered a variety of art-making opportunities, which encouraged them to see themselves as artist-

collaborators

- While professional artists (a playwright, a director, actors) led the script development process, community members collaborated deeply and got to see their contributions in the finished piece
- The piece was performed in the same community setting in which it was developed, allowing residents complete access to the finished work and a sense that their stories still belonged to them
- Audiences included a mixture of the collaborating community members, experts in the field, and general theatregoers, allowing the piece to speak differently to different people and to offer different experiences
- Audiences moved around to different locations, a simple tactic to make the viewing experience less passive
- Part of the project included connecting to funders and elder-care experts who could disseminate the model widely, building broader social aims into the fabric of the work

For Rohd and the company of Sojourn, the idea that theatre can serve as a spur to encourage deep dialogue around community issues (the kind of dialogue that might yield real change) has always been integral to the work and process. By reaching out broadly to include communities in the shaping of work, then carefully designing the context for seeing their productions, Sojourn has succeeded in creating a kind of community conversation that reaches past convening a supplemental panel after the play or getting people to argue about the issues a play raises on the way home.

When Sojourn created a piece dealing with the challenges of public school education in Oregon, they performed it at school board meetings around the state, deliberately aiming at the audience that had the most capacity to shift the issues the play described. For their upcoming project, *Town Hall*, Sojourn is collaborating with The Team, a New York-based ensemble, to travel around the country exploring the history of civic discourse and what Rohd calls "the particular polarized moment we're in now."

Rohd has large ambitions for this piece.

"I just want to see whether theatre done in a really complex but articulated way can get at the challenge of listening and communicating today in America," he says. "I want the show to be a play with a story, but it also needs to be a piece of applied creativity where an audience goes through the process of collectively imagining better ways to have public discourse."

In a way, "imagining better ways to have public discourse" sums up a lot of what Rohd and Sojourn try to do all the time. Rather than holding aspects of the theatre form sacred, Rohd and his team continually explore how a professional theatre company can use different modes of participation to engage audiences while still "putting on a show." That said, Sojourn, by design, is compact, nomadic and efficient, which in part allows them to take on such challenges. For artistic directors at larger institutions, it can be trickier to figure out how to shift to a more participatory mode–but it's becoming increasingly essential that they do.

Ben Cameron, former director of TCG and now head of arts funding at the Doris Duke Foundation, likes to compare the current culture shift with the Protestant Reformation. It was a time of great change, he explains, a time when new technology like the printing press was taking away the need for intermediaries like the Church to facilitate people's relationship with God. He parallels that with the advent of various technologies that are allowing for an un-intermediated engagement between the art and the individual—You Tube videos, "concert-quality" sound through headphones, higher-quality on-demand television and movies, professional quality recording and editing capability in the palm of your hand. Who needs an institution in that world? As Cameron says, the Reformation was not a great time to be monastery.

Some disciplines seem to be getting Cameron's message faster than others. For example, a quiet revolution has been happening inside museum curation. Curators were once expert authorizers, the arbiters of whether an art object was worthy of inclusion in a collection or an exhibit. As the ones determining what objects were displayed in what order and how those objects were described, curators were the invisible shapers of viewer's experience, the framers of the story, the ones who elevated certain facts to "important" while relegating others to inconsequential.

Now, their role has shifted profoundly, as more and more museums make changes as seemingly small as having curators sign their labels (eliminating the idea of an invisible expert, reminding viewers that this is just one person's take, however expert) and as radical as asking visitors to choose which art will be displayed and participate actively in creating work for exhibition.

As theatres struggle to survive and innovate through the Great Recession, they are opening up (or being forced to open up) to conversations about the changes in cultural participation. Rohd explains how he'd like to see changes in other disciplines translate into the theatre field, moving beyond "leaning forward in your chairs" towards engaging in discussion before and after the

175

work and even towards participating in the unfolding of the performance event:

> There's *interpretation*: that's the leaning forward and engaging in participation by interpreting your own experience. Then there's *commentary*: that's being given technological tools to be involved in discourse around the event either during it or before and after. And then there's *impact*: that's layers of participation where you impact dramaturgically what happens in the trajectory of the event. The other fields are past number one, and they've been practicing number two for years. Number three is where the real action is.

Inevitably, many industry conversations are framed around changes that will ensure institutional survival. "How," go the conversations at professional conferences, "can we tap into younger, more diverse audiences and the new ways they want to engage with art, so that we can arrest the decline in ticket sales?"

Cameron further warns that when the Reformation was over there was still a Catholic Church and many monasteries, but the time of their absolute ascendancy had passed, never to return. Cameron argues that, without innovation in how institutions perform the "gatekeeper" role—the way they attempt to curate an artistic experience for the audience—many institutions won't survive the cultural reformation occurring today.

The most pressing question, then, is not how we can band together to "save the big theatres," but rather what is the necessary role arts institutions might fill now that their historical job of curation and intermediation is shifting. How can theatre artists help our communities, and how can institutions facilitate that interaction? What do theatre artists and theatre institutions have to offer to the project of redressing injustice, bridging difference, and repairing the world? What kind of storytelling, what kind of ways of gathering, collecting, and sharing stories through live performance, would further this work? How could theatres play a more essential role (or any role at all) in building healthier, safer, more equitable communities or a stronger democracy?

Artistic directors, of course, operate inside real-life institutions, not tidy research case studies. They deal with board members they haven't selected, legacy programming that's hard to escape and increasingly impossible financial models. They are beholden, to some degree, to the individual donors and high frequency patrons whose financial contributions are so crucial and worry that pursuing new audiences might mean abandoning the ones they have.

So, given that, how can change happen in real life? Does moving towards more and different types of audience participation necessarily mean abandoning the theatrical canon, the mission of the organization, or the subscribers and donors who still support the older model? What kind of practices support incremental or even radical change?

There's been a lot of discussion recently about the sector being "overbuilt," especially in terms of the many administrators on payroll at large theatres. Listening to the artistic directors at larger theatres who are trying to move towards new kinds of engagement, I began to see the scale of effort that large staffs can bring to experiments in participation. Done well, deep community engagement is both time- and resource-intensive, especially if community relationships are to be sustained long-term. Participatory audience experiences can mean reconfiguring spaces, exploring alternative venues, adding time for artists and challenging normal design and production practices. Perhaps the resources of large theatres, with their sizeable staffs, could be used to create deep and meaningful community conversations and to offer audiences a host of different ways to encounter and even co-create performance.

If broad-based change is going to happen in the theatre field, such change must include the larger institutions. The engagement work that has been happening for years at community-based theatres like Cornerstone Theatre Company in Los Angeles, or in small experimental companies around the country, can begin to filter up into the work of institutions where it can increase in scale and impact.

This year, I've been invited to lead a project like that in the San Francisco Bay Area. The California Shakespeare Theater (Cal Shakes) and Intersection for the Arts have come together to create the Triangle Lab, a space for experiments in making theatre more participatory. Jonathan Moscone, the artistic director of Cal Shakes, is passionate about infusing his theatre with Intersection's ethos of community engagement.

"I want to stop saying 'audience' and start saying 'participant,'" Moscone insists.

Intersection for the Arts comes to the partnership with a tried and true "open process" by which they invite community participation into new play development. In partnering with a larger theatre with much more traditional programming (Cal Shakes historically has presented an outdoor summer season of Shakespeare and other classics), the artists at Intersection hope to see how their methods work in new contexts and how they can be tested and shared with more people. Both theatres believe that by working together they can push their work further towards their shared goal of a meaningful civic role for theatre.

"Triangle Lab, " the name of the partnership, came from the realization that we were examining the triangular relationship between artists, institutions, and communities. We wanted to find ways to strengthen each side of the triangle, and to make sure we were putting equal value on each of the corners. It should be, this name proposes, that we always consider the community a play might engage as much as we consider what artists we're working with and that we carefully work to connect artists to communities at every stage of the process.

The Triangle Lab has just begun work, and we don't pretend to yet have discovered any answers with universal application. What we have found so far is that language matters enormously — for example, if participating in the work of the theatre is going to mean more than just buying a ticket to the season, should we stop saying "the mainstage season?" What should we say instead? We're also discovering that advancing change within a institution (even a medium-sized one with an artistic director devoted to change) requires the collaboration and support of every department, so this work is necessarily beginning to affect the ordinary divisions of labor, bringing marketing staff into conversation with the education department, and involving guest artists in developing community engagement strategies.

Not every theatre wants to (or should) focus on devising community-based work or creating work with explicit political aims However, many theatres are beginning to take some steps towards a more inclusive, open, democratized way of working, developing a set of methods that invites more people to participate in more ways. This kind of opening is necessarily gradual, and if we want more theatres in the field to begin to change, we must chart these early steps and acknowledge the importance of beginning.

This won't look like never doing *Hamlet* again, but it may look like telling stories from other traditions as well, developing new work in concert with the communities we hope to engage, gradually blurring the lines between professional and amateur, and creating other programs that receive as much focus and investment as the performance of classic plays by professional artists.

Many of the questions we're beginning to explore in the Triangle Lab are at play in the innovations taking place at Woolly Mammoth Theatre Company in Washington, DC, the American Repertory Theatre (the A.R.T.) in Boston, and Mixed Blood Theatre in Minneapolis. Working in different communities, and beginning from very different histories and missions, the artistic directors of these organizations described how they're looking at:

- Connecting the work of the theatre with important issues in the community
- "Designing" audiences specifically for a particular play
- Blurring the lines between professional artists and "civilians"
- Multiplying the kinds of discussions offered to the community before and after a performance
- Changing the expectations about how audiences interact with the play in the performance space

At Woolly Mammoth Theatre Company in Washington, DC, Howard Shalwitz and his staff are several years into a deep exploration of engagement. This work, funded by the Doris Duke Charitable Foundation (who also was a major funder on Theatre Bay Area's intrinsic impact research), began after Woolly convened a conference on "Theatre, Democracy, and Engagement" several years ago. That conference, which brought guests from around the country together to help Woolly think about how they wanted to engage with their community and audience, encouraged Shalwitz to make major changes in his staffing structure. Most significantly, he designed a new position he calls "connectivity director" who is tasked with creating new ways to engage audiences with the work of the theatre.

"We're in a state of evolution about how we think about our role in relation to our audience," Shalwitz explains. "We're still working from our historical emphasis on challenging our audience, but with an increasing emphasis on trying to doing plays that connect with pressing conversations that are happening in our community."

Rachel Grossman, who was, at the time of this interview, Woolly's first connectivity director, elaborates, saying, "The big picture idea, of course, is to ask, 'What is the role of theatre in our community and in this city?' …[W]hat conversations are actually happening among people now, and how Woolly can participate actively?…How we can be a hub for civic discourse that is already occurring?"

At Intersection for the Arts, Program Director Sean San Jose describes his process a little differently: "We think about a question we're interested in exploring and then find artists who want to be part of that exploration. Or sometimes an artist comes to us with a question they've articulated. Then it's about exploring that question with the community it matters to."

The team of artists working to develop a new play, he explains, might be only one method of exploring an issue, with parallel explorations going on in, for example, a youth writing workshop or a series of public discussions with community groups.

Each artistic director employs a different balance between letting artists lead, and choosing artists who connect to issues the theatre is interested in exploring. Diane Paulus at the A.R.T. has begun seeking out artists who can jumpstart dynamic engagement around issues:

> …[I'm] always looking for artists that have, in a way, that larger question they're asking. That's the kind of work I gravitate to. Like Steven Sater, with *Prometheus Bound*, who sends me his translation of this Greek play and says, 'Prometheus is the first prisoner of conscience.'…Artists that think that way lead to these kinds of moments. So it's always looking for an artist who is going to have a larger worldview on their work.

In an effort to engage audiences in grappling with the ideas of the play she forged a partnership with Amnesty International. A.R.T. adopted different human rights cases and presented them to audiences at performances of *Prometheus Bound*. After each performance, audiences were invited to stay, learn more from Amnesty staffers about that evening's case, and then participate in a postcard signing campaign. Paulus concludes:

> To me, it's exactly what you hope for from the theatre. You don't hope that you make a theatre event, and then the ushers ask you to leave, and then that's the end of it. You work very hard in a theatrical way to transform an audience so that the next thing can happen. We were really using the Prometheus story to say, "Here is the first prisoner of conscience"—and then to ask the audience, "How can his story relate to human rights cases and prisoners of conscience who are working all over the world today? How do their stories resonate?"

If Paulus is specifically seeking artists who are interested in activating this kind of audience connection, looking at, as she says, "What kind of noise this artist and their issues and their energy are going to make at my theatre," then the Woolly Mammoth staff go one step further, explicitly asking playwrights, "Who do you imagine is the audience you want to be talking to with this play?"

This is what they call "audience design," and it's part of a shift in the role of the organization away from curating work for the audience the organization has and toward curating the audience required for the work. As Rachel Grossman says:

> "What we call audience design is really looking at filling out, shaping out, "finishing" the audience, if you will, as an artistic gesture of the show. Saying, from an artistic perspective, we're looking for people who are going to complete the story of the play. Who is going to make the conversation that the play tees up more meaningful by their presence in the theatre?"

Engaging the playwright in this type of conversation can have surprising effects, as it did with Robert O'Hara, a gay African-American writer whose play *Booty Candy* was part of Woolly's last season. *Booty Candy* was comedic, but also challenging and confrontational, and Shalwitz and Grossman figured that O'Hara would simply want the piece to speak to the gay African-American community of Washington, DC. Instead, as Shalwitz says, "Robert said something very, very surprising. He said that he wanted to talk to black churchgoers. He wanted to talk to the unconverted part of his community— the people that weren't comfortable with all of these images of black gay men dealing with their history and identity questions."

This was a transformative moment for the staff, he explains, and ended up having a significant effect on the way the show was marketed and what kind of supplementary programming they created. Shalwitz is quick to add that Robert's wish was tricky to fulfill, and he's not sure if they succeeded in reaching that population. However, Shalwitz notes, this conversation reminded everyone "that you don't want to just preach to the converted."

"That's one of the key points," he continues. "It's not just about all those elements of diversity, but it's also getting people in the theatre who, in fact, will find what's being said provocative."

The idea of reaching out to particular communities for particular plays may not sound like any kind of radical participation model—until you start thinking about how few people really do it. When you hold such a model up next to the subscription model, in which theatres create a package of 4-6 shows they can sell to a large group of long-time patrons, often sharing many demographic characteristics—or even the newer single ticket approach in which each show must both attract subscribers and be jazzy or well-reviewed enough to attract the occasional or first-time buyer, it's a very different approach indeed. What Woolly Mammoth staff are describing is a subtle but profound shift away from thinking about what kind of work the people who currently attend your theatre want to see, towards asking what sort of audience would match a new play, or what sort of play would match a new audience. Given the grave mismatch between the demographics of most theatre audiences, and the demographics in the surrounding community, this approach can jumpstart efforts to diversify audiences, and, at a minimum, shifts the organization away from feeling responsible only to a narrow group of long-time patrons.

Jack Reuler at Mixed Blood Theatre in Minneapolis agrees that matching the audience to a particular play is the best way to achieve his mission of promoting cultural pluralism: "Traditional marketing says you try to get somebody in the door and then you try hard to get them to come back. We said, "What if we put that on the back burner and say, 'Who's this play for? Let's find them.'" Since he programs a variety of shows aimed at different communities, Reuler measures his success in terms of reaching the people the show is about, and doesn't worry as much about whether those people attend his other programming. Describing a recent survey in which he looked to see how many people who came to his first show returned to his second, he says:

> ...[W]e found that there was *zero* overlap of single ticket buyers. *None* of the people that saw the second show saw the first show. For some theatres, that would be a sign of catastrophe. For us, that's a sign that the targeted marketing we're doing and the aim of the script and what we're trying to do is on the path we want it to be.

This year, Mixed Blood has made an even stronger commitment to their vision of "revolutionizing access" by making all of their shows free of charge, a project they call "radical hospitality." It's too early to tell exactly what effect

182

this will have on who comes to their work, or how sustainable the plan will be for the theatre, but it's a powerful evolution for a theatre that already leads the field in efforts to reach diverse audiences, and an interesting experiment in determining how much cost is truly a barrier to inclusion.

At Roadside Theater, developing plays and developing the audience for those plays have always gone hand in hand. Based in Virginia, Roadside was founded in 1975 as the theatre wing of Appalshop, a federal project to provide employment opportunities to poor Appalachian youth. The aim of the company from the beginning was to tell the stories of Appalachia "from the inside out," in the voices of the community. Their play development processes engaged the local community deeply, and brought the people to see the shows whose stories were being told on stage. However, when the company began to tour its work, it became challenging to ensure that presenting theatres had the tools to attract the kind of diverse working-class audience the work was made to play in front of.

Roadside collaborated with Junebug Theater (an African-American theatre in New Orleans) to create *Junebug/Jack*, a play exploring the historical relationship between the black and white working classes in the South. Cocke explains the challenge they faced on tour:

> So, the trick, for us while on tour, was how in the world are we going to get black and white working class people to come to the play? And if we don't get black and white working class people to come to the play, haven't we defeated the play's purpose?

After some experimentation, they settled on the tactic of requiring that a theatre that wanted to present the play had to create an ecumenical choir, inviting participation from both black and white churches. Roadside sent the show's music to the choir ahead of time, then rehearse with them for a few days after the touring troupe arrived. This choir, Cocke explains, would end up sounding different than anything the community had heard before, because these voices had never been heard together before, and by the time the show opened, all different communities were in the audience because they wanted to support their friends and see this new choir they kept hearing about. This elegant solution helped create the audience that could best appreciate the play, and helped set up a new kind of conversation about race after the performance that could never have occurred just by watching the play.

This Roadside method might suggest an interesting next step to a theatre like Woolly Mammoth interested in drawing a line between the impulse of the artist, the work of the theatre, and the audience that ends up in the room. What if a playwright (or a director) who expressed a wish for a certain audience, then built in a mechanism to attract that audience into the structure of the play or production?

"Audience design" (as the Woolly Mammoth staff call it) is one way to begin experimenting with different audiences and different ways of engaging them. Another area of exploration for all these theatres is improving methods for what Alan Brown calls "enhanced engagement." A step up from just watching a play, this category includes the program note, the talkback, the panel, the conversation in a school classroom, and myriad other ways to invest audiences more deeply in preparing for a performance experience and reflecting on it afterwards.

"Enhanced engagement" may still fall shy of active participation, but, writing about shifting cultural patterns in his essay the "Art of With," British thinker Charles Leadbeater, identifies it as one of the key ways audiences connect to art. Leadbeater identifies three main ways audiences can engage: Enjoy, talk, do. He goes on to explain that technology tools have shifted the balance between these categories, so that his parents might have had 90% of their cultural experiences in the "enjoy" category, while his ten-year old son has at least 50% in the "do" category. While the balance may have shifted, he goes on to explain, arts organizations still need to find ways to offer all three experiences, and most individuals are seeking each of them at different times. For theatres that aren't able to easily offer the "do" experience, it's worth investing significantly in enhancing possibilities for audiences to "talk" about their experience, online, in-person, in large settings and in intimate ones. Brown's intrinsic impact research in fact demonstrates that the surest way to deepen the impact of a performance, and the lastingness of that impact, is to get patrons talking about the show afterwards.

When American Repertory Theatre (A.R.T.) recently produced *The Gershwins' Porgy and Bess* (with revised book by playwright Suzan-Lori Parks), the project provided an opportunity for an unusually comprehensive set of educational activities surrounding the show asking (as Paulus frames the question) "How do we make this not just about the art on the stage but rather a point of departure to discuss African American history, issues of race and representation in art, culture meets politics in American 20th century history?"   A.R.T. created a kind of city-wide seminar on this set of topics with activities ranging from classes in high schools and colleges, lectures in a variety of community venues, and even dinner parties in the homes of audience "ambassadors" featuring combinations of Jewish and African-American cuisine along with the opportunity to discuss the production.

Enhanced engagement activities can also begin to carefully blur the lines between professional artists and "civilians."   Shalwitz describes how they have begun to shift the content of their post-show talkbacks away from discussions of craft, and towards a discussion of the issues underlying the play. It's important, he adds, for the artists participating in these talkbacks to be asked to respond to the play as themselves, as people in the world like the audience, rather than as experts:

> We've been using the phrase "a citizen artist." You're trying to value their participation, not just as a craftsperson but as a human being. For example, in the post-show conversations around *Clybourne Park* that included actors, the actors were asked to talk about their neighborhoods in relation to the content of what's in the play. That's an evolution.

This kind of conversation begins to offer the audience an experience not unlike conversations around the table in a rehearsal room, where each person is asked to connect to a play out of their own experience. Shalwitz took this concept further during Woolly's production of *Oedipus el Rey*, Luis Alfaro's adaptation of *Oedipus* to the world of Chicano gang-members. Instead of creating panels with experts discussing the issues of the play, Woolly worked with community organizations to get people with relevant life experience into the audience, then invited selected individuals to speak as what he calls "citizen-witnesses" after the play, sharing with others how they responded to the play, including sharing whatever piece of their personal history they chose to. This way of working is profoundly democratizing, demonstrating that we each come to a play with our own ways of receiving and interpreting it, and that each of us has something to share with others that might deepen their experience.

This language (citizen-artist, citizen-witness) helps shift our perspective, agreed Dudley Cocke, who also uses the phrase "citizen-artist" to refer to community members who participate in creating or performing Roadside's work. At Cornerstone in LA, they use the lovely phrase "first-time artists" to refer to the community participants that almost always play roles in their productions, as in "when working with a cast composed of a mixture of professional and first-time artists, it's important to…" This phrase reminds those of us in the field that each of us was a beginner once, and that our craft is not an impenetrable mystery, but rather something that can be shared and taught.

Sean San Jose, with whom I work in the Triangle Lab, has been experimenting with a method that bridges between amateur and professional performers, creating what he calls a "street team" composed of young actors of color, mostly recent college graduates. In his role as program director at Intersection for the Arts, he works intensively with the group, providing training in interviewing, writing, videography and the creation of devised pieces, then sends them out as artist-investigators, tasked with gathering material that relates to a particular creative investigation. For a project currently in development about street artists, this has included conducting interviews with street artists, photographing graffiti in different locations and helping to develop movement and text in response to what they've observed. The street team works in conjunction with the rest of the creative team (cast, playwright, etc.) serving as a conduit between communities and professional artists.

At Roadside Theater, "enhanced engagement" has evolved into a method that extends the development of a piece into the conversations that happen with audiences after a performance. Instead of talkbacks, Roadside uses story circles to follow performances, inviting audiences to share their own stories that were called up by the show. These stories often help actors deepen their roles, or find their way into a revision of the play. This back-and-forth connection with the audience is part "of the DNA" of Roadside Theater and essential to the work they're attempting to accomplish:

> When one of our plays is successful, it takes you into different places, intellectually, emotionally and spiritually, and with that experience, the stories that then come out in the audience circle are very, very rich. At such moments they realize their own potential as artists and as shapers of narratives. And that idea of animating and empowering the community voice is why Roadside…got started in the first place.

Space also plays an essential role in shaping audience participation. Sojourn's shows are all site-specific, with location being integral to the experience they are trying to create. In her few years as artistic director at A.R.T., Diane Paulus has received tremendous notice for her radical experiments with space. After a wildly successful run of *The Donkey Show* (a *Midsummer* adaptation) in a club space, A.R.T. began to consistently program work in this alternate space, including the US premiere of *Sleep No More* by the British group Punchdrunk, an immersive piece that asks audiences to don masks and chase actors through the space as each audience member decides for themselves which *Macbeth* character they're interested in following. In this club setting, lines between audience and performers easily blur, entering and exiting is informal, and audience members can shape their own participation. Paulus is also extending these experiments into her mainstage space with this season's production of *Three Pianos*. She explains the piece:

> ...[I]t recreates a *Schubertiade*: a salon that Schubert held with his friends in which he played his music for them. So built into the conception of the show is a total embracing of the audience's presence. Wine is served and poured multiple times throughout the evening. The audience becomes a participant in this salon. The evening transforms from just these three guys playing piano as themselves to a journey through Schubert's life and inspirations.

Serving wine and asking audience members to roam may not seem like radical news, but if you've ever tried to take a drink into a theatre that doesn't allow it, or (god forbid) take our your cell phone to tweet about your response to a play, you've likely encountered the strict participation rules that still hold sway in most theatres. Teachers bringing student groups are likely to be met with hand-outs and speeches aimed at "civilizing" groups of young people who may never have seen a play before and theatres seem to have more signs telling you what not to do than most hospitals. Is it any wonder that audiences may not feel invited even to "lean forward in their chairs" in this environment?

The iron-clad divide between audience and performers, broken only by a request to turn off your cell phones, is actually a recent artifact in our culture, explains Dudley Cocke, who find that the communities he works with have no such conception of a "fourth wall." "We speak directly to the audience, and the audience is invited to speak back. And that isn't just some imposed, formal convention; it's part of the culture here. And it's part of the culture in many communities – for example in southern black churches, where we've often performed."

Imagine for a moment a theatre where conversation back and forth with the performers was allowed and expected, a theatre where you could move freely around the space and decide what angle to watch from, a theatre that perhaps you paid nothing to attend. Imagine that you or some people you knew had been part of story circles that generated the material for the performance, and that you were invited to share stories from your life that connected to the play after you watched. What if community members with no professional training were included in the performance? What if the theatre held a meeting to ask neighbors what issues they'd like to see addressed in plays? What if artist-investigators traveled the streets of your neighborhood, inviting you to contribute material that might wind up in one of the plays? What if the local theatre was really part of local life, community discourse, and offered a spectrum of amateur and professional performance? Cocke describes the moment he knew Roadside had really become part of the community it was trying to serve: "Out of the blue, we got a call from a woman asking us to please come and sing several of the songs from one of our play's at her dad's funeral. Then we knew our theatre had become part of the community's daily life." Is this kind of community integration only possible in a small town with a "community-based" theatre?

What if our large regional theatre aimed for deep community engagement and a spectrum of possibilities for participation? There's a democratizing wind blowing through our culture, and a growing sense that everyone deserves the opportunity to be a maker. Theater institutions can be part of making that possible, or they can continue to be gate-keepers, deploying their formidable resources on behalf of just a few anointed artists, performing in front of ever-shrinking audiences. Transformation is happening all over the arts sector and I hear the beginnings of change in larger theatres. Let's identify and celebrate these early moves towards a more participatory theatre while continuing to reach for deeper change.

Visualizing the Artist/Audience Relationship

What follows are the twenty word clouds generated from our conversations with artistic leaders from companies large and small across the country. Word clouds are best read sort of like those Magic Eye images that were so popular in the 1990's: unfocus your eyes, pull back from the page, and see what floats out of each one for you.

Look for example, at the relative prevalence of different words that one might think should figure into a conversation about audiences. How prevalent is the word "audience?" What about "community?" What about more progressive words like "experience," "engagement" or "conversation?"

When I look at these clouds, I see a diverse set smart people grappling with how to address the dramatic changes that are occurring in our audiences, our funding model and our form. Some of them, the words show, are interested mostly in staying the course, while others of them, a relative few, speak strongly of new concepts of inclusion, engagement and experimentation.

As a start, here are the numbers of interviews for which, when I did the Magic Eye thing, the following words showed up prominently (let's say in approximately the top 5 words):

Artist/Artistic/Artistry	3	Want	3
People	9	Need	0
Audience/Audiences	13	Get	3
Community	4	Think	8
Work	6	Know	3
Show	6	Impact	2
Play	4	Experience	1
Theatre/Theater	3	Conversation	2
Like	4	Engagement	1

Keeping in mind the findings of the WolfBrown report, namely the importance of anticipation, accurate expectations and pre- and post-engagement—and that startling finding that single ticket buyers are actually more impacted by the work they see than subscribers—what do these clouds, and these conversations, say about our way forward? – CL

Anne Bogart
SITI Company

Howard Shalwitz and Rachel Grossman
Woolly Mammoth Theatre Company

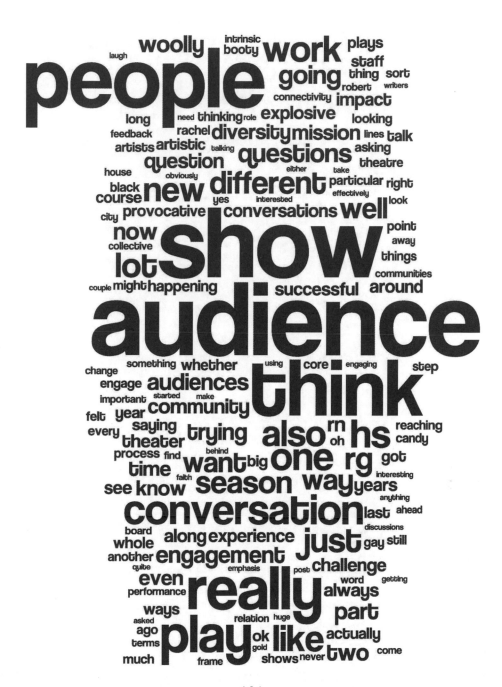

David Kilpatrick
La Crosse Community Theatre

Bill Rauch
Oregon Shakespeare Festival

Steven Glaudini
Musical Theatre West

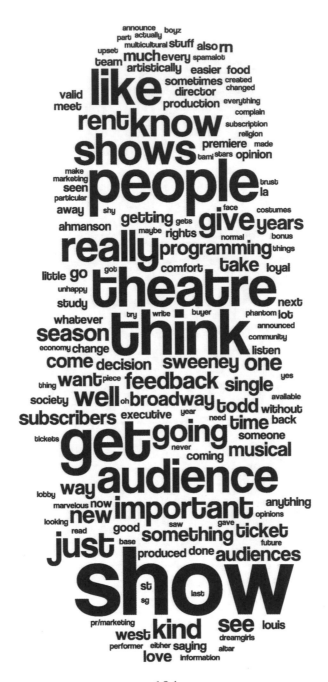

Martha Lavey
Steppenwolf Theatre Company

Rob Melrose
The Cutting Ball Theater

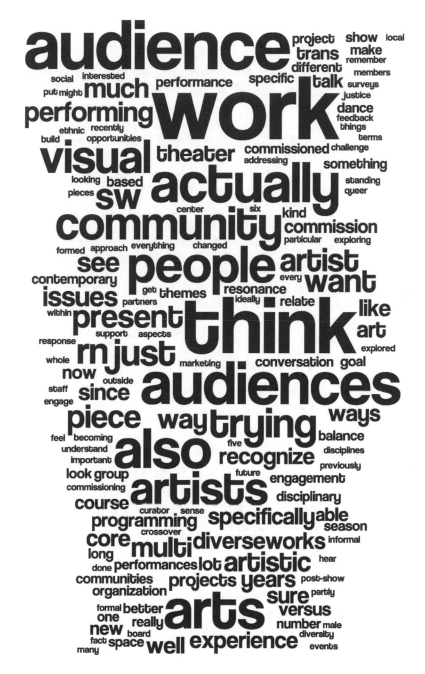

Todd Haimes and Jill Rafson
Roundabout Theatre Company

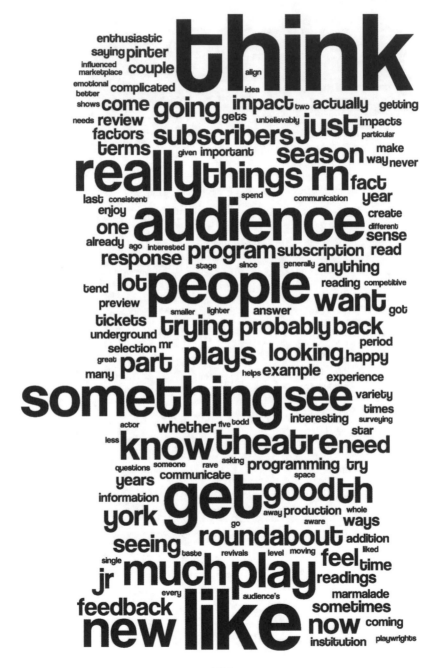

Oskar Eustis
The Public Theater

Jessica Kubzansky and Michael Michetti
The Theatre @ Boston Court

Susan Atkinson and Keith Baker
Bristol Riverside Theatre

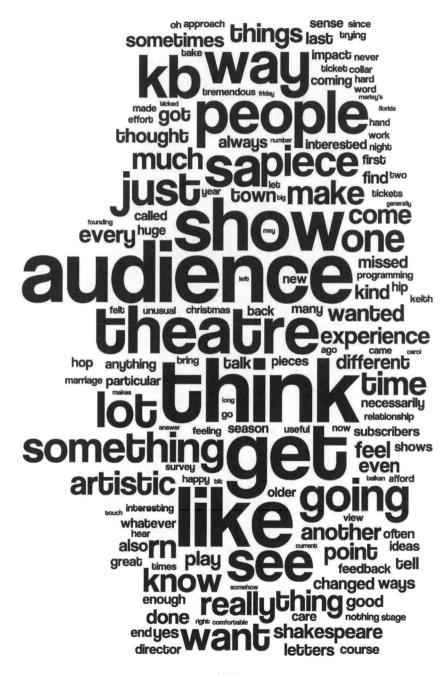

Tony Taccone
Berkeley Repertory Theatre

Michael Rohd
Sojourn Theatre

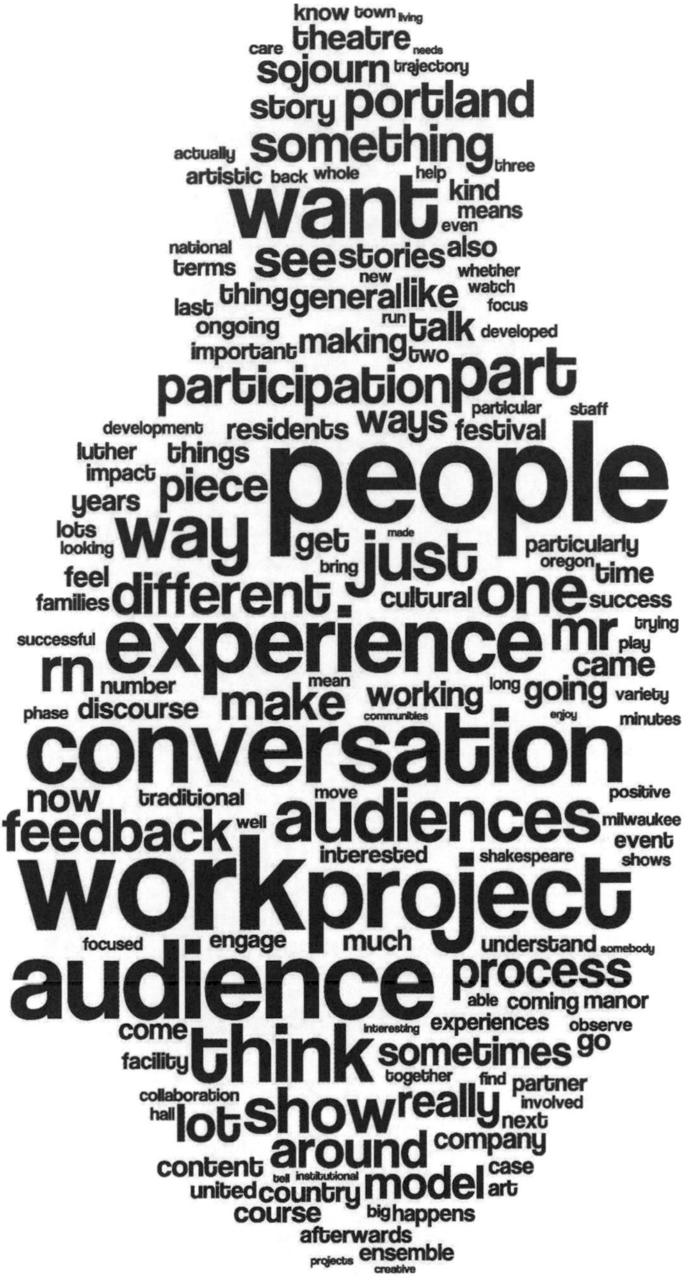

Jack Reuler
Mixed Blood Theatre

Dudley Cocke

Roadside Theater

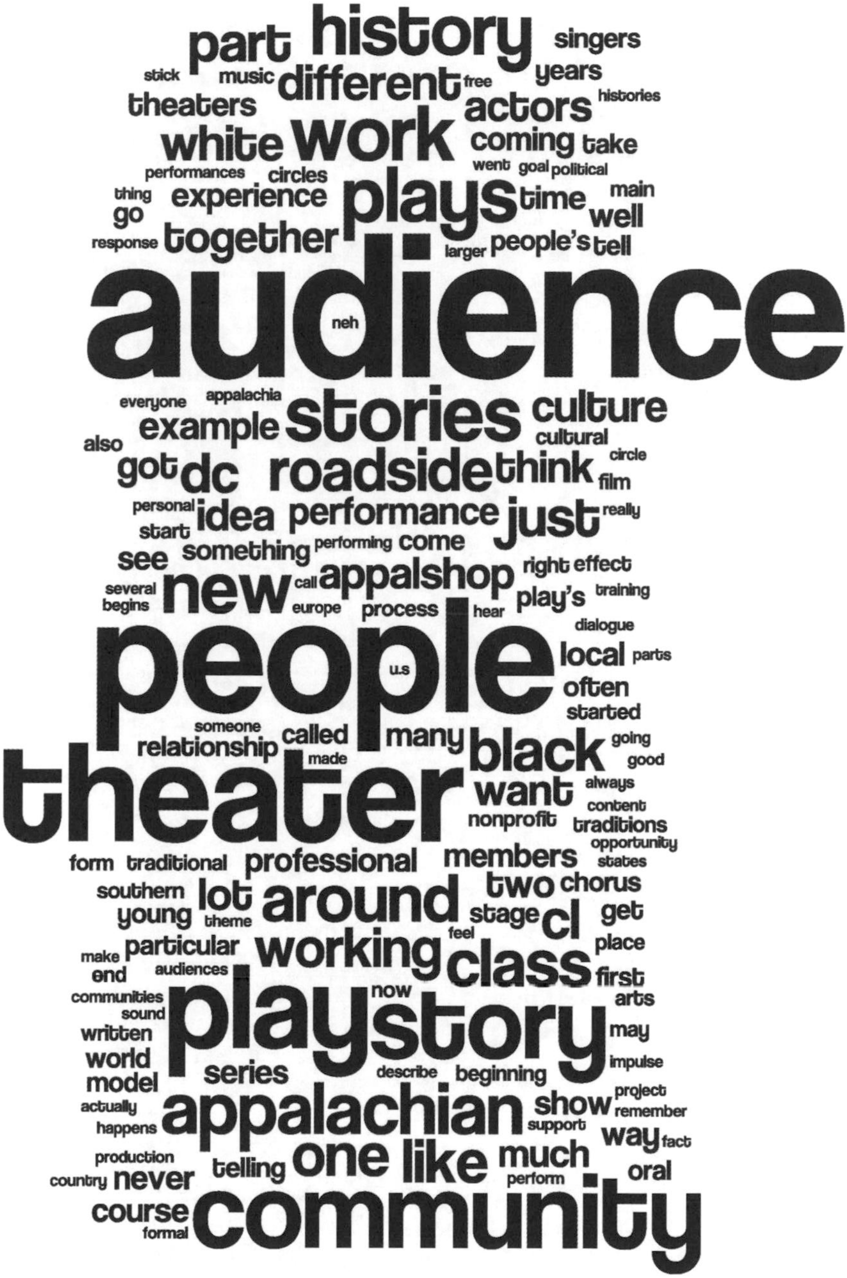

Terrence Nolen
Arden Theatre Company

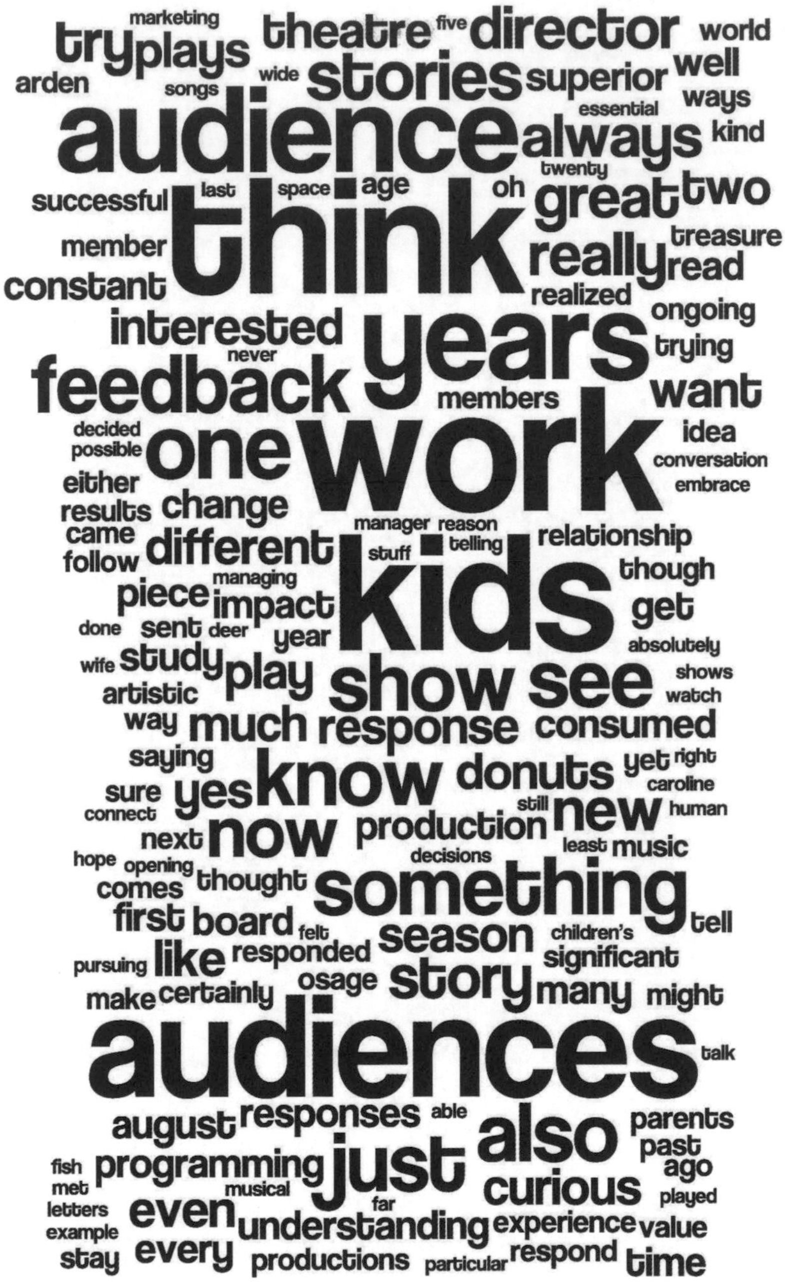

David Dower
Arena Stage

Bonnie Metzgar
About Face Theatre

shows works festival much art got
mission sort audiences reason
ways performances two relationships bodies
speech now show piece questions done
oh choice weeks
taylor story something project
night group read less
thought community certain curtain
trans older issue
maybe impact come always
good strategic respond getting
actually xyz love
mainstage year want able
need projects stories
artists face also success coming
planning means people's
make
feedback audience
first loved act program wants discomfort
many going came
cool choose event
guys get part important focus
trying whole
one thing theater ask right
house
different bm artistic
interested selecting kind
people new
advocacy understand
programming go every things
season think see just lot
talking company horizon way
four like experience still chicago
members
long work play big
next time
change
anyone expectations terms reach build
rn everyone may plays building youth
talk asking artist interesting working know

208

Diane Paulus
American Repertory Theatre

Artistic Leaders in Conversation
What is the role of audience feedback in the artistic process?

interviews conducted by **Rebecca Novick** and **Clayton Lord**

Anne Bogart

SITI Company

I know that your company has, of course, a very around-the-country audience and a different model. My first question is to ask you how you typically seek feedback from audiences in terms of what their experience was artistically.

I think I can encapsulate the entire question of the audience into one little anecdote which was spoken by Alfred Brendel, who is a concert pianist who is very well known for his Beethoven sonatas. He says that, when he is playing Beethoven, he will get to just before the final chord of the sonata and he'll lift his hands and in a sense ask the audience how long they'll let him wait until he plays that final chord. To me, that's the deal. It's not about audience surveys. It's about how an audience is breathing with a play. If the audience is breathing wrong, as a director or actor, we know it acutely, and we change what we're doing. If the audience is breathing correctly, then we keep what we're doing.

That's very deep listening that you do.

Yeah. I've always been an admirer of—and it'll sound funny that I'm saying this because I'm not known for commercial work—the notion of the old-style Broadway show where they would go to out-of-town tryouts and the creators would pace around in the back and listen to the audience. Then they'd go up to their hotel suites—because they usually had suites afterwards—and rewrite the play based on what the audience told them in terms of listening. I believe in that.

I think, essentially, that the theatre is an art form, unlike film and television, that actually demands audience participation, creative participation. You can tell physically. If an audience is leaning forward, then you've got them. If they're leaning back, you don't.

Film and television are made to lean back.

I enjoy that when I watch film. I want to lean back and eat my popcorn. In the theatre there has to be a loop. What's important as a director is to stage just enough (but not more than enough) so that you leave room for the audience to play.

Can you think of a time when you felt like the audience was breathing wrong with the play and you made a significant adjustment?

It's usually when you tell too much. We did a piece about the life of Orson Welles. And I had always thought that he would appear at the beginning of the play as in an overstuffed costume, like a big fat man with a beard, at the end of his life, and that the audience would meet him then and then go back into his life. And in the rest of the play, you would sort of go back to his beginnings, a la *Citizen Kane*, but in the version, it would be Orson Welles' life.

The minute that we had an audience, it was very clear that this old fat guy with a big beard coming out was telling the audience too much. If you actually have a young Orson Welles come out and talk about being at the end of his life, the audience has something more involved to do than look at this stupid costume.

The role of the imagination in the audience is much more acute in the theatre; they actually are part of the playwriting event.

As you're initiating a project or choosing to work with a particular writer or artist, do you consider or discuss what kind of impact you're looking for?

I was brought up in the downtown theatre world. And in the downtown theatre world back in the '70s and '80s, there was a joke, which was not a nice one, that downtown theatre artists made theatre for other downtown theatre artists. And I always felt a little odd about that. And I thought there was some truth in it, but I also resisted it. And one day—not one day—I decided to do a play that, in that spirit, would be a love letter to a theatre audience, a downtown theatre audience. And it was using the theoretical essays of Bertolt Brecht.

And I did that play saying, "Okay, this is a play that is simply a love letter to theatre people." And that turned out to be one of the most accessible plays that I ever did. So the lesson to me was that, if you aim for a big audience and you say, "I'm going to reach the widest possible audience I can, the most diverse audience," you usually get into trouble.

I'm more of a believer in what Umberto Eco called the "ideal audience," that you have what he called "the ideal reader." It's that, "Who is the reader for this piece?" And sometimes, if you say that the reader is a very specific person, it turns out to be very, very, very accessible to a lot of people because they can feel that it's not being written to please everybody but is really being written as a direct letter to an individual. Which then, in turn, makes it, oddly, widely accessible.

So do you feel like that ideal reader is different for different projects of yours?

I absolutely do. But here's another thing. I'm going to tell you another anecdote that, I think, has a profound effect on this notion of who you're speaking to.

Years ago, just before I founded SITI Company, I was invited to do a play at San Diego Rep, which is in the basement of a mall in San Diego. And I thought, "Okay, what kind of audience,"—meaning, what kind of play—"shall I select?" I thought, "Southern California Mall Audience" and I proposed to do Clare Boothe Luce's *The Women* because I thought, "Okay, it's a screwball comedy." It's about a really angry woman who's actually very, very funny, and it will appeal to a southern California audience.

So I did it. And I got 16 really fantastic women. I decided that each of them should be able to play Medea, rather than the third salon mistress from the left, that each woman that we cast should be sort of voracious. And they wore fantastic clothes, and they were great actresses.

And on the second preview—we all know, second preview is awful—the play was just not going over. The audience just didn't meet the actresses, and I got in a deep, deep funk. And I had to get on a plane, that night actually, to go back to New York, to receive, oddly enough, an award. And I got on the plane and I thought, "Okay, I can't do regional theatre anymore, because what am I going to do when the next regional theatre calls? Am I going to do *Harvey* next? What can I do?"

Well, so it turned out, thank God, that it was just a second preview. The rest of the run was a huge success. So that was good. But I had this horrible feeling when I was on this plane, I thought, "Okay, I'm starting this company"—which turned into SITI Company—"I'll go to Saratoga Springs and people will have to make pilgrimages to see my work." I was so angry.

And then, of course, that "E-word" came up. I started thinking, "Elitist...I'm being elitist, and this isn't good." And I kept thinking, "Who's my audience? Who's my audience?"

It turned out that it was just a bad night in the theatre. It went on fine.

A few months later, the founding summer of SITI Company, I was in Japan at Tadashi Suzuki's summer festival, which is way up in the mountains. And

> I believe it from the depths of my soul, that we do not have a specific audience, but we speak to a particular part of every single audience.

Tadashi Suzuki actually came to watch a run-through of Chuck Mee's *Orestes*. It was an afternoon run-through, and I really respected him a lot, and I was really excited that he was coming, but also nervous, because he's one of the great theatre directors of our times.

And he walked into the rehearsal studio. And suddenly, the actors saw him and got really nervous. And we proceeded to have an awful, awful run-through. And the actors were sweating, and I was standing there looking at everything I was doing, saying, "Oh my God, I haven't dealt with this and that..." And it was just a bad run-through.

And when it was over, Mr. Suzuki, who had mostly looked at the translations, didn't really look at the stage that much, got up and very sweetly said, "Thank you," and walked out. I was so upset, and the actors were angry. And I took a walk with Leon Ingulsrud, Suzuki's translator. He's now a member of my company; he speaks fluent Japanese, although he's a Minnesotan. And I said, "What just happened, Leon?"

And Leon said, "Well, actors know that when Suzuki talks to an actor, he'll say things like, 'A professional sees this in your work.'" And I thought, "That is really interesting." Because, as an American, I'm brought up populist and I'm brought up to think, "Will Joe Schmoe in Peoria understand this?" But Suzuki looks at the work and says, "Will the person with the highest level of perception understand this?" And I thought, "That's something that, as an American, I wouldn't be able to do." But then I had to question that.

What I learned from that, and this is key—and I realize, again, that this is theoretical for your intrinsic impact research—but I believe it from the depths of my soul, that we do not have a specific audience, but we speak to a particular part of every single audience.

In other words, when you go to a theatre, in the first five minutes, you know which part of you is being spoken to by the creative team. You know if they want you to laugh like, "Ha, ha, ha," or if they want you to laugh in a very

216

different way, or how they want you to participate.

So rather than saying now, quite so simply, "I am doing this as a love letter to a theatre audience," I'm saying, "I am writing a love letter to the part of every person who comes in the room who might love the theatre," or whatever the subject matter is.

It's very important to understand that every high school student who comes in has a part of them that could relate to this play, might not, could not. But that that's who I'm speaking to: a very particular part of every human being who comes in the room. And if they're past the age of seven, it's accessible.

Do you have a sense of having an ongoing conversation? Is there a national conversation you feel like you're in, or is it about repeat engagements in specific locations?

I think it's about repeated engagements in the same place. I know that best from working in Louisville, Kentucky, where we worked for about 12 years, every year. The first year I was there, I felt the audience bristle and say, "What's this?" The second year, I felt them say, "What's this? But I think I can take it." By the fifth year, they were rolling up their sleeves as they walked into the hall and saying, "What are they going to do next?" I don't think that blowing into a community, doing a show and leaving is particularly great. We have to create an appetite and an audience for the work.

I think that it's really important and I hope that your research is asking these kinds of questions. It's not about exposing a community to something and then something else. It's not like a sampler plate. You actually have to have some kind of follow through and some sort of development, because it takes time.

Do you feel like there are particular things you've gotten to do, somewhere like Louisville where you've been over and over? Is there an ideal of this relationship with the audience that you've arrived at or gotten to?

I've always felt that the best theatre is like a gym for the soul, so that people feel like they've had a workout, that it's not particularly always the easiest thing they've seen and that there's something in it that should actually challenge them to stay with it. But I think that the illness in the theatre is to, in a sense, try to simply make the theatre only pleasurable. I think pleasure is about one-tenth of what it can do. But there are nine-tenths, 90 percent of other things that

I've always felt that the best theatre is like a gym for the soul, so that people feel like they've had a workout, that it's not particularly always the easiest thing they've seen and that there's something in it that should actually challenge them to stay with it.

include. You can learn from it, you can be challenged from it, you can take a journey with it.

One of the most painful experiences I've had was when we took our show, *Bob Rauschenberg America*, to Paris and to a very political theatre, Bobigny. In the first moment, an American flag is revealed. And to feel the bristling and hatred of the French to see that event happen, that shut them down completely. So I think context is hugely important, the context.

Or, that same piece, we made it before 9/11, and how the meaning of the piece changed and the meaning of an American flag changed. Almost every piece of text and every song in the play changed radically after 9/11. Similarly, 9/11 changed the meaning of another piece we've done for years called *The Radio Play*. It's *War of the Worlds*, and after 9/11 the meaning of Martians landing in New York changes. So it's, again, the time and the frame around which this temporal event is happening.

I think that every good theatre piece has a sense of showmanship and showbiz and an entertainment streak, but you'd have to offer a lot of other things. So I can feel, even if it's a community where we haven't been before, if it's landing or not.

Is the audience game? Are they up to it? There's nothing worse than when you feel like they're not.

Howard Shalwitz
and Rachel Grossman
Woolly Mammoth Theatre Company

How do you currently measure audience response to a performance?

HS: If you'd asked us this a year ago, the answer would be very different. A lot has changed over this past season. We've been through *Oedipus el Rey*, Mike Daisey's show *The Agony and the Ecstasy of Steve Jobs* and *Booty Candy*, and the remount of *Clybourne Park*, and we're moving into a season where we're really trying to flex our connectivity muscles and to frame a season long dialogue.

We started about a year ago, doing an official post-production assessment process. We're still experimenting with how to make that as effective as possible. It happened on the board level and also on the staff level. That's been the vehicle for collecting our data and reflections, and has run parallel to our work in the whole intrinsic impact thing.

What are the components of this assessment process?

RG: Well there are two things. First we work to generate and collect thoughts from the board, the staff and participating artists. Then there are subsequent focus group conversations with the collective of board, and collective of staff.

HS: The starting point was like a 22-question questionnaire. We're not happy with it so now we're redoing it. It had a series of questions about the relationship between the show and our mission, and how well it reflected our mission. Then it had a few questions about the quality of the show and how well the script was realized, and how well the direction and acting were realized.

Then it had questions that covered how effectively it was marketed and the image of the show, whether it matched what they believed the show was. Also, there were questions about connectivity and how effective that programming was.

There were questions even about fundraising; did we effectively use the show

219

as a platform to raise money? So it really looked at the show as in a way the centerpiece of a whole body of all this activity over that period of time, with different people who had expertise in different areas answering the questions that were appropriate for them.

When we did this at its best, we also supplied to people—and we only did this a couple of times—a data sheet that went along with the questionnaire that said, "Okay, here's our data about ticket sales. Here's the publicity we got. Here's a copy of all of the reviews." That's when we really did this well.

It was a formal process that built itself up over the last year that we're now re-examining. And then on top of that, we had a variety of surveying instruments for the audience as well.

RG: Yeah. I think, of course, the intrinsic impact work significantly colored how we were communicating with our audience and really let us deeply explore different ways of measuring audience feedback about the performance. It also allowed us to grow our thinking about the impact of post-show discussions and other live engagement activities. We were so interested in the questions that we also created a mini-survey based on the intrinsic impact questions that we ran on other nights.

We also instituted a Google doc for our ushers (that they were trained on as part of our Usher Program) to have them record what they have overheard during the show. This year we're implementing that for our front-of-house staff as well, encouraging them to say, "What did you hear?" We're finding it's a great way of recording literally what people are talking about.

In general, there is a considerable amount of observation, certainly from Howard and the artistic staff and from me. At a certain point, I don't actually watch the shows—I end up watching the audiences watch the show. Documenting what we're seeing and trying to create some sort of standardized form like that is in the dream future of recording feedback. The intrinsic impact work gave us a huge jump forward, and kicks in the pants energetically, to think about how we were doing it and the possibilities of what it could be.

HS: The interesting thing was the way we unified a lot of this around our mission. So we have a very powerful mission statement which begins, "To ignite an explosive engagement between theatre artists and the community" by doing a bunch of stuff. By producing, developing new plays, and by engagement in our community. So we've really seized on that opening phrase of our mission statement, which has been our mission statement for over 20 years. But in the last two years I'd say—wouldn't you say about two years, Rachel?—we've really been seizing on that and saying, "Okay, if we say we're going to ignite an 'explosive engagement,' what do we mean by that? What really is 'explosive?'"

In fact, we took this question so seriously that some of the mini-surveys included a question to test the accuracy of that language in relation to people's perceptions. It asked them to rank their engagement, and the word "explosive" might have been one of them.

RG: We created a number of phrases that could describe a theatrical experience without any numeric ranking or value assigned. Phrases like "distant investigation," "direct confrontation," "passive observation," "standard interaction" and "explosive engagement." And then we said, "Okay, what do people choose?" So we're actually able to see how would people using those five phrases describe their experience?

And what did you find?

RG: "Explosive engagement" came out either top or near top for all three shows.

HS: But not necessarily a majority, but a plurality.

RG: But a plurality, yes. Absolutely. Thank you. But I think what's interesting for us now is we're saying, "Well, how much of that is the success of our mission influencing the descriptions that people are using, and how much of that is people describing their experience in the theatre?" Then there was also a follow-up question asking, "If, in addition to this, there's another word or phrase you would use to describe, fill that in right here." So there's a blank, and then people would say, "No, it was freaking' amazing!"

HS: There are also certainly online opportunities for people to give feedback, although in most of our engagement activities online, we're not generally asking people, "What did you think of the show?" And even in post-show conversations, we're generally not asking that question. We're asking them to engage in what the show was about.

In fact, in the last few years we have even gotten away from craft-oriented

> We've been using the phrase "a citizen artist." You're trying to value their participation, not just as a craftsperson but as a human being.

discussions with our audience. Which is not to say we never do them at all, but for the most part, even when we invite artists onto the stage after a performance, which happens quite a bit still, we're asking them to engage with the audience abcout what the show was about and not about: "How did you learn your lines?" or "How did you come up with that set idea?" or "How difficult was it for you to develop your character?"

RG: We really are interested in directing the conversation in a different direction, but also allowing for artists and audience to engage with one another back and forth.

HS: We've been using the phrase "a citizen artist." You're trying to value their participation, not just as a craftsperson but as a human being. For example, in the post-show conversations around *Clybourne Park* that included actors, the actors were asked to talk about their neighborhoods in relation to the content of what's in the play. That's an evolution.

When you're selecting a season, when you're initiating a relationship with a particular play or a particular artist, how do you think about the impact you'd like to have on an audience?

HS: Historically, the core word at Woolly Mammoth is "challenge." It's the word that shows up in our original manifesto 35 years ago. We want to challenge our audience, and we usually talk about challenge along two lines. One is in terms of aesthetic challenge: innovations in the form or in the way the story's told or a time frame or style or whatever. And then there's challenge as it relates to subject matter: relevance or provocation in relation to what's happening in our city or our lives today.

I've always said that the ideal Woolly show does both. It challenges people both in terms of its content and its aesthetics. So if there isn't some sort of provocation or challenge component along either of those lines, it's very unlikely we'll do a particular play. Sometimes we might do a play just because it has a stylistic innovativeness and it's by a writer who we've been connected to over a long period of time. But usually it's not just that it is innovative; it's that it's provocative in some other way as well.

That's old and longstanding Woolly language, and it has never gone away. It's still part of our thinking. And then this change started happening when we moved to our new space downtown. You walk out our door, and you can see the National Archives. So we're just a couple of blocks from the National Gallery and from the Mall. You walk two blocks, and then you can look to your left and see the Capitol and look to your right and see the Washington Monument. So we are right in the heart of the capital of the United States.

And because of that, I think we became very, very conscious of our work in that context, and started thinking more about our role in the politics of the capital and civic discourse.

For our thirtieth anniversary a few years ago, we hosted a conference around the theme of "Theatre, Democracy and Engagement in the 21st Century." That was the conference from which the whole connectivity concept really sprang. We invited a lot of guests from around the country to talk to us about their ideas of how Woolly could be engaging with our community and our audience. And now we're in a state of evolution about how we think about our role in relation to our audience. We're still working from our historical emphasis of challenging our audience, but with an increasing emphasis on trying to do plays that connect with pressing conversations that are happening in our community.

What we're experimenting with right now—and it is having a big impact on our season selection—is thematically linked seasons. So the season that we just finished that *Oedipus* was a part of was a season called "Strip Tease of Your Subconscious." And it was really all about sexuality and gender issues from a whole series of provocative angles.

And the season that we're just heading into right now is organized around the question, "Does our civilization have an expiration date?" And it's a series of pieces that imagine either the end of the world or ways in which our society is collapsing or how we might survive a collapse. I have to say it's a lot of fun stuff, and it comes at it from a variety of angles.

This year, we're trying to better understand how to frame a conversation over the course of the whole season more effectively—this, in addition to the

> From an artistic perspective, we're looking for people who are going to complete the story of the play. Who is going to make the conversation that the play tees up more meaningful by their presence in the theatre?

conversation we want have around each play, since each one still comes at the larger theme from its own unique angle.

And I think that question—what is the conversation and who wants to be part of that conversation—is actually becoming a central season planning question and a play selection question.

When you're thinking about a season-long conversation, what is the universe you're aiming for? Are the people you want to have a conversation with your "loyal audience" or are you reaching for different communities with different pieces? How does this relate to the different circles you are encountering or trying to serve?

RG: The big picture idea, of course, is to ask, "What is the role of theatre in our community and in this city?" So I think the conversation is about looking at what conversations are actually happening among people now, and how Woolly can participate actively—how we can be the artistic work for civic discourse—how we can be a hub for civic discourse that is already occurring. I think who we're looking to engage is, on a show-by-show basis, people that are connecting from a personal place in those conversations that are happening in the community. "Stakeholders," we call them.

Where this starts filtering down, of course, is to what we call "audience design," which is really looking at filling out, shaping out, "finishing" the audience, if you will, as an artistic gesture of the show. Saying, "From an artistic perspective, we're looking for people who are going to complete the story of the play. Who is going to make the conversation that the play tees up more meaningful by their presence in the theatre?"

That makes for a richer dialogue for everyone that's there, whether they are the "stakeholder" in that conversation, or whether they are the standard veteran single ticket buyer, or a subscriber who is always up for digging deep or interrogating into another topic, social issue, political issue.

HS: There's this balance between picking plays that speak to your existing audience and picking plays for other audiences that may be out there. I think that we crossed a bridge two or three seasons ago where we certainly knew that subscriptions were not going to be the wave of the future, though it was never a huge part of Woolly's picture. Now, subscribers are maybe a third of our audience, not two-thirds like a lot of regional theatres. Woolly's always been driven, I would say, by single-ticket success.

There came this point where I felt frustrated with the audiences we had—that sort of older, committed, loyal core—and felt like if we weren't reaching out to new audiences, we weren't actually bringing energy that refreshed their experience.

Rachel hit the nail on the head. We need that core audience, and we need to be reaching out to new audiences, but I think our emphasis has tipped a little bit more towards the reaching out to new audiences, even if the price we're paying for that is that some audiences are coming to certain shows and not to that many others.

They're coming to a show because we've helped them to find an affinity for to the show. Our connectivity and marketing departments aim for repeat buyers, but I think we've learned to value people who come once as much as people who come 10 years in a row and see every show.

RG: You never know who you're affecting. And it's so important to really look at every show as its own opportunity.

HS: But in some ways, when we think about framing the conversation that's happening in post-show discussions or online and stuff, I think we frame it for the audiences we want for that show who haven't been to the theatre before, rather than framing it for the audience we've already got. And that's a big change.

RG: Yes, and I think it allows for new and fresh language and a new and fresh line of questioning for every show, because it's not being supposedly "tailored" to a specific, and somewhat generic group—especially here at Woolly, because while most of our subscribers do have a typical "Woolly subscriber" mindset, they're all over the map as far as type of people, where they are in their life, where they're from. Where they're common is that they all are inquisitive and interested in the new and the different.

HS: And I should say, our core audience is a great audience to begin with. I don't mean to dump on them. I just think that you have to always reinvigorate.

Howard, in terms of different people in the theatre, it sounds like you're expanding generally. But are you also specifically looking at reaching out to communities of color, immigrant communities? Is that part of who's not in your current or core audience?

HS: There's a number of things that we sort of are after, and that when we're successful we pride ourselves on. One of those things is diversity across age, and another is diversity in terms of race and ethnicity. Race and ethnicity are such huge factors in our city—even larger than in most cities, and we're also an international city. And then, too, there's economic diversity. And in some ways I think economic diversity might be the hardest thing to achieve. We think of diversity along all of those lines, and we have strategies for trying to achieve all of those.

I think it begins with the work itself. It's definitely true that when you represent somebody's world on stage, they're more likely to come and feel that they can identify with what's there. So obviously, doing plays by writers of color, and women, and men, and older writers and younger writers, those are very, very important. And they're built into the DNA of Woolly anyway, since we have such a focus on emerging, newer American playwrights.

You know, we're a theatre that is—and this may be an advantage for us in a funny way—we're a theatre that is most often offering a season of plays, none of which anybody has ever heard of.

RG: There's something relaxing about that on some level, you know?

HS: Yes. Though, of course, that makes it harder to market, because there aren't big titles, or last year's New York hits, or anything like that. But at the same time, our stage is, in a way, an equal opportunity playing field for everybody. It's not like your tickets are being snapped up by the audience that reads the *New York Times* and knows that X, Y and Z plays were big hits last year. So I think for us, it's really all about what Rachel said. It's about, "What's the play about? What's in the play? What's the conversation that the artists want to have, and then who are the audiences that bring meaning and energy to that conversation?"

We now do an interview with the playwright, Rachel and the dramaturge on each show, and the whole staff a couple of months in advance of the show. And one of the questions we always ask the writer is, "Who do you imagine is the audience you want to be talking to with this play?" So we did that for *Booty Candy*, we talked to the playwright, Robert O'Hara. And with *Booty Candy*, which was really a play very much from a black, gay identity, Robert said something very, very surprising. He said that he wanted to talk to black churchgoers.

You don't just want to preach to the converted.

He wanted to talk to the unconverted part of his community—the people that weren't comfortable with all of these images of black gay men dealing with their history and identity questions. And that was a pretty tough order for us. Because, of course, that's an audience that we knew would be pretty offended by what was in the play. So, ultimately, we were, not surprisingly, quite successful with a lot of outreach with the GLBT community—those that were going to identify most strongly with what was in the play and also be challenged by the play because the images of gay and African American identity in the play were not always comfortable ones.

But I don't know whether we had any success with the church crowd or not. I think our assumption was, if we did, they'd probably hate it and walk out. So, it's tricky. But regardless, the lesson was important. Robert reminded us that you don't want to just preach to the converted. That's one of the key points. It's not just about all those elements of diversity, but it's also getting people in the theatre who, in fact, will find what's being said provocative.

With our current play, *A Bright New Boise*, there's a similar kind of challenge. It's a play about an evangelical Christian who is trying to reconnect with his son who was taken away from him when the son was just a baby. And it's a very complex look at faith and how it helps or gets in the way of our lives. So it's a very complex play for people of faith—and honestly, it's just as complicated for people who don't believe in God at all. But I know that one of Rachel's first steps there was to really try to reach out to communities of faith, even though the truth is that probably the churchgoing crowd is not necessarily the theatre crowd.

RG: It really is thinking about diversity. Robert O'Hara, at one point, said,

"Everyone is welcome, no one is safe." It's really diversity in all ways, shapes and forms, and *A Bright New Boise* is only really going to be successful if the audience isn't just filled with cynical, cultural Jews like me who are like, "Oh, the crazy fundamentalists," you know?

I'm clearly reducing myself, but you get the idea. That's going to limit the audience's collective empathy for the protagonist, and won't encourage a willingness to change the mindset. There is more likelihood that I'm going to broaden my perspective if I'm seeing other people experience the show in a different way.

HS: The thrilling thing about *Booty Candy*—it was a wonderful show and it was quite successful for us—but the thrilling thing about being in the audience was the way in which gay, straight, black and white audience members cued each other and gave each other permission to laugh at very incendiary material.

It's like a straight person would see, "Oh, a gay person's laughing, so it's okay for me to laugh," and a black person would see, "Oh, a white person's laughing at that, so it's okay for me to laugh." It was really, really interesting, and a lot of this show's dynamic was this kind of conversation between the audience and actors, about where our collective comfort zone begins and ends.

They all got each other on board. It was an amazing show, that got cheering and standing ovations, most nights, but every audience member went through some harrowing moments because nobody got out unscathed in that particular show.

Can you think of a time when you changed a programming decision because of feedback you were getting from audience members, whether that was about a particular show you did or didn't do or whether it was about a change in future direction?

HS: Hmm. Well, there hasn't been a case in the history of the theatre where we've announced something and then decided not to do it because—we haven't been through like a *Rachel Corrie* experience or anything obvious like that.

But on a more subtle basis, I would say that we have adjusted programming around a show in response to what we were perceiving from the audience. A good example might have been last season's *House of Gold*, a show that was very provocative, very sort of *avant garde*. It was about the myth of Jon Benet Ramsey—obviously an incendiary topic—and it was told from the point of view of this little murdered girl. We felt that people weren't getting it. There were things we weren't happy with in the production and felt that it in some ways or another it wasn't coming through to a lot of people. Or a lot of people were just plain hating it.

We knew that it was a show that people would have trouble processing. We did an awful lot of things to give them tools for doing that. But we also scheduled post show conversations after every single performance. What we said was, "Okay,

> We want to be one step ahead of the audience, but not two. One step means someplace that they haven't gone before. Two steps means we've left them behind.

whatever people's reaction is, positive, negative"—because it had rabid supporters who loved it as well—"let's make a forum for that." If people wrote in and emailed or something saying, "My God, why did you pick that play?" we picked up the phone and called them. In other words, we said, "Let's be proactive in creating and engaging this conversation rather than running away from it."

RG: I think what we really got out of *House of Gold* is we said to ourselves, "If we're going to keep pushing to the edge of theatrical style, as we're charged in the mission, we have to stay proud of the work, and learn from that place. Our job is to engage people in the excitement about the art." So I think if anything, as opposed to telling ourselves, from that reaction, "Oh, we shouldn't do this show," or "We should do it differently," we learned we needed to tell ourselves, "Stay proud of the work, and talk with people about how they're processing it more."

Because that's what's important. We're going to keep doing this work, so we need to check in with ourselves and ask ourselves, "Are we questioning this? Are we saying, 'Oh, I don't know' and being preventative? Or are we actually saying, as we should be, 'We're excited about this work. We want to be engaged with the work, and with you. We want to be curious with you.'"

HS: There's a long standing Woolly mantra that we want to be one step ahead of the audience, but not two. One step means someplace that they haven't gone before that really feels different and new and fresh and provocative. Two steps

229

means we've left them behind.

We are sometimes less than one step ahead, although I don't think very often. And I think we are sometimes more than one step ahead of them where they feel left behind. You can't always hit the nail on the head. I want to be off the target as much on one side as the other over time and keep trying to find that place where you're really pushing the audience to move forward but where you feel you're successful in bringing them along with you.

We have a lot of those shows—*Booty Candy* is a perfect example—where I think it pushed a lot of buttons and we were reasonably successful in bringing the audience along with us. *House of Gold* was clearly a show where it felt two steps ahead and the audience couldn't process it and catch up with it.

We think about this problem both financially and programmatically: how do we protect our ability to take big artistic risks over the long-term? To us, you can take a bigger step forward if you help the audience along. So in that sense, investing in this relationship with the audience is obviously a key to long-term stability. Over time, if you're more successful at engaging people in the conversation about the work, giving them tools to think about it and process it, letting them know that that's part of the experience of the work, it ought to allow you to take even more artistic risks and be more provocative over time. That's the contention behind a lot of what we do.

David Kilpatrick
La Crosse Community Theatre

What's it like, trying to learn more about your audience?

This weekend, we had an audience member who left his card because he wanted to talk to me. He was very concerned that what we were doing was collecting data in order to report to the government in order to motivate the government to do things, and to try to get money out of the government. He just knew there was an ulterior motive and wanted to know who was going to do the survey and where it was going to go.

His experience had been that sometimes people would ask these innocuous questions and then label him as something. He related a story about his mother getting called and being asked, "Do you believe that healthcare is good for people." And of course she said, "Yes." But then he'd see the numbers and it would say that we all support Obamacare, and "that's not true," he was screaming. "That's misusing the data and being unfair."

I'm the executive director here. I'm the head of all administrative staff, but we have an artistic director who is then the head of the artistic staff. He and I, like with many theatres with the split heads, he and I work very closely together, and swap and share, and I give him responsibility and power where it belongs, and I work as a sounding board, and then I work as a liaison with the board—to free him up to be an artistic director without worrying about anyone looking over his shoulder—he has just me to worry about that.

You've kind of lived in both worlds, the artistic side of things and the management side of things?

Yeah, I enjoy both, I guess probably management would be my passion. The stage manager in me says that if I can put my skills to marketing and audience development and fundraising and that kind of stuff to allow artists to be artists then I consider myself successful. But, like all artists, we want to jump in every once in a while to do it ourselves, too.

How does your organization gather feedback? I noticed on your website you have an ongoing survey asking for feedback about a possible new building...

> Our audience members are volunteers; we cannot make them do anything they do not want to do.

We had put that out there early on this year. We're in the starting phase of our capital campaign as we speak, and one of the things that was important to the architects was to make sure that we've got some input from the audience members. Rather than trying to do a rash, really fast meeting, we decided to do this survey and see who responded. We got some good comments, no real surprises, and they took it as an opportunity to comment on our artistic direction as well. Still, it was a very targeted and focused survey.

We got about 150 responses. We were actually very pleased because we have an active mailing list of about 1,500, and not everyone is going to have an opinion on what they want the building to look like. And you know that 1,498 of them want to make sure we have more women's rooms.

Some still commented on the quality of the productions or the direction or selection, stuff like that. I passed that information on to the artistic staff. As with any response and survey, you have to recognize that if someone has bothered to write that down, they're representing and speaking for a few people, and not necessarily is that always going to change what you have to say, but it at least allows you to look at that as a perspective and say to yourself, "Hmm, what's the validity of this. Is this something I should be concerned about, or does it really go counter to our mission and I'm not going to address this?"

As a community theatre, do you think that gives you a different mandate in terms of the balance between what the audience wants and how your artistic decision making is driven?

Unfortunately, I don't know that it necessarily has to do with community theatre as much as it has to do with the balance of funding: how much are you totally dependent on ticket sales versus how much are you dependent upon donations. To me, that allows us to have some flexibility in terms of meeting our mission without necessarily making our audience happy.

Let me try and clarify that. I recognize, as an executive director—and my personal business philosophy is—that our audience members are volunteers; we cannot make them want to do anything they do not want to do. And I'm very conscious of that, so work from community standards. And, having traveled around the country and having worked in a number of theatres, I recognize that the community standards really aren't that different. People are still afraid of the F-bomb, and still want to be careful of using the Lord's name in vain, things like that. They're still going to conscientiously be aware of that. I think that there are certain smaller theatre companies that have built an audience based on using that, and the audience knows that, but that's not necessarily your bigger, more commercially-oriented theatres, community theatres, where you're mostly dependent on a string of volunteers.

One of the things: we're currently in our production of *Doubt* right now, which is, you know, or could be a controversial play—it's been made into a movie, and everyone knows what the subject matter is about, if they've been paying attention. We did this play, and it's not selling as well as our comedies, and definitely not as well as our musicals, but we've talked about this as a staff and decided that this is part of our mission, to make sure that we don't just exclusively do the sex farces, because that's not doing anybody any good, and people will get tired of that just as fast as anything else if that's all we produce. So we said to ourselves, "For this production we keep the costs low, we don't go crazy on our production, we don't spend too much on the set, we just make it a good quality production and then those who come do enjoy themselves." It's important for them, it's important for the rest of the audiences to know that we produce this as well, we can do this as well as we can do our comedies. And it's also good for our grant applications and other sources to be able to say that we're a bit more balanced than just exclusively "commercial theatre."

Talk a little bit more about the part of your mission that you feel that is fulfilling.

Part of our mission is about raising the quality of life through education and theatre. And so a situation like this, where we said to ourselves, "You do need to experience a little bit of the power of theatre," it was manifested through talkbacks. We have a talkback for every show this season; we've met on Thursday nights. We have always sold it as, "Come meet the staff, the designers, and learn a little more about theatre." At our musicals and comedies, we would get two people, four people that would stay. And most of those were staying out of politeness or because one of their friends was a staff member.

For this particular play, we set out and said "No, we're not going to do it in

233

house." So we invited somebody from the media, somebody from the law and someone from philosophy and ethics from the university, and they were our panelists. We did it on a Saturday night, which is our most popular night, and we had 75 people sitting in this theatre for an hour and fifteen minutes after the show. Now, was it the panel, was it the play, was it doing it on Saturday night? All of those are variables, and it could be all of them combined. But to have 75 people sitting there and discussing a piece of theatre, especially a play like *Doubt*, saying "I *know* what it's about!," it was a powerful experience, and that's just as important to us as getting 99% of our house sold to see *West Side Story*. This is part of our theatre education mission, and it's important to present a situation where we do challenge our audience, and to celebrate those few who share the challenge with us.

When you are selecting plays, how does that work?

Selecting plays is a bit of a collaboration. We have a playreading committee comprised of volunteers, a board member and the artistic director. For several months they're asked to read plays and write up brief little one-page reports on them, and then we meet as a group and try to advocate for various plays, reduce the list down a bit, and then we go to our artistic staff, the technical director and designers, and say, "What do you think, what's your reaction to these?". And then the artistic director kind of whittles it down a little bit, and then he and I sit together and, primarily, I play devil's advocate, to just ask questions about this play or that play, and he works hard to sell it to me. And we look at balance, and what the season is. Then we present it to the board. Previously, the board got more involved in the selection of the season. But at the present, they've reached a point of trust in the artistic director and executive director, because we're the ones who have to deal with the consequences. We finally convinced them that, just because they don't recognize the title doesn't mean it doesn't exist.

In what ways do you think about impact on audience when you're going through that process?

Crass and commercial as it is, we must appeal to the audience. We look at play titles, actually – I wish we could tell playwrights the world over, "Pick better titles." The title of a play has a significant impact on whether we think it's going to truly appeal or draw, or if there's a way to get past the title and still sell the story. That's the first thing. The second thing is that we try to make sure that we're not telling the same story. We don't want to do four versions of the sex farce, however it's couched, whatever period you're sticking it in. It's still the same basic plot, and we like to avoid that as well.

> Crass and commercial as it is, we must appeal to the audience.

We did *West Side Story* this year, in September, and our artistic director has really wanted to do the play *Blood Brothers*, which in many ways has some fairly similar themes and concepts and ideas. As a selling point, we can say, "You liked *West Side Story*, you'll like this one," when I'm talking to the board. But we also have to recognize that we did this play in September, so we have to wait until following May, at least an 18-month separation between the two, so that people won't say, "Oh look, they just remounted *West Side Story* with boys instead of girls."

Then we also do look at what's the play that is, for lack of a better term, the "drama." Sometimes it can be a classic, like next season we're doing *Glass Menagerie*, and this year we're doing *Doubt*. We just want to make sure that we—I'm a staunch believer that you can't have one size fit all. So if we can offer six mainstage productions, each with enough variety, then maybe we'll win some fresh people each show, and maybe a few of them will become season ticket holders.

We feel the impact of productions through letters, and one of the things we have noticed this year is that we haven't gotten any letters. We have not received letters of complaint of any kind. A part of me is thinking, "Uh oh, are we not pushing them enough that we didn't get any pushback from anybody, or have we figured out their standards, and now they're just enjoying the play so much?" We get the occasional email as a reply to our e-news, "Love the play, had a good time," but how often do people write you to let you know what a wonderful and exciting theatrical experience they had? But boy they'll sure let you know when they're mad, and we haven't gotten that—and a part of me is worried.

We do a patron's pick that picks one of the six mainstage productions that we present. One of the plays, we set aside and we call it our patron's pick. In the past, quite simply, the artistic staff would pick two plays and write up descriptions and mail out the ballot to the patrons (individuals who have given

$100 or more), and they would mail it back, and they would just pick the play, and whoever got the most votes would be produced the next year. When the artistic director arrived, he said, "We've got to do this more significantly." And he set it up so that we actually do readings. He picks two plays from the shortlist that are like in nature, so one year it'll be a comedy and one year it'll be a drama (he says he doesn't want to leave the musicals with the audience because they'll always just pick the most popular musical). The two plays are comparable, for example, last year they put *Doubt* against *Frost/Nixon*, so clearly, you know, very small cast, easy set, etc. Then we do a reading for up to an hour for the public on a Friday night, if you're not a patron you have to pay $5 to vote. We get guest directors to direct it, and guest actors to do the reading. They rehearse about six hours, and we turn it into this big event, and then they come and they vote on it. It really truly feels like an evening that the audience owns.

And then you abide by their vote?

Absolutely! Although as the artistic director says, he does not put up these two productions if he's not willing to do either one of them. They have to be equal – he's not going to throw his favorite and least favorite in and hope, and we're pretty conscientious to not try and sway the vote. So two plays, comparable in size, comparable in budget, comparable in production values and style, you know, he's not going to put a drama against a comedy. And this year we had about 65 or 70 people participate in the process, plus another 20 or so who vote by mail.

Can you give me another example of a time when feedback from an audience changed your programming in some way?

We had an executive director who was a bit controversial when hired, and kind of set out to do some big sweeping with a broom, without necessarily taking into consideration much of anything. It had reached a point where this particular person fired the artistic director on Wednesday before a show on that weekend. The cast got very up in arms and threatened to say something to the audience at the end of the curtain call, and so this executive director cancelled the production. Totally devastating. This was a year and a half ago. But the troops (actors, volunteers, patrons, anybody who was committed to the theatre in such a fashion really got activated) rallied via Facebook and other social media, and the result was that the executive director got fired and the artistic director got rehired. With the switching of staff again, *Driving Miss Daisy* happened, and it was one of the biggest sellers they had had, because people were very supportive of the program and supportive of the production, and that support carried over to some very committed donations that took place over the course of the year. There was a real rejuvenation of energy, and it was a very powerful presence by the audience, the volunteers, the donors, the cast members—and as a consequence, the theatre became stronger. That was a massive impact.

Part of being a community theatre, when your billing, is, "We're your community theatre," there is ownership. It's owned by the community, and it's shared by the community as well.

Part of being a community theatre, when your tagline, your billing is, "We're your community theatre," there *is* ownership. Ownership extends to sponsorships, to advertising sales, to board member commitments – it's owned by the community, and it's shared by the community as well. So we're very conscientious of our presence and our impact on our participants.

From my standpoint, one of the areas that impact assessment might help with is to rely less on anecdotal evidence. Prior to this, with the exception of the patron's pick, there really had not been any kind of formal process of evaluating the audience. When I showed up I asked, "What do you guys know about your audience?" And they said, "Nothing." And I said, "Well, we need to learn something," and just about that time is when Arts Midwest called us and asked if we wanted to participate.

There are enough people that request that quantified number, and it will be helpful to share with the board. The purpose of this study is to put numbers to something that really is not numbers-based. It helps just give us, for lack of a better word, more ammunition in our exploration, and helps justify and support what we do and how we do it and why we do it.

Internally, it's going to be one more lens to look at. And it may prompt a few more debates amongst the artistic staff, or between the artistic director and myself. I might turn and say, look here's some numbers that substantiate my viewpoint, and he, as a convicted, passionate artist is going to say, "Well that's nice but you know what, I disagree with them." So this data might evoke better, richer conversations, discussions, debates – because otherwise we're just swapping anecdotes or feelings. It allows us to try and anticipate not only plans A, B and C, but plan O.

I would say that relying exclusively on this is just as inappropriate as relying on any other method exclusively. Don't erase what you're currently doing, use this to supplement and round out the perspective. That's what I'm looking forward to. Because it would be wrong, and just as inappropriate, for a bean counter to whip these numbers out and say this is why you have to do this because we're looking at a percentage, and those who are willing to respond, but we're not looking at individuals. And we still have that – our audience, as much as we'd like to think of them as "the audience," it's really 300 separate individuals with 300 separate perspectives and opinions. So, from my standpoint, it would not be the only weapon, though weapon is the wrong word, to badger and beat on the artistic staff and say "here's these numbers!" It just gives me supporting insight if I'm having questions about whether we've brought in this perspective, and it allows me to ask what they think about addressing that side of the coin. But it's one of many tools, not the only tool.

Bill Rauch
Oregon Shakespeare Festival

How do you or your artistic staff seek feedback from your audiences? How do you figure out what people thought of the show, how it landed for them, what the experience was like for them?

Well, I speak to the audience in a lot of different ways. We have an audience here that really takes ownership of the work. I get a pretty steady stream of emails and letters and people grabbing me on the street and grabbing me on the Bricks, which is the courtyard area in front of where the three theatres meet, and giving me their opinions. We also have weekends for donors and I speak to groups at those. We've got post matinee discussions that I do at least a couple of every season where I talk to 200-300 people. I'm trying to think how else...

I assess the season. I give a very unvarnished view of what I thought of each show at the September board meeting. After I talk about my opinions about a play, they weigh in with theirs and we go back and forth and have a dialogue.

If there's an artistically controversial thing happening, sometimes there's tension between us and the marketing department about the appropriateness of a choice. This year, for example, we had a character in *The Imaginary Invalid* who was a musician and who was playing in front of the theatre. He appeared to be a street musician, and he actually collected money that we were going to distribute to a local school system for the arts.

The marketing department was very upset that we were tricking the audience, while we in artistic were very adamant that this was an appropriate thing to do. So we actually did a survey on the preview audiences, and we found that the majority of people did in fact think he was a street musician and not part of the show and people ranged from being absolutely delighted when he entered the stage and they realized he was in the show to feeling betrayed.

In the end, we compromised by having him play in front of the theatre, with people thinking he was a street musician, but not having him collect money. It seemed like the greatest part of the discomfort was in people giving money

> **The greatest part of the discomfort was in people giving money thinking it was for one thing and then learning it was something else.**

thinking it was for one thing and then learning it was something else. That betrayal was something we decided some audience members wouldn't be able to recover from and it wasn't worth it. That's an example of a very targeted communication with the audience, in that case through an email survey, to get artistic feedback.

Are there moments where you are conflicted about what to do about audience feedback?

We have had some pretty traumatic cases. We have a high percentage of audiences in both the spring and the fall, what we call our shoulder seasons, who are students, so we have to set age guidelines. And I will be absolutely honest with you: I hate that we do it. I hate it, but the teachers and the parents and the school administrators really demand it.

We set these things long before the show is in rehearsal. I think the education guidelines go out in May or June and some of these productions don't go into rehearsal until the following May, and so it's just so ridiculous trying to say what age the show is appropriate for. In my tenure—we're wrapping up my fourth season as artistic director—I would say that every season we've had to change an age guideline during the season.

Those changes can be fairly dramatic, both the change and the process of the change, in terms of audience feedback and weighing in. A lot is at stake in terms of, "What is artistic censorship?", "What is giving in to a conservative bent in the society versus what is being professional and appropriate and communicating clearly and honoring what we've communicated?".

It's the difference between bringing your own 10-year-old to a show and having a group of 10-year-olds in a class come to a show. I've got a six-year-old and an 11-year-old and what I feel is appropriate for my kids is obviously completely different from someone else.

The question becomes: How important are the Catholic schools and the religious-affiliated private schools to us? Are we willing to lose that whole chunk of audience for a given project or maybe long-term based on an artistic

240

choice? This is not about our work across the board. This is about the work that we market as being appropriate to student audiences and what happens when the production finally exists and people feel that it's not appropriate.

I also get really worked up because it is so much about sexuality, of course. It's never about violence. Julius Caesar is played by a woman as a woman this season and she's stabbed brutally in front of the audience. There's never a peep. Never a peep, but two people are dancing suggestively in *Measure for Measure*, fully clothed, and it's a travesty. Or there's a transgender character in *Measure for Measure*, a man playing a man who identifies as a woman, and the bile that has come from some of the school groups about this choice, it's really intense.

> I get audience response that I just completely disagree with, so I want to keep my heart open, but I also don't want to be reactive, in a knee-jerk way, and change things that I don't believe in changing.

Then there are all the people who talk about how their lives have been changed and how moved they've been and how encouraged they are by what they're seeing on the stages.

There's been a lot of dialogue with the audience over the years about race and ethnicity as it relates to casting. There's a lot of good say on that and, again, we can get into that as much as you want. We have a deaf member of the acting company who performs his roles in American Sign Language.

The fact is, I get audience response that I just completely disagree with, so I want to keep my heart open and I want to listen to trends, but I also don't want to be reactive, in a knee-jerk way, and change things that I don't believe in changing. Trying to really gauge my own meter about which concerns and criticism have integrity and which don't is a very interesting part of this job.

When you're in that phase of choosing a project how does that process work? How do you think about impact on the audience?

Well, we're a rep company. We perform at the very least four plays in rotating rep at the same time. Most of the season we're running nine plays in rep at the same time from June all the way through the first week of October. So for us, it's never about one play. It's about the combination of plays. Absolutely we talk a lot about trying to push the envelope in terms of audience comfort. We talk a lot about the kaleidoscope of rotating repertory and how can we make the colors brighter and the contrast sharper, so that your jaw drops open that this story and that story are juxtaposed within our season—are juxtaposed in the same theatre—so that you can come and see one in the afternoon and the next in the evening and see some of the same actors in the same space and they're wildly different.

We talk a lot about trying to build in a sense of unpredictability. The rep is so rigorous. Everything gets locked into place so far in advance and there are certain patterns that have been here for years and years and years. A lot of my job as an artistic director has been trying to, hopefully in an intelligent way and not just a random way, trying to subvert those expectations and trying to do this kind of play in this kind of slot that's never been done before, this kind of play on the outdoor stage, this kind of play in that special slot that opens in April.

That's really important. We talk a ton about the audience because we have to look at every slice of the season. What are the four plays that are running in rep in February? What are the six plays that are running in rep in April? What are the nine plays that are running rep in June, which are different from the nine plays that are running in rep in July because two close and two new ones open?

There are seven or eight different slices of the season that we have to look at with the audience in mind, with school groups in mind, with the general audience in mind—to maintain balance.

Is there a balance tonally in terms of comedy and tragedy and everything in between? Is there a balance of Shakespeare and new work? What does it say if you have a play written by a woman that's running these months but then it's not going to be running the rest of the season, or you take this story that you know really kicks ass in terms of student groups but it's running in the summer when there are no student groups?

There's a lot of debate in terms of culturally specific stories and where they belong in the season and when they're going to have the greatest impact. We have two slots that run all year, from February all the way through the first week of November, so we have to ask ourselves, "What are the stories—the statements we make with those stories—that can not only sustain an audience for 121 performances but can challenge an audience for 121 performances?"

During my first season it was really important for me to expand our classical canon outside of the European and American canon. We had never really done classical work from other parts of the world. I knew that in my first season as artistic director, which was 2008, I wanted to do a Sanskrit epic called *The Little Clay Cart*.

It's a 2500-year-old Sanskrit play, so I said, "Come on, it's going to be very hard to get people to come to this." I was determined to do it but I was trying to keep it in a shorter slot. It was either going to open in the beginning and close or open late in the season and close but it's certainly not going to have one of the longer slots. And then a guy in our marketing staff, at one of these meetings, kind of banged his fists on the table and said, with great passion, "I don't understand why we're trying to bury this play in a short slot."

He said: "If we feel so strongly about expanding our classical canon outside of the Western canon then we should run this play all year long so that no matter when somebody comes to the Oregon Shakespeare Festival they can see *The Little Clay Cart*."

That was so radical because it had always been Noel Coward, Oscar Wilde, Kaufman and Hart. It had always been a British or American comedy that had run in that slot all year long alongside of Shakespeare. To do an ancient Sanskrit play was radically outside of the box, but that's what we did.

Hopefully we strike a really good balance. I'd say we work really hard to strike a good balance, being savvy about the pressures on the different slices of the year in terms of audience, but also making sure we're challenging our audiences and ourselves with the choices that we're making.

Tell me more about your season selection process. It sounds complex.

The season selection system, which I inherited, is called Boarshead, named for the tavern in the *Henry IV* plays. It started some years back, long before my time, with all the department heads getting together and reading the plays that the artistic director was thinking about so that they could weigh in. The costume department head could say this one has too many clothes for this slot, that kind of thing. We've expanded it since I've arrived so it now also

243

includes company members-at-large. There are six or seven members of the acting company on Boarshead and then there are five company members that are not.

You might have an usher, a carpenter, a stitcher from the costume shop, a lower-level administrator as part of the group. There are 45 to 50 people. They're huge, these meetings. We put out a reading list of 12 to 15 plays every two weeks for everyone to read, and then we get together every two weeks on Fridays in September, October, November and December and we talk about them.

We assign two lead readers out of the group to each play and they launch the discussion about the play. It's just fantastic. Ultimately I have to make the choices about what plays we're doing and I work very closely with colleagues in the artistic office including our director of literary development.

The conversation that happens in these meetings and the way people really hate plays, really love plays, the way people disagree about plays—the insights people have about why the stories are urgent or irrelevant, how the stories might land with our audiences or not—how the stories might pull new audience members in—it is all invaluable, that feedback that I get. It absolutely shapes the decision making in a very profound way.

Do you include folks outside staff or artists, like board members or patrons or donors?

We've never had board members on Boarshead as far as I know. In preparation for our 75th anniversary season, which was in 2010, we opened it up to audience members and some audience members wrote a little essay about why they'd like to be part of it and then we selected two audience members. It was very interesting and very useful to have them in the room but we didn't continue it because some of us felt that it was maybe inhibiting. I'm of two minds about it. I can imagine going back to trying it in the future, maybe in a different way. For example, we've done focus groups within departments and we've talked about doing one of those with audience members to get their opinions that way.

This may be different since you operate as a destination theatre, but when you think of who the theatre is serving, who are the people you think of when you say "our audience" or "our community?" How do you think of those circles and do you think that's something that's been evolving in your tenure there?

Yes. We have a large audience, though it's hard to talk about the audience as a monolith. Last season was 414,000 people; 414,000 ticket holders. That represents probably 100,000 individuals, because folks see on average about four plays. There's the real core audience, which we define as people who come at least twice a year to make sure they see all 11 or 12 shows. That's part of the audience we think

We think a lot about the audience of the future and not just the audience of the present.

about. There is the larger membership and they usually come every year but they don't come more than once a year so they might come and see three or four plays but not everything. Then there are student groups which we've talked about some already. Then there are the single ticket buyers who will come from far away.

We have 18,000 member households. Then single ticket buyers, and then there's our local audience. We live in a town of 20,000 people. This part of southern Oregon is fairly rural and isolated. We live in a very progressive little town in the middle of a hugely conservative part of the country. It's an area that's largely white but with a growing Latino community.

We just had a two-hour company call, our last company call of the year, where people gather from across the entire organization and we present our financials for the current year and our budget for next year. And we unveil the marketing images for next season's plays and we talk about pressing issues facing the company.

Then we do a slideshow retrospective of the season. It's very moving. It's very, very powerful. There was a 25-minute presentation on audience diversity and where we're at and where we're headed. Five people in leadership in the organization and I formed a taskforce and we created an audience development manifesto. We spent a year creating this document. A year.

Then we've been very slowly and with purpose rolling it out, first to our board and our company-at-large and—we're just at the beginning of this part—now to the public. It is very much a guiding document in terms of the philosophy we have about wanting to increasingly diversify our audience. We think a lot about the audience of the future and not just the audience of the present.

> We *are* driving away some of our core audience. There are some people who hate what's happening artistically and I hear from them loudly and clearly. I feel like it's all in service to the mission, and there does come a point where you just have to say, "Oh well. It's not for you anymore, and that's fine. I'm not going to change what I care about."

There's a lot of discussion about how do we include and involve and retain the audience of the future without driving away the audience of the present. There's a lot of fear, I think, that some people have that, as an artistic leader, I'm more interested in the audience of the future than the audience of the present, and that therefore I'm going to jeopardize the organization's fiscal health.

That leads to some really interesting organizational tensions, though the longer I'm here, the more muted those become. Not muted but diminished, those concerns, because in fact 2009 and 2010 were highest attended seasons ever in the festival's history. I think the fear that I was going to drive away the core audience has been mitigated to a degree—though we *are* driving away some of our core audience. There are some people who hate what's happening artistically and I hear from them loudly and clearly. They say, "I've been coming for 30 years and you've ruined this place for me and I'm never coming again." I think it's probably a pretty small minority view, but each one of those letters is like a dagger to the heart.

I feel like I'm building on 75 years of history, and I feel like it's all in service of the mission. And there does come a point where you just have to say, "Oh well. It's not for you anymore, and that's fine. I'm not going to change what I care about." Still, it hurts.

Are you finding that there are particular changes you've made or particular directions you're going that are the problematic ones?

It varies, but there are common themes. Shakespeare not being done in distant historic periods is one. There was a lot of backlash about artists of color in

Shakespeare plays here, but you never hear that anymore ever, ever, ever. There are no longer complaints about that nearly the way there were maybe 15 years ago. If people feel it they're keeping it to themselves. I never get that. Marian the Librarian in *The Music Man* being played by an African American woman, though? Multiracial casting in American classics, I got a flood of letters about.

It's like the target has moved. It makes sense and it gives you hope in terms of progressive politics. It's like we can't think about Shakespeare without thinking about it with actors that are diverse. That's normal for Shakespeare. It's become normal for this audience, too—which is huge. But with the American classics it's like, "Wait a minute, there's a particular cultural context here."

"Come on," I say. If we were doing Shakespeare in its original cultural context everybody would be male, everybody would be white. That's not what we're doing. I think because the cultural context of the American classics is a little bit more recent people feel more disturbed and confused.

There are people who are uncomfortable with depictions of gay characters on the stage, so that comes up. And some people are unhappy and feel like this is a classical theatre and there shouldn't be such a strong focus on new work. And for me there's a certain kind of exuberant humor which I think is very, very Shakespearean, but then some people want their Shakespeare and other plays to be more respectful, so that comes up.

Politically, of course, any number of the things that we've talked about and themes in plays become part of a "leftist political agenda," which for some conservative audience members is hard. Although we did *American Night*, a Culture Clash piece about immigration, and it was quite beautiful because there were some really hardcore conservative, Republican donors and other audience members who loved it.

In that case, the politics of the piece were right on the sleeve, but the deeper thread was a love of this country and calling this country to task, wanting it to be its best self. People responded to that regardless of their political affiliation.

In my first season we did a play called *Welcome Home, Jenny Sutter*, by Julie Marie Myatt, and it was about a female marine returning home from Iraq. We were really worried. It was a brand new play written by a young writer that the audience would not have heard of. Plus, you know, this feeling of "Oh great,

> It's not about picking a fight with your audience. That doesn't get you anywhere. It's about asking, "How can we expand the dialogue?"

a play about a marine coming back from Iraq." It's going to be a screeching, antiwar diatribe and nobody will want to see it: this was our fear. Partly because of this fear, but really mostly because it felt like the ethical thing to do, we offered free tickets to any veteran or active duty military personnel.

We had 1,500 tickets given out to vets and active duty military personnel, but way beyond those 1,500 tickets and the loss we took to make those free, way beyond that was I think that we sent out the message that this is a play that needs to be seen regardless of one's position on the war in Iraq. It wasn't just a polemic with one point of view.

The play was, in fact, pretty harshly critical of the war, but that wasn't the point of the play and we got that message out. It did extremely well at the box office. People were very moved by it. I had a gentleman come up to me and grab my arm at the opening and say, "I'm a wounded marine vet and you people nailed it, and I thank you." He was tearful and I was tearful.

Having spent 20 years with Cornerstone [Theatre Company in Los Angeles], I believe it's not about picking a fight with the audience. That doesn't get you anywhere. It's about asking, "How can we expand the dialogue? Who do we want in the room and what can we do both in the choices we make and how we communicate those choices to get as many people in the room as possible?"

Do you find some of that is about putting events or engagement opportunities around the performance experience? Are there development moments where audience is involved, or do you feel like the dialogue is happening largely in the performance for you?

It's a great question. This year we will have 835 education events. We do preshow prep, what we call "Prologues and Prefaces," some for student groups, some for general audiences. And then we have workshops with student groups and even workshops with classes. You can do what is called "An Unfolding Weekend" where you dig deep into the issues surrounding one production then you take a whole bunch of classes over a weekend.

I would say our education department has done spectacular work over many,

many years around the idea of being better prepared for a play. What I'm as interested in that we don't do as well is the process of processing a work of art *after* you've seen it. Encouraging and empowering the audience to able to dialogue with itself and with company members after seeing a work of art.

We do do post-matinee discussions after every matinee, which tend to be led by an actor—who generally have not had any kind of facilitation training, so there are some very awkward things that happen—but they're very valuable.

As we look at the long-term space needs of the organization and expansion of the campus, one of my dreams is to create what I think of as the Welcome Center, although there are probably a million discussions to be had about what we would call it. I see it as a patron and education center with classrooms, with a lot of big, open public space to encourage dialogue to happen here on our campus.

Because OSF is a destination theatre, our audience is here. There are people who want to go rafting or who want to go shoe shopping or want to have a leisurely dinner but there are just as many people who, if we gave them more opportunities to dig deeper in dialogue with each other and with ourselves, they would take it.

As we talk about expanding this stuff, some of the dialogue has to be about the fact that the entire community of Ashland is here to support these discussions. Bed & Breakfasts: at every Bed & Breakfast in Ashland during the Festival, the dialogue over breakfast is about who saw what last night and then discussing the plays. In the lobbies of the hotels, the school groups get together and talk with their teachers about what they've seen and processed. What is our role versus what is the community-at-large's role? What should we be doing as a theatre that we're not already doing, and what would be poaching from others in the community?

Where do you guys stand in terms of how your talkbacks and other audience engagement currently are or where you'd like to take them?

With *Welcome Home, Jenny Sutter*, the play I referred to earlier, we did a panel of vets from four different wars talking about the experience of coming home. Yes, I'm deeply interested. Why did we put the play on in the first place and what kind of dialogue can we have that isn't just, "How did you memorize all those lines?"

249

Why are we doing theatre and why are we telling stories and what are we trying to learn about ourselves?

Those craft-based discussions, whether they're at a very elementary level or a more sophisticated level, are useful and I think help people fall more deeply in love with the art form and have more context with the art form, but I completely agree that the best discussions are ones that get at the heart of the matter, the issues raised by the play itself: why are we doing theatre and why are we telling stories and why are we telling these stories and what are we trying to learn about ourselves as a human species from these stories?

Yes, yes, yes, yes, yes.

Steven Glaudini
Musical Theatre West

What kind of tools do you currently have in place at your theatre to solicit audience feedback that comes to you as opposed to going to marketing folks?

Pretty much, it all stems through our PR/Marketing team. They send out surveys after the show, getting their feedback on particular performance and Musical Theatre West, and I just get forwarded reports and charts and stuff. Really, artistically the only thing that I'm ever involved in is when we ask them to give their opinions on the five shows they want to see. But it's never has anything to do with the experience of coming to Musical Theatre West. That's through our PR/Marketing team.

I stand in the lobby before every show and after every show and get the feedback at intermission or afterwards. Our executive director does a curtain speech as well, and he's been around for 40 years of our 58 years, so he's really the face, but I'm kind of the person that artistically picks the shows and gets the quality of the shows up. So we're both in the lobby, readily accessible to our audiences to have them rave about the show or say, you know, the air conditioner is too cold. Whatever it is, they find a reason to complain or praise.

We don't get a lot of letters complaining. I think the one show that got the most complaints was when we did the regional premiere of *Altar Boyz*. Religion is just something that they say just don't take lightly, our audiences. But everything else from *Full Monty* to *Sweeney Todd* to *Rent—Rent*, we did last year as a bonus show, and our people were very appreciative that we gave them the option to not take the show as part of the season. We have a lot of people who tend to write emails; we're doing this world premiere that people are saying is one of the best things we've done. So they're very open to having their opinions be heard.

In your process of selecting a show, do you think about the kind of impact you want to be having on your audience?

We definitely do. We have really loyal subscribers (we're at a 93% renewal rate), so they're kind of game to whatever we give them. But we're sensitive, too. Like next season, we have a lot of new shows so we said we should probably give them a little comfort food, we haven't done *Man of La Mancha* in thirty years, and in a season that has *Hairspray* and *Spamalot* and *Forbidden Broadway*, we should also give them a little meat. It's like painting a canvas. You just want to make sure there's a symmetry to what we're doing. We had a really artistic season last year, where we gave them comfort food, we opened with *Meet Me in St. Louis*, then *Sweeney Todd*, *The Marvelous Wonderettes*, *1776*, and we had the bonus show of *Rent*. And out of that season, the one show that made the most money out of everything was *1776*, which no one knew would do the business that it did. The audience really glommed onto *Sweeney Todd* and *1776*, which I thought was really fascinating. And they brought in a single ticket audience, too, which is important. Our subscribers are so loyal that I need to get the new people in, the audience of the future, so it is important, when we're programming shows, that we get those titles that are of interest to the single ticket buyer. Like when we did *Rent*, 87% of our audience had never been to a Musical Theatre West show. And of that about 78% of that group came back to see *Sweeney Todd*. So that's really important, too, for our future, because let's be honest, our subscriber base, if they're not renewing it's because they're dying or they can't get to the theatre.

Whenever someone hasn't renewed, we contact them, and it's, "Oh, I've lost a spouse and I have no way of getting there." It tends to be that, as unfortunate as that is. Long Beach is really multicultural, and we do try to do shows that bring in a multicultural audience, but we don't find that that's really it at all. For us the main thing is age. People are aging out.

When I saw *Spamalot* on Broadway, it was the first time I'd ever seen a show on Broadway where it was obvious the men were dragging the women to the theatre. So it's important we do those shows as well, but without alienating our subscribers, because they are the backbone of our organization. We couldn't do it without our subscription base.

We have an executive director who has produced all but 18 shows in our 58 years. He likes to revert back to 1977 when we were a community theatre. He's so loyal, but at the same time it's like getting him to think outside the box—which he's been marvelous at since I've been there, which is four and a half years—to take those bold steps in building a new audience and getting the people to our theatre for the first time. When you do *Meet me in St. Louis* our matinees will be packed, but no one on a Friday night is saying, "Hey, let's go see *Meet Me in St. Louis.*" It's just not that kind of show. So while I know it comfort food for Joe and Martha our subscribers, it's not doing anything to get new blood and new people into our venue, which really, I think, has to be our immediate goal. We can't pick a season for subscribers, because we know they're tried and true and they've come to trust us in whatever we give them, even if they don't think it's up their alley. Like with *Sweeney Todd*. I had many patrons say, "Now listen, I may not have loved the storyline, but the show could not have been better produced." The way it was done, the people were floored by the talent and Sondheim's score. Do they

> We can't pick a season for subscribers, because we know they're tried and true and they've come to trust us in whatever we give them, even if they don't think it's up their alley.

think cannibalism and slitting throats is a way to spend a Sunday afternoon? Maybe, maybe not—but they could not argue with the way it was produced and presented to them.

What I do, like if we have the exclusive LA rights to *Next to Normal*—yes, it's a depressing show, but it's also a Pulitzer Prize-winning, important piece of theatre—so when we program a show like that, what I try to do is to get a performer who our audiences love. Sometimes, you know, it's an easier pill to swallow if they're seeing Tami Tappan playing that role. Instead of bringing out stars, we've kind of created stars, and it helps our audiences when they know, "Oh, Tami Tappan's in this." They just love her, and it's an easier journey for them to take with a performer they love. I do think about that in programming, but I don't shy away from doing a show like *Next to Normal* because I think it's an important piece. And for where we are in the LA community—we tout ourselves as Southern California's premiere musical theatre company—it's important that we get the rights to those shows. It's important that we get the newer stuff to support the single ticket audience, but also how can I make this easier on our matinee audiences, as well?

Can you think of a time when feedback from the audience changed a programming decision?

You know what? No, not changed a programming decision. They get more

> I would say that we do listen to every complaint, but it's an opinion. If I have two people come up to me and say they don't like something, I think, "Well, good." Isn't that what theatre is about?

upset when we change a programming decision. There was a time when we had announced that we were doing *Dreamgirls*, and then the Ahmanson announced that the pre-Broadway tour that started at the Apollo was coming to the Ahmanson. And it was right when the economy crashed, and you're looking at, "Okay, *Dreamgirls* is an expensive show." We've already seen our single ticket sales pretty much stiff, because in this economy as a single ticket buyer, are you going to go see this new production at the Ahmanson with music from the film, or are you going to see the production at Musical Theatre West. We saw the writing on the wall, and we were looking at losing $100,000.

I had just acquired the Broadway set and costumes of *Little Shop of Horrors*, and I told our executive director, it's got three African American women who actually appear as the Supremes, so let's face this and go we can either lose the money or we can do a show with seven actors and a five-piece band, and I have the Broadway sets and costumes, so it's going to have the bling. People get more disgruntled when we announce something and then decide not to do it, rather than feedback making us change the show. We've made the decision that once we announce it we have to commit to it.

I would say that we do listen to every complaint, but it's an opinion. If I have two people come up to me and say they don't like something, I think, "Well, good." Isn't that what theatre is about? If it's good theatre, it's going to move you, either to love something or to hate it. When I ran a theatre in Riverside, California, I had a couple walk out during *Company* saying they hated the show, and I said, "Well, you've not seen it. You've walked out on a pot scene because you don't agree with the situation. But if you were to go back in there and follow the show, and Bobby, until he gets to 'Being Alive,' then I'd listen to your opinion."

Unfortunately, we've become a squeaky wheel society. We've created a society that can just complain. And sometimes they're valid, and sometimes they're not valid. And for someone to hear me say that their opinion isn't valid—well,

I have to think of the greater good, I can't think of the couple people who will be upset if we do something. Then give your tickets away. Give you tickets to your kids. If you come, I guarantee that the production will be fantastic, but if it's not your cup of tea, I can't change that.

I just trust our instinct and guts. And— even if *Altar Boyz* was distasteful to some people, would it shy me away from doing another show that deals with religion in that way? Probably not. But we would be prepared to get the feedback that we would anticipate. You have to prepare to massage the people that you know are going to be unhappy. There's always going to be someone who is unhappy.

Like with *Rent*. The people who complained about *Rent*, we said, "You know, it wasn't part of your subscription. You should have Googled it, it's not like *Rent* is an unknown commodity." To come into that without the information—I think that now, in this society, in 2011, there has to be some audience responsibility. It's not like before we had the Internet—if you come in now and you act shocked because you don't know what the *Rocky Horror Show* is about, well then shame on you. Because the information is available. And we give as much as we can. And for you, as an audience member, not to take any kind of ownership, I think that's irresponsible.

Knowing what you do about the study, are there particular ways that you're hoping the study will be useful to you?

I'll read anything. I actually am one that will read what people have to say. And that's what I think is invaluable about this study – we need all the help we can get in somehow judging what they want, where they're coming from, what's going to keep them here. All that is absolutely invaluable. If there were some really clear-cut, high-percentage things on certain shows, of course we

> I think that now, in 2011, there has to be some audience responsibility. If you come in now and you act shocked because you don't know what the *Rocky Horror Show* is about, well then shame on you. For you, as an audience member, not to take any kind of ownership, I think that's irresponsible.

have to pay attention to that. This is more of a real survey – the questions that are included are intelligent. It's not like, "What shows do you want to see?", and they all write *The Phantom of the Opera*, and they don't know that the rights aren't available for *Phantom of the Opera*. I think yes, there's much more mileage to get for my marketing team and for us artistically. I'm very interested in reading the results.

Martha Lavey
Steppenwolf Theatre

For you, or for your artistic staff, what are some of the ways right now that you hear from audiences about what their experience was at the show? What are the formal and maybe informal ways that you tell how the show has landed for your audience?

Well, of course, the principle venue for that is we have a post-show conversation after every performance. We get the immediate response from the audience and those are all led by a member of the artistic staff. That doesn't necessarily mean someone who is part of the artistic office, but perhaps was the assistant director of the play.

We train those people to do the post-show discussions because what we're interested in, in that situation, is talking less about "How did you memorize those lines?" than to put the play in the context of the season theme and have them just talk about the play and be interpretive about the play. That's the first case.

Also, at every performance we do a register-to-win survey to win a dinner at a local restaurant. We've been doing that for years. Those are collated for me and the other staff to read at the end of a run of a play. We have a blog, which sometimes elicits response relative to the performance or the play itself, but is more engaged in a conversation about the art and the artist.

Our front of house files a report every night for staff that really is about gauging audience response. That's for all of our shows in all of our theatres. The stage manager, too, records things like audience response specific to lines. They talk about standing ovations, all that kind of stuff.

That's how we keep the pulse on it. We also do some video interviews, reactions, through the marketing department. For each of the shows, there's audience response, which they film and which gets posted.

Some organizations have a short email address to write to the artistic director or some kind of direct line for subscribers. Do you have a mechanism like that?

> The guiding star, the North Star, of all of our programming is, "How does it serve the ensemble as artists?"

Yeah. There's a customer service line and the person who minds that sends all of that stuff to me and I respond to those personally.

As you're beginning to think about selecting a season or initiating a relationship with a particular play or playwright, in what ways do you think about impact on your audience? Are there particular kinds of effects you're trying to have with every play or with every season? How do you incorporate that into your process of choosing an artistic project?

A lot of the decision making around programming is guided by the service to our ensemble of artists. We have 43 ensemble members, most of whom are actors, a number of whom are both actors and directors, and then two who are just exclusively directors. We always describe their conversation with the artistic office as a "two-way conversation."

Either they are bringing projects to me, like Frank Galati saying, "I really want to adapt E. L. Doctorow's *The March*," and going through that process, which he'll also be directing this season, or Tracy Letts writing a new play, Anna Shapiro saying "I want to direct it." Or it is us, the staff, because we're obviously the collection points for new plays from audiences, either the things that we've commissioned and have developed or submissions that we get.

We'll mull those over with the ensemble. Is this a role you'd like to play? What about this? The other source would be extant plays and me saying to Tina Landau, "I know this is a crazy idea, but would you think about directing or are you interested in directing *Diary of Anne Frank* or *Time of your Life*."

The guiding star, the North Star, of all of our programming is, "How does it serve the ensemble as artists?" And then, "How effective are those pieces in this idea of a season theme?" And the theme is stated in a capacious enough way that it's really permitting of a lot of different kinds of plays.

The evolution of the theme happened for kind of interesting reasons that had to do with, really, my decision to have post-show conversations after all of the plays. The presiding metaphor that we use at the theatre is to say that Steppenwolf is a public square that's activated by the work on our stages. At

258

the center of that metaphor is dialogue. My feeling is that having a theme allows that dialogue to have more points of view.

It's not like a filtering principle like, "Oh well, we can't do that play because it doesn't fit into the theme." It's more like, "Oh, here's a good way to talk about it."

And it can also spur our imagination about the kind of play we might want. You know, "Oh, we didn't think of that. But if this is a season where we're really looking at this question of faith, what would that mean?" Thus, the ensemble said, "Oh gosh, we really should do Beckett in that context." You know, stuff like that.

> The presiding metaphor that we use at the theatre is to say that Steppenwolf is a public square that's activated by the work on our stages.

So you have a real two-way exchange with the ensemble. Is there a parallel kind of exchange with your audience or community?

Do you mean, does the audience participate in, "Here's a play I think you should do?" I'll have personal communication with people who say, "Gosh, I saw this really great play in London, what about this?" But that tends to be stuff that we're aware of already.

Do you connect with community organizations, or the public, on a bigger level? Do they participate in the theme?

We don't, actually, and we've talked about that. But no, we don't. Now, might that ever be true? Might that be an evolution to say, "What do you guys want to talk about?" We actually have posed questions like that on the blog. But we haven't done that per se. We haven't said, "This season the audience is going to...we're going to collate their responses, and they're going to generate theme." We haven't done that.

It sounds like you might end up with a slate of projects that you're interested in that come out of this exchange with the ensemble.

Right.

And then there are your audiences: your subscribers, your single-ticket buyers. Do you think about what will grab them? What will "keep them happy?" How do those things sort of play into these other considerations?

> The standard contract with the audience has stopped being the principle and enduring model of how a theatre and an audience member interacts. Our bet is that the more that the audience knows about the work and about the artist, the stickier their connection will be, and the more they'll have a sense of ownership.

We don't tend to be formulaic in that way. I was just meeting with Anna Shapiro and Tracy Letts today, who are artistic associates here. And I was just saying, because we were thinking about 2012/2013, I was just saying, "I like a season when the iris opens and contracts."

From the point of view where the audience member is sitting, I like that this season we're doing a play that has a kind of epic sweep with *The March* or *Three Sisters*. And then it comes up close for *Time Stands Still*. And then we have a kind of, as Bruce calls it, a comedy of manners like *Clybourne Park* that takes us and spans 50 years for us.

I like that kind of variety. I like that the audience has to sit in a different chair perceptively. Rather than, "Gee, I want a funny one."

And then, of course, just as one constructs a season, you think about things like, "Okay, well how many 15-character plays can I do in one season?" And honestly I have to say our executive director, David Hawkinson has been so smart about encouraging the board to think about our planning in more like a three-year-cycle rather than a year-to-year budget cycle, which is the reason those big projects can be endeavored. That's been very helpful. And it's freed us even more over the last number of years from having to think, "Okay, now we need the little play."

We're very fortunate in that because this is a theatre that got generated out of an ensemble, there was an aesthetic that was theirs and presumably to which people are attracted. So we're not required to behave like the only game in town. We don't have to do a musical and do a Shakespeare, because we're not representing the theatre diet for a whole locality. We're part of an ecosystem in Chicago where you go to Chicago Shakespeare and then you go to Goodman and then you go to Lookingglass....you know. Plus you go to the 200 storefront theatres that are sitting there.

When you think about your audience and use that term (if you do), are you thinking primarily about your subscribers, or about the subscribers and single ticket buyers, or do you think, "We serve the Chicago theatregoing public?"

Well, in the last number of years in particular, the standard contract with audience has stopped being the principle and enduring model of how a theatre and audience member interacts. Instead, we're trying to form an engagement with the audience that is different from the standard membership model. Our bet is that the more that the audience knows about the work and about the artist, the stickier their connection will be, and the stronger the connection, the more they'll have a sense of ownership. Thusly, of course we love our subscribers and blah, blah, blah. But we don't treat them differently from a single ticket buyer who still considers us a home, because what we discovered in our research is that there are people who are not subscribers who consider Steppenwolf their theatre.

So we talk to our audience in that context. We talk to *all* of our audience. We consider our home audience Chicago, but we know that there's a kind of interest in Steppenwolf, I'm very grateful to say, as a national theatre. It even has a reputation internationally. But we always do the work, first and foremost, for here, for now.

Rob Melrose
The Cutting Ball Theater

Talk to me a little bit about what kind of feedback, formal or informal, that you've solicited in the past from your audience. Has that been you, or ushers, or artists - and what has that feedback been like?

We've never done anything systematic as far as surveying those kind of things. We started a aggressively surveying our audience about three seasons ago and what we were asking for, we gave away a bottle of wine a night, and we were asking for mainly demographic stuff, what their income level is, what age they are, what ethnicity they are, what marketing they saw, and would they be interested in getting involved with The Cutting Ball Theater.

So this year, with WolfBrown, is the first year of asking any kind of question about their experience at all. Which probably shows how small we are that we haven't gotten around to doing it yet. But I was just saying that I wish we were doing the survey last season, because last season was like our best season ever. I kind of felt like this season would be similar, and we've gotten great reviews and I've been really proud of the shows, but they just haven't been selling nearly as much as they did last year. It's got me doing some soul-searching into, you know, "What are we doing this year that's different than last year?" It's crazy.

I just don't know what it is. We've spent more money on marketing this year, I feel like our marketing has been better this year. And it's really hard to tell what's making things different. And I kind of thought that because of our success last year this year would be easier. I thought, "Well hey, now we've proved that we're an important theatre to a big number of people, and they'll all come back next year." And they didn't.

What about in terms of your own informal conversations? Do you have regulars that you talk to for feedback on shows?

I would say it's almost like there are concentric circles for me. In the center of the circle is a conversation between me and [wife/co-founder] Paige about how we thought it went. Then the next circle is probably the staff and the artists, and then the board, and then the next circle out is probably—we have people who have been coming to Cutting Ball since the beginning, and they're really big fans and they tell us what they think. A couple of them have blogs, and they write an essay, usually after the first preview—a pre-review—and then, you know, we definitely, I read every review, and we take that in. And then definitely, lots of talk in the lobby, especially during previews and opening. With two kids, though, and I know this is the difference between a good artistic director and a bad artistic director, and I'm on the bad side, but once opening happens I'm usually at home for the rest of the run, because I've usually neglected my kids for a month, and while it would be nice for me to be at the play, the play will still go on without me there. I know that really successful, really good artistic directors are there all the time, and really cultivating their audience, and I wish I did more of that, but I can't.

When you're in that process of, "I'm interested in the piece, are we going to do it or not?" Are you thinking about what sorts of impacts you're going to have on the audience? Or is that not a way of thinking that you use?

Our mission is to do experimental plays, seminal *avant garde* works and re-visioned classics, so our first question is, "Are we hitting those things? Has it been a long time since we've done one of those three things?" And I have a list of those things that I want to do, and they're usually being developed. A number of things go into "Are we going to do it or not?" One is just everybody's excitement about it—the artists and the audience. "Have the workshops we've done struck a chord with anybody?" We have in the past workshopped some things and no one seemed very excited about it, and that's easy then, we're not going to do it. But then we also ask, "Do we have the right artists to do this?" And then, especially a theatre our size, "Do we think that a foundation will fund this?" If something is really fundable, it's more likely that we'll do it, because you know, if I know that a foundation is likely to fund something, or if we apply for something and get the money for it, then we're kind of committed to doing it. That's the part of the decision-making process that I think is probably unique to being a small theatre, because if you have something you want to do and people are excited about it, and you get a grant—some grants cover, you know, half of the cost of doing a production.

I know that one of your big desires is to build an audience for this type of work. So, what's a homerun for you in terms of audience response?

The big one, just on an individual basis, is "Wow, that really blew my mind."

> There was a time that I knew what the sell out shows would be for Cutting Ball. But we've done all those plays now. I don't know how to sell out anymore; I don't know what a safe choice is for us anymore.

Or "That was surprising to me." Or "That really engaged my imagination." Those are the ones I really like, where it seems like we've done something new and exciting. "Oh my god, that was *something*," that's what I like. For us, what building the audience means, and this is where I haven't gotten there yet, but in doing this experimental work, my strategy is to say, "Okay, let's do a really exciting, innovative production of *The Bald Soprano*, which many, many people have heard of, and let's get lots of people, you know, 2,000 people, to come to see it." And then my hope is, when we do something no one has heard of, you know, 1,000 people come to see it, to take a chance on it. But that's not how it's been. It's not translating into this year.

Are you familiar with Oregon Shakespeare Festival? Libby Apple ran it for years and years, and she really wanted to go out with a bang. So in her last year, she picked shows that she knew would sell out. And what's funny is, there was a time that I knew what those shows would be for Cutting Ball. It's *No Exit*, it's *The Maids*—but we've done all those plays now. I don't know how to sell out anymore; I don't know what a safe choice is for us anymore, because we've done the obvious safe choices for us already.

So what's the balance for you between a personal response you have for a play and your sense of whether an audience may or may not go for it?

You know, other theatres have an identifiable audience that they know are their audience. And I'm still trying to find my audience. We're trying to develop audience for a specific kind of work. So there's really no sense of, "My audience hates this, my audience doesn't like that." There is a sense of, "What do I think is too obscure to run for five weeks in San Francisco?" And there's the question of the limits of what I'm able to do in terms of obscurity and darkness—there's also some work that I just love that I think is just a little bit too dark for San Francisco. I love Heiner Müller, I'd love to do *Quartet* and *The Task*, but in some ways that kind of hits two bad areas. It's too obscure, they're like the fifth and sixth most famous plays that Müller ever wrote, and they're also the darkest ones. So that's my level. I guess my audience is San Francisco, but I don't have a subscription audience, so it's different. So I have to ask myself, "Are there a thousand people in San Francisco who will actually come to see this?"

So your audience is who you can get to come, as opposed to a base of people who come again and again?

My dream is to have developed a subscription audience who really likes theatre that I like. I'd love to be boxed in that way.

Exactly. Although my dream is to have developed a subscription audience who really likes theatre that I like. That would be terrific. I'd love to be boxed in that way.

So how could this study be of use to you along that path?

Especially because we're doing experimental work, I'm really interested in knowing what people's actual responses are. Because of course the people who talk to me are usually the people who really liked it, and really connected to it. And it's interesting; it would be great to know if I'm underestimating what a San Francisco audience can take, or if I'm overestimating. And I think that's something I'll really find out from looking at the surveys.

On one level, I think of San Francisco as a really progressive place, the place where Beat poetry happened, and performance art. A place that's really game for a lot of stuff. But I feel like that there isn't the same hunger for experimentalism that you'd find in downtown Manhattan, and certainly not the same tolerance for experimental work as you'd find in Europe. It's amazing to go to theatre in Poland, because what would be totally edgy for Cutting Ball to do is basically being done at their version of ACT.

Do you have any example that you can call to mind where feedback from the audience changed your programming?

It's never like we hear feedback and were like, "Now we've got to go in a completely different direction." But one of our board members who got involved with us very early on, when it was a little bit more "The Rob Melrose show," and the philosophy was more, "Hey, this is some crazy thing that I want to do, if people want to see it great, if people don't want to see it who cares." Back then it wasn't so much about building an audience as it was about doing a play that I wanted to do. She really liked those days, and, you know, we had these years where we were doing *No Exit* and *The Maids*, *Bald Soprano* and Shakespeare, all these things that were totally meant towards broadening the audience, and saying we're not going to give you *Roberto Zucco*, we're not going to give you *Hamletmachine*, we're going to give you something you've heard of, something you probably read in school. And she sort of said, "I miss the cool wacky weird stuff." Getting that feedback from one of our oldest audience members made us think, "We don't want to lose the people who got involved with us from the beginning, because that was good work, too." One of the reasons we're doing this, for us, more conservative work, is to build an audience to present more risky work, but it's easy to look at what we've done in the past few years and say, "Oh, we're just becoming more conservative." That's not what we want, so I'm grateful for her speaking up.

Sixto Wagan
DiverseWorks

Can you start by telling me a little bit about how things work at DiverseWorks?

We were formed in 1982 as an alternative art space, visual and performing arts, multidisciplinary art center where we operate out of two warehouse spaces north of downtown. A typical season is September through May/June. In the visual arts galleries we present about five to six main gallery exhibitions. We have a 100seat black box theatre where we present approximately five to six national and international projects as well as a number of residencies from local companies. Much of what we do is about commissioning and developing new work. Unlike Intersection [for the Arts, a San Francisco-based multidisciplinary organization], our work is not specifically social justice, but there is some social justice that is involved in what we curate and commission.

Right now, we actually just transitioned our leadership. Previously we had a co-directorship that was formed from our previous visual arts curator performing arts curator. At this point, I am now the artistic director to cover all aspects of programming. We will be bringing in guest curators or another staff member in order to take over aspects of the visual arts or performing arts as necessary.

How do you get feedback from your audiences, specifically about their experience of your productions? Not so much those kinds of questions like "how did you hear about the show?" and "were the lines too long?" or whatever, but really trying to figure out what their experience was watching or what they took away. It can be formal ways like you do surveys or informal ways like you stand in the lobby. I'm interested to hear what the range is for you.

We generally do a lot of question-and-answer sessions post-show or discussions, particularly since most of the work is commissioned and premiered here. It is to engage both the artist and audience in getting that evaluation. Then, of course, we have more informal ways of evaluating like just standing around outside and listening and talking to people about the piece. We are trying to do more of this and get better at it. We also have an artist board who we've utilized as the sounding board, as well. We've made sure that they see the performances and are actually part of the audience so it's not specifically

> **Memorableness is a goal. I want the audience to be able to remember the work and talk about it. I also recognize the fact that some of the pieces that people remember most are the ones that they hate.**

just staff-driven. And since we do a lot of partnerships and community engagement, we also do the formal evaluations with our partners post-show, or post-residency, in order to talk about the artistic product as well as the process.

We are looking for new and innovative ways to do that in the future. We don't do much surveying because they yield hasn't been all that great previously, but we are looking at what that could be in the future.

As you're selecting a piece to present or an artist to commission, what are the ways you think about audience? Do you think specifically about what kind of impact you're trying to have on audiences, or do you mostly lead from your response to an artist or an artistic work?

All of the above? I've been with this performing arts community since the mid '90s. I've grown up with many of the artists who are creating work. A number of the performances I commission relate to the aesthetics that I see that people are exploring, so that it has resonance. Most of the commissions relate to issues or themes that are prevalent within the communities that we want to engage with. Ideally, we have a multi-disciplinary approach and are able to carry through that idea or theme in the visual arts as well.

Then, of course, there are the other pieces where I have an artist whose vision I think is amazing and I just want to be able to support them. Mainly it is about whether an artist's project or artistic vision will resonate with the community here either by pushing boundaries or by addressing and highlighting themes in a different way than people here are already addressing them.

How would you describe the effect you're trying to have on your audiences? Is there a way you think about a kind of particular response that signals success for you, or does that change with every project?

It changes with every project because, I think, each one of my projects has very specific goals for me artistically as well as community-wise. It's a challenge, in the best sense in term, because I want the audience to be able to remember the work and talk about it. I also recognize the fact that some of the pieces that people remember the most are the ones that they hate. But they will talk about them years, because it was something that stuck with them and resonated with them. What's important is how we actually define the nature of the performance and understand what actually sticks with the audience. Memorableness is a goal—a kind of continued resonance?

How do you think about balance over your whole season? What engagement are you trying to create when you look at a whole cycle?

Our organization is called DiverseWorks. I feel we have to be able to appeal to that diversity in terms of ethnic origin and really also supporting voices of communities and artists who aren't normally heard from. Since we are a multidisciplinary art center, I look at the balance of disciplines: dance, theatre, performance, and the multiple disciplines in the visual arts. I also look at a balance of male/female, artists of color, artists who are from New York or LA versus artists who are not. I recognize that these are overarching themes. Some years I do much better than others. But some years I also recognize the fact that the people who I am most interested in, whose projects have the most resonance, might actually be white dancers out of New York. I am cognizant of that, and I try to make sure the next season doesn't have a similar homogeneity.

Recently, we've been doing a lot of work in the trans community. We've been trying, over the course of many years, to use theatre and performance and visual art to bring up these issues so that the dialog doesn't just exist within one community. It started, I'd say, over a decade ago when we brought in Lauren Cameron, who is a female-to-male photographer. We also produced *TransFest*, a 12minute-max showcase of local artists who explored trans issues. A few years back we co-commissioned Scott Turner Schofield's *Becoming a Man in 127 Easy Steps* and recently with Q-Roc Ragsdale, a Dallas-based artist exploring male-identified lesbians and also issues of class and race.

I think we are trying to build a safe space for trans issues to be explored and to also make sure that the work is not just ghettoized in gay culture and is instead put into a much larger artistic conversation. We're doing our work with other communities so that, even if it is not something that particular people attend, they actually recognize why we are doing it, what its purpose is, and why the need is for us to support and commission projects like this.

> My goal is to actually have audiences see work that is not simply about their representation on stage. I want them to understand that there is a universal experience.

When you have a piece that is with a trans artist or dealing with issues in that community, how do you think about who you want in the audience for that piece?

My goal is to actually have audiences see work that is not simply about their representation on stage. I want them to understand that there is a universal experience or human experience because I want our audience to be multigendered, multiethnic, multigenerational, so that the work they see can be experienced in all those different levels.

There are conversations that only can happen or be sparked from that work and because of that experience. Since most of the work at DiverseWorks is commissioned, I also want to make sure that the audience is receptive to the piece and the work. I do a lot of work with other community partners to make sure that there is appropriate representation in the audience, but then also that there is enough context around the work so that the artists feel they can safely present the piece. The goal is to have the diversity of conversation. The reality is that most of our marketing happens specifically as mixed marketing to target the people who would most relate to the piece. Because of the way that audiences run here in Houston is that we have very specific audiences for dance or contemporary dance versus ballet versus theatre versus text-based theatre which is devised. It becomes a niche market for everything.

Ideally, of course, we do actually have audiences who are crossover audiences and who do actually come just because it's presented by Diverse Works. We value a sense of people crossing into something they don't always tend to see, especially with the multidisciplinary aspect. I think it is really important for us to see people who are predominantly visual actually coming to performances so that it is builds a better contemporary conversation and not just about a discipline or a form.

When you think of your audience, do you think of a core group of returning audience members, or is it very different show to show? Who do you mean when you say "our audience?"

There is a core group of performing arts audiences and a core group of visual arts audiences. Then there will be targeted audiences for specific events. Actually, I think there is more crossover now than we had believed between core visual and core performing. But most of those audiences, I would say, are 25 to 45, educated, at least a degree, and middle income. That's what our surveys say.

Can you think of a time when you've changed a programming decision, or the way you approach programming, based on audience feedback?

Yeah. I'm trying to think of what I've done. I guess one of the things that we have done is recognized, and this is long-term, that we do present a number of queer artists, but when we put their work out there in context, we rarely talk about their sexual orientation because people continue to think of us as only a queer space, which was far from the case.

I think the way we actually started contextualizing the work changed drastically. That's a simple, broad way we've looked at it. And we've also programmed events sometimes that are more related to audience engagement than artistic challenge. An effort that I think was partly board-driven (in terms of audience numbers) was partly about recognizing that certain artists have been longstanding members of the community, and not necessarily the most "challenging" artists.

We're trying to recognize people's role in our community even though they might not be the most forward-thinking aesthetically, but they continue to build audiences for contemporary art.

Now that there are other opportunities for people to present or self-present outside of DiverseWorks, DiverseWorks does not have to be everything for everyone and focus on the presentation and commissioning, and not as much as a service organization. As those other opportunities become more available, it is becoming easier for me to be strictly about mission and programming.

Todd Haimes and Jill Rafson

Roundabout Theatre Company

I was reading over your initial information, and saw that you have set up a special email for subscribers to reach you directly with their responses to the work. Have you gotten a good response there?

TH: Not as many people as you'd think, although we publicize a lot, given the number of subscribers as we have, not as many people as you'd think would email. I probably get five a day, you know, and so far I've been responding to them all personally. Sometimes Jill helps out. And it's…sometimes they say something that is helpful or informative to me, either about a production, because we have long preview periods here, so things can actually change during the preview period, and sometimes I'll get a really articulate letter from someone that will make me think of something that might be a good idea. But 99% of the time it's more "I liked it"/"I didn't like it." That's not unhelpful, however, because if you get enough people saying "I didn't like something" or "I'd like something lighter"—which is a theme we've noticed since the recession, that people love to not be depressed—that has an impact on me in terms of planning the season.

And in terms of other ways that the theatre currently collects audience feedback or does audience surveying, does most of that come to you, or are the other mechanisms more about marketing?

TH: It's much more marketing-related.

JR: We do a series of donor readings, actually, for people who are already part of the Roundabout family, and for the last season or season and a half, we've been surveying them on the way out of the reading, and they tell us about the project that was being read, and their thoughts on whether they'd like to hear from us about new plays or revivals, and so on. Since we use those readings as a way to try out material, we actually read that feedback to get a sense of whether they responded to that reading, because they're the audience we would be doing it for.

Jill, has that influenced some decisions or direction for you in the recent past?

JR: To some extent, yes. Most of the time, they're very enthusiastic, and they understand what the purposes are for doing these readings, so when we sometimes will read an older play, they say things like "This was a great old revival, but I'm not sure you should do it; it's kind of dated." And that reaffirms exactly what we're testing out by trying to hear these things out loud. And usually their tendency is to be more enthusiastic about the lighter fare, as Todd was saying, because it's a one-night affair and they can feel good as they leave. So they tend to have a better response to those.

> I have a sense of what our subscribers like that has been developed over the years. I like Pinter but our audience really hates it, so if I do a Pinter it's rare, and hopefully with a great actor.

Do you feel like asking those questions of them affects their experience of these readings?

JR: It seems like that. I think they enjoy feeling like it's not just an exhibition evening; that their opinion actually counts. It genuinely is read by us, and I think they feel good that we really want their opinions because we're trying to program for them.

Todd, let me ask you, would you agree with that? When you think about season selection, would you phrase it that way, that "we're trying to program for them?"

TH: Yeah. I have a sense of what our subscribers like that has been developed over the years of doing this job and so I'm acutely aware…the problem is that there are lots of other factors that go into play selection here, like trying to get stars. But, for example, I'm very aware of the fact that I like Pinter but our audience really hates it, so if I do a Pinter it's rare, and hopefully with a great actor. That's an example of a case where the audience's taste might be different than my taste. The hardest part is to make all of the pieces come together. It's one thing to say that I want to do two comedies and a drama and a musical. In the New York marketplace, I think uniquely, we need to get stars and we need to get directors who are unbelievably busy, so making it all happen at the right time is a huge challenge—a much bigger challenge than just picking the shows I'd like to do.

273

> When we program,
> we know when
> we're pushing our
> subscribers a little
> bit, and we know
> when we're doing
> a disservice to the
> play by putting
> it in front of the
> wrong people.

TH: So many other factors. But having said that, I still keep them in mind in picking plays that I think they would like.

JR: One of the times that I think we could say that the audience feedback affected programming, and really launched a whole new program, was in 2005 when we did Noah Haidle's play *Mr. Marmalade* on our off-Broadway stage, the Laura Pels Theatre. This was a play that everybody here loved, this dark comedy, kind of twisted, and we were really enthusiastic about it going in. And our audience pretty much rejected that play. It had a young sensibility, it was the major New York debut for this writer, who was a young guy in his twenties, and we got phone calls and emails and a lot of negative feedback about that.

And the response that we had to that was not to stop doing edgier, riskier plays, but to instead create the Roundabout Underground. Todd's idea was to start a program that was specifically geared toward being a safer space with less of a spotlight on it for more emerging playwrights, so that they weren't given the huge pressure that comes with doing a million-dollar production at the Laura Pels Theatre. Instead they get a 62-seat theatre, and they get all the things that anybody gets working at Roundabout, they have the same rehearsal period and preview period and get to be a smaller part of the larger institution but without that glaring light on them. We're building a whole new, younger audience down in that space, and that all evolved from the response we got from our subscribers to *Mr. Marmalade*.

I think that when we program, we know when we're pushing our subscribers a little bit, and we know when we're doing a disservice to the play by putting it in front of the wrong people. That's something that we just have to be smart about.

So when you're looking at season selection, do you think in terms of a particular impact that you'd like to have on an audience over the course of the season?

TH: I don't think about it like that. I want them to be happy—I don't mean happy, "joyous," but happy with the variety of the selections. Unfortunately, in the New York market, a lot of that has to do with not only doing good productions but getting actors that they're familiar with, who are famous, to do them. So, there are some advantages and disadvantages to being in New York. I don't know if you'd call that an advantage or disadvantage, but that's the reality here.

With our new plays, which is a smaller part of our programming, we try to get as much feedback as possible, and we try to do plays that we think our people will enjoy. The Underground has been incredibly successful, and out of the Black Box some of those playwrights are now writing for our medium-sized stage. The first one of those is happening this fall, so we'll see how it goes.

> We pick plays that we like and that we think are interesting; we pick plays that we think are well-made. We tend to look for plays that are relatively traditional in their construction because, with something that is a more *avant garde* play, our audience can't really cope. And that's okay.

But, you know, I would think that someone like Oskar Eustis would give you a much more dramatic answer about challenging the political realities etc., but I'm embarrassed to say that's not really what we do. We pick plays that we like and that we think are interesting; we pick plays that we think are well-made. We tend to look for plays that are relatively traditional in their construction, because, with *Mr. Marmalade* being an example of something that is a more *avant garde* type of play, our audience can't really cope with that. It's the same reason they can't cope with Pinter. And that's okay. Some other theatres will do Pinter.

JR: With the Underground, if our goal is anything, it's less about the impact being from one specific play and it's more about getting an audience that is excited about continuing to see new work. Because we need that. We're just trying to create lifetime theatregoers. We're trying to create a season each year that will have people coming back to the theatre over and over again. Hopefully to Roundabout over and over again, but in some ways we just want theatre as a medium to continue.

> The effort is to try and make subscribers realize that, in addition to the fact that they get a good price, the best seats, all that stuff, that they're part of something that's important, an institution.

What do you think are the elements of the experience that keep people coming back over and over again?

TH: I think that's a complicated answer. Fifteen years ago, if you asked me that same question, I would say, talking about subscribers, "The tickets were half-price, and they got a variety of plays, and they liked the majority of them, so they came back." But now we're in a much more competitive marketplace—New York is unbelievably competitive, because we're competing with commercial theatre in addition to other not-for-profits—and discounting is rampant. So a sense of why people subscribe to a theatre in general and Roundabout specifically is becoming more complicated to communicate and define, but the effort is to try and make them realize that, in addition to the fact they get a good price, in addition to the fact that they get the best seats, all that stuff, that they're part of something that's important, an institution, that they feel good that they'll see a variety of work that probably they wouldn't have the inertia to go see if they didn't have a subscription. That we do other things like have an incredible education program that helps the city.

We spend a lot more energy focusing on the fact that they're a part of something, an institution that's important and that needs them, and they need us—a sense of belonging—which, as I said, is a much more complicated message to communicate than just saying, "Well, the tickets are half-price."

We communicate a lot with them. I mean, in terms of positive communication, not asking for money. Before every show, I write a letter on what they're about to see and why we did it, any other information we think they'd like. Five years ago, we didn't do any of this—first of all, we didn't think of it, and second of all the technology didn't really exist.

JR: And I think that there's something about the consistent level of quality that also keeps them coming back. There are certain shows that feel very much like they're in the Roundabout wheelhouse. The subscribers know that every year when they renew their subscription they're probably going to see a couple of really fantastic play revivals, like last year *Present Laughter*, or this year, *The Importance of Being Earnest,* and that they're going to probably get a couple musicals, and then a couple of things that are off the beaten path. It's a mix of meeting the expectations that they have for this company and throwing in the things that they wouldn't necessarily seek out themselves but that they're generally excited to see because it's part of the package they bought.

TH: For example, we're doing a revival of *The Milk Train Doesn't Stop Here Anymore*, which is a lesser-known Tennessee Williams play, and I feel pretty confident 90% of our subscribers wouldn't come if they weren't subscribing. But generally from the feedback I'm getting, 90% of them are really happy they saw it and really turned on by seeing a Tennessee Williams play they've never seen before and probably will never see again, done well.

You're not looking at moving away from a subscription model?

TH: No. Though the last couple years have been tough, they've gone down. But now, we're not looking at moving away from the subscription model. But there's more pressure financially now on single tickets, and single tickets tend to relate to one of two things, either a rave review in the *New York Times*, which is something you can never guarantee, or a star. In fact, a star is probably more important than a rave review in the New York Times.

So as you're looking at all these ways that you're thinking about your audience and programming, what are some ways that you're hoping that this new tool will be useful to you?

JR: I think that in the long-term we're really interested in how much people want to know going in the door, and how much more do they want to know leaving. I think that's something some companies do more than others, and my personally curiosity is whether that's something we need to be increasing, or whether we're satisfying their needs. And I think knowing their emotional and intellectual impacts after seeing a production will really be a window into that. Do they want an in-depth study of the playwright we're doing? Or do they just want to know why we decided to do this play at this particular time?

How should we continue that level of communication that we've had with our audience? In terms of future programming, I think that the question is going to be about what gets them to come back for more. Because we're trying to get people to have a consistent theatre habit. What gets people to come back over and over again? Some of those questions are about, "Would you now see anything Roundabout does?" "Would you now see anything by this author?" "Would you now see anything this actor is in?" And seeing how audience members parse that out, and who they assign responsibility to when they enjoy something, or when they dislike something, is going to be really interesting for us. We need to figure out what they're looking for that we're already doing and what they're looking for that we haven't yet provided.

TH: I just think more information is always better, always.

JR: I'm most interested is seeing how the intrinsic impacts align with those factors that we already know about. How much are audience impacts influenced by a good review or a bad review? What's the audience's reaction to seeing a star? Do they not care?

I think what's going to be interesting is seeing how the numbers align with the intellectual impact and the emotional impact. Do they have things in common or are they totally different: how people spend their money versus what they get out of the experience?

Oskar Eustis
Public Theater

Tell me what kind of methods you use for yourself or your artistic staff to collect feedback from the audience.

It is entirely informal, and there are two main components to it. One is that I sit in the audience and I listen and just feel what their responses are. And for anyone who has spent a life in the theatre, that's

> I sit in the audience and I listen and just feel what their responses are.

actually amazingly accurate. You get a sense not only of what they like and dislike, but what they connect to and don't connect to. And the second thing is really boring but it's also true, which is that you just look at ticket sales: who shows up?

There are certainly occasions where there are shows that we feel are unjustly poorly attended. Sometimes, that's because a critic or a set of critics completely doesn't get them, and therefore we get bad reviews for something that we know is actually great. Sometimes it's because we don't get enough of the core audience for the show in to spread the word of mouth. I can use the example of Dan Beaty, who I think is a really wonderful young black actor/performer/writer. He did a show called *Emergency* down here in my first season. It was just a fantastic show, but it's natural audience was really a kind of black, church-going, middle-class, civil rights-engaged audience—and the Public is not their natural home. And we know, although it did fine and we managed to extend for a couple of weeks, it didn't begin to tap the people who would have loved that show, because the Public isn't really on their radar. And we've used that as an example since: there are shows that certain audiences would love who don't naturally come to the Public. How we get to them is harder than how we get to the audiences that are used to coming here.

When you are designing a season, what are the ways that you think about impact on audiences?

My own artistic response to plays is where I have to start, because I don't really

279

My artistic response to plays is where I have to start, because I don't really have any other tool. I comfort myself with believing that I was hired for my taste. But then what I also have to do is put that through a certain sieve. I have to problematize my own taste.

have any other tool. I comfort myself with believing that I was hired for my taste, and so therefore it's appropriate for me to exercise my taste. But then what I also have to do is I have to put that through a certain sieve. I'll use the example of me and the Public very specifically: what I recognized very soon after I arrived here is that if I just followed my taste, the various slots in my season would be clogged up *really* quickly with hyper-verbal, intellectual, historical, left white males who just coincidentally happen to be a lot like me. I was going to have to really put some brakes on, because as broad and Catholic as I like to think my taste is, ultimately I'm just like anybody else, I'm just a person, and other people who speak to those qualities tend to feel centrally universal to me. And I have to problematize my own taste.

I try to do that by who I hire on staff. I try to do that intellectually, thinking, "How am I going to get a different kind of work in here?" "How am I going to find a different kind of artist?" And I try to do that by changing myself and expanding my sense of who I am and who I feel comfortable with, so that hopefully I become a bigger person in the course of the work, and that changes my taste. And over the course of the years, I have to say that I feel like that has worked.

And how does the audience or your sense of the Public's audience play in there?

Our members are a small enough number, we have about 7,000 members or a little over, that economically it doesn't have a huge impact on the theatre. So I don't experience what a lot of my colleagues experience in subscription houses where they actually feel like they have to play to who their subscription audience is or they get into trouble. I don't really have to do that, partly because it's a small enough group, but also partly because even for those in that group, the Public Theater's profile has been so determinately diverse and aesthetically and cultural broad for so long, that the people who are members tend to want that.

I have literally never gotten—of course, I've gotten negative feedback on shows—but I have never gotten anything that suggests that by doing this kind of programming I'm in danger of losing an audience member. I have audience members complain about certain shows, but I never have them complain about the kind of programming. And I think that's one of the huge advantages of being at the Public. It's understood that our mandate is broad.

> **I don't have to worry on a show-by-show basis whether this show makes them happy or that show makes them happy.**

Can you think of an example of a time when you've changed or shifted your programming because of feedback from the audience?

No. But let me put that in context.

I got to play a bit part in the HBO movie of *Angels in America*. I commissioned and developed it, so they cast me just as a favor, which was sweet. And I was talking to the President of HBO and he told me that the cost of the film was the most expensive made-for-television film in history; it was going to cost about $80 million. And I said, "Oh, are you going to make that back?" And he said, "Well, we don't know." And I said, "What do you mean, you don't know? You're running a business."

And what he said was just beautiful. He said, "The great thing about being at HBO is that, because we have subscribers to our cable service, and we have big providers that add our channel to their line-up, for any individual show, we don't know how it does. We can't measure it the way commercial enterprises measure the first weekend's gross, or TV measures the Nielsen ratings. What we try to do is elevate the brand, and in the long-run of course it's going to make a difference because if we don't do enough high-quality work people won't subscribe to HBO anymore and we'll lose money. But we don't have to measure on an exact show-by-show basis, which frees us up to think in the broad terms of what is going to elevate the brand, what is going to lift HBO as a whole."

And I thought, you know, what's so interesting about that model is that's a

> I want to be accountable to my audience; I have no desire to make shows that nobody wants to see.

commercial model that does the same thing that we do in the non-profit model. I don't have to worry on a show-by-show basis if this show makes them happy or that show makes them happy. But on the other hand I'm going to get in trouble if I don't do shows that, taken as a whole, are perceived as attracting an audience and fulfilling the mission of the theatre. And that's as it should be. I want to be accountable to my audience; I have no desire to make shows that nobody wants to see. But it frees me up to take risks on individual shows, because I don't need any individual show to be a success.

I think I respond to the audience in a sort of indirect way that feels in no way artistically inhibiting to me. It feels like as I get to know my audience, as I get to know the theatre, as I get to know what's exciting...I get to respond to that, but over a long arc of time, not over one focus group asking people, "Will you like this play or not."

Jessica Kubzansky
and Michael Michetti
Theatre @ Boston Court

So let me just start out with this: you guys are co-artistic directors, right?

MM: Correct. We are the founding co-artistic directors and have shared the job since the theatre's inception.

I wanted to start by asking you all how you get feedback from your audiences about their experiences of the show?

MM: We have not done any formal polling about any artistic things prior to this survey, but we do have a number of informal ways we get feedback. We do at least two post-show talkbacks, and every Friday night after our show opens (we don't do it during previews), we keep the lobby open after the show, serve some complimentary wine and Chex Mix or something, and do what we call a Late Night Salon where we essentially invite the audience to hang out, have some wine, talk to one another, talk to the staff, and talk to the artists about the show. Because we do thought-provoking theatre, we often hear patrons saying that they talked about it all the way home, were thinking about it the next day, had arguments with their spouse about it, and that kind of thing. We thought, "How can we enable some of that conversation to happen while they're still at the theatre?" So it's very informal, it's entirely unstructured, but we do hang out there and talk to people. And since we do shows that are often challenging in one way or another – whether it's about themes or about structure--we often hear from people about their enthusiasm, their confusion, their uncertainty. A lot of times when you do something that is an unfamiliar idea or an unfamiliar way to present something theatrically people don't trust their own opinions. So I find myself responding, "Well what did *you* think that was?" and they end up saying, "Well I think it was blah blah blah," and it's like, "Well that's exactly right." But without the conversation they're not sure that they can trust that what they thought had validity.

JK: It's interesting, because our executive director stands in the lobby almost nightly, which is really about fundraising, continuing relationships with patrons and potential donors, etc. And we also often do stand in the lobby

283

> **When we're planning a season we are trying to gauge the impact of the on the whole. But I have to say that from the moment we started, we promised ourselves that we were going to create art and seasons that were going to excite *us*.**

after the show, if we're there, either singly or together. The challenge there is that people probably feel freer to make an uninhibited comment to him than to us. So it's not clear that the people who talk to us after the show are being honest, because they know who we are... Or rather, we've definitely had people come up to us and say, "I'm not sure I got that," but I don't know that people who actively hated something would come up to us and say, "That was the worst thing I've ever seen," you know? We do also sometimes get feedback from people because when Boston Court sends out an e-newsletter, we'll sometimes get comments from people in return, or sometimes people do the very old-fashioned thing and write a letter. And when that happens we tend to respond. But as Michael said, we've never formally polled them.

In the process of selecting a season or choosing a project, do you think about what sort of impact on an audience you're looking for, or is that not a frame you use?

JK: One of the things that is really important to us--this is an unofficial part of our mission--is that we really want to engage the cultural conversation. And it is also a sort of unofficial part of our mission that we think it's really important to give people a unique experience at our theatre that they can't have at any other theatre in Los Angeles. So there's no question that when we're planning a season we are trying to sort of gauge the impact on the whole—what the season will mean as a whole, its breadth and depth and variation. But I have to say that from the moment we started, we promised ourselves that we were going to create art and seasons that were going to excite *us*. Because it was incredibly important to us that we stay true to our sense of integrity as artists and to our vision, as opposed to starting to worry about what the audience might think. And so it's been a really guiding principle that we make sure we are true to what we believe would be an exciting season, would be an exciting set of plays to offer. And that can't help but be about what kind of impact we're making on the audience, but I don't know if that's exactly what you mean.

Would you describe yourselves as having "an audience," or does it vary show to show?

MM: We have a lot of people who are regulars. We have a membership model which is really largely a subscription model with a different name and a little more flexibility to it, but our membership is not enormous. So we certainly rely on return single-ticket and new single-ticket buyers for each show. And we do find that when we do a show that is targeted to a particular audience—when we do a play that is dealing with specific thematic material, or material that is dealing with a certain ethnic group, socioeconomic group, a gay-themed play, etc—we end up getting some audience that is interested in that particular show. But one of the things that's important is that when we began this, when we created the theatre, there was not an audience for it. And so we created a mission statement and a sense of guiding principles for what we were going to program, and decided we would try to be as consistent about that brand as possible and find the audience that wants to see the work we do, rather than trying to program for some imaginary audience.

> When we created the Theatre @ Boston Court, there was not an audience for it. So we created a mission statement, and decided we would try to be as consistent as possible and find the audience that wants to see the work we do, rather than trying to program for some imaginary audience.

We're now in our eighth season, and we do find that there are people who are coming more and more. In our early years, it took a while for people to catch on to who we were, because they didn't know what Boston Court was, and because they needed to see a certain number of pieces of the puzzle to see what the picture is that is being created. We are at the point now where our audiences are consistently larger than they were, and we have many more repeat customers. It's always been our goal that people come not strictly because they recognize the title--because we do very few recognizable titles-- or even because the blurb sounds good; we want them to come because they're interested in the work we do, and they just want to keep coming back because there's a consistency in the excellence of the work and a sense that we do the kind of theatre that they want to see. And as it happens we are finding more and more people to be our audience.

JK: Absolutely.

MM: Though the truth is that we're always continually struggling to find wider and more consistent audiences.

JK: Our trajectory has certainly been that in the early days we would do plays that no one had ever heard of and would have 20 people in the house in a night. And then by accident we started a season with a known title—we did a re-envisioned *Medea* set in a catering kitchen—and all of a sudden the houses were full, and we were like, "Oh, see, people know what Boston Court is now and they want to come see our plays." And then the next play was a new play with a title that no one had ever heard of and we were back down to 20 people. We realized that for a while it was going to be about title recognition. And I think for us, the way that we've been able to track progress is that last year we did, as it happens, an all-world-premiere season (although *Oedipus el Rey* is certainly a title that people could figure out), and we had our best season ever and extended all of our shows. And so it became clear that we had crossed that imaginary threshold to get to a place where people were starting to have faith in the art. We sometimes have season announcement parties, and one year we invited this woman to come and hear the season announcement and see what we were going to do next, and, in one of our favorite comments ever, she said, "Why? I'm not going to know any of the titles and I'm going to come anyway." We loved that because, ideally, it's about them getting on board our ride. And I think what we have started to establish is that they have trust that they're going to see a really terrific production. Whether they like the particular content of *that* play or not, they have faith that they're going to see a quality evening of theatre.

Have you ever had a moment where audience feedback has actually made you change something in the way that you program?

MM: We are very careful not to pander. We only sell 99 seats four times a week, so we don't need to look for an enormous audience pool to draw from here, and that gives us much more freedom to take risks. That said, a couple of years ago we had a little bit of a creative crisis of faith because we were doing a number of shows that we were very proud of, that we thought were really beautiful and exciting, worthy theatrical explorations, and they were things that were significantly less linear, less literal, challenged the audiences even more than our general fare, and we found that there was some audience resistance to that. People were not quite as satisfied with the experience, our houses weren't quite as large, that kind of thing. So we're continuing to try to straddle the line—certainly not selling out or pandering, staying very true to the kind of work we want to do, but finding the right balance of things that, while still challenging and inherently theatrical and a number of things that are part of our mission, are maybe a little more linear in terms of the storytelling or—

> We are being watchful about how much we challenge. We don't want to challenge them so much that we challenge them out of the theatre.

JK: In some way a little more accessible.

MM: Exactly. And the possible balance of that against one or two plays in the season that really take even greater theatrical risks, so that even in a model where "challenging artist and audience" is part of our mission statement, we are being watchful about how much we challenge. We don't want to challenge them so much that we challenge them out of the theatre.

JK: And sometimes critics affect things. I think we're lucky that we have found audiences are willing to try us no matter what. But we have at times worried about doing certain challenging plays and feeling like we were consigning our playwrights to a critical bloodbath. And we just felt guilty.

MM: There was a period where, in particular, in the *LA Times*, we were being assigned a couple of critics who just didn't like the kind of theatre we did. Over and over, we were doing new plays and they were giving them terrible reviews, and I kept saying they were sending food critics to boat shows— it's not that they're bad critics; this just isn't the kind of theatre they like, so they're never going to like what we do. So there were as period where that was fairly frustrating. That seems to have subsided somewhat, thankfully. But that's one of the challenges too, because part of what we'd love to be doing

> We want to make sure we're pleasing enough people, satisfying enough, and yet it's not about the most easily offended being happy or the one who wants their theatre feel-good or wrapped up neat and tidy. That's not the person we're looking to please.

creatively would be to give playwrights a first opportunity to work on their plays so they can take them out to have long healthy lives in the world, and there are some examples where we're afraid that we've contributed to their early demise.

JK: It's a tricky thing, because we *must* stay true to ourselves, that's incredibly important to us, but I guess we have also discovered that inside that paradigm there are some parameters. And also, I feel like there are times in the world where people are up for more adventure than others. This crisis of faith happened around 2008/9, when money was tight, and people were less willing to take risks even in the types of theatre they wanted to see. So that was a sort of interesting *sub-rosa* influence as well.

MM: We have never done a show that everybody loves. It's inherent in the kind of programming that we do that there will be people who dislike it. And we have had some shows where we have very regular and consistent walkouts either because of style or content or whatever. So it's a little tricky because I know there are many theatres that feel like if they get one or two angry letters from somebody they can never program like that again. We certainly expect that we are going to get some resistance to some of the work we do, and it's really not about trying to please everyone. It's a careful balance because we want to make sure we're pleasing enough people, satisfying enough, and yet it's not about the most easily offended being happy or the one who wants their theatre feel-good or wrapped up neat and tidy. That's not the person we're looking to please. And again my feeling has been that if people come to see three or four plays at our theatre they'll know what we're about. And they'll know whether we're the right theatre for them or not. And we're clearly not the right theatre for everybody, and we're not trying to be.

JK: During one of those Friday late-night salons, while we were doing a musical adaptation of *The Seagull* called *Gulls* set in 1959 in New York and LA, there

288

was a group of people who clearly were trying us for the first time. And this man said to me, "Have you seen any plays at the Pasadena Playhouse?" (which is four blocks from our theatre). And I said, "Yes, I have." And he said, "Because they do *nice* musicals there." Clearly these will not become our patrons, and that's okay—that's wise, actually, because they would not enjoy the work we do.

What tools are you hoping to get out of this work?

> We very passionately resisted audience surveys, I think because we were terribly afraid that we would be influenced away from our hearts.

JK: I know I loved the questions, because when we initially resisted audience surveys, I don't think we ever envisioned asking them the kinds of questions you're asking. I think we're hoping to learn things we don't know. I think there are certain assumptions that we make about how people are receiving work, or what experience they're having as a result of coming to Boston Court, and I'm personally looking to be enlightened—to be told some of the things I don't know, and because I am all too visible in our community, I never get to hear those things. No one would ever come up and tell me the things that I hope they'll say when they're an anonymous form-filler-outer.

Are there any things that you're concerned about?

JK: In our early days, Michael and I very passionately resisted audience surveys, I think because we were terribly afraid that we would be influenced away from our hearts. And maybe in the early days this would have been true. So we've sort of had to go on the faith of our gut about what's important to do. But of course knowledge can't hurt that, as long as it doesn't sway our artistic integrity.

MM: I would say that the thing that worries me the most is that it might shake my *faith* in what we are doing, not that it would necessarily change the way that we do what we do. It's a tricky thing, too. When you are doing something that is inherently trying to push on forms and try new things, there's no question that you're going to get more resistance, more negative reaction. And there's that conundrum that theatre exists only briefly in time—Van Gogh could never sell a painting in his life but subsequently we'll look at him for centuries as a genius. It's different when a play has but a six-week run in which people can receive it and respond to it, because then, although the play will continue to exist as text, the three -dimensional production is gone. There's something about the ephemeral nature of theatre that always makes taking chances a little scarier. If you are doing something that is strictly being created for its commercial appeal, then you know that the goal is: if you get 10 people off the street, nine people will love it. We don't do that, and I'm quite sure that we'll have some negative reaction. I'm prepared for that. And I think that, if there are things that we can learn that will give us a better understanding of where the audiences will go and where they won't, and so are able to adjust within our mission, we could have a very beneficial result. We could learn by degrees what kinds of things our audiences are up for and what they're not. But I don't think there's any risk of us losing track of what our approach is, what our mission is, what our vision is. The biggest risk, I think, would just be a personal crisis of faith.

Susan Atkinson and Keith Baker

Bristol Riverside Theatre

So, Keith, you're the current artistic director, and Susan, you're the founding artistic director?

SA: Yes. I'm the founding director. We've sort of split it up, it's a crazy name, I do both sides of the coin.

KB: Yes, I'm the current artistic director.

What are some of the ways that you as the artistic staff receive feedback from the audience about their artistic experience of the show, either formally or informally?

SA: I normally, at the end of the show, I say good night to everybody, and they let me know what they think. And I've done this since the beginning of the theatre, mainly it was from the point of view that if people can tell you they're upset about something, they're a lot less likely to say, "I'll show them, I just won't subscribe." And it makes it more personal, and it also allows me to give them my point of view on why we chose a show or how we felt about it, and to express a sympathy if they didn't care for it. It's very anecdotal, but we've done it since the beginning of the theatre.

Do you have a process where attendees can send email or letters?

SA: Oh yes: good, bad and indifferent. Generally, they come pretty much directly to my desk. Sometimes to Keith, but mostly to me. They don't yell at him, they yell at me. And I respond to every one of them. And no, I don't back down, I explain to them why we made the decision we made or whatever. We got a fair amount of them this last show because we changed shows on them, and it was a little bit rough-going for some of them, this show, rather than a more classic American play. So yes, I do answer every one of them.

Would you say that you're influenced by those letters, or your sense of how people felt about a particular show?

SA: I hear what they say, and more importantly I sense what they feel. And of course you don't do theatre to disappoint your audience. You do theatre to

291

> Of course you don't do theatre to disappoint your audience. You do theatre to excite, inform, to have them have a mutual experience with you.

hopefully excite, inform—not necessarily to make them comfortable, but to have them have a mutual experience with you, and if you sense any sense of shutting down, that's the last thing you want. I don't care if they get ticked off; I care if they shut down.

KB: We do talkbacks at the end of each of our previews, and we also have something we call a Friday Festival, which is a special evening at which there's a lot of interaction between us and the audience. And they're very expressive about the way they feel. At the Friday Festival, we do a lecture or a talk, a stage talk, before the show, which illuminates for them not so much why we *chose* the show, but why we're doing it in this *way*, and what they should look for in it to get the most out of it, and why did we make the choices we did about this show. And so we get a lot of feedback that way, we get a lot from the talkbacks after the previews, and we also do on every single show of the season a pre-show talk for subscribers. We hear a lot from them at that point about how they feel about what they're about to see, how they feel about what the rest of the season was. I think you have to be careful, because one or two or three letters does not an audience make. And certainly I agree with Susan that you do theatre to entertain people, but you also do theatre to stir the waters, and to try to expand the perspective of the audience on different aspects of life. That's always been the case, from ancient times through Shakespeare and all the rest, examining human nature. You can't do that without kicking up some mud in the water sometimes, and that's a good thing. It takes them by surprise. It more often than not leads to conversation, not only with us, but often on the way home, and with others they came with. So I think it's important that the ideas presented at your theatre are ideas that, from an artistic point of view, you feel are crucial and critical to discuss and to gain different feelings than you thought you had.

In selecting plays, do you think about what kind of impact you'd like to have on the audience?

KB: Yes, I do very much.

SA: Mhmm.

KB: I think, for a theatre like ours, which is a medium-sized regional theatre in the suburbs between Philadelphia and Trenton—this is not an automatic theatregoing audience. That has had to be cultivated, because it's not a natural response; it's not a habit of theirs. So they've got to be somehow coaxed a bit, offers offering free tickets or cheaper tickets on the whole, just to get them through the door. Because there's nothing that they're going to listen to until they get through the door. So a lot of that has to do with titles, a lot of that has to do with pieces that they might possibly have heard about even though they know nothing about them. There has to be some familiarity on some level. So it's this balancing act. I really think it's a balancing act all the way along, about everything, because at the same time that you want to have an impact on your audience, part of the impact you can have on your audience is to bring them tremendous joy, and a tremendous entertainment. Not just a nice show, but something done with skill and expertise, timing and precision. Where it becomes artistic, and an artistic expression—that has a tremendous impact on them.

> You do theatre to entertain people, but you also do theatre to stir the waters, and to try to expand the perspective of the audience on different aspects of life. You can't do that without kicking up some mud in the water sometimes, and that's a good thing.

SA: One of Keith's favorite things to say is that your relationship with your audience is like a marriage, and a lot of times you've got a lot of stuff to work out. And sometimes it's just wonderful and goes along with no bumps in the road, and then you get these great big bumps in the road as the relationship between the audience and the theatre gets worked out.

KB: I had a theatre in Florida, in South Florida, in the 1980's and one of the reasons I left was because in that marriage they only wanted happy endings. They just were not interested in having any ideas of theirs challenged, or in any examination of anything they'd believed and thought throughout their lives. They didn't want anything that was sad. They didn't want anything that wasn't going to bring a smile to their faces and make them happy on

293

> ## My experience has been that people don't really have any idea what they like.

the way out. Period. And you could call it whatever you'd like, but essentially their experience needed to be a happy, pleasant and preferably funny one. And I left that because that's not the kind of marriage I wanted.

And this audience in Bristol is different?

KB: They sure have been. They've gone on real journeys with us. They have seen things that have been very unusual for them. Unusual for a lot of theatres but certainly for them, and they have stayed with it. When I first got here in the mid-90's, I did a piece by Eugene Ionesco called *Macbett*, which is his take on the Shakespeare play. It's a huge absurdist piece. The last time it was done, at that point, had been at Yale with Robert Brustein. Since then I was invited to Armenia to get to know the artistic directors there by the State Department, and when I was there I saw some pieces I really wanted, and developed a cultural exchange and brought back an Armenian drama to Bristol, in English of course. That was a very hard piece for them, because they didn't get it, and it was filled with Eastern European techniques and ways of dramatizing things, it had its own absurd qualities about it. I did a piece a while ago called *The Balkan Women*, which was a very harsh piece about the war in Bosnia and the use of systemized rape as a political tool. Those were hard pieces for them, but they didn't run. They may have said, "That's not my cup of tea," but they came back.

SA: It's interesting, over the years with the ones that are hard… We have a very loyal audience. It's interesting how many times things like *Balkan Women*, or *Forget Herostatus* or *Macbett* or *What You Will* will come up versus *My One and Only* or *Evita*, even, or *Brigadoon*, things like that. Those won't necessarily come up again. Even if they were ticked off like crazy, they'll remember something about those harder shows, something else will trigger something, and then they'll say, "Oh, I didn't like that either." And that gives me the opportunity when I'm saying good night to them to say, "Have you ever thought about what bothered you about those two shows?"

KB: My experience has been that people don't really have any idea what they like. And they don't know until they see it. We did a piece not long ago called *Lady Day at Emerson's Bar & Grill*, about Billie Holiday and her heroin addiction and the last part of her life. *No one* wanted to see that piece, but we did it because we liked it, felt it was important, and because it was financially doable for us at the time, and it was during the winter, and we get a lot of snow, and sometimes we have to cancel performances, and on big shows it's harder. They came to see this, and it was their favorite show of the year. They had not a clue that they were going to like that—in fact, they were sure they were *not* going to like it.

Which we've seen this year, on a couple of occasions, where they really thought they weren't going to like something and they did. Or they come to a musical on occasion and they walk out with some sort of lackluster feeling about it. And so what they thought they were going to like they didn't like as much. It seems to me it has much more to do with the way we do it than with what it is. And in terms of the way our audience is going to respond, at least in my mind, in my head, when I'm directing, it is about how to make whatever piece this is have a particular effect on an audience. What do I want them to get from this? Why should they spend two hours with us in a dark room? And how should they feel about that? And in some ways I think it's almost more about how you do it, the themes that you're promoting, the ideas that you want to bring forth, the kind of performances you're getting as much as it is about the piece itself.

SA: The more passionate I am about a piece, generally, the more they love it. I think that carries over into the production and the experience of it. Let's face it, we're all faced with the situation of doing things for financial reasons, especially now. Somehow I always end up directing those. But anyway, I find that when I really love something and am very, very passionate about it, I find it makes a huge difference. A huge difference.

KB: Not long ago, I did a piece based on Shakespeare's *Twelfth Night* called *What You Will*. It was a kind of radical hip hop version of it, and I only say radical because the other hip hop versions of Shakespeare have always been take off points – the Shakespeare was a launching pad from which they could then go off on what they were talking about. My objective in this was to do the whole play, word for word, which was unusual. There was an awful lot of our audience of a certain age that wanted nothing to do with that. This coming season, our last musical is *Rent*, and we already have numerous people who have said, "Can't we just get a four-show season, we don't want anything to do with that?"

> This is not a theatre town in any way, shape or form. They like to come to see their friends. The programming doesn't really matter. They're not interested in "coming to the theatre." Do you know what I mean?

What needs to be explained to them is that they're not the only audience, and that it's necessarily to engender goodwill in another generation. We owe them something as much as we owe our loyal subscribers.

SA: And also, this is a story you can identify with, even though you think you can't. People think they know, but they don't.

Can you talk about the working class quality of the town? How does that affect the selection?

SA: Our community is definitely a very blue collar area, and I would say our audience is split about 50/50 blue collar and white collar. It's interesting. It does affect us, because we find ourselves second-guessing ourselves on purely intellectually-driven pieces, just because the touch points with the audience are not necessarily as great as they would be—*A Moon for the Misbegotten* would touch people more than *The Real Thing*, the Stoppard play.

KB: I have a somewhat stronger feeling about the town. This is not a theatre town in any way, shape or form. More than that, this is not a ticket buying town. They like to come to see their friends. The programming doesn't really matter. They're not interested in "coming to the theatre." Do you know what I mean? So therefore, what we have done as a theatre is to approach them from a different angle. For instance, every year now for over a decade, we have donated the theatre and our services for the scholarship concert for the Lions Club and Christmas time. From that, from them coming and doing that and actually coming through the doors, we have begun to get numbers of them that would never have normally come to participate in the theatre and to buy tickets.

So do you feel like you make an effort in your programming then to tell the stories of this town, or let people see themselves on stage, or that's not really how you approach it?

KB: We make every effort to approach it in a way that they can see themselves

296

on stage. Of course. I think in particular in a comedy if that isn't there then you just have missed the boat. So of course we do. But you can't make all of your effort that way, because that leaves a lot of people out in the cold who are really interested. The point is that we try, in every way that we can, to get them to come in and—I've had so many people in town actually say to me, "Well how do I get a ticket?" And I tell them, and I often offer them a ticket, for the first time, and I will meet them here, so that they have a comfortable feeling about being in the space for the first time. They just don't have the habit, that's all.

Let me ask you about whether feedback from the audience has ever changed a programming decision for you?

SA: I guess an example would be the number of negative reactions we have had to *Rent*, but I don't think we'd have changed it.

KB: On the other hand, we just changed *All My Sons*.

SA: But people wanted to see that, that was a totally different reason. I'm just trying to think, but I can't think of any show that we changed.

KB: I don't think it's going to be anytime soon that we do another hip hop Shakespeare.

SA: But that's only because we can't afford it.

KB: But even a show like *Jacob Marley's Christmas Carol* – the older audience absolutely hated that piece, and we never had so many young people in the audience, and no one could have predicted that in any way, shape or form.

SA: Total surprise.

KB: and there was so much negativity from the older folks about that show. And they weren't interested in the hip hop Shakespeare.

SA: And the younger people were.

KB: But I don't think we'll be doing that exact thing any time soon. We just can't afford to have that many of our subscribers not like it. In point of fact, the show got great reviews, the reviewer from *The Inquirer*, every time he sees me he's going, "What's happening with that play?" The New Victory Theatre in New York City wanted it—and one of the things that we've been trying to promote as a theatre is our connection to New York, doing new work here

> **We just can't afford to have that many of our subscribers not like it. So what do you do in that situation?**

and taking it there—and yet our audience, older audience definitely did not care for it. So what do you do in that situation, where on one hand you're trying to get your theatre to expand in a way that is better for everyone all the way around, and on the other hand you can't put up another piece that displeases your audience like that or you're going to begin losing subscribers at rate you can't afford.

How do you think the results of this study might be useful to you in your process?

KB: The thing is that, I think it's very easy for all of us to get isolated. To get wrapped up in our specific and particular challenges. And one of the ways that a study like this is helpful is determining trends, seeing where breakthroughs have been made in which the relationship between the community and the theatre is most successful. How that happened, what caused that, what tools were used.

SA: And often you don't get the kind of specific answers or reactions that you get anecdotally. You get four letters or five letters, not three hundred. And so in general you don't have a broad enough sampling. So I'm hoping this will give me a broader take on how people responded to a show. You hear the anecdotal things, and I can tell, at the end of a show, because I'm good at reading people, how it went. But it would be great to have a broad enough sample to know when you've hit or when you missed, what was it about what you hit or missed—sometimes it isn't enough to know you missed, then you go, "Oh crap, I missed, I'll never do another show like that again." Which may not have been the case at all!

The problem is that, on the feedback in general, we don't have enough information to make it useful. Maybe marketing thinks it's useful, but from the artistic side I think it's difficult to really read the kind of snapshots you can get now. Because the survey is of, "What do you want to see?", and as Keith said before, people don't know what they want to see until they see it—that's 98% of the time. Maybe we're not telling them what they're going to see correctly, but I think that's another thing this will tell us too. When you describe a show,

298

when you present a show, are we missing the mark with the way it's presented to the audience for the first time? Do they even understand what we're talking about? Are we using the right words? I thought I was going to see this, and here I am sitting, thinking, "Well I gave marketing the right words to talk about it, but obviously it didn't work." That's another thing I think is significant.

KB: When I was mentioning before about audiences not knowing what they want to see, what I mean is that, when we do those usual surveys about what you'd like to see, you always get the same answers back. They want to see musicals and they want to see comedies, period, and you think you're doing this survey and you're learning something, but you're not. This survey is significantly more in-depth, and is asking much more sophisticated questions as to the overall experience and how you interpret that experience. Which is another thing, I think.

I always find myself backing up on the way I interpret something, because sometimes I think we jump too quickly to think we understand something, to think we know about something, and I find myself that it takes a lot of questions, a lot of different ways of looking at a thing, to really come up with a true answer. Like, with *Jacob Marley's Christmas Carol*, what in that would have so alienated the older people? That's too strong a word. They weren't "alienated," they just didn't get it. They just didn't like it. Whereas the young people, they got everything. And this wasn't done as a concept production that was far out or inaccessible. So you think about that and you go, "What is it in there that I'm not understanding about them?" And if I'm going to do a play like that, then how can I do it in a way that is going to address *that*. Whatever *that* is.

Tony Taccone
Berkeley Repertory Theatre

So, you're the artistic director at a very large theatre that's been participating in this intrinsic impact work. How involved have you been in this work so far?

I've been indirectly involved. I've been in contact with [marketing director] Robert Sweibel and [managing director] Susie Medak a lot, and they're very involved, and so my information has been relayed through those conduits. It's a bit of a contradiction, dealing with the audience in my particular job. Because obviously you want to be in tune with "the audience," but I always think it's a big issue when you start generalizing with the audience because you can make so many false assumptions.

As an artist, I don't want to be a slave to the audience, because I don't believe you can actually create great art by thinking first about the audience. I don't believe that. I think if you were to do marketing surveys, which some theatres do, you know—"What do you want to see?"—that's sort of the opposite of how we work. We tend to be artist-centric. I don't even tell artists what to write about, because I found that that always backfires. We try to find the most talented people and see what they're interested in and give them some sort of reign over their own work. I try not the let the audience into my thinking too early, because I feel like it would create the wrong set of passions about where the work gets created and how it gets done.

Having said that, it's not like I'm unaware of the audience. It's my responsibility, of course, to create a body of work that a significant number of people can enjoy and engage with and continue to support. But that's largely an intuitive thing, and even though I look at the surveys—I look at the responses from the audience that Robert so diligently puts together, and I even read parts of some of the surveys about what the individuals are saying about each show—it's got to be a balance between being aware of it and being overwhelmed by it, to where it becomes like paralysis.

Do you yourself have any kind of process by which you seek audience feedback? Are there subscriber interactions or other ways you receive direct feedback from audience or is it all filtered through other staff?

It is filtered through other staff, and I think it's filtered through because I'm an artist. It's tricky because artists need to be actually protected from that in some ways, because what you don't want—we've entertained all sorts of ideas, you know, "Why don't we put up computer kiosks in the lobby and have everybody respond to the shows as soon as they see them?" or "Why don't we give them the emails of the directors?"—No, absolutely, positively no, the answer to that is No. And on the other hand I don't *dislike* the audience; we want them to be able to have access to us. So the filter is really important. There are some artists who want to know what the audience thinks and some that don't. So we have to have a device where it isn't the same for everybody. Like reviews. A lot of artists don't read reviews, but some like to read reviews, so we make them available to anyone who wants to see them. And myself, I'm in a tricky situation because I'm a producer, and as a producer I want to know the information, but as a director I don't want to know so much of that. But that's a fairly common response, I think. Directors want a little more protection from the flow—the onslaught—of criticism, because what's really unhelpful is the unformed critic, which is, "That was really bad," "That was really long," "Me and my daughter were really pissed off."

So who is the filter for you?

I rely on my staff a lot. As a producer, I rely on my staff to tell me the hard stuff. And I also pay attention: I read the reviews. I don't read all the reviews for each show, but I definitely get a sense of what the reviews *are* for each show, including my own. I want to know what the information is, I want to know how hard or easy it's going to be at the theatre, I want to know what arguments I have to put forward to the board, I want to know what risks we're going to be taking. As a producer I need to know that stuff. As a director, like I said, it's a different thing; every artist has their own small, small group of people who they usually rely on to give them the God's honest truth.

However, you're catching us at a very interesting moment. As you're fully aware, there's a brand new interest with the new [social media] technology

We're led by the art.

in including the audience in some kind of "cyber loop feedback system." So we've got our Facebook page, we've got our—I don't tweet—but people are talking about that, we've got our blog. There have been some interesting discussions about the blog. There's much more interesting conversations going on about streamlining the audience into some sort of process-driven thing. And I'm really interested in the technology. We, ironically, have kind of been in the vanguard of technology; almost every single show now has a video element. And just in terms of aesthetically streaming images and relaying information in different ways to an audience experiencing a play, we've been doing that a long time. And there are more and more artists who are thinking in a different way about creating audiences and creating some kind of different dialogue between an audience and a show, and so in some ways the art is at the forefront in this stuff.

If you're doing *The Rivals*, you know, a seventeenth century play, you're probably not going to be involved in streaming the audience… But you never know – people are thinking of all sorts of ways of doing things, and the sense of "event" has increased exponentially, and I think that as artists channel that more into something that is a creative voice, you're going to be able to see more interesting projects, plays.

So you're led by the artists?

We're led by the art. The culture is so increasingly aware of the issues of marketing, and there's this obsession now of trying to get your brand out there, and there's this hyper-capitalistic marketplace, everyone's got their own little space. The obsession with trying to increase that space and trying to get it into people's consciousness and using it for various things, the reiteration of that, and the redoubling of one's efforts to try and expand that space—that's in a lot of conversations now where it wouldn't have been before. So I think we're getting it from both the artistic and administrative ends.

Let me talk to you a little bit about season selection. For you personally, what's the balance between your personal responses to a play or artist and your sense of what audience response might be? How do you balance those things as you're planning?

I tend to think of it more as an overall seasonal issue than an individual play.

Most people think, "Oh Berkeley Rep, cool, this play is perfect for you," and it's a 70-character play about the apocalypse, because we've got this reputation that we're edgy, we're willing to take on topics that nobody else is. And so we tend to get a lot of artists giving us their darkest, most meaningful, most impossible play. And I say that only half being flip. It's obviously great having the reputation that we have, but because artists see the world in a particular way, and because the world is how it is right now, a lot of the plays we get are dark. The world is not a fun place right now, and artists reflect what's going on in the world. So getting the balance in the season—"balance" is a world I think about a lot, because we can't do seven plays about the apocalypse—getting the balance to the season in terms of both form and content.

> To the extent that we have a strategy or a formula, it's based on eclecticism, it's based on surprise, it's based on having the audience be delighted and entertained and surprised by what they "like."

To the extent that we have a strategy or a formula, it's based on eclecticism, it's based on surprise, it's based on having the audience be delighted and entertained and surprised by what they "like." For example, we did a play called *The Laramie Project* a few years ago, which was about the murder of Matthew Shepard, the gay kid in Wyoming. And that's the type of project where I think the audience didn't necessarily think they'd like it before the saw it, and then they saw it, and they were blown away. They were blown away, they were moved, they were enlivened. It was just so—that response to a play like that is what I live for. Because that's where people go, "My God, I won't try to pre-judge as much, I won't try to eliminate possibilities because I think the play's about a particular thing."

What we're trying to do is to create enough work that is consistently fun and enlightening and engaging, that is just *good* in a variety of ways, so that people just trust us, and not the familiarity of the title, or the recognizeability of the playwright or the actors; they're just coming to Berkeley Rep. And I think we've done that enough that our people now are doing something that is pretty rare: they're buying into a season of plays that they largely don't know anything about. Which is awesome.

> # The marketing department will tell you, "People buy what they know," and we're trying to get them to buy what they don't know.

The thing that I have to consistently do is make sure we that we don't fall into any categories. And it's a trick because of course the marketing department will tell you, "People buy what they know," and we're trying to get them to buy what they don't know. So it's a real challenge. And the only way that I get to exist outside of the conventional wisdom is by doing stuff that people consistently enjoy. They don't have to enjoy it in the same way, but they have to enjoy it and they have to respect it.

So how I think about the season is this: I think we have to get a wide spectrum of pieces and projects that run the gamut from tragedy to comedy, that run the gamut in terms of form from how, let's say, how Mary Zimmerman tells a play to how Sarah Ruhl tells a play to how Lemony Snicket tells a play. There's a lot of different ways and a lot of different voices, so one minute you're seeing *American Idiot* and the next minute you're seeing Tony Kushner. Really eclectic branding, with a spectrum of experience that is joyful and moving, intellectually challenging and simple. That's my strategy. I think that surprise wakes people's senses up more than anything else. I will frequently hear people say stuff like, "What are they going to do now?" It's filled with both terror and excitement. Hopefully we can get both.

This study is trying to quantify this kind of ineffable experience of watching a play. How would you say that this connects to this desire to surprise people? Do you think this work will be useful in this thinking process, or are you concerned that it will drive artistic process into focus groups?

I'm always concerned when things get reductive, and I think the nature of studies is to get a little reductive, because you don't just want people to fill out essay questions. I would be interested in some focus groups where the audience was selected from a variety of people that were representative in some ways—I think a focus group like that would be as interesting for the audience as it would be for the recipients. Because one of the things that is most successful for a successful show of ours is that the audience becomes aware of itself, and they're aware that they're not the same. I get a lot of letters by older members of the audience that say, "Look, I know that you have to do these younger plays because it's good to have younger audience members but..." or "I know that you didn't really want to do this, but you had to..." Those are my favorites. Kind of a benign way of forgiving me. But they're wrong.

I don't know if there's any way to scientifically measure engagement. I think one question would be, you know, "Has going to Berkeley Rep increased your appetite for being surprised?" "Has going to Berkeley Rep changed any of your preconceptions about what theatre is?" "Has going to Berkeley Rep increased your doubt about the theatre's ability to do work which is consistently enjoyable?" It's all in the asking, and I know that the way you frame the questions gets you the answer you want.

If you were able to ask those questions, would that be useful information?

Yeah, I think it would be. At the heart of that question is, "How do you change people's perceptions? How do you change people's experiences? How do you continue to invite people to look at things in a new way?" That's what our goal is. Because I don't believe you just put the art out there without providing any tools for people to understand what you're doing. So another thing I think would be helpful is to know which of the tools that we provide gives you the best access to the work. I'd like to know that. Are there ideas that they have that they think would increase their sense of enjoyment with the work. I'd love to know that.

With all of this obsession about social media, is that really true for them, or not? Do any of them really have time to participate in the process more than they were? Do you really have time to do all this shit that we're spending a lot of time figuring out how to do? Or is it a waste of time? How many of you really, really would like to get on a blog that talks about the plays more, really? Given the fact that there are three million blogs out there now? What are the tools that would really, really excite you? Would you like to go to rehearsal? Really? Or would you not? Are we slavishly just kind of going after this

305

> **Is complaining really the only way people want to talk to us? Can we change the complaint into a suggestion, or, even better, into participation? Complaint is not participation.**

crowd? A lot of this stuff is really for twenty-year-olds, who won't be subscribers and are only going to participate to the extent that they're going to participate. I'd love to know some scientific answers to this as opposed to this general, "We gotta do this!" Do we?

And I would ask also, "Is complaining really the only way people want to talk to us?" The major mode of the internet is complaining, and I think that that's real, and we've created this culture of opinion which is encased in sort of absolutes. I understand some of this is part of a larger cultural thing, but is there some other way that we can talk to people? Can we change the complaint into suggestion or, even better, into participation? Complaint is not participation.

We're in the business of engagement so anything we can do in this study that increases our understanding of how we can get people involved in a way that make sense is really valuable.

We're about to start this big project, this new center we're going to start for playwriting and developing new work, and there's a lot of thought for including the audience more in some of the projects. I would really like to know if there's an appetite for that, and not just among the same fifty people. I think every theatre is kind of doing some of this, everyone is now actively trying to…and I think it's driven by the fact that nationally, subscriptions are flat, so you're really driven by single ticket sales, which actually are good, but the work that it takes is different and more intense. So it's that issue, and that's the same issue – it's more like niche marketing. More like, this play is saying this, how do we get these people into the space? The problem is, it's really labor intensive. It used to be that you wanted to turn people into subscribers—now you're sort of giving up on that, so we need to make sure that every play stands up on its own, which is basically making every play into an "event," which takes more time. It's a bigger deal.

Can you think of a time when feedback from audience members changed a

I think every year is a reaction to the year before. This year, there's no question that the degree to which *The Composer is Dead* polarized the audience will absolutely have a significant effect on how I think about next year. That piece should not have gone in the mainstage year; it should have been an extra add-on show. There were a lot of people who felt it was targeted at too young an audience for them to appreciate. The people who came with their kids or grandkids had a fantastic time, but it's just like a Pixar film: if you go with the kids it's a different experience than if you go alone.

> Season selection is really strategic, and it lives inside my body, and that's the only body it should live inside.

I heard a lot of negative feedback that people were pissed off that the program was too young for them. And I thought that the craft of the show alone would be impressive enough to win those audience members over, and to a large extent it was. But for some it wasn't. So I won't ever program a show that is a kid's popup book as part of the five-play offering. Cause it was a mistake. If it had been an add-on show and been properly marketed...you know.

There are things that happen every single year that informs the following year. And usually how it works is I will step way out on the gangplank one year, a lot of world premieres that are a little risky, a little edgy, and the next year I'll hold back a little bit, make sure there are some more titles that will reassure some folks, while all the while trying to push my agenda forward. It's really strategic, and it lives inside my body, and that's the only body it should live inside, because I don't want [my artistic associates] Les Waters and Madeline Oldham and Amy to be thinking the same way. I want them to feel freer. If they're free, they're not burdened by the compromises I have to make ultimately, and I want to hear from them in a free way before I get to constricted or too afraid to go forward. I think that's why you construct a staff in the way that you do. They're not doing the same job, and they shouldn't.

So, in your role as artistic director you're actually aware of the audience and you're filtering for your other artistic staff?

That's right, that's exactly right.

Michael Rohd
Sojourn Theatre

Michael, you ended up on the list because we wanted to talk to somebody whose theatre doesn't work with a consistent audience. As I understand it, you guys work in all different communities, and it's really dependent on the show.

We've been based in Portland for a long time, but a lot of our work now happens in different parts of the country—sometimes hosted by institutional theatres, sometimes created with hosts or partners who are not institutional theatres. We have experiences with lots of different kinds of audiences and, particularly, lots of different definitions of what a "successful" engagement with an audience means.

Let me start there. How do you or other members of your ensemble typically seek feedback from audiences? Do you have formal ways that you do that? Is it really about a series of conversations? How do you tell what people thought of the experience?

I think there are probably a variety of ways, but one of the things that frames it is that we don't have a one-size-fits-all model for how we make work, nor do we have a one-size-fits-all model for how we figure out who our audience constituency will be and how to relate to them. We tend to, when we initiate a project, whether on our own or with a partner, talk about what the project will mean in terms of success, and what we want to accomplish, and how we'll learn about that. A lot of our work is developed with the people who are going to be a part of not just the project development, but who will help us find other stakeholders and people who will invest in the success of the project, the content of the project and the discourse around the project that we're trying to host in a variety of ways. Some of our shows are articulated as civic-dialogue projects, but not all. Some of our projects are really art-focused, creating events that focus on spectacle and aesthetics…I think we try to find the language for each one.

In terms of feedback, honestly, the most important feedback, what we're most interested in, is not from the random audience member who came because they saw about it in the paper. The audience that we're interested in being in conversation with, in terms of whether we succeeded or not, is generally people that have been involved in the project, and have invested in it. By "invested," I don't mean that they helped write it, but they have something at stake in the making of it, in the way it lands and the way it is received, and what it articulates, and the kind of experience that it embeds in a community conversation. That becomes the "audience" that we want to be in conversation with. Then the people who come because they go to theatre events, and they want to see it, we talk to them afterwards.

We rarely do surveys. We more sort of chart whether they jump onto our mailing list and become a part of the conversation that we have, in general, with people around our company.

There are things that continue in the spirit of the project afterwards. For example, I spent the last three years working on a project at Oregon Shakespeare Festival for which our core partner was the United Way of Jackson County. Initially, when we exploring some of the very early content, we met with them because we knew we wanted to engage people who were not traditional audiences at the festival. The United Way offered to partner with us and help us reach people who did not go to the theatre for a variety of reasons, didn't even necessarily know about the festival. Through them, we did story circles and workshops. I did interviews.

We set up this whole process and brought some of them over to the festival to be in conversation with us. The executive director of the United Way, she took 50 people from their organization, staff, board members and constituents, to the show on this past Sunday. And she wrote me this lovely email last night and just said really positive things. That it was an amazingly positive experience for them, that she feels that it completely adhered to the values that are core to their work. That some of the people who were interviewed didn't see their story in the show, but saw other stories from their lives, and were super fascinated, and kind of confused, like, "How did they get those stories? I didn't tell those stories."

She just thanked us for making something that she felt was going to be a part of their ongoing work, in terms of conversation and the spirit of the event.

I sent that comment out to my Sojourn partner, Shannon, who is my main ensemble collaborator. She's a designer. She and I led this show together. I sent it out to the whole cast and crew, and the staff at OSF and I said, "Granted, lots

We define success in proportion or relation to stakeholders in the process, not just supporters.

of feedback is important but, frankly, this is the feedback that matters."

Her feedback means more to me than 150 people out of 5000 who "Sort of didn't get it," or said "This wasn't a play." I cared about this feedback much, much more than I care about anyone else's. That's what I mean when I say we seek to find the feedback of the people who we feel matter. Partners and collaborators and the people they cared about. We want to understand their experience of coming to see the thing.

We want the general audience to have a positive experience, and we make it, of course, for the audience we've never met as well as the one we have. But I think for us, we define success in proportion or relation to stakeholders in the process, not just supporters.

Sojourn did this big project, *The Penelope Project*, over the course of two years. That was a collaboration with the University of Wisconsin, Milwaukee, the Center for Age and Community, and Luther Manor, which is a long-term care facility outside Milwaukee. We worked with all those collaborators on a site-specific adaptation of *The Odyssey*, particularly focused on Penelope's story of waiting.

It was a multidisciplinary experience of using different forms of artmaking to gather stories and images and thoughts from the residents at the Luther Manor facility. The focus was on the residents living with Alzheimer's and dementia, and their families and caregivers. Over a long period of time, as the staff at the Luther Manor led art activities, playwright Ann Basting developed a script and then we went through a devising process with our company, her, and residents, and families at Luther Manor.

Out of that came a play that took audiences on a half-mile journey through the facility to see the show. We were there, in this facility with the residents and their families and a general audience from Milwaukee, as they came through the space.

The relationships that developed over the course of making the piece and the experiences that caregivers and families and residents had, collaborating in this creative way—we have a lot of those stories. And those stories allowed us to witness the kind of relationship building that was important to us on this particular project. Similarly, there were people that came in from around the country to see the show to look at it as a potential model for creative work inside care facilities of Alzheimer's and dementia patients.

Those people have now been taking the model out across the country. We've already been in three conferences. We'll be at another one in two weeks in DC, where it's being put out as a best practice model. There's funding now coming together that's going to have the model happening in different facilities around the country.

To me, that speaks to an audience experience that allowed them to feel and observe the value of the work as an artistic experience but also, in this particular case, as an applied model.

I have to say we're not so interested in a model where we make something, the audience experiences it, and we reshape the thing a little more to what they want. That's not so much it, although certainly in the process of making we are trying collaborate with audiences so that not only are there access points but we are indeed in conversation with what people are looking for when they come to a theatrical experience beyond, "I want to sit in the dark and by moved by a transformational story." That's part of what we do sometimes, but lots of places do that so we're not looking to push that audience button and get feedback on how well we pushed it.

Would you say that there's a piece of your process that is in response to how you see things happening once it's in front of audiences? Do you feel like that's very much the endpoint for you?

We bring audiences in before previews. Audiences have to be part of our rehearsal process, for one because a lot of our work is site-based and actually journeys audiences through geography. The only way to understand the relationship of geography to dramaturgy is to actually work with human beings and learn from their experience, both by talking to them about it and by observing them. It's super interesting.

We bring in audiences, full-sized audiences early. And we'll do the "Let's stay afterwards and talk" thing, but the truth is I just walk around and watch them. You move around with an audience for ninety minutes through an experience.

You watch them and listen to them, and there's not a lot you're going to hear in the conversation afterwards that you weren't able to observe in the experience with them. Learning from them but the learning is as much in the moment as it's in any focus group situation.

Can you think of a time when you observed something or heard something in one of those settings that caused you to make a significant shift in the piece or how you approached a future piece?

All the time. I can think of a lot of instances where I learned something from the audience before a show opens or even as the show is opening and made big changes. If the thing isn't successful in the ways we've defined success, if the thing isn't compelling and entertaining in ways that make the experience able to be something we are hoping to occur, we adjust.

Our vocabulary around participation says that an audience needs to be moved through a "watching phase," then a "choosing phase," and then a "doing phase." If we move through the work in a supple, intentional way then we're able to move them beyond a traditional experience. We certainly have grown in understanding that trajectory and how to deploy tactics that help that function usefully.

Back in '07 or '08, when we started working more and more with participation as a part of our artistic palette within performances, we would discover these trajectories of participation that were successful, and others that were bumpy. Sometimes we wouldn't really understand which trajectory was which in a nuanced way until we were in a run. Then we would be in the run and discover they needed a little more opportunity to watch.

That's probably the biggest area where we'll observe mid-run: what if we go back five minutes and this had just been altered here? How does that impact when we're trying to make strategy choices in the next piece if we're going to engage participation in that next piece?

I heard somebody else say, in reference to cultural experiences in general, "Enjoy, talk, do." People sometimes just want to enjoy a cultural experience and sometimes they want to talk about it and sometimes they want to do it.

Everything is changing—all the notions of coauthorship and collaboration and what participation even means. I was at a TCG event last year and they were having a conversation about participation. The person who runs a traditional regional theatre in Chicago was like, "Well, what participation means to me is when people lean forward in their chairs."

I was like, "You know what? The rest of the art world—other disciplines—think we're children when we talk like that. We just seem like children."

People hold very tightly and very conservatively to two boards and a plank, catharsis.

There's interpretation: that's the leaning forward and engaging in participation by interpreting your own experience.

Then there's commentary: that's being given technological tools to be involved in discourse around the event either during it or before and after.

And then there's impact: that's layers of participation where you impact dramaturgically what happens in the trajectory of the event.

The other fields are past number one, and they've been practicing number two for years. Number three is where the real action is. But we can't get out of number one. People hold very tightly and very conservatively to two boards and a plank, the story, catharsis. Great, that's a part of the palette. That was actually a challenge up at Oregon Shakespeare Festival, with a few actors more than anyone. Just those notions of what theatre is and isn't. It was very interesting.

You were working with the Oregon Shakespeare ensemble. That must have been a very different kind of work, though I suppose their work has been changing pretty radically in the last few years in general.

You know, I think it hasn't. It has in *content*. But it hasn't in *form*, particularly. They're doing amazing work up there in engaging new voices. They're doing wonderful work in offering more for different audiences. But the process by which they make plays, other than the Black Swan Lab where a playwright can come in and have their work read and get feedback, the process of how they rehearse and build plays in general is not so different than what's its always been. It's very challenging when you bring something other than that in.

So your project sounds like it was a real stretch for that group.

I think it was.

When you set out to devise a new project or think about what the next several

313

> I want the show to be a play with a story, but it also needs to be a piece of applied creativity where an audience goes through the process of collectively imaginging better ways to have public discourse.

things Sojourn is going to engage in are, how do you think about what you want the impact on audience to be?

It really depends. We've started this project now called *Town Hall* which we're working on in collaboration with The Team, which is a New York City-based ensemble, and it'll go up to Kansas City Rep in winter 2013 before it goes on the road some. The work of that project is looking at the history of civic discourse in the United States and the particular polarized moment we're in now.

What I've been passionate about for this one is, I want the show to be a play with a story, but it also needs to be a piece of applied creativity where an audience goes through the process of collectively imagining better ways to have public discourse.

I would say this project has succeeded, both in the course of development and then in the course of an audience coming to attend it, if it fosters a sense of a more nuanced and dynamic conversation about how democracy functions. Can this engage people more actively in 90 minutes than the Internet or the news, or are we just part of the echo chamber?

I want to figure out how this show engages audiences to a degree, with some interactivity, but I also just want to see whether theatre done in a really complex but articulated way can get at the challenge of listening and communicating today in America.

So in the case of *Town Hall*, **you're responding to what you see as a civic or a national issue and you're also pushing the limits of your own methodology. Is that's a usual combination as you're picking what you want work on next?**

Yes. As we work on *Town Hall*, we have a simultaneous project starting up in Portland with [the theatre company] Portland Taiko. Portland Taiko approached us about making a show together and a bunch of artists from the company said that's really exciting. Their artistic director wants to make a piece about identity and memory.

314

So in that case, the work comes out of a formal interest, and then the content will have to be something that we're interested. But in that case, the content is coming second to this desire to collaborate.

Are there people who come to many Sojourn shows, come to most of your work? Are there groups or individuals that you're having an ongoing conversation with?

We more see ourselves as part of a national cultural conversation, but it happens in Portland. It happened particularly in Portland, I would say, between 2002 and 2008. There was a big Sojourn audience that came to shows and accumulated. When we were back there in 2010 with *On The Table*, a lot of those people came out again. We're there with irregularity now so I don't think I could claim that we are a part of the ongoing cultural conversation there the way that we once were.

I know there were a lot of reasons that you made the decision to let go of Portland as a home base. Why did you do that? Did having an ongoing conversation with consistent people begin to feel less important to you or was it just that that wasn't a very sustainable way to be working?

I think it's some of both. I think the truth is, in Portland, small to midsized nontraditional arts organizations are not sustainable if you want to pay artists any kind of semi-living wage. At a certain point, I chose to prioritize the work of the company and the development of the company's aesthetics and missions over place. Sustainability became a priority. There wasn't a lack of interest in a place-based conversation, and I think in various ways we still are part of a Portland conversation. But we did have to make that choice.

It's funny. For me, personally, before Sojourn I spent 10 years on the road as an artist in residence for Hope Is Vital. My whole artistic life before Sojourn was working in different communities, never an exclusively place-based conversation. And I have found that both because of the Internet and the way communication happens among people involved in the cultural and policy conversations around the country, I do feel that we are part of a certain discourse right now.

I'm a believer in place and locality, and have been passionate about that and committed to it for a lot of periods in my life. But I also don't mind us being more focused on the national conversation than the local one for a period of time.

Jack Reuler
Mixed Blood Theatre

What kind of process do you use at your theatre to gather feedback from your audience for the artistic staff?

The surveying we do on our own is more demographic in its focus. And, as a matter of fact, we collect it before the performance ever takes place, so there is no opportunity for the audience to say, "I had a great experience," even if they wanted to. There is not opportunity for that qualitative feedback.

This may just sound pretentious as hell, but it is my impression that it is our job as leaders of nonprofit theatres to lead the audience to see that which they don't yet know they want to see. And in doing so—to me, the big divide between commercial theatre and nonprofit theatre is that it is commercial theatre's domain to say to an audience "What do you want to see?" and provide that. But it's the domain of nonprofit theatres to say, "We need to have programming that realizes our mission and that has the highest professional standards." But the decision should not be based on, "Is this what you want to see?" If you know what they want to see, then there's something you're not doing quite right as an artistic director. You need to be guessing what they want to see and try to take them to that place.

When you start from that point—that your job is to take them someplace they haven't been—how do you know if they've gotten there?

I'm there a lot, in the house and in the lobby. There are three or four criteria I use when a show is over to see how we did on it in terms of mission realization, in terms of entertainment factor. I look inside and ask, "Did that turn out how we wanted it to, whether 12 people came or 10 million?" And then the biggest

> This may just sound pretentious as hell, but it is my impression that it is our job as leaders of nonprofit theatres to lead the audience to see that which they don't yet know they want to see.

question for any nonprofit, maybe for any business at all, is, "What are you trying to do and how well did you do at that?" So we ask that – what were our aspirations and how did we do according to our own standards, and then we certainly also have the anecdotal experiential audience reaction by being in the room with people. And a lot of the time, given our mission, the "who" that comes is more important than how many of people come.

It was, for us, a real turning point in about 2000, when we made a decision— traditional marketing says you try to get somebody in the door and then you try hard to get them to come back. We said, "What if we put that on the back burner and say, 'Who's this play for? Let's find them.'" It's much more labor intensive, and as a result, the numbers of people that come aren't necessarily the reflection of the success of the project, but *who* made up the numbers that did come can be far more telling. And so we do that demographic data collection in a much more aggressive manner than the intrinsic impact survey is being given.

And that's why I think that there are certain inherent weaknesses in what we're doing in this survey. It's happening to everybody in the same way, but there are certain people who are disinclined to participate in that kind of survey. We're actually putting it in their hand, giving them a pencil, and then looming over them politely, and before the show starts we've collected those surveys. And so we can look a little bit at the disconnect between what our surveys are telling us demographically and what the intrinsic impacts are, but that's just about survey collection.

There's critical response, which one takes with a grain of salt. But that's certainly part of the thing. We go back and say, "How did we do by the media? How did we do by our own standard? How did the audience experience it?"

And so what's interesting about this survey is you're asking us to guess how the audience response is going to be before they see it, and then to see how it compares. I find that part of your methodology fascinating.

It's really intriguing, thinking about "Who is this play for?" instead of "Who can we get to come back?" Can you give me an example of a recent show of how you talked about that, how you figured who you thought the play was for?

Take the first show that we surveyed, the adaptation of *House of the Spirits* done in two languages. We were definitely aiming to get a bilingual audience since

317

> **Surprise is not only a factor we take into consideration, but has become one of our core values.**

we did the show in Spanish and English, so it's probably the only Spanish-language theatre in the area over a period of time. Attendant to that, we were trying to get Latinos to come, although in our surveys, interestingly enough, a lot of the bilingual people that come do not self-identify as Latino. So there were a lot of Spanish-speaking Anglos who were attending. And then what we don't do is dig deeper and say, "We're succeeding in getting 26% of those self-identifying as Latino," we don't break that down deeper. But each show that we do, whatever the topic of the show is, and whatever the population of the characters of the play, really targets our marketing.

When you're in that selection process, do you think to yourself about what kind of impact you're trying to have on the audience?

One of the core values of the organization is "predictably unpredictable." Surprise is not only a factor we take into consideration, but has become one of our core values. That is reflected not only in the choice of the material, but we have a flexible, reconfigurable space so what the relationship between the audience and the performance can change.

There are many factors that go into season selection. The first one is always, "Is this a reflection of our mission?" And our mission really has to do with a multiplicity of peoples coming together in the world of the play, usually for common purpose. So does it do that, model pluralism successfully? That's always the first question that we ask.

And then we have at different times, different focuses that we aim at. We realized a few years ago that we had been remiss in not having disability be a manifestation of our mission. So we now do plays that are by, for, about and with people with disabilities, but there are many different disability universes out there. So we will specifically select a play whose content is about disability, and then other plays whose characters might have disabilities or the actor playing the character might have a disability. All of which helps us taper our reach for audience.

So when you have this "predictably unpredictable" idea, are you looking for that

to be the case for every show in the season?

Sometimes that predictable unpredictability comes through in the way in which you do it or the way it's written. So I'd say there's some element of that in everything – there aren't shows that are more or less so. And that's a little bit of an "eye of the beholder" thing, too. What's surprising to one person is humdrum to another.

> The creation of a season is like the creation of a restaurant's menu. You want a series of entrees, and you don't want them to all be similar.

The creation of a season is like the creation of a restaurant's menu. You want a series of entrees, and you don't want them to all be similar. One of the things that we did this year that was very telling in our own survey work was, we solicited the patrons of the shows for contributions after they've seen the show. And for *House of Spirits*, the second show of the season, the first one you were involved in, we were only going to solicit those that also saw the first show, called *Cool Drink of Water*, and we found that there was *zero* overlap of single ticket buyers. *None* of the people that saw the second show saw the first show. For some theatres, that would be a sign of catastrophe. For us, that's a sign that the targeted marketing we're doing and the aim of the script and what we're trying to do is on the path we want it to be.

So now we'll crunch the numbers on the next show, *Agnes Under the Big Top*, and look at our own surveys and data capture and ask ourselves How many people saw that that saw the other two? And if the answer is small or none, it's really not a bad thing.

So your reach then ends up being much, much broader over the season...

And "retention" just has a different meaning for us. For 22 seasons in a row we've done Latino-focused work, and for a dozen of those we've done the shows bilingually. So I think the much more interesting thing is who has come, where's your repeat attendance between those shows. So your retention isn't between Show A and Show B, it's between bilingual show this year and bilingual show next year. I just think those are more interesting indicators.

For you, you've talked a lot about the really clear mission-focused nature of your planning. What's the balance between a kind of personal response you have to a play and your sense of how the audience might or might not go for that choice?

319

> I'm hoping that people are buying into my vision and taste rather than into that particular script.

Here's my ego talking, as I answer that, but just because I've been here for a long time, I'm hoping that whatever the overall aesthetic of the theatre has been has come out through those mainstage choices. I'm hoping that people are buying into my vision and taste rather than into that particular script. Over a body of work I've figured something out in terms of realizing the mission of the organization. Of course, for any given show, walking that fine line between the commerce of the play and its box office potential, and its artistic ability to realize both high-quality theatre and an audience—good artistry is all one big question, it's not ten different questions that you try to integrate.

And that proceeds on kind of a gut-level for you, on a kind of identification with the theatre and its audience over a long time?

And sometimes, as we go into these phases—we've redoubled our efforts in areas of disability, in areas of our own neighborhood and the populations that make that up, in disability-focused work. And so, putting that menu of entrees together, there are also other things that weigh into that: Here are particular initiatives that we're trying to get better at, for example. So it's not just my five favorite plays that realize the mission for the year, but "What are these things we're trying to do?"

There are relationships between us and playwrights and us and development centers, like the Lark in New York and the Playwrights Center here in Minneapolis, there are a million agents. We're a member of the National New Play Network. So there are all sorts of ways in which we're accessing scripts that will be on topic. And we also commission a number of works. Almost everything we do is a first, second or third production—although I say that somewhat guiltily since we currently have *Avenue Q* running, which is completely on topic for our mission, but it is not the sort of edgy, new play world that I think we're usually part of.

When we do the kind of work we do, it isn't out of the hope that people can learn about the other. It's really so people can see themselves on stage, reflected in important ways. When we do an African American play, if the audience that isn't African American say, "Oh, I now know something more about African Americans than I knew when I came in," that's a by-product. It's nice that it happened, but that's not at all the design of why that play was chosen; it's for people to see themselves. So if you're going to say, "We want people to see themselves," you better have those "themselves" in the audience, seeing it.

> If you're going to say, "We want people to see themselves," you better have those "themselves" in the audience, seeing it.

Can you give me an example of a time when feedback from the audience changed your programming?

You know, here's an example, I don't know if this I the right one, but…two or three seasons ago, in this bilingual, Latino-focused programming that we do, we did a play that was very much in the Chicano style: the archetypes were bigger than real, the characters were probably, you know, two-and-a-half dimensional. And to some, it looked like over-the-top cheap sitcom theatre, and to those that knew Chicano theatre, or the Chicano community even if they didn't know the theatre style, it really worked. And so I had this dichotomy reaction from "That's the worst crap you've ever done" to "That's my favorite show you've ever done." And it got me back to, "For whom are you picking this," and "Who are you hoping to see this?"

That really made me look at, as I share these plays with people, who is giving what kind of feedback on them. We now have a small advisory council who this year read a half-a-dozen Latino-focused plays that we were looking at. We wanted to hear what the reaction was, and it was a multi-generational group—and probably the one that I thought the fewest of the older group would like, I was completely wrong. It was wild and raunchy and political. So, coming out of that Chicano show, it's changed the way in which we gather feedback on the shows, we gather broader feedback now.

As you are beginning to see how the Intrinsic Impact survey is working, what are some ways that you think the findings and tools from this survey might be useful in your artistic process or selection process, or programming choices?

I think the idea of filling out the form for myself and the others on staff prior to the show opening and then seeing what the results are is really a great idea. And I think it lets one know, for each of us on staff, whether we have our finger on the pulse or not. The results, because of certain people's fundamental distrust of filling out those surveys, I think that the homogeneity of those filling them out, when compared with the demographics of our own surveys, which we force feed to them and then take back, it's less comprehensive of the whole audience. I wish we could figure out how to have those two things go hand-in-hand.

If you just say, "Fill this out," there are certain bodies of people who just aren't going to do that. I do think, though, that as we look at the results it's going to be fascinating—what we thought the emotional response was going to be and other areas.

Will it impact season selection? I would think so, especially after we have two or three shows under our belts. Once we know whether we're getting better at guessing what the audience's reaction was going to be, or that we're consistently wrong in certain places, that will factor into not just season selection, but how I do my job.

Dudley Cocke
Roadside Theater

Why don't you start by telling me a little about Roadside?

Roadside Theater is the professional theatre wing of a larger organization called Appalshop, a part of Appalachian Workshop. Appalshop began in 1969 as a War on Poverty program to provide a head start for Appalachian youth in film training. The federal Office of Economic Opportunity set up a dozen such programs around the country with the rationale that the training would enable young people to escape their impoverished communities. Appalshop was the only rural and white program. The others were in the inner city, the so-called "ghetto," so Appalshop's orientation, from the beginning, was around communities of color that were likewise disadvantaged economically.

As I said, Roadside is Appalshop's theatre wing, and there is also a documentary film production and distribution division, a radio station, and a record company. We continue to train young people to become community leaders and citizen-artists. We occasionally publish and work in still photography. We have a major archive project.

All of this work begins with the Appalachian voice – with the impulse to understand the life of our region, of our place. Like the message coming from the 1960s black southern civil rights movement, we, too, were ready to proclaim, "We are somebody" -- and we are definitely not the stereotype you think we are.

Within the reality of Central Appalachia, there was always this idea that part of what Appalshop needed to do was to tell the Appalachian story from the inside out. The Appalachian story had been told to the nation by lots of other people. But not by people from Appalachia. It was within that exciting context that Roadside Theater was formed in 1975-'76.

This idea of projecting from the inside out: is the goal, then, to create local work that is distributed beyond the Appalachian community? Or to create work locally for locals, so they can see their own stories on stage?

Both. Roadside makes theatre that is, in the stock phrase, "of, by, and for"

The soul of Roadside's plays just shrivels up without a diverse audience.

Appalachian people, with the idea that by telling our particular story with skill and care, that story can appeal to people anywhere. And that turned out to be the case. Our work begins here, but it travels around the United States and occasionally overseas.

From the beginning, our relationship with our audience and our local culture has shaped the form and content of our plays and how we produce and perform them. For example, our work has no fourth wall. We speak directly to the audience, and the audience is invited to speak back. And that isn't just some imposed, formal convention; it's part of the culture here. And it's part of the culture in many communities – for example in southern black churches, where we've often performed.

What happens when you take a piece of yours to Europe that is designed that way? Does it change the interaction that you seek to have with the audience and that you actually have with the audience?

Getting diversity in the audience is a key thing when we take the work outside of our own rural, working class culture. That's been an issue when we tour in the U.S., and it's also an issue when the work has gone to Europe. Professional, nonprofit theatre in the United States is largely viewed by well-educated, economically well-off people. Since our work comes out of a working class culture, of course, we want to reach that working class audience whether we're in Europe or whether we're in Nebraska. And that's taken a lot of effort, because it's not the usual audience that one finds as a touring theatre. Getting this more diverse audience to attend when you're sponsored by an arts presenter or a university performing arts series requires a lot of strategy.

Let me make an analogy to give you an idea of what I think is at stake artistically. Shakespeare wrote for the gallery and the pit. Can you imagine what happens to the actors playing the low parts when everyone in the audience is rich and powerful? I witnessed that watching the Royal Shakespeare Company perform *As You Like It* in San Francisco for an audience that had paid $140 a ticket. Those poor actors with the low parts just died right there before me – nothing they said or did could elicit a response. I thought they might fail to reappear after intermission! Likewise, the soul of Roadside's plays just shrivels up without a diverse audience. And the irony is that the shriveled, disfigured version may actually be popular with the wealthy audience -- but it's not the play Roadside wrote.

In the late '80s, with support from the Lila Wallace-Reader's Digest Fund, we, along with a bunch of other theatres, tracked our audiences over six years. The findings for us were almost the exact inverse of the rest of the theatres being tracked in the sample – for example, 73% of our audience earned less than $50,000 a year and 30% of those earned $20,000 or less annually.

Our audience diversity success derives in part from our artistic understanding that the audience is part of the show.

Our audience diversity success derives in part from our artistic understanding that the audience is part of the show. Often it seems like our plays occur in some third, ephemeral space, which is neither where the audience is seated, nor is it on the stage where the actors are playing. Remember, there is no fourth wall, and we prefer non-proscenium spaces. This intimacy and the opportunity for spontaneous call and response between the audience and actors can cause what I can only describe as a levitating effect. It's probably akin to what athletes describe as "being in the zone," but in the theatre of participation, everyone can go there together -- and without losing their individuality.

In your play creation process, what does "audience input" look like to you?

The two main heritages here are Scotch Irish and Cherokee, and both are narrative-based cultures—so we're a narrative-based theatre. After showing a work in progress, we like to hear more stories from the audience about the story the play is trying to tell. We have a particular storytelling methodology—it's a formal story circle method—that we use. It provides a form, and forum, for audience members to tell their personal stories about the themes in the performance in which they have just participated as audience members. Parts of some of their stories eventually may be incorporated into the play. This process is repeated as the play develops, with the goal of deepening and bringing more nuances to the story we are telling. In that way, the play develops from these deepening iterative stories that the audience is telling around the themes.

We do the same thing when we take a finished play to a new community. Say

> To see your own story on the stage for the first time is shocking, and can be a life-changing experience.

we put on a play about that moment here in the coalfields when people made the change from a small subsistence farm economy to an industrial economy. That's a theme that you can find in places around the world. After the play, rather than having a talk-back with the audience, in which someone says, "Well, why did the actor or director make this choice?" or "I like this better than that" or "I didn't understand this"—rather than that, we go into story circles with the audience to hear their personal stories called up by the performance. As a bonus, these new stories help the actors develop their roles.

When one of our plays is successful, it takes you into different places, intellectually, emotionally, and spiritually, and with that experience, the stories that then come out in the audience circle are very, very rich. At such moments they – the audience – realize their own potential as artists and as shapers of narratives. And that idea of animating and empowering the community voice is why Roadside and Appalshop got started in the first place.

So, this connection with the audience is part of the DNA of Roadside Theater. The people who are in the plays all came up in this culture. They're not actors who've trained at some academy somewhere else. In the main, they've received their training as folk artists—they're trained by the community as storytellers, as singers, as musicians.

We've been asked, at different times, what's given you the fortitude to continue as an ensemble for thirty-odd years? And my answer has always been that we've endured because we place the audience at the center of our work. That's been the secret ingredient. When we travel around the country, we often run into audience members who have Appalachian roots, but there's been so much stigma around working class and poor "hillbilly" culture that they may feel ashamed of their background. They arrive at the play incognito, and then when they see something of beauty and truth on the stage that reflects them, the pride that swells up is huge. To see your own story on the stage for the first time is shocking, and can be a life-changing experience.

As we've gone around the country, we've encountered many, many people who've had that experience while being part of one of our plays. It's emotional, and they now want to reveal themselves by sharing their own stories -- and then just stand beside the actors in this circle of new-found intimacy. That's one very good reason that when our plays end, and after bows are taken, we have no curtain.

Several years after we got started, there was a moment when I knew that Roadside was succeeding. Out of the blue, we got a call from a woman asking us to please come and sing several of the songs from one of our plays at her dad's funeral. Then we knew our theatre had become part of the community's daily life.

With such connection to the community, how do you make decisions about programming? Do you start with the topic and then go solicit the stories? And is there something particular that you're looking for as a reaction to those stories when you first start?

We've approached the making of our plays in many different ways. We don't have a formula. In fact, we think of ourselves as an experimental theatre. For example, we made a series of plays, in the early days, which retold Appalachian history from the people's point of view. Starting in the 1890s, at the end of the Appalachian frontier period, the official history of this region started being written by absentee corporations. So you have this official written history and a parallel people's history -- a classic counter narrative. And so we did a series of plays over a dozen years that retold the history from this people's oral history. For those plays, we worked a lot with community stories. We collected oral histories and pored through recordings and transcripts from the local WPA Oral History Project.

One of those early plays is *Red Fox/Second Hangin'*. It's about the coming of the industrialists to the mountains and the two hangings that result from their new coalfield law and order. We set out to test which of the two radically different versions of this important story was more accurate: the written history or the people's oral history.

We collected a lot of oral histories. We got up into the old courthouse, found the actual courthouse records of the two trials that led to the two hangings. Got into the newspaper morgues in the different states. Crafted a play, and started performing it around here.

In the warmer months, we would pitch a revival tent up the hollers hereabouts in

> **The idea of taking offense at interruption is actually a minor tradition in the history of theatre. It just happens to be the one that's prevalent in the U.S. right now.**

eastern Kentucky, southern West Virginia, and southwest Virginia. People are used to revival tents, and we would paper the holler with fliers, knock on doors. In the afternoon, we'd do a free kids' show of traditional Appalachian tales and music, and then the big show that night. People would stream in to hear about the coming of king coal, a story in which they still had a stake.

I can remember on many occasions that we'd be somewhere in the middle of this play and an audience member would just interrupt the performance, and say, "Well, you're missing a piece of information here." And then, he or she would rattle off the information. Or, someone would interrupt and say, "Well, I heard a different story and it goes like this ...."

That's the kind of ownership of the play local people felt. And we encouraged it. It turned out in this instance that the people's version was more historically accurate than the version written by the industrialists.

So you take interruptions and conversation as a positive thing as opposed to, for more traditional theatres, the idea that an audience interrupting the narrative and the emotional flow as a negative.

I think the idea of taking offense at interruption is actually a minor tradition in the history of theatre. It just happens to be the one that's prevalent in the U.S. right now. If we were to survey theatre around the world, I think we would conclude that call and response in some form is more the rule than the exception.

How would you describe the effect you're trying to have on your audiences? What do you want to happen to the audience in the course of experiencing the work?

We want the audience to find a closer relationship with their own story and with the stories of others -- and the Other. We, for example, do a lot of intercultural work. One of the ensembles we've collaborated with for almost three decades is a black theatre company from New Orleans called Junebug Productions. We've made a lot of plays together, including a play called *Junebug/Jack*, which examines through music and story the historical relationship between black and white working class people in the South.

So, the trick, for us while on tour, was how in the world are we going to get black and white working class people to come to the play? And if we don't get black and white working class people to come to the play, haven't we defeated the play's purpose?

So, we had a problem, because black and white working class people, in the main, do not attend professional touring theatre. In fact, in the main black and white working class people don't typically go on social outings together. We solved the problem, after some amount of experimentation, by saying that any community wanting to present the play had to pull together an ecumenical choir to perform in the show. This would be some singers from the black church, some from the white church, a few from the women's chorus, maybe some from the high school. An inclusive community chorus, if you will.

We would send the new chorus the show's music several months in advance of our arrival. They would select someone from their community to serve as chorus master to conduct their rehearsals. And then a few days before the performance, I would arrive and stage the chorus members into the production – even giving them some choice lines to memorize.

Well, a lot of things happened in the course of this process. For starters, the play's presenter had to begin thinking about her whole community. The singers didn't come together because of the play's theme of the relationship between race and class. They came together because they loved to sing, and this professional play looked like a good opportunity to shine. In the course of rehearsing the music, the singers hit on a new sound that had really never been heard in the community, simply because all those different voices had never been brought together before, and certainly not with the particular intention of the play's content.

The word went around that there was a kind of new sound going down. And it was local: "It's our sound, it's coming from so and so who lives just six houses that way." Young people got interested because it wasn't the same-old. So, by the time the show went up, all the community turned out. And of course it didn't hurt that all the churches had to show up to support their choir members.

Because the performances enabled people to feel confident about their role

329

> We want the performance to be meaningful to the people who are in the audience. They take the risk of attending, because they think they're going to get something meaningful out of it.

as singers and about their own traditions, cultural chips on shoulders fell away. Everyone was eager to witness and to learn more about the other traditions; to experience how the black people sang, or how the white people sang, or what inflections young people brought to the song.

It really took off as a community happening. And then, from these performances, we would break into our story circles. And the community would now be charged up and feel a new permission to tell stories that maybe they had never told to each other, because white and black people and young and older hadn't been together in that trustful way before.

In those circles, you would often get a recounting of some local racial incident. But instead of hearing it in one dimension, you were now hearing it from two or three different, distinct personal perspectives. And so for the first time the community was telling their own story to themselves in a new, more complex way. That really charges up a community.

Your model relies on the storytelling as not only the formal part of the presentation, but also as the way that audiences interact with the experience afterwards. I imagine that makes for a very memorable performance. Is that a goal of Roadside's, to have performances that stick in the brains of the people that see them? Or is that simply a side effect?

Well, we don't say to ourselves we want this performance to stick in the brains of the people who see it, but you're right. We want the performance to be meaningful to the people who are in the audience -- the majority of whom are not accustomed to attending professional theatre. They take the risk of attending, because they think they're going to get something meaningful out of it.

As we know, people who are on the short end of the economic stick don't have as much free time as people who are wealthy. So, they have to be intentional about how they spend their time and money. That is important to us. When we're creating a play, before we get very far into the process, we think, "Here's our theme, what effect do we want to have, and how might it be useful to audience members?"

So, in the *Junebug/Jack* example, we wanted the play to help the community open up a much more realistic dialogue in the present tense about race and class. And that means coming to some understanding of the history of race and class generally in the South, but also, then, through the story circles, moving into the particular history of that community. We want to stimulate dialogue and then to leave something in place so that the dialogue will continue after we leave.

So you are always working from a larger impulse. Theatre is a means to a larger end, a bigger conversation.

Yeah. And it used to be that wasn't so unusual. There was a lot of action around this idea, coming out of the '60s, into the '70s, and even continuing into the '80s. And then you have something happen with the election of Ronald Reagan. Before that, nonprofit cultural organizations inspired by the southern civil rights movement, like the Caribbean Cultural Center in New York City and Appalshop, were as much about the public humanities as they were about the arts. For example, until 1981 the NEH, not NEA, was Appalshop's largest source of public support.

In the late 1970s, Appalshop began receiving a series of grants from the NEH to plan, script, and produce a seven-part documentary film series on the history of Appalachia. We had just finished the pilot film of the series when William Bennett took over as NEH chair and immediately—and without discussion—canceled all future funding for our project. And that begins a political trend of suppressing people's voices and histories in the little nonprofit arts and humanities sector.

That has certainly been my experience, based on what has happened to Appalshop and its peer organizations, and in such political circumstances one then has to spend significant time fighting for a different culture policy just in order to carve out some space to be able to do the creative work.

And that political trend has led to a solidification of what might be called the "traditional theatre?"

331

If by traditional theatre, you mean the Western European canon – yes. That tradition gained added strength after the Second World War with the rise of the nonprofit regional theatres. But even those theatres, when they were first created, had an impulse that was much closer to Roadside's, which was to tell their region's story. And then those regional theatres moved to an industrial assembly line production model. From the beginning, Roadside was an ensemble theatre, and never went toward that model -- of course, you can see how that model would be antithetical to what we were trying to do. I think that model is slowly fading in our new post-industrial era. If we remain a vibrant democracy, I expect U.S. theatre to return to its deeper roots – and thereby develop a much stronger relationship with so-called world theatre.

The fact that there was no professional Appalachian theatre before Roadside has been a great advantage in many ways. Every possibility was open to us. We felt very free to experiment, and we have continued to experiment with both form and content, drawing on our own indigenous theatrical traditions and co-creating plays, which are often bilingual, with other theatres steeped in their own cultural traditions. And we were lucky in that, pretty much right out of the chute, we were able to go to New York, where we were well-received, favorably covered by the press, and so on.

We never got caught in that psychology of feeling like, well, we may be good at home, but nobody would like us beyond here—which you would hope wouldn't matter, but it does. Never being burdened by that, we ranged out, experimented, and all the while tried to stay true to our founding values.

Once, I remember, we were performing at the Manhattan Theater Club, close to the beginning of our theatrical journey, and at intermission, I overheard two older women who were the type that had probably seen a play a week for the past 30 years. Clearly they were extremely knowledgeable about New York theatre. So the taller one leans over to her friend and says, "You know, Helen, these actors have the best Appalachian accents I've ever encountered."

Terrence Nolen
Arden Theatre Company

How old is your theatre now?

This is the 23rd season.

And you were one of the founders, right?

Yes, that's right.

How do you as the artistic director seek feedback from the audience about their experience in the show?

There's a constant stream of feedback. I include my email in the welcome letters included in our Stagebills, asking people for responses to a certain work, and there are a significant number of audience members who will email me after every show about how they responded to it. In addition, there's constant dialogue with board members and key stakeholders. Our annual giving group is called the Sylvan Society, and, in addition to all the opening nights, we typically host at least one Sylvan event per production, so there are lots of opportunities to continue the conversation.

We just closed *Superior Donuts*, and we invited our donors to join us during intermission for a donut and coffee, and either myself, Amy, or Ed Sobel, our associate artistic director, was there every night talking with our patrons. We're also constantly surveying our audiences; that's one of the reasons we're very interested to learn the results of this survey. And there's also a constant stream of reviews posted online as well as responses to our Arden blog entries and Facebook and Twitter posts, other kinds of new media conversations going on, and I try to stay apprised of all that. There's no shortage of feedback.

So it sounds like you really stay in the center of that, it doesn't get filtered through your marketing director. You're really hearing directly from a lot of audience members.

Yes, absolutely. Now, we send out a letter after every show to single ticket buyers saying, "Hey thanks for coming, what did you think, here's the next show." That comes from either our managing director or our marketing director.

> **If I look at the most successful productions throughout our history, most of the ones that have been most successful I never would have expected.**

And any feedback that comes in during the show to a house manager or a box office manager or through those letters gets sent to me as well.

We do a wide range of work at the Arden. We do work for kids, and it's a very different audience. I want to know what kids themselves think. After every show, I ask kids for suggestions of other stories, to figure out what they're engaged by, and what the most popular current books are, that I might not have heard of. With the kids work, we find that there ends up being two different responses. You have the full student group, 375 students and 25 teachers, versus our evening and weekend performances, when there are more parents in the crowd. I want to know what the parents and teachers – the gatekeepers – think; but more importantly, I want to know what the kids think.

We also do musicals and new plays, so I'm curious to see how different audiences respond to the wide range of work we're doing. We also have a lot of ongoing relationship with artists, with whom we're in constant communication. We've done, for example, eight productions of new plays by Michael Hollinger, over the past fifteen years. I'm always curious to see how audiences value that ongoing conversation with the playwright. It's something I really treasure, and I hope that our audiences do as well, but I'm trying to make sure my assumptions are based on as much feedback as possible.

How does that kind of play into your selection process either for the season or for development? Do you think about the impact you're trying to make on the audiences for a particular choice?

That's a very tricky question, obviously. In the past 23 years I can think of two examples where we chose something because we thought it would sell. One was twenty years ago when we were opening a new space. We thought that the name recognition of this piece would launch the space and expand our audience base. And no one came to see it. It was a really important lesson. If I look at the most successful productions throughout our history, most of the ones that have been most successful I never would have expected. So I've learned to embrace the idea that I don't know, so season selection can't be based exclusively on those guesses because at best, they're faulty. And that's something that I try to communicate to our board and staff, we just don't know for sure what will be popular with audiences. We have to follow our passions.

Do you think about specific ways that you want audiences to respond to shows?

Absolutely. Our mission is pretty simple; it's to tell great stories by great storytellers. And I think stories are a way to organize, at least through one lens, the complexity of living in this world and the complexity of being human. So I think more often than not our work tends to have a very human perspective. We're achieving, even if the work is epic in some way, this very intimate relationship with the audience.

How do you find the balance between your own response to a play and your sense of what the audience's response will be?

I can't think about it. I can't judge, so I don't. I gather as much feedback as possible, and I'm curious to see *afterwards* if my response matches or doesn't match the response of our audiences. But I don't think there's any value in that conjecture beforehand. Because I don't think I know. I try to follow my hunches yet embrace the unexpected.

Many years ago, I knew Jeanine Tesori, and I was sent a couple songs from her musical *Violet*, and I thought, "There's something about this voice that's just great. And there's something about what it's trying to do with the American musical that's different, that's truly unique." So even though it was only two songs, we decided to do it. And it wasn't until I was directing it, that I realized how deeply personal it felt, how connected I was to that piece, and how the spirit of her music carried with it so much beauty and meaning to me.

So a couple years later we were talking, and she was telling me about *Caroline, or Change* and working with Kushner. She sent me the script; I hadn't seen it yet. I read it and I just didn't get it. And my wife picked it up, (she's also the managing director of the theatre) read it, and came downstairs sobbing and saying, "We *have* to do this." And I said, "You're kidding me. Really?" So I read it again, and I had not listened to the music. In listening to the music I realized that I was drawn to it, and felt that I had a personal reason to do it, to try to enter into that piece. And I just ended up loving directing it, it was

> There are essential stories to tell. I am determined that we seek to bring to our stage stories that get at some essential part of what it means to be alive in a complex world.

as amazing a learning experience as any play I've ever done. It was remarkably successful in so many ways. And our audiences just—everything my wife first responded to when she sobbed, our audiences responded to, too.

So I try to stay open. And yes, there are certainly times where someone loves something, or a playwright with whom we have an ongoing relationship gives me a play, and I read it and I just don't get it, I don't feel compelled to do it.

I also have two boys now who are eleven and seven. They have helped refine my understanding of what kids are interested in. We were doing children stuff before they were born, but I now understand in my bones what kids are looking for in a theatrical experience, what kind of stories they're driven by.

There was a wonderful story told by a teacher on NPR, she was a kindergarten teacher who won a MacArthur Genius Award for her work with kids. And she was saying, for kids of that age, there's one story that they're consumed by: There was a baby deer and he was alone and he was walking through the woods and he met another deer and they played. There was a little fish that was swimming through the ocean and she met another fish and they played. And she said, "I could tell variations of that story all day, and they'd be consumed by it each time, because they are so consumed by the idea of, 'Will I be able to make and keep a friend, now that I'm leaving my parents? Is that what awaits me in the world?'" I retell that story time and again to remind our children's theatre writers and directors – and myself – that there are essential stories to tell. I may not be able to guess how an audience of kids will respond to a specific piece, but I am determined that we seek to bring to our stage stories that get at some essential part of what it means to be alive in a complex world.

So, over many years, you've developed your own responses and your understanding about how those can be a barometer.

Precisely. And there are artists with whom we've worked for many years that if they're really passionate about something, even if I don't fully understand it, even if I'm conflicted, I will follow their passion.

So they're also trustworthy choosers to you?

Exactly.

Has there been a time that you can remember when feedback from the audience affected your programming choices?

Sure. When we were launching our kids programming, we were doing stuff for age 6 to forever. And then, in our second year, we decided to move into work for teens as well. We did that for about five years, and some of the scripts were great but some were not. They weren't always telling great stories, they weren't always great plays, and they were sometimes "good for you" plays. We also realized that there were productions in our seasons like *Caroline, or Change*, which thousands of teens came to see, and that sort of programming was far more significant for them than the work that we were doing specifically for kids their age.

The last thing we wanted to do was work that a teenager would see and say, "Oh, I hate theatre." So we discontinued that programming.

Next year we're doing Tracy Letts' *August: Osage County* after producing Tracy Letts' *Superior Donuts*. This past year. Our production of *Superior Donuts* was extraordinary; audiences just went crazy for it, and there's so much excitement about *August: Osage*. So while *August* was not a show that I chose because of the success of *Donuts*, knowing that we have an anchor like that in the season is a extremely helpful as we program and budget for next season.

You were preparing the audience in a way?

Yes, that was certainly the hope. If people didn't like *Superior Donuts* we still would have been doing *August: Osage*, but we try to capitalize on those opportunities when they happen. It's more about capitalizing on success rather than making decisions dictated by it. We're still very much aware that if there's not the passion on our part for the production, there's no reason to do it.

How do you think these new tools in the intrinsic impact study will be useful in your artistic process?

I am very curious to see the results of this study. Especially since we've surveyed audiences for three very different plays, I have a very strong hunch of what those results will be, and I'm curious to see whether they'll match my

337

hunches or not.

I value feedback; I crave it.

I want our work to change lives. So I think more than anything, this type of work parallels what I'm most interested in understanding about our audiences, and have been interested in understanding for the last twenty years.

I treasure the anecdotal evidence of how our work can have a significant impact. Such as the board member who fills up with tears when he talks about the new play we produced and the scene when two older sisters re-enacted a childhood game. This board member is politically very conservative and yet even though our politics are very far apart, when it comes to this depiction of family and legacy, we connect. Or when kids talk about their favorite children's theatre production from five years ago, or have seen shows at the Arden for ten years and can talk about how this one or that one made them feel. That's what I treasure most. I have no idea how that might be quantified in this intrinsic impact work, but. this study certainly sounds like it's pursuing what we've been pursuing.

So you're interested in gathering these anecdotes of change in an audience member?

Yes. Now how the information from this study will affect what we do, I don't know. I think I'll always invest first and foremost, in passions and dreams. I'll always begin there.

But I value feedback; I crave it. And that informs future decisions. For example, with our work for kids, we are always building on what our audiences have taught us. The first time I watch a show with an audience, there are these light bulbs: "Oh, that's how they are seeing this story. That's what they're consumed by." And though we've been creating work for kids for years now, I never know how a story might connect until I watch the first audience. All of a sudden there'll be a particular response from the kids and I'll think, "Oh, of course. Of course they're silent there." A little tiny bit of…something… that is very powerful.

David Dower
Arena Stage

The first place I wanted to start is to ask you, what types of audience feedback are currently shared with artistic staff?

The main avenue of artistic response from our audience is through the talkbacks, and those are run by the artistic team. At least five and often many more times during the run, somebody from my office is sitting with the audience to talk about the show. Just about half of the projects we do each year have some sort of humanities-related event where there will be experts on the content. Generally, they take place on the weekends after matinees, before evening performances, and there'll be an expert on stage talking about their experience of seeing the play and inviting the audience to talk back about it. So it's more anecdotal. And then, a number of people in the artistic staff and I, we spend a lot of time in the lobby. So that's the main way we get it, is anecdotally.

In terms of actual research, when the marketing department is doing their research, if artistic impact is addressed in any way, or artistic feedback is collected in any way, it generally goes to Molly [Smith, Arena's artistic director], if there is some. And then there are always very marketing-focused series of focus groups that go on around the announcement of the season and how to talk about the season. And so there's not really any formal method at play here for understanding the audience's response to our artistic decision-making for sure.

Elsewhere, Molly has referred to the volume of letters she gets in response to the work that goes on here. Does she share them?

Molly is sort of a first-name artistic director here. People call her Molly and write letters to, "Dear Molly," which we have encouraged, and so people have that sense of her as being on the other end of the letter when they mail it—and she actually is. She shares some things. What is shared are the positive letters, and where there's something critical, I may hear about it indirectly, but it's not generally shared. So it's maybe a discussion between her and I don't know whom, and possibly me. But, I think mostly the negative things aren't shared.

In terms of impact, is this play addressing a stakeholder community that is not otherwise adequately addressed in the season?

For example, with *Next to Normal*, we got a lot of letters from our older patrons that the show was just too loud. Half a dozen letters, which is a lot about the same topic, and so there was pressure going toward the production to deal with the volume, and I didn't know its source until I went back to Molly and asked her, "Why is there so much tension about the volume in the theatre?" And she said, "We were getting these letters so I asked them to turn it down," which of course the producer didn't want to do. So I know that there are those kinds of moments that I don't really see, but as the artistic director she would see them.

When you're in the process of looking or choosing an artist or production, are you curating impact? Are you thinking about what kind of audience response Arena sort of desires overall or particularly?

We know that we have a number of different constituencies, though these are more from marketing research and given to us in the artistic department. We have this group of people, the largest group of people, who are sort of event-based single ticket buyers that respond to the classic American musical or to comedy blah blah blah, and that's the biggest part of our audience. But we also have a very significant African-American audience. They sometimes crossover into events or into comedies and vice versa. We have a small audience that is driven by new plays, and we have this sort of stable, though not necessarily growing, subscriber audience that is really attached to the institution and just needs to know why this play is part of the institutional strategy.

And so we end up having to address all of that as a matter of first priority in the season planning process: "Are we talking to those various constituencies?" "In terms of impact, is this play addressing a stakeholder community that is not otherwise adequately addressed in the season?" "Are we over-focused in this group of projects on any particular affinity group within our general audience?" And so it's much more of a market-driven set of questions.

After the fact, we end up trying to figure out, "Okay, so these are the choices we've made, how do these start a conversation? What are the conversations being started?" It's kind of where my job really picks up—once we've gotten through the decision-making process then it's my job to make sure that those plays achieve the overall goal of the season in terms of why we selected them as a group, and then individually what were we expecting this play to do in terms of community impact and audience impact. So that's how we allocate resources to things like which ones have panel conversations and which ones we focus primarily on groups and getting our artists out in the communities where there are groups of ticket buyers to interact with in that way. So, in a way, we get much more involved in the intrinsic impact of the decisions *post-decision*.

Can you give me an example of how you've phrased the desired community impact of a particular recent play?

Oh, sure. Anna Deavere Smith's *Let Me Down Easy*. She, as an artist, had already articulated why she wanted to be in Washington. She wanted to be in Washington, she wanted to be at Arena, because she wanted that peculiar mix that Washington can bring of power brokers, policy makers, local educated theatre audiences, and a community impacted by the issues of the play. And so she was particularly interested that this play created a dialogue at the intersection of these communities. So we spent a lot of time, for example, reaching out through healthcare worker unions and the Community Health Foundation, and other places to make sure that some of those stakeholders in her work were in the audience. But then we hired a separate publicist to go get Kathleen Sibelius and Eric Holder and the Supreme Court justices and all those people in the audience. That person also set up events for her at the National Institutes of Health, and she did one at Sibelius' office for all the employees in the department. She did appearances on the Hill and at the White House that were all associated with the play and followed on people having come to the play first to see it before they had a conversation with her. She did events at the Aspen Institute and other things that are kind of Washington-based opportunities. Then we also surrounded the play with a series of panel conversations on different aspects of the issues, every weekend there was a panel and then a whole series of talkbacks. We often are more apt to start from the artist than anywhere else to say, "What's your goal for the impact of this project here?"

Ruined is another perfect example. We have so many partnerships with *Ruined*

> Everything becomes analyzed on the level of its ability to discharge that responsibility to the community effectively and inside the art, rather than creating separate events outside the art to do it.

in the global NGO world right now, it's kind of overwhelming, the number of different community partners there are on this play right now. And it's very interesting—there's almost more of that activity than there is regular audience activity because the play speaks so immediately to activists, and when you read the marketing copy it's a little scary to the casual theatregoer.

So, your work on impact generally comes after choosing the play?

Yes. But—it's a conversation at the time we're choosing plays. We're sort of anticipating—for example, in the choice of *Ruined*, knowing that we were going to be balancing this heavy subject matter with the importance of the play as a tool to create awareness and activism around the issues. In the conversation around choosing it, we were already trying to understand, is there a value in its favor on the level of its community impact… we kind of talk about it from a stewardship standpoint, I guess, I'm struggling with the word a little bit. And this comes from the fact that we have just built this new building and there's $30 million worth of city money in it from a city that didn't have any money to give to it, in a way. It's a huge investment they made in this building, and so we take a serious responsibility, and we're held to a serious level of responsibility as a citizen of both the local community and the federal community. We have to understand whether we're speaking to that responsibility.

So when we have *Ruined*, then we know we're doing the part of it that has to do with civic discourse around global issues that matter in our community. When we're doing even something as simple as *Music Man*, it's really immediately about, "What are the opportunities to involve the school communities that we are committed to serving?" "What are the opportunities for school bands to participate in the event of *Music Man*? How does that become an opportunity for us to play with them, and for this to be a place for them to play?"

So pretty much everything, because of the stewardship responsibility that we took with this public money, becomes analyzed on the level of its ability to discharge that responsibility effectively and inside the art, rather than creating separate events outside the art to do it.

As you're looking at all those different factors in choosing plays, what for you is the balance between your personal response to a play or an artist and how the audience may or may not go for that choice?

Since I'm ultimately not the decider, I get to spend a lot more time in the pure world of, "This is an important play regardless of what the audience response is going to be, and we should be good enough as an organization at this point to go find the audience for this play." I always come back to that great scene in *Slings and Arrows*, that terrific lunch where the managing director is asking the new president of the board for more money, and the president responds, "I sell *water*. And it's *free*. You should be able to sell tickets; you don't need more money for me. I sell *water*." I often find myself sounding like that guy: "People buy *water*! *Water*! Of course they're going to pay for this play!" But that's only because I'm not ultimately responsible, you know.

Another artistic director said to me that one of the things he feels like is that it's his job is to protect the rest of the artistic staff from having to think too much about the audience response.

I wouldn't say that it's that formal here, but that would be nice. Molly says, and she means it, that she has to own something in her gut, it has to really belong to her as a choice in order for her to do it. So she'll wind up in places where I'm often the one who is pushing for opening the lens wider than just what she owns naturally. And sometimes that's beneficial, and sometimes we end up in a situation where there's a play that isn't resident in her gut and I'm still trying to make it go here, and that's a big challenge.

And that's back to that thing that we all know, that there's all these other factors, but ultimately the artistic director has to love the play.

Yes, and part of loving the play has to be loving the potential for the play to achieve whatever its purpose is. This stewardship role, that's a big factor for her. What is this play going to do in the world?

I was surprised and delighted when I got here. It's one thing to have your general audience and your Berkeley professors, who are a big impact community as well, in terms of the way issues develop and are framed in our culture. But to really be talking directly to the Congress, to actual members of Congress, at a moment when they're talking about defunding the arts in general—that's a different level of immediacy to what is going on in Berkeley.

Can you think of a time when feedback from the Arena audience changed programming decisions?

Absolutely. One of the areas where we're still finding our confidence and our voice is in the programming with the African American community. *The Good Negro* is a perfect example. We were very interested in the play, pretty much planning to do it, and then we did a reading of it here. But there were significant reactions that caused us to back away from the play. Molly ended up programming *Resurrection* in that slot instead, because it was a much closer match to the feedback that she had gotten from the audience. They just were not interested in that story about Martin Luther King. And what ended up happening, the result of that change, is that we did a play that wasn't ready, that was not fully embraced artistically as we were moving into it. Ultimately, in the end, pretty much the same set of people who had reacted to *The Good Negro* felt as though this play was going backwards in terms of the dialogue around African American men in our community.

Now, Daniel Beaty has since turned *Resurrection* into a solo piece called *Through the Night* that is still running in New York, and he's had great success with it. But for sure, the African American community in DC, they have had an impact on our decisions by virtue of doing the development process on work.

And I think, I'm not sure, but it's probably true that it has happened in other readings. But that was the first time that that had happened to me, and I was very surprised by it. It was a very extreme turnaround, and we were actually in conversation with two other organizations about a three-way co-production on the premiere of the play, so it was very disruptive to everyone, not least the playwright and the director, that we didn't do it. It was bad.

Do you have any concerns about how this research into intrinsic impact might play out? Worries about how the tools will be used?

The only way in which I would have a concern is if it goes opposite to how I think it's going to go. One of the challenges that we always have here, and I think it's not unlike other places, though I think it's perhaps extreme here—because of the balance in our revenue model (we're now at seventy-something percent earned income now, which is just nuts), because of that balance we're already overly determined by the marketing projections on our artistic ideas. And so I have been really interested in this study as a way to have other ways to talk about why we could or how we could value these choices as a hedge against simple thumbs up/thumbs down based on box office potential. The only way I feel like this could become a challenge is if the findings somehow become more marketing focused and driven, so they become yet more of a litmus test for artistic choices to pass some market test. Right now, we are without defenses against a strong case from the marketing department that a choice is not going to serve us budgetarily. I think I could make the intrinsic impact case as an antidote to that, to weaken that sort of lock-step response around the numbers. But if somehow it becomes first and foremost a tool of the marketing department to measure toward the same end, if it becomes sort of euphemisms for box office success, of what's the easiest thing to sell, then I'll be in trouble.

On the flipside of that, what are some things that you're hoping will come out of the study that will help you and help Molly in your artistic process?

To my view, it's much less about helping Molly or helping the artistic staff than it is about coming up with ways to help the rest of the staff understand the artistic purpose at the center of our mission. It's quite easy to become enamored of the sort of P&L analysis of nonprofit theatre producing, and also to be looking for the things that are going to make some part of these challenging lives we lead in the theatre easier. So, to put people back in the frame of, "The reason any of this is happening at all, the reason to spend any ounce of energy, or the first penny, on this work, is because it matters to the quality of life in the world around us"—that's what I think this is for. My hope is that we will come through this process with a better understanding of the ways in which our work matters and will be able to better articulate it within the staff and beyond, within our donor community and our media relationships—all these places that help determine whether or not the artistic life of the organization is viable and responsible to its purpose. So to me it's far less about helping us understand ourselves and our work.

The other thing that I know it's going to do is help us understand how and where to allocate resources like money and personnel to expanding and activating the full potential of something in a way that can fully impact an important community of ours.

Right now, we make these choices based on the artistic staff looking at the season and saying, "Oh, there are sort of obvious links here, reasons we would make it go off in the community." Really helping to understand the "what" and "why" of something like *Virginia Woolf* on an intrinsic level—what actually happens to the audience here when they see something of such quality from another city without having to travel to see it: to go beyond the kind of thumbs up/thumbs down, to discover what else mattered to them about it, to be able to activate in the less obvious moments and go deeper into some of the less issue-driven, less obvious groups of people involved here. Like our subscriber community—they come to everything we do, but I don't think we fully understand what the intrinsic values are that they're looking for when they come, or are getting when they're here. This work will help us better talk to them as an artistic staff, here in the building or before they come. It will help us set them up for that impact.

Bonnie Metzgar
About Face Theatre

How do you currently seek feedback from your audience about what they thought about a show, what their experience was?

I'm really interested in what you guys are doing and think it's really cool. At About Face, we have two main components of what we do. One is the mainstage season, which is kind of a professional theatre that is both a mainstage season and this XYZ Festival of new works that's ongoing. Then we have our youth program. We do present work that's created by the youth program as part of our mainstage season, but also have a tour through Chicago Public Schools.

One thing that we can do as artistic directors and artistic leaders is prepare the audience for what the experience is that they're going to have. I think for my audience, they want to know, "Is this going to be something that at the end of the play is going to have me get up and want to take an action? or, "Is it going to be more of an artistic event, where it's a story that I'm going to be reflective and perhaps more of the intrinsic impact that you guys are thinking about?" How do you measure the footprint in the sand? Were they surprised and did they like being surprised?

We're in the middle of a really intense strategic planning process here, and we're starting to do something you guys might think interesting, although somewhat provocative, I think, where we're contemplating splitting our programming into two different veins, one being "art" and the other being "impact." Because in some ways, About Face is much more comfortable in the role of the intermediary between advocacy and art, because when we're teaching our youth program, we're right out there, saying, "We are nurturing young artists and activists—and therefore leaders." But in that work, what people want from their artistic experience is very different.

In our mainstage work, we have surveys that are in the program. The return rate of those is not great, though it depends on the show. Some of our shows we do a curtain speech, and when we plug the survey in the curtain speech we get more people who fill it out.

> A lot of my work here has been about preaching the good word that discomfort is okay and community building is good but hard.

Does the survey ask questions about what they thought about the show or does it just ask more demographic questions and that sort of thing?

It definitely asks what they thought about the show. We're interested in these really specific ideas. We ask questions like, ""Is this the kind of work you think About Face Theatre should be doing?"

About Face is up against—and this is true of everyone but slightly different for us—the LBGT community is experiencing this big generation gap between people who identify as lesbian and gay and who are older, maybe 40-60 and have long been supporters of the work that we're doing, and the younger generation who experience our work.

Because of their own experience and history, these older patrons are still very hungry for coming out stories; they want to be told narratives in a certain way. They are, by and large, our core membership support. But then there are younger audiences who are much more fluid about identity, are much more sophisticated in a lot of ways, and want trans romance stories and things that my older audiences...well, it's outside of their comfort zone.

We want to get as much of that kind of feedback as we can, to be able to count who is in the audience. How is it breaking down in terms of their expectations and discomfort?

I am always around About Face. A lot of my work here since I've been here, and this is my fourth season, has been about preaching the good word that discomfort is okay and community building is good but hard.

We have got to get new people. We've got to convince them of why our work is important to them. We have to listen to what they are doing. We have to go into their communities. It takes time. We have to prepare ourselves for a new kind of success and "a new kind of success" may mean having very few people in the audience at certain moments. Yet those 10 people who came from that new community, who four or five years down the road we're going to have a vibrant relationship with, that's a really important group of people.

Now for the immediate bean counting, that can be perceived as not a success. But if you only count bodies and you're not looking at who those bodies are, you're not seeing everything. Are 30 people of the small group that has supported us over a long time, are they worth the same as the 10 bodies of this new community that we are cultivating? What's the goal, what is the message that we're using to reach out and build this new audience? What are these events that we are creating with them? What are our expectations?

> What's the goal, what is the message that we're using to reach out and build this new audience? What are these events that we are creating for them? What are our expectations?

I feel like that's a lot of what I spend my time on now. It's going to pay off, as we are building our future relevancy with larger groups of people. The work of About Face Theatre is to get into communities that are not as comfortable with who we are, and are not part of this dialog every day, and who we want to be talking to and we want to be having our work in front of.

And we need to measure who those people are. So, yes, I'm asking demographic information, but I'm also asking other kind of questions about "how they respond to the story" and "were there new things they had never thought about in the story," that kind of thing.

We also have moments where all the documentation is done over the phone. We talk to audience members—either my artistic associates from the show or myself. People talk to us at intermission. We ask them. We want to know from anyone who is there what they think about the show.

It sounds like you do a lot of balancing between asking your audience what stories they want to hear and then also trying to, as you said, "Preach the gospel of discomfort." Can you talk about how that balancing act works for you when you are selecting a play or selecting a season?

In general, when I make theatre in the context of a theatre company, I like a lot of involvement by a lot of people. About Face has this incredible group of artists, these artistic associates. One of the things I've done while I've been here is really activate that group. They have a lot of input in terms of season

What I want is to be working the muscle of advocacy in all aspects of what we do.

planning. Really what I want is, again, is to be working the muscle of advocacy in all aspects of what we do.

They are welcome to advocate passionately for any of the projects that are on the table. I give them scripts and invite them to make the argument. When you submit a play to About Face Theatre, as a playwright, you not only submit your play, you've got to write me a letter and convince me just from the letter before I see your play why your play sits inside of the mission of About Face Theatre and why we should read it. It's not until after I get that letter and I get that argument, that advocacy, that I say, "Yes, I want to read that play." This is in our mission.

Our mission is to advance the national dialogue on sexuality and gender. You can act from the negative side and say "We don't have enough right now," and focus on that, or you can focus on "What are the opportunities I have right now? What are our opportunities to get out of this mess? Where do we want to build first?"

Okay, a hurricane came and knocked down all of our houses. Where do we want to build first? You can spend a whole lot of time focusing on the friggin' hurricane that came through and that our house is knocked down, but ultimately if you can get everyone building houses and get them excited about why you're building this particular house, then the next one's going to be that house over there then all of a sudden everyone's moving in the same direction.

There's got to be a lot of dialogue. That's what we do. At the same time, I have a board that is eager to also have measurable box office success because it's a company that has, at different times, seen more box office success.

I always have many more projects that I want than I'm able to shoehorn and squeeze into the season, so we have to choose. We have to choose from which community outreach or impact show are we doing and for what reason and why is that one coming first before the other?

It's really about testing within this ecosystem of About Face Theatre, asking myself, "What are we all the most passionate about in terms of the different projects?"

350

I really allow each project to have its own goals and its own success. That may mean it has its own particular audience. It's not about trying to sell a season that all the same people are going to want to come to. I believe if we do the right thing, we are articulating this discomfort—the challenge of crossing the culture. If you can make a work seem beautiful in its challenge, people will want to come.

That's some of what I'm doing. For example, I just did this Sylvan Oswald piece, a trans love story. There is nothing that makes people more uncomfortable right now than trans people, even my audience. You've got to include glossaries. You have to have handouts at the lobby. There's a post-show discussion for anyone that wants to come.

All that kind of stuff where you're ready to talk to them, and be able to talk about why the work is important, and hear what they think, and all their questions and things they never thought about—that's the important stuff. And for each show it's different, so with season planning, I really treat each show very much as its own project. Then, once they're chosen, I look at them and ask, "Are these the five endeavors we want to be doing next year?"

Once we understand what they are, are there overlaps? How can I bring this thing into that project? Once they're chosen, we sort of lace them more together.

Is that how it works with the XYZ Festival of new work, too?

Our XYZ Festival, which we do every year, is different. It's really about making the organic messiness of us making things really apparent to the audience. They come along. Sometimes they're in a gallery and someone's just shoved a bunch of video in their show and you see 45 minutes of just a big mess and then they talk to the artist. The whole idea with the XYZ Festival is, after every single piece, the artists talk about where they are in the process and what they've been working on for the two weeks or however long they've been working.

It really is more like an open lab structure where it's about getting input directly from the audience, not only their thoughts on the artist's work, but also the audience experience. They're set up like labs.

When you're selecting work, is the group really limited to your artistic team, or does your process somehow include your audience or community—the people

> We all want something different from the theatre. We are all very individual audience members who want something different.

We have not actively included the audience in the selection process. The only way that we've ever really done that is that in the XYZ Festival, in which we have a People's Choice. It's an open submission, and we get somewhere between 200 and 300 submissions. Those submissions, they go out to a first round of readers across the country. Each project goes out to two readers. They come back. Internally, we narrow it down to 20 that then go out to a panel. Now, we are committed that every year, the XYZ Festival has at least one Chicago-based artist, usually there are more. But, with this People's Choice, what we do is we choose two plays. They are both by Chicago playwrights.

The playwrights are asked if they want to be part of the People's Choice. Then PDF's of those plays are made available for anyone who would like to read them. Then we basically have a night at the bar that anyone can come to, the XYZ People's Choice night, and anyone who wants to can come and vote.

People come and they vote for the people's choice and that then is included in the XYZ Festival, whichever of the two plays. It's really fun. It does require people to read two plays, however.

You talked about dividing the work into "art" and "impact?" How would you characterize the difference between the outcomes of those two sorts of projects?

Well, here's the thing. I'll tell you the reason that we're doing this. As I was saying—and although this is obvious, we don't, in the theatre, really acknowledge it all the time because it's difficult—but we all want something different from the theatre. We are all very individual audience members who want something different, right?

I teach a lot of playwriting. This is something I teach all the time. There is not a "good play" and a "bad play." There may be a play that someone thinks has more craft or one that resonates more with more people. But we all respond differently to plays.

My mother always wants a happy ending. You don't ever want to send my mother to something where it goes badly at the end because she's going to hate it, and she's going to be angry.

The same is true for programming. The company where I used to work, Chip Walton, who is the artistic director there, in his curtain speech every single night, would say, "If you like everything we do, we are not doing our job." Because the whole idea is, we're a risky theatre. Risky theatre means that we're going to do some things that you don't like. If you say that, people begin to understand. "Oh, this is all an experiment. People like different things. It's cool. If I don't like it there's something interesting in the experiment that I can focus on."

But it requires talking to people about that. So, here at About Face Theatre, we've been asking ourselves this question about relevancy, but I think when we ask different people, they think it means different things.

Some of my board members, some of my artists, some of my youth, half of them think that what we should be doing is "art." Art requires no explanation. And, in fact, the better art, it's like the Richard Serra sculpture. If you walk all the way around it, you still don't know what shape it is. When we make art, there is something mysterious about what we do, which is what draws us to it. I think that is sort of what you guys are getting to in this study. And so part of what we need to focus on at About Face Theatre is making excellent art—and not art-in-dialogue with these questions of sexuality and gender. There's a group you thinks it's really more interesting as art if those dots are not connected.

And then there's this other half of my stakeholders who believe, "No, we need to be putting out narratives that incite people to action—that make them want to go out and change the world. We need to have programs for youth that train them to act with integrity and have principles that are designed specifically for community impact."

Where I have come from, from the beginning of being here, is, "Oh, my God, the most beautiful thing about this organization is that we are trying to do both these things, and that we're not always only speaking to just one kind of people." We're not only speaking to people who like things a little more obtuse and challenging and sophisticated. We're not only talking to people who want advocacy and messaging. We actually, at different times, are creating work that uses all of these different strategies across a really beautiful horizon.

Some of that may be because I was at the Public Theater for a long time—a company that also serves a huge aesthetic horizon, a huge cultural horizon, etc.

One of the ways that we thought about doing this is we said to ourselves, "Perhaps our audience doesn't appreciate that we do both of these things. Would it be interesting for us to begin to think and inform our choices by calling?"

We haven't quite figured out the terminology, but that's one of the things that we are focusing on in the course of our strategic planning.

So, is the implication here that the kind of work that would live over in the "impact" category would it be less artistic? Would it be less "good?" Or would it be more that you would judge its success less on artistic quality and more on its impact?

Do you see a big dichotomy between artistic excellence and community impact? Can they exist together?

I don't think it's a question of quality—it's something else.

We perform often in short format. We do a lot of event performing that is invisible. Some of this is for people who are really, really jazzed and engaged with that aspect. For instance, we marched in the Pride parade. We had a big, big bunch of people who wanted to march with us. Now, is that either artistic *or* impact programming? I don't think so. I don't think that is. Because we didn't actually perform. In that case, we were just representing as a community.

What I would define as "impact" work is more when we do something that is specifically in partnership with a community organization dealing with a certain issue of some kind. It's much more issue-oriented, and maybe more narratively directed just at an issue. And that can be artful, too, but it's first about the issue. If we were doing a piece on marriage equality, for instance, I think there are still lots of ways that would be artful, but impactful, too.

So these are more labels. It's more a way for the audience to identify, "Oh, I really love those impact events that they do. What are the next three of those?"

I think ultimately it frees up some of the art projects from always having to carry that "issue" piece.

You're sort of sorting out the impulses a little bit, and helping the audience understand which thing they're coming to.

Right.

Looking at this from a slightly different angle, can you think of an example when feedback from the audience has caused you to make a shift in your programming?

A couple of things come to mind. The first thing, and this is more about Chicago—when I first came, I had been in New York for many years. Then I came to Chicago and I took this job. And the first thing that I did was I presented Taylor Mac, this performer and playwright who's based in New York, who at the time had just run two solo shows in rep that had sold out for all the months of the summer. He's a trans clown, and he's almost like a Shakespearean fool.

I brought Taylor out, and because Taylor is, as you know, he's incredibly charismatic and lovely, and his stories are amazing and they're full of magic. I thought, no problem. Well, I presented it at the Center on Halsted, which is our LGBTQ center here in Chicago for four weeks, which is much shorter than a usual run. Nobody came. It got warm reviews. They weren't raves, but they weren't "don't go see this play." It was like, "Oh, this is kind of a nice thing." The audiences that came loved it so much. They loved it, they loved it. All I got was positive feedback. But it was a 150-seat theatre, and we had a number of nights where we did not even have 10 people.

And what I learned in that situation was that the Chicago community is sort of consumed with its own ecosystem of performance and theatre. There's a reason why the Museum of Contemporary Art, when Yunjin Lee comes, it's for two performances over a weekend. It's because the curiosity of seeing something new here is somewhat tempered. You have to bring someone for two performances the first time, and then the next time for four performances, and then the next year maybe for two weeks. In New York, there is a desire to see the next really, really new thing. That drives everyone, because you're kind of embarrassed if you haven't seen it. That's just not the way that Chicago works.

And yet, I knew that from the feedback I got from the audience, there is a really

I wanted to be successful for the artist and for everyone.

interested audience here. It's smaller than I might have wanted, but it's an important audience. I want them to come and I want to build it. I just have to be better about how I can reach them, and again, I want it to be successful for the artist and for everyone. So here, what that means, is I need to present something like this for a weekend.

Another part of our strategic plan is getting into "many, many, many" rather than just having three or four shows that run for a long period of time. Because we want to do all this community building, we're going to start doing a lot more event-driven programming to reach all these different audiences in all the ways that they want to be reached, with many different relationships to artists, with many different relationships to the story, with many different relationships to each other.

It's cool to design programming that meets the audience where they are. It's not a failure. Bringing Taylor Mac for four performances where people love him and it's packed, that's a success. But we have to have the right expectations, because having our expectations being wrong—we have to change our visioning in order for our success model to change. We have to meet our audience where they are and recognize, "Oh, we're actually presenting work for you to come to. How many of you want to come? What shape should that take?" We have to respond to what our audience wants. That's success.

Diane Paulus
American Repertory Theatre

What are some ways that you currently, you or the artistic staff, seek feedback from the audience?

Well, the most common and frequent way we receive feedback is actually through a post-show email survey with every audience member. It usually includes 10 questions, and we always ask what they thought of the performance, as well as the administrative questions, like how they heard about the show and when did they buy their tickets and all that. We always ask for response to the actual content and what their experience was.

We also have a very active online community, and we receive a lot of feedback through social media. Comments that come to us via our website, Twitter and Facebook are forwarded on to administrative, front of house, and production staff.

I regularly get emails from audience members who just write in talking about the show or talking about their experience. So those are very powerful and very informative, especially with *Porgy and Bess*, which we just finished this past weekend. A primary audience development and outreach initiative for this production deepened our partnerships with schools and community organizations who attended the performances on substantially subsidized tickets alongside master classes, post-show discussions, and in-school workshops. Families, school children, and the elderly from underserved communities had access to the performances and enrichment activities.

And then, of course, because you've developed these relationships, there's a very logical and vibrant follow up. You're always receiving letters from students and from group organizers about the experience.

None of this is rocket science. I'm sure you're hearing this all over this country.

We also do a huge amount of post-show talks that give us immediate feedback in particular about the artistic work. And because we are affiliated with Harvard

University, we have a whole relationship with the student community. We teach classes that relate to the shows in our season.

So we have feedback coming kind of "hot off the presses" in the classroom from students who are seeing the production and then talking about it in class. So there are a lot of avenues that come to my ear.

And we've also done work encouraging our ambassadors. Of course, we have board members, but we also have an ambassador group made up of volunteers who help promote the theatre and talk about the shows and get out there in the community. We've encouraged, in a way, self-organization to happen. There are board members or friends of the theatre who have organized their own groups where they gather 10 to 20 friends in a home.

They do a meal, and the theme of the meal is related to the show. For *Porgy and Bess* they did a whole African American meets Jewish cuisine in one instance. And they have a discussion about the show. In that case we just had the person who organized it write into us and share all kinds of feedback that was bounced around at the dinner table about the production.

Porgy and Bess is an example where we were really committed to making conversation about the production. It was part and parcel of why we took the show into our season as part of what we were doing. It was simply too enormous of a project, with too much potential, to have it be just a "show with post-performance talkback" situation. It was really, "Let's make this educational."

I taught a class about *Porgy and Bess* in performance and context last spring. I gave lecture demonstrations about the history of the work in various venues leading up to the actual production.

We had members of the cast out in the schools working with kids. It was really, "How do we make this not just about the art on the stage but rather a point of departure to discuss African American history, issues of race and representation in art, culture meets politics in American 20th century history?"

That was the impetus around doing a show like *Porgy and Bess*.

Would you say that those efforts were sort of unusually comprehensive, or is that your usual level of engagement?

There was a lot of effort put into this show, I'll tell you. It would have been enough for our theatre to just undertake the largest-scale musical we've ever done. Huge orchestra, huge cast, big, big production. So it was unprecedented, I think, the amount of work we did side-by-side with it.

That's not to say the theatre hasn't done that sort of thing. We did a project last year that was really comprehensive. We were doing *Prometheus Bound* on our second stage and we were doing *Ajax* by Sophocles on the mainstage. And we did a discussion about war, war in our world, and what does it mean to look at these ancient Greek plays and meditate on current military situations and post-traumatic stress disorder.

To me, it's exactly what you hope for from the theatre. You don't hope that you make a theatre event, and then the ushers ask you to leave, and then that's the end of it. You work very hard to transform an audience so that the next thing can happen.

We partnered with Theater of War to moderate panels with cast members from *Ajax* as well as current conflict vets and active service persons. In the case of *Prometheus Bound*, which was presented on a smaller scale—it was a show in our club theatre where the capacity is 260 people—we partnered with Amnesty International. With Amnesty's guidance, we adopted different human rights cases from around the world which were shared with the audience following each performance.

So the performance of *Prometheus Bound* ended and part two, we called it, of the show was an Amnesty event. The audience was encouraged to stay, learn about whichever human rights case we were dedicating the performance to, finishing with a postcard signing campaign.

To me, it's exactly what you hope for from the theatre. You don't hope that you make a theatre event, and then the ushers ask you to leave, and then that's the end of it. You work very hard in a theatrical way to transform an audience so that the next thing can happen. We were really using the Prometheus story to say, "Here is the first prisoner of conscience"—and then to ask the audience, "How can his story relate to human rights cases and prisoners of conscience who are working all over the world today? How do their stories resonate?"

What is the reason for this theatrical event? What is the necessity for this show to happen? In my opinion, it's not good enough that it's good art. It has to be, what are the reasons why an audience is going to make time in their lives to come and engage?

As you're selecting a season or initiating a relationship with a play or a playwright, what kinds of ways do you think about impact on an audience? Are there particular kinds of impact that you're always shooting for, or a range of them over the season?

I think I'm always looking at, "What is the reason for the theatrical event?" And usually for me, "What is the necessity for this show to happen?" And then by necessity, it very quickly relates to, "What is the issue, what is the secret cause, what is the rallying cry that is going to get audiences out of their very busy lives to the theatre?"

In my opinion, it's not good enough that it's good art. That's just not enough anymore. It has to be, what are the reasons why an audience is going to make time in their lives to come and engage?

"Engage" is another important word for me. It's not about being passive. It's not about seeing a good piece of theatre that I take like it's my vitamin. No. Why do I have to go? What is the issue? What is the engagement? What is going to make me feel like I can't miss this?

And for me, it's always looking for artists that have, in a way, that larger question they're asking. That's the kind of work I gravitate to. Like Steven Sater, with *Prometheus Bound*, who sends me his translation of this Greek play and says, "Prometheus is the first prisoner of conscience."

And this is a play that was written 2,500 years ago that speaks to the issues of our day. And let's partner with Serj Tankian (of System of a Down) as the composer, who is a major human rights activist and writes for Amnesty. And let's get Amnesty International as a partner.

Artists that think that way lead to these kinds of moments. So it's always looking for an artist who is going to have a larger worldview on their work. How does what they're doing fit into the issues of our time, the necessity of what it means to be alive? How does what we're doing engage people as citizens more fully

360

in the world we live in?

Those are the kind of artists that I'm interested in nurturing or collaborating with, because I know that it's got to start with the work. You can't start with a work and then slap all this stuff on top of it. It's got to come from the inside out.

People have such different kinds of places they begin. So when you're programming and especially when you're creating a whole season, how do you balance between your own response to a play or to a particular artist and a sense of your audience or your sense of what audience response might be? How does that balancing act work for you?

Again, I very rarely think, as an artistic director, "I like this artist. We must do this artist." I really don't think that way. As much as I adore artists and I'm their greatest fan, I very rarely think about an artist and my personal interest in them. I'm looking at an artist and looking at who they are, what they're doing with their work, their form, and their issues. For me as an artistic director, I'm looking at what kind of noise this artist and their issues and their energy are going to make at my theatre.

> I very rarely think, as an artistic director, "I like this artist. We must do this artist." I really don't think that way. As much as I adore artists and I'm their greatest fan, I'm looking at what kind of noise this artist and their issues and their energy are going to make in my theatre.

And it's not, "Oh, our audience only likes this or only likes that." It's really, "What is the potential for engagement with this project?" That's it. That's a better way of saying it. What is the potential for engagement? And by "engagement" I mean engagement with the work, engagement with the issues, engagement with the dialog the show will create, engagement with our community, engagement with the thought leaders in our community who will then participate in the production and get excited about it.

So all of that, that's the core level at which I'm thinking about programming.

How does that play out over a multi-show season? Do you feel like there are different priorities with different slots or with different selections that you're

361

> **Engagement is intellectual. It's visceral. It's entertainment. It's social. Those are all valid forms of engagement for me.**

balancing against each other with this kind of as the overall?

I think about the quality and the level of engagement. There are different kinds of engagement. So we have a *Porgy and Bess*, which is all about the history of this work and the meaning of *Porgy and Bess* in the 20th century, how it's changed, where it's going, how is this production the next chapter in the history of this work. How do we inform people about what was radical in 1935 theatrically, what has changed over time? That's the priority. There is a lot of engagement to be done. How can we share this with the most diverse and broad audience in Boston?

The next show we have coming, which is *Three Pianos*, that's a different kind of engagement. I'm interested in that because of the show's form itself. I don't know if you know that show, but it recreates a *Schubertiade*—a salon that Schubert held with his friends in which he played his music for them. So built into the conception of the show is a total embracing of the audience's presence. Wine is served and poured multiple times throughout the evening.

The audience becomes a participant in this salon. The evening transforms from just these three guys playing piano as themselves to a journey through Schubert's life and inspirations.

So I'm looking at the show as, "Okay, it's Schubert. It's learning about his music and his life history, but you're also talking about an engagement that's a social engagement in the very form of the show." And, sure, does that kind of fit with maybe a holiday slot? Great! And it's kind of fun to come out of the cold when it's wintertime in Boston and everybody wants to come inside and feel like you're in a community and near each other and drinking wine with each other. Sure.

And then *Wild Swans*, which is the premiere of Jung Chang's best-selling memoir about 20th century China and the Cultural Revolution, that's a different kind of engagement. That's engaging with the largest international student body at Harvard, which is Chinese. And then you do a match, because you're not going to do that one in the summer when none of the students are here.

You're going to do it at a time when the students can take advantage of it.

So you're always looking at what's the quality and strength of the engagement and how do you program it at the right time of the year that will maximize our ability to make the engagement happen.

So engagement is sort of a constellation of things in your mind and then you're sort of looking at different aspects of it.

Yes, absolutely. It's intellectual. It's visceral. It's entertainment. It's social. Those all are valid forms of engagement for me.

And how do you know if the audience has been engaged in the ways that you hope? You talked in the beginning about some of the ways you are hearing back from people. Is it a kind of observation of the audience or is it about the level of response? How many emails you get, how many people stay for talkbacks?

Well, of course you're looking at how your box office is doing, because if a show picks up and word of mouth spreads you can feel there's a call to arms and word is spreading. I think even when a show doesn't ignite as fully as you'd hope at the box office, there is a test of how much the audience that is coming is engaged. And that does have to do with the quality of energy in the theatre, the vibrancy of the talkbacks.

When we did this one-man show about Buckminster Fuller, we went into the production with a "Bucky and Me" series with architects and scientists and biophysicists speaking at every show and installations in the lobby and interactive activities for kids. But it all came because that material was so rich. You could feel it.

It drives back to the choice. The A.R.T. is very committed to engaging the audience to create an experience of theatre that's not just the work on the stage, but what happens before, during, and after the event. So we're looking at programming shows that give us that food, give us that material that will allow us to create social moments, to create intellectual moments, to create community moments. That's how we're picking our shows.

Can you think of a time when feedback from the audience caused you to change a programming decision, whether that was a large thing like deciding to do a different show or not to do a show or whether it was around something smaller scale than that?

You know, to me, what I've learned from audience feedback is not as qualitative

> It's like when you have a sports team that people are passionate about. And they can criticize them freely and criticize the players for not playing well in a game, as the greatest sports fans do. We can't be afraid of that.

as—not as definitive as—"Oh, let's not program that, because of x." Its more, what I've learned from the audience feedback is the necessity and the importance of how you speak with your audience, and how you dialogue with your audience. The most important thing is that you're communicating with your audience.

My interest as an artistic director has been to try to make the audience care enough that they're engaged, and they're able and feel entitled to express opinion. It's never about, "I have to like everything." But if I can care enough that I can express my opinions and ideas and responses. It's like when you have a sports team that people are passionate about. And they can criticize them freely and criticize the players for not playing well in a game, as the greatest sports fans do. They'll criticize the referees, they'll criticize the coaches, they'll criticize the players.

We can't be afraid of that. We can't think, "Oh God, we're going to change the game here." No. It's rather, "How can we be in a dialogue with our audience, and talk to our audience?"

To me, you learn so much more if you're willing and able and committed to talking to your audience, and being in a relationship with them.

When you say, "my audience," who is it that you typically mean by that?

We have our small cadre of loyal subscribers. We have a growing membership base, which is an alternative to subscription. And we have the ever-growing single ticket buyer populace that is discovering the A.R.T. on a show-by-show basis, which then our challenge becomes about bringing them back. So I think when I talk about our audience, I think I'm talking about the audience of all those categories. Everybody.

And one may speak differently to those different constituencies, because a subscriber or a member has already indicated an interest across shows. And a single ticket buyer might very well just be interested in one show. And then the task becomes, "Will they convert? Will they remember their experience and therefore come back?" That's a different dialogue.

How do you talk to your audience about the choices and the work and getting them to have questions and reflect and think and not just say, "I liked it," "I didn't like it?" It's a much deeper, longer-term, more complex and more vibrant relationship to have, that dialogue with your audience.

It's a much deeper, longer-term, more complex and more vibrant relationship to have, that dialogue with your audience.

But I think that's the most important relationship to build, because that's the longer-term, deeper relationship. It's like a pedagogical relationship with your audience. You do that with your cast. You do that with your staff. You do that with your board. But what about your audience?

4 THE VALUE OF ART

No study on audiences would be complete without hearing from some of the people who actually fill our seats and donate to our companies. As part of a pilot project working from a set of questions developed by WolfBrown, we conducted four interviews with what might be termed "super consumers" of theatre—four people from different lifestages who all share a common, deep passion for theatre. The interviewees range from a former financial executive to a computer programmer, a high school student and a shy eleven-year-old and her mother. They are as idiosyncratic and revealing as one might hope, but underneath they also carry echoes of the intrinsic impact constructs: stories of social isolation giving way to communal experience, of aesthetic enjoyment leading to strong emotional response, of works that made these people think, care, dream, empathize and hope.

After gathering these interviews, we approached Arlene Goldbard, a well-regarded scholar and arts activist, to do a careful read of the four interviews and write an essay in response. What she came back with is out-of-the-box, completely unexpected, and exactly right for the assignment: a modern, arts-centric take on Plato's famous Symposium, *with seven dinner guests voicing various sides of the argument around what art does and how we should talk about it.*

We open this section with that essay, and then we close with the four interviews, a journey right the way round from anecdote to data and back to anecdote, proving most profoundly the need for both in this vital conversation about the impact of theatre on audiences.

Would you like to contribute your thoughts about why art matters to you? We have set up an ongoing survey that asks the same questions asked of these patrons, and will be periodically rolling out more responses through the web. Please visit http://www.theatrebayarea.org/intrinsicimpact for more information.

Symposium
Seven Characters in Search of an Audience
(with apologies to Plato)

by **Arlene Goldbard**

SETTING:

A private dining room at Symposium, a bar-restaurant in San Francisco. It's a comfortable room, with wood-paneled walls and upholstered chairs. There's a low hum of voices beyond the door, the occasional clink of dishes reminding people that they're in a restaurant, but nothing loud enough to disturb.

The Advocate has invited six guests to join in a convivial after-dinner chat. The six are comfortably arrayed around a long oval table, sipping from cups and glasses and nibbling on bits of cheese and small cakes their hostess ordered for them in advance. But she hasn't yet arrived. The subject is theatre.

PARTICIPANTS:

The Advocate *works for an arts service organization. She's in her late thirties, fast-talking, energetic, intelligent, hearty. Her father is Italian, her mother Chinese-American. She likes to confound members of each group by fitting into both, speaking a little Italian and a little Cantonese, joking about growing up on chow fun Marinara and provolone-filled bao.*

The Artist *is a playwright who works closely with a small theatre company she cofounded. Some of her plays have also been produced by other companies. She's still young, ambitious, half Lebanese (her mother's side) and half Irish*

371

(her father's). She constantly fusses with her mop of dark curls, often twirling a strand around a finger as she talks, deliberately, with long pauses. She's drinking red wine.

The Connoisseur *is a self-described intellectual, an aficionado of serious, mostly experimental performance. He is thin, pale, intense, with thick black-rimmed glasses: black shirt, black jeans, nearly white-blond hair, long on top, short at the sides, green eyes. He explains the eyes by saying, "Irish, on my father's side. I learned to love theatre as a choir boy." He's sipping black coffee, and at 29, young enough so it won't keep him up all night.*

The Exec *is a retired corporate executive. Mid-sixties, tall, expensively dressed, African American, gray at the temples. There's the tiniest hint in his speech of his Trinidadian heritage. He has season tickets to a couple of major repertory theatres, and serves on the board of the region's largest African American theatre company. His habitual expression is an amused half-smile, friendly, confident and tolerant. He holds a brandy glass, warming the liquor between his hands.*

The Amateur *acted in school and community plays from early childhood through adolescence. He now attends as many plays as possible, although he loves musicals most of all, and never misses a Broadway touring production. He has a cheerful, open, ruddy-cheeked face and thinning light-brown hair: he could be 40 or 50. He's wearing a blue pullover sweater with a collar, buttoned up. His vowels retain a hint of Upper-Midwestern roundness.*

The Acolyte *goes to nearly a hundred performances each year, almost every available production. He has olive skin, dark gray hair and deeply seamed cheeks. He could be Latin American or Arab—he speaks a little Arabic in fact, learned from his Egyptian Jewish mother. He has a retro-arty way of dressing. Tonight, it's all autumn colors: deep gold shirt, moss-green tie, tweed jacket with a touch of rust.*

The Teacher *works at a public high school. Her family is from Mexico. She speaks Spanish at home and English at school, with a girlish Californian cadence. She wears loose salt-and-pepper curls (mostly pepper, still), a soft green sweater and half-glasses on a chain. Her wide smile gives her an ageless quality, but she's probably in her early fifties.*

"So how did you all come to be here?" asks Teacher, grinning. "Do you know Advocate?"

"Not really," says Connoisseur. "I wonder where she is? It's a little odd to invite us and then not be here herself." People shrug: who knows?

"Perhaps she's just running a bit late," says Connoisseur. "I met her for the first time last night at an extremely interesting one-person show. She was sitting a row in front of me, two seats over. Just before the lights went down, she turned and whispered that if both of us weren't there, it would have been a one-person audience too. At intermission, she told me that she was working on that very problem right now, how to build the audience. We talked about it a little. After the show, she invited me here to continue the conversation. Quite an interesting notion, I thought."

Artist sighs. "God, I've known Advocate for ages. She texted me last week to ask if I would do this thing, so of course I said yes. What can I say?" Artist rolls her eyes, shrugging. "That's my policy: say yes unless there's some major reason not to. You never know how opportunity's going to find you. So here I am."

Exec lifts his glass, catching her eye. "I'll have to keep that policy in mind."

Artist looks momentarily flustered, rakes her fingers through her dark curls, then turns back to Teacher. "So what about you, anyway. How do you know her?"

"Well, not personally," says Teacher, polishing her glasses with a corner of her sweater. "But I already worship her. She has been getting my kids free tickets to shows for the past year, so of course, when she asked me to come, I said yes."

"Your kids?" asks Acolyte. "How many have you got?"

Teacher laughs. "The old woman who lived in a shoe? I have two of my own, a boy and girl. But I teach high school. So, in that sense, quite a few. Have you got kids?"

"No," says Acolyte. "But I spoil my niece and nephew. Are you a drama teacher? Ever since *Glee* started, that's been my secret dream job."

"Really?" says Artist. "You look like an architect."

Acolyte is startled. "How did you know?"

"The clothes," Artist says. "You look like an autumn leaf. Although I would have had to see your handwriting to cinch it."

Acolyte, a little deflated, takes another sip from his scotch rocks.

"I'll say this for *Glee*," Teacher tells them all, "it has attracted a much more interesting group of kids to try out for school plays." She turns back to Acolyte. "I teach English, actually. We no longer have a drama department—cutbacks, you know. A few of us take turns directing. It is fun. Exhausting sometimes, but fun."

A disembodied voice interrupts the conversation: "Truth time, people. How many of us were in a school play?" Advocate walks in trailing a little cloud of noise from the dining room. She's balancing a cardboard box in one arm while struggling to hold her other hand aloft. "Confession time. Show me your hands, people."

Teacher, Acolyte, Artist and Amateur raise their hands. "I played football," says Exec, chuckling. "Does that count?"

"What it lacks in character development," says Connoisseur, "it makes up in plot and action, hm? Ah well, it's all spectacle, I suppose."

"I knew you guys would hit it off," says Advocate, removing her coat. She tosses her head to get her long black hair out of the way. "Now, I want you to know that I'm not late because the freeway was a parking lot. Oh, no. I planned it this way to give you time to get acquainted."

"Whatever you say," says Amateur, looking affably skeptical. "You're the boss. Or maybe you're Hercule Poirot. We haven't quite figured it out. Waiting for the big *J'accuse!* speech."

"That's right," Advocate tells them, rolling up her sleeves. "I'm the boss here, and in a minute, I'm going to lock the door and not let you go to the bathroom for the next six hours." She scans their uneasy smiles. "That's a joke, friends."

"Glad to hear it," Exec says. "But since you are the boss—or at least the host—do you mind explaining why you asked us here?"

"Not at all." Advocate clears her throat, stands a little straighter. "I invited you because theatre matters to you, each in your own way." As she speaks, Advocate removes a small recording device from the cardboard box, setting it up in the center of the table. "And because I need help. I think you know the situation we face in the Bay Area. It's not much different from other parts of the country: there's an amazingly vibrant theatre scene, and nearly everyone in it is struggling to survive. Most theatres can't support themselves on box office. Competition for public and private grants is off the charts. And meanwhile people have less money to spend on tickets." She sighs.

Artist, Amateur, Acolyte, and Connoisseur nod. Exec and Teacher remain still, waiting to hear more.

Advocate continues: "So, my organization keeps studying the situation. That's our job. We know that the old way of doing arts advocacy isn't working anymore, if it ever did. The patrons and donors are not exactly flooding in. In real dollars, the National Endowment for the Arts' budget is worth way less than half what it was in 1980. We tried to convince legislators that theatre was good for the economy, or raised kids' test scores, or did all kinds of other things that people were supposed to consider worthy. But they still didn't want to pay for it. In fact, they keep wanting to use it for target practice in Washington.

"So now we're trying a different tack. Instead of spinning theatre as economic development or the cure for juvenile delinquency, we're trying to figure out what going to theatre actually does for people. You, the person who is sitting there in the dark, what that person gets out of it. And then, what that might mean to advocates like myself. How could we use it?"

Done with her introduction, Advocate smiles and gestures at the walls. "Nice place, hm?"

Murmurs of agreement fill the room.

"Well, full disclosure," Advocate continues, "it's no coincidence that I picked Symposium, and it's not just the goat panna cotta with pomegranate granita, either—although it is truly scrumptious, and if you stick around till the bitter end, I might order a round for everyone. Actually, I'm taking a cue from Plato. *Symposium*, you know? I'm guessing some of you have read it."

Connoisseur clears his throat just as Teacher opens her mouth to speak. Smiling, she defers to him. She can spot a star pupil at fifty paces. "The dialogues were written about 2400 years ago," he says. "They emanated from an oral tradition, and the writing reflected that. Plato explored complex ideas about love through a group of friends at a drinking party. No one knows whether it was based on real conversations or not, but the speakers touch on different aspects of philosophy, medicine, law and so on. Each of them delivers an encomium, a speech in praise of love, until at the end, a crowd of even more intoxicated guests arrives and several of the original group fall asleep."

"Thanks," says Advocate, briskly. "So that's what I want us to do this evening." She gestures at the recorder. "Only it's theatre, not love. I'd like each of you to take some time and say whatever seems true to you: anything you want. You can comment on what the person before you said, or just ignore all that and say your own thing." She checks the time on her cellphone. "And since it's a school night, I won't make you sleep here."

"A speech, without any time to prepare?" Connoisseur looks a little peeved.

"Well," says Advocate, "not a speech like The State of The Union. A rant, a rap, a riff."

Connoisseur points to the recorder. "And will we be quoted by name?"

"Not without your permission," Advocate tells him. "I promise. And maybe not at all."

No one says a word. Advocate, taking that as a sign of assent, continues. "I didn't want to load you up with too much stuff to read in advance, so I decided to give you just one piece of our research. You all got the transcripts of four interviews with people who go to a lot of theatre. We call them 'high-level consumers.' I'm kind of interested to know if your own experience matches theirs, and if it does, what you make of that. But don't feel you have to be limited by what they said. Tonight, it's your ideas that count.

"And one more thing," Advocate says. She sounds casual, but something about her posture suggests it's not an afterthought. "The interviews I sent are part of a much larger research project. One of the things it tells us is that most of the people who go to live theatre are older and white—like a couple of the interviewees fit that profile, and they're typical of the people who attend the most. But I think it's easy to over-generalize from statistics. Just because a majority fits a certain demographic, that doesn't erase everyone else. This region has every type of theatre in every type of community there is. Which is why I gathered a diverse group, to try to reflect that. But I'm not asking you to represent anything or anyone but yourselves. I'm not up here speaking for Italo-Asian-Americans, and you don't have to be speaking to any category either."

"*Gracias*," says Teacher, with an ironic smile. "That's a relief."

Exec tilts his head and makes a small salute.

"Okay, everybody?" Hearing no objection, Advocate proceeds. "Plato went from left to right. Wait, I wrote down the exact words." She declaims:

> I mean to propose that each of us in turn, going from
> left to right, shall make a speech in honor of Love.
> Let him give us the best which he can; and Phaedrus,
> because he is sitting first on the left hand, and because
> he is the father of the thought, shall begin.

Advocate turns to Artist. "So Artist, because she is sitting at my left hand, and because, as a playwright, she is a mother of theatre, shall begin."

Artist's Speech

Artist drains her glass, setting it down carefully. She drags both hands through her curls, staring for a moment at the ceiling. Taking a big breath, she sits up straight.

"Okay," she says. "Never let it be said that I was at a loss for words. Before I was in kindergarten, I knew I wanted to make theatre. I mean, I didn't have those words for it, it was more about racing down the block on my bike, rounding up all the other kids: 'Let's put on a show, it'll be fun!' And it was fun, or at least it was for me, because mostly, they let me boss them around. I mean, even then, it wasn't all fun and games, you needed to take care of business. Back on the block, I learned everything I know about casting—my little sister didn't want to play the captive princess all the time. Sometimes she wanted to be the one doing the rescuing instead, and casting against type often worked. Producing was intense, we had to persuade people's parents to let us have old clothes for dress-up. The props, the venue, all that. The more it changes, the more it's the same, right?

"But I had a knack for making up stories, and I loved doing it the most of anything. The other kids knew that if they gave me some latitude, I could keep the story flowing. And I was really addicted to the power of that. I lived for those moments when we were all in full-on pretend mode, when ordinary reality just melted away, and we were whatever we wanted to be. We became other people—or monsters, fairies, whatever we wanted." Artist laughs a little, shaking her head. "God, that was delicious. It still is.

"So you could just say: here is someone who is good at stories, making them up and acting them out, and who managed to make a profession out of playtime. And there would be some truth to that, I admit it. When I told my father I was going to major in theatre, he looked at me like I had brain damage. 'And who's going to support you while you play for a living?' he asked me."

Artist grins. "I had no idea at the time how often I would have to respond to variations on that question. I should have thanked him for giving me a glimpse of what I would be up against, instead of what I did, which was storm into my room and slam the door hard enough to rattle all the dishes in their cupboards, three rooms away.

"I have this sign up over my computer," she tells them. "It says 'Art is

Sacred Play.' Because at a certain point, I realized that my father was both right and wrong about that play thing. Seeing something as play does not equal seeing it as trivial. I mean, it's kind of ridiculous that I even have to point that out in a country where sports are a multi-zillion dollar industry. We take our games seriously—and so does just about every other nation on earth: the soccer riots and all that.

"But with sports, the driving force is more or less tribal, right? True fans identify with their teams. They have a lot invested in their teams winning. When they do, some of that triumphal sense of accomplishment trickles down to even the lowliest fan, whose only connection with the whole thing was yelling at the TV while he watched the game. And they don't see anything wrong with paying huge sums of money to a talented player who leads his team to victory.

"Remember in the interview, the guy who compared theatre to baseball? What did he say?" She rifles through her papers, picks out a page, and reads:

> When somebody hits a home run at a baseball park—you don't say, "Oh, I guess I should get up, everybody else is getting up." Everybody just gets up, because it's so exciting. You're so involved. You've been waiting for something to happen and then bam it happens and you connect with it.

Artist pauses and holds out her glass. Advocate refills it. "Thanks. So, the excitement and involvement he's describing, I see that all the time at my theatre. The only thing missing is the tribal part. I've often wondered, is it about getting people to feel the same identification with a theatre company as with a sports team? Isn't that what the whole season subscription idea is supposed to be about? We want you to be part of us, we want you to feel loyalty, we want you to promise to buy tickets to all of our games…I mean shows."

"But then I think back to those little shows we put on as kids. Most of my friends from back in the day did not wind up in the theatre like me. But their hunger to make up stories and act them out was almost as intense as mine. I bet you all had that experience."

Teacher says, "Doll theatre. Weddings were very big. My brother absolutely would not have called it playing with dolls, but he was just as involved in acting out toy-soldier battles with his friends."

"Exactly," says Artist. "So whatever that is, it seems hard-wired into human beings, no? I think it is even more primal than tribes. Ellen Dissanayake compares making art to making language: learning to speak is universal, even though every culture develops a different language to do it. I think she nails it. Whether you're talking about images, songs or stories, it's the same. Denis Dutton says art-making is a survival trait for natural selection. Imagine us back in the Pleistocene. Say there was someone in your extended family who could act out stories in a really vivid, compelling way. Everyone would learn from that. And just like people would want to mate with the best hunter, they'd want to mate with the best storyteller.

"So I think of an ancient ancestor, a woman standing in front of a campfire, casting shadows on the cave wall. She's bending her body into the shape of tiger, to show people how one sprang out of a thicket to attack a hunter on his way home with fresh game. She's showing them what the hunter did to escape being prey. And I ask myself the same question she did: what stories are needed now, when the balance of life seems so fragile? This theatre is my campfire. What stories can I tell that honor the true value of stories in human history, of stories as the secret of survival?

"Ancient Greek theatre keeps drawing lines between gods and humans, reinforcing the virtues of honor and bravery, warning against hubris. Shakespeare is telling us something about the intensity and impact of human feelings at a time when individuals and what they want starts to matter a whole lot more. In the 1930s, there's all this work about social issues, the *Living Newspaper*, and theatre focuses on the mess we're in right now and how to get out of it. Fifty, sixty years ago, playwrights are demonstrating the absurdity of social convention. I don't mean to over-simplify, but if you take the long view, you begin to see how those answers change and change and change with the times."

Artist picks up her glass, smiling. As she speaks, one finger winds and unwinds a lock of hair. "Fast-forward 12,000 years and that's how I came to write my new play on the Tea Party. Loosely based on *An Enemy of the People*, of course, only instead of being vilified for warning the people about poison in the water, my protagonist warns them about who's really destroying the economy." She tips her glass to her companions. "Let me know if you want comps."

When Artist stops talking, the room is silent. The low rumble of the world outside can be heard, making everyone feel cozy, like hunkering down on a rainy night.

"Thank you," says Advocate, softly breaking the silence. "I like that idea, Artist. Just pretend this recorder is a campfire, and this room is a cave, and we've got it. Right?

"Connoisseur," Advocate says, looking to Artist's right. "You're next."

Connoisseur's Speech

"Very interesting," Connoisseur says to Artist. "I have to admit, though, that I tend to be suspicious of explanations grounded in evolutionary psychology, because they all cleave so tightly to normative ideas of the human subject. Remember watching cartoon cavemen?" he asks.

Nods and grins all around.

"*The Flintstones*," says Artist.

"*Alley-Oop*," says Acolyte, and then, noticing Connoisseur's puzzled expression, "before your time."

"The archetypal caveman," says Connoisseur, "is dressed in animal skins, dragging a woman by her hair. That isn't very different from the picture that sociobiology draws today, which tends to be an essentialist account that justifies—that seems to validate and ratify—one or another stereotypical privilege. Why men can't be monogamous or why women should stay at home with the children. If we accept these explanations, we don't have to interrogate those assumptions anymore, because we have the ultimate reason: it's all foreordained by biology."

Connoisseur turns to Artist. His black attire seems to disappear into the gloom of the dining room, leaving a disembodied head, the light glinting off his glasses and blond hair. "It's not that I'm disagreeing with your point that stories are intrinsic to the human subject. How could I? Once we're done eating and sleeping and having sex, practically all we do is tell stories. And before you say so, I'll stipulate: we like to talk about other meals as we eat, we like bedtime stories and pornography—which has some kind of story structure, often. So, yes, with the human species, it's stories all the way. Let's be *Homo fabulans*, the storyteller, which is just as good as *Homo sapiens*—man the wise, or *Homo ludens*—man the player.

"So I ask the same question you did, Artist: what stories now? But I come up with a different answer. I don't see a ribbon of time stretching forward from the Pleistocene to today. I see radical breaks, ruptures, in our self-understanding, and each rupture changes our relationship to that question. The center of life moved to industrial cities, and plays reflected that. The devastation of World War I completely changed what people wanted to see onstage. Now we're facing climate change, maybe the end of the planet, and what do we have to say about that? Whatever it is, it won't be *Hello, Dolly!*.

"Of course, most stories exist to ratify a particular social order. We hear enough of them, and that constructs an embedded expectation that is almost impossible to dislodge. All the frames that politicians play off of: the patriarch who belongs at the head of the family, the faithful woman and children who exist to serve him, the rich and powerful man who earns his good fortune, the lazy ne'er-do-well who squanders his." Connoisseur taps the side of his head. "They all live in there. So do we let them take over, or do we disturb the peace?

"I can't simply accept the blanket category, theatre, as if it were a unitary whole. It covers too many contradictions. We have to unpack it. Look at all the theatre seats that are occupied on any given night in this city. The vast majority will be people who are getting an emotional massage from some piece of hummable drivel or heartfelt family drama that reinforces all of their unexamined assumptions. That kind of theatre has absolutely nothing to say about what we really need, which is to deconstruct the old stories and use the broken pieces to create something that hasn't been seen before. The stories we need aren't so much stories as hammers that can shatter the trance of stories."

Connoisseur pauses, looking each person in the eye. "Look around. We're in San Francisco, where you can't walk a block without noticing that the old gender story doesn't capture reality anymore, if it ever did. The best theatre in this city takes on that challenge, by showing us people throwing their bodies on the machine, insisting that the world acknowledge them, that we take the time to know what they are thinking and feeling and stop pretending they don't exist. It would be wonderful if there were money to do that work, but most of those artists don't have any illusion that the hegemonic structures they oppose are going to underwrite their work. They hold day jobs and throw house parties and pull it together however they can, because making the work, getting it out there, is their imperative and their reason for living. It's not just about art. They recognize that today, under dominant conditions, life itself is *bricolage*."

Teacher raises her hand tentatively, like a shy kid in back of the class. "*Bricolage?*"

"It means pulling whatever you need from wherever you can get it, making something new by juxtaposing things that aren't meant to be used together," says Connoisseur. "Like using old pieces of machinery to create new musical instruments, or positioning bits of advertising and soap operas and Shakespeare to make a new dramatic language."

Connoisseur drinks the dregs of his coffee, even though they are cold. "When I read those interviews that Advocate sent us, I thought, most of these people's sole criterion for theatre is that it makes them feel something for a little while. It's the dramatic equivalent of fast food. If that's all it is, I can't make myself care much about it. I'd rather talk about how people like that could be dislodged from their comfort zones and made to see something like the piece Advocate and I saw last night.

I probably wouldn't have heard of the performance if I wasn't on the playwright's mailing list from when we worked together in the editorial group of a critical journal on gay theatre. I don't care about the audience for most of the stuff your 'high-level consumers' love," Connoisseur says, turning toward Advocate as he makes air quotes with his fingers. "But I care deeply about theatre where both the story and the telling are new, and where experiencing them changes the way we perceive other stories in future."

When he finishes, Connoisseur looks a little defiant, chin a bit more forward, mouth slightly set.

Exec's Speech

Exec, sitting on Connoisseur's right, is quick to reply. "You made me think, man," he says. "I have to give you that. Both of you," he adds," looking at Artist. "You are passionate, and committed, and you explain yourselves quite well." He holds each of their eyes for just a moment.

"But I have to tell you both, you are truly full of it."

Artist and Connoisseur both look a little shocked, like someone who misjudges a chair and sits down too hard.

"You heard me right," Exec says. "And I am speaking from the perspective of someone who is living right here on planet earth, not in the art world. I was in business for over forty years before I retired. Do you know what I learned? Lesson number one? If people don't want something, you can't make them pay for it.

"You convinced me about the stories, you really did. I buy the notion that we learn from stories, and I also agree, that way of learning seems hard-wired into us. That's how religions teach morality—*Bible* stories. That's how parents teach their offspring about the world. My two begged for it: 'Tell me a story

382

about the olden days, Daddy!' Hell, when I was a kid, we even made a story out of a basketball game. You go for a lay-up and you're writing the narration as you go: 'He shoots, and he makes it again! The kid can't lose!'

"But come on, it's not like stories are in short supply. We are swimming in them: TV, movies, video games, comic books, audiobooks, Kindles, spindles, bindles—you name it. It's a long leap from saying that human beings love stories to saying they should want to go to live theatre, let alone give extra money so it stays afloat.

"My last job was head of branding for a soft drink division. Saying everyone needs stories is like saying everyone gets thirsty. Okay, fine, stipulated. Now what? You're talking about branding, folks. I didn't hear one thing in what you said that proved to me that your way of telling stories is better or worth more than any of those other ways.

"When we looked to position a new brand, we started by finding out what people were seeking when they satisfied their thirst: refreshment, good taste, fun, friends, health, sex—sex sells everything. And whatever it was, we made the case for why our product could deliver that better than anything else. We tried to show that it tasted better, or cost less, or we connected it to friends and fun in a memorable way. If people swallowed what we were putting out, they bought the product, and we all went home with money in our pockets. It's that simple."

Exec sips his brandy. "You art worlders, you've been making huge branding mistakes, so huge you might not be able to fix them. You made theatre a luxury item. That was a seriously bad move. How many people go to the movies every Friday night—these days, they can easily spend eight, ten dollars a ticket—or to a rock concert, where ticket prices are about as high as theatre seats? But those people would never think of going to live theatre. Why? Because in their minds, you have to dress up a certain way and be on your best behavior, you have to work hard to understand it, you spend a lot of money, and in the end, you haven't really had all that much fun. It's a luxury item, and they don't see it as delivering the same bang for the buck as other luxuries.

"And then on top of that, you theatre people have your hands out all the time. It's like—I don't know, a panhandler in a tuxedo. 'This is a very elite activity, mostly for people who have money to burn'—look around you the next time you pop into Marines Memorial, for instance, you'll see a sea of prosperous white faces—'and we need you to pay through the nose for tickets plus give us even more money, because ticket prices are about as high as the market will bear and it's still not supporting us in the style we prefer.' Come on! Do you really not see why this isn't working?"

"Well," says Acolyte, a tight little smile creasing his tan face, "you make it sound like the last days of Pompeii. Do you really think all the actors who are working day jobs to support their habit of performing at those theatres are living in the lap of luxury?"

"Now you're getting into labor-management issues," Artist says, twirling a lock of hair around her finger. "My theatre could live for a year on what those theatres pay for props and costumes. But at least during the run of a show, we probably pay cast members more."

Exec shakes his head. "You're not convincing me; the opposite. If I give more and it doesn't trickle down to the artists, doesn't that make it worse? And those ticket-buyers, do they even know if they are in a nonprofit or a for-profit theatre? Do they actually care? Half the time, you people talk about this as if you were living in a little bubble labeled 'the arts,' and all those other storytellers—the TV, the movies, video games—that make up this multi-mega complex where people spend money like water—as if all that didn't exist. You act like they offer nothing of value. And what's more, there's this fastidious feeling, like if you get too close to them, you'll be contaminated. And yet that's the so-called mainstream, where people choose to spend their time and money. You, Connoisseur, you go one better and say that even most live theatre fits that category!"

Connoisseur raises one eyebrow, opens his mouth, shuts it again.

"So what I'm saying is, let up for a minute on tooting your own horn and look at it from a branding perspective. What message are you putting out? To me, it sounds like this: 'What we do is probably too good for you, but you should support us anyway because only we are wise enough to know what's good.' How many bottles of juice do you think I would have sold with a message like that?

"I like to go to the theatre," Exec says, leaning back and smoothing his dark silk tie. "And for me, that is two different things. At the theatre where I sit on the board of directors, I'm a successful black businessman who is supposed to bring some wisdom about money to an African American company with drive and ambition and not enough resources. There are parts of that work that remind me of my father as a deacon in church: you're there to support the community, to put a certain face on things, and you are given to understand that this a responsibility that comes with success. So I fly the flag and I go to every opening, and I'm as proud as if they were my own kids. We should have black theatres that are as honored and as well-funded as the biggest white theatres in this country, and it's a disgrace that we don't.

"Apart from that, for me, theatre is a social activity: I like to go to dinner, take friends, sit around afterwards and talk about what we've seen. I like it to be a special occasion. I feel a nice sense of affirmation in my orchestra seat, like belonging to an exclusive club. I don't go to those funky little theatres in someone's garage, because I don't like the way they look at me when I come in, all surprised: what are you doing here? And I don't like it that no one smiles and shows me to a seat and thanks me for being there. I'm not one of those liberals who pays to be dissed.

"But when the theatre has upholstered seats and velvet curtains, and an usher has handed me a nice program and helped me find my seat, then I like it a lot when the lights go down and there's nothing to do but stare at the stage. I like sitting there and wondering if the talented people onstage are going to succeed in fooling me this time. Will I get caught up in the action? Will I be moved to tears? Will I laugh out loud? Or will it be like watching a puppet-show where you can see the guy pulling the strings? Sometimes, it makes me feel so much, I'm excited and glad to be alive, and I feel privileged to witness something unique, like the people in the interviews say: it's live, it will never happen exactly that way again, and I was there! But you know, just as often, I'm looking at my watch and thinking about what I'm going to do when it's over. I remember how much the tickets cost me, and I think I should have waited for the DVD.

"So, as a board member, I ask certain questions that I want to ask you right now. What is your unique brand? What is the essence you're trying to put across? If there were suddenly no live theatre, what would people lose? You can't say they would be deprived of stories, when there are so many of them in other places. The bottom line is this: if you can't come up with something that sells me on the idea, how are you going to sell all those people who don't know anything about live theatre in the first place?"

Connoisseur seems ready to respond, but Advocate cuts him off. "Let's do all the speeches first," she says, "then talk. Intense questions," she says to Exec. "Thanks for asking them. And now it's Amateur's turn."

Amateur's Speech

"I'm not sure where to start," says Amateur, "because I come at this from a few different perspectives, and each one has something to say on the subject." Amateur pauses, thinking it over. He pulls at the collar of his blue sweater, absently undoing the top button. He plucks a small, square cornmeal cookie from a plate and breaks it in half, setting one half on his saucer. After a few seconds, he sets the other half down without eating it.

"I guess I'll begin with my own direct experience, because that's the perspective that's been with me the longest. I'm very like one of those people in the interviews: I started acting in community theatre and school plays when I was just a little kid. *A Christmas Carol* every year, which was a big deal in Minnesota, a really big deal.

"So I was imprinted with the two sides of that experience. There was the fun and satisfaction of learning a part, of impersonating someone you could never be in real life, and playing with other people who were doing the same thing. If you enjoy that, it's addictive, the same way team sports are addictive. There are many reinforcing factors, and when they converge, you want to repeat the experience. And then there was the magic of being in the audience when you saw all of that come together with a great script, skilled actors, wonderful sets, all adding up to that feeling of being transported, along with everyone else in the theatre, to another world."

Amateur gazes into the distance of memory, brushing stray strands of light-brown hair off his forehead. "The first play I really remember that way was *Peter Pan*, a touring production with Sandy Duncan as Peter. I must have been in fifth or sixth grade, which you'd think would be old enough to not be quite so impressed. I was sitting pretty close, too, so I could see the wires when Peter flew into the air. But it didn't matter. To me, he was flying, and it was simply amazing. For weeks afterwards, every time I went to sleep, after my parents said good night and closed the door, I got up and opened the window, just in case Tinkerbell came to get me. Of course, I knew it was all pretend, but there was a little part of me that wanted it not to be. And since I was already acting, it brought home to me that I could be part of creating that kind magic. Well, it's never lost its enchantment for me."

"I'll never grow up, never grow up, never grow up. Not me, Not I, Not me-e-e-e-e!" sings Teacher. "Sorry," she says, looking sheepish. "Couldn't help myself."

"Nor I," smiles Amateur. "Which is why one thing I want to say is that the answer to Exec's question is much more compelling, I think, when the experience of watching is combined with the experience of doing. Every child should have both opportunities, to act and to see live theatre. Doing both provides an instant feedback-loop that teaches so many things: how illusion and misdirection work with suspension of disbelief; how we can affect other people through things like tone, posture, and gesture; how empathy is activated. These are important lessons about the human cognition that can't be learned by watching a film or playing a video game. You have to be able to perceive how human beings do these things—not merely that they do them—for the learning to come through. Participating builds confidence. It creates social opportunity for kids to interact with peers and adults they might not otherwise encounter. It gives young people a way to comprehend ideas or experiences without having to go through them in real life. It gives them a way to rehearse life.

"I could make a pretty convincing argument that my involvement in children's theatre led directly to my work today. I do research in cognitive science. At one point I realized I probably wasn't going to have a career on Broadway—I didn't have the looks or the talent or really, the drive—but that I could make a contribution by studying the human capacities that underpin theatre. Whether we're talking about ancient ritual drama or the latest special-effects extravaganza at the multiplex, human beings have this desire to enact stories and spectacles. Why? What does it do for us?"

Amateur smiles. "What are the perceptual and cognitive aspects of story-processing? How does it activate memory and imagination? What are the behavioral and neural correlates of learning, skill acquisition, and brain adaptation when someone takes on a role? Well, I'm not going to bore you with the details of my research, but I'll just mention a point or two. Mirror neurons? You've heard about them?"

"Yes," says Exec. "I was reading about long-jumpers practicing for meets by watching track films."

Amateur nods, continuing. "Being able to observe the human brain while it's processing experience has been a remarkable boon to research. One thing we've discovered is that when you or I pay close attention to someone performing an action, the same parts of our brains are activated as when we perform that action ourselves. My colleagues disagree as to whether specialized neurons are responsible, or whether all neurons sometimes have this mirroring function. And we haven't fully explained yet how the effect is aggregated into an understanding of other people's feelings and actions. But we all know from subjective experience that when we form an attachment to a character through the first two acts of a play, what we feel closely resembles our real-life experience of emotional attachment to someone we know. And if we cry when that character dies in the third act, we are feeling very much the same things that would accompany the loss of someone we cared about in real life.

"We've proven that watching performances helps expand our experience of empathy and connect with other people's feelings. It helps us see into other people's motivations and thought-processes, and understand more about their choices. If you are the performer, the effect is increased, because you have to get inside a character's head to play that role effectively. But even if you're only an observer, the effect kicks in.

"As for it all being the same—TV, movies, video games—maybe so, a story's a story. But Artist asked what stories are needed now, and that is where I think theatre comes in. Unless you're trying to recreate a blockbuster movie onstage—think *Spiderman*—the scale of theatre makes it possible to explore more diverse, complex, and interesting stories. Most plays wouldn't be picked up by Hollywood, because entertainment moguls wouldn't think that millions of people would want to buy a ticket. That's too bad, because a lot of that theatre wrestles with important questions or portrays people we need to know and will never meet at the multiplex.

"Exec is probably right that the average theatregoer can't tell a for-profit theatre from a nonprofit," Amateur says. "But there are some important differences: if a nonprofit theatre can get grants, that can provide a kind of buffer zone for the development of new work that might be too risky for commercial investors. I'm not saying they always do that, or that commercial theatres never take risks, but there are risks and risks. You earn nonprofit status by providing some type of public benefit, instead of your prime directive being to make money. That could be presenting theatre by people who aren't well-represented in the mainstream media, bringing new voices into the cultural mix. We always say we're a nation of immigrants, but you might not know that from for-profit theatre. That could be theatre that focuses on social issues."

Amateur pushed up the sleeves of blue sweater. "My son is still in high school, and he and his friends play video games all the time. Most of the stories Mike and his buddies like are things like *Call of Duty: Black Ops* or *Grand Theft Auto*. What capacities are being developed? What are we preparing them for? Violence, mayhem, a dog-eat-dog world? An emotional gamut from rage to triumph? The stories we need aren't going to spring out of Hollywood based on 90-second pitches and focus groups aimed at catching the 18-to-25 male demographic. They have to be worked out on a small scale, with actual human beings at the helm, giving it all they've got. For example, I'm biased toward stories that show immigrants in a fully dimensional way, rather than the way my son and his friends sometimes start to see foreigners after charging their adrenaline in multiplayer world for a few hours, more or less as targets.

"Not that I'm spending a huge amount of time in lofts and garages, either," Amateur says to Exec, "though I do go to some, and people don't seem to mind having me there. I love musical theatre more than anything, though, and that usually takes a more substantial effort to pull off.

But then, I'm not a snob," says Amateur, turning pointedly to Connoisseur. "If Peter Pan changed my life, who am I to judge someone else's taste? I'll stop there for now." Amateur pops half a cookie into his mouth.

Acolyte's Speech

"I am delighted to be next," says Acolyte, jumping right in. "Because I've been waiting for someone to talk about what theatre is to me, and what it also seems to be to some of those people in the interviews." He swivels from face to face, making sure he has everyone's attention. "A place of worship."

People laugh, but Acolyte keeps his tan, lined face straight, his dark eyes still and open. "Seriously," he says, "we go to church—or synagogue, mosque, temple—for reasons. We go to declare that we are part of something larger, and to connect with other people who share that awareness. We go to be reminded of the good we are capable of doing, and the harm, and their consequences for ourselves and others. We go for moral lessons—not only stories in the sense that everyone has been deploying that word, a story about this, a story about that—but a grand narrative that all our individual stories fit into and that helps all of them make sense. We go to connect with our best selves, to refresh that connection regularly, so that we don't subside into the busy, uncaring self that is lurking inside us. And when I think about theatre in that light, I see that it's true: I go there to worship.

"I'm Jewish," says Acolyte, "which might strike you as odd, because when people think of religion and theatricality, Catholicism usually pops up, right? The cathedrals with all their attention to staging, the costumes, the props, the music, the ceremony. But each spiritual tradition has a different way of conveying its meta-story: the *Ramayana*, the *Jatakas*, the *Passion*. If you go to services for a year at most Jewish congregations, you'll work through the whole cycle of Torah readings, the first five books of what Christians call the 'Old Testament.'

"Some of the readings, you have to strain to comprehend their spiritual significance. When the Israelites are wandering in the desert, for instance, God commands them to build the mishkan, a portable shrine. The text goes on for pages and pages about what types and colors of wool should be chosen to weave the coverings, what animal skins, how they should be decorated, their exact measurements. And once the thing is built, the instructions are just as detailed in describing how sacrifices and ceremonies are to be performed. Or you look at the part earlier in Exodus where God instructs Moses on how to go to Pharaoh and say, 'Let my people go.' The language is exactly like stage directions: you'll stand here, and he'll stand here, and you'll do this, and he'll say this. God gives Moses a script.

"Growing up, I had to think, why is this stuff in here? Why is it given such close attention? It seemed to me then—and it still seems now—that the text is saying we have to be really mindful about worship. We can't just toss it off. I think it is true to say that the Torah portrays God as an artist, directing all of us, like characters in a vast play. Any old story in any old setting isn't going to align our spirits with our best selves. To make memory and meaning, the kind that stays with us and has lasting effects, it has to be well thought-out and well-executed. There has to be all kinds of intentionality.

"Understanding that had two effects on me," says Acolyte. "Like Amateur, it set me on my path. I became an architect because I wanted to design what seemed to me sacred spaces—the places where we bring our full intentionality, and our full awareness of the beauty human beings can create when we set our hearts and minds to it. For me, that's been libraries, theatres, concert halls, and even a few houses of worship. When I've succeeded, everything comes together: the physical space is inviting and comfortable, there's a feeling of welcome and rightness about it. There's some grace and rigor, some purity of impulse expressed in the design. And whatever use human beings make of the building seems to infuse it with spirit, with higher purpose.

"I'm not so religious anymore in the conventional sense. I don't go to services all that much. But I still go to the theatre, and like the people in Advocate's interviews and some of you, I'm sure, I go many, many times each year. It's not just a metaphor to say I am a devout theatregoer. And there's another word that comes to me when I think about what that means. The word is sublime. In aesthetic philosophy, the sublime has a greatness that can't be entirely captured by calculation or measurement. It puts us in touch with the awe that is our natural condition, what Abraham Joshua Heschel calls 'radical amazement.' You can feel it in relation to the natural world: standing at the rim of the Grand Canyon, for instance, we experience awe mixed with an overwhelming awareness of beauty, so intense that we feel we can barely contain it, that we may burst. Whatever gives us this feeling is worship. It reminds us of our true place in the universe, how insignificant we are in relation to the scale of life, and at the same time, how we are the center of it all, in that our own perception enables the world to exist."

Acolyte pauses, looks around, shrugs the tweed jacket into place over the gold shirt. "I can't be the only person in this room who has felt that in the theatre, can I?"

Heads nod, telling Acolyte he is not.

"So is theatre a brand, Exec? Is it a new way of telling a story, or a story that speaks uniquely to this time and place? Does it make our mirror neurons jump? I don't think anything I have said satisfies the criteria others have offered for getting people with money to support theatre. But tell me, why do so many people give money to churches and synagogues? I think it's because they recognize that somehow, somewhere, we have to be reminded of the deepest meanings we have given our lives. That reminder gives us the inspiration and energy to go on making meaning. Honestly, I don't know if any foundation or government agency values this. But—and this is the least humble thing I could say right now, so if that bothers you, apologies in advance for my *chutzpah*—if they don't, it's not because I'm wrong. It's because they've lost touch with what's really important.

"I have to say, that prospect worries me. The fact that we're all trying to justify what we value according to some rules that don't really fit, instead of pointing out how our society's values have to come in line with what really matters. Maybe we need to be less defensive." Acolyte pauses. "My two cents."

"Amen," says Artist.

Advocate looks at Teacher. "You're last," she says.

"Oh, no," says Teacher. "You are! Do you think we are all going to take a turn and let you off the hook? That is not how it works in my class."

With a half-smile, Advocate assents.

TEACHER'S SPEECH

"If anyone here needs a definition of 'a teachable moment,'" Teacher says, "I think we have supplied it." She pauses for the laughter to settle, taking a

391

sip of her white wine. "We public school teachers have become kind of expert in that, you know. That is the way we handle hot-button issues like abortion, same-sex marriage, or evolution. We cannot come down squarely on one side of the question and disregard the rest. So we teach the controversy.

"It is a defensive strategy, of course. But I have come to think that it is the best approach, in that when we teach that way, students learn three things at the same time. First, they are listening to all sides of the issue, so they're getting a lot of information. They are learning the discourse around that issue, 360 degrees. And second, we are demonstrating how to be respectful even when you disagree, by showing how their teachers rise to the challenge of explaining opposing viewpoints without caricaturing or short-changing them. Third is that by exploring the controversy without identifying with a particular position, they practice seeing things clearly, separating awareness and emotion.

"I am not saying that they come into the classroom without ideas—about evolution, for instance. They have heard something at home or seen it on TV or read it on the internet, and they take it as their own position, often just because it sounds good, without too much thought. More than half of my kids are first-generation, with parents from Central America, Southeast Asia, the Caribbean. Young as they are, they remind me of my parents. Their parents listen to the church, on questions of personal morality, they are conservative. The kids are very polite. They've been taught not to disagree with authority figures. To me, they need a way to start thinking for themselves. They might end up with exactly the same positions, but I want them to arrive there on their own steam.

"That is why I always start by teaching them about confirmation bias, which our friend the cognitive scientist can probably explain better than I. I just say that the human mind is disposed to look for confirmation of what we already believe, and to ignore the rest."

"I couldn't have done it any better," says Amateur, tipping an imaginary hat.

Teacher dips her head, a sort of sitting curtsey. "*Gracias, señor.* I tell them that the best way to test their arguments is to try to disprove them," she continues. "And after that, they start to see holes in arguments they agree with, not just in the ones they reject.

Teacher lifts her left hand to count on her fingers. "I have one, two, three main points to make about holes in the arguments that have been made. First, there is an implicit assumption circulating that I would like to question. The

392

four people whose interviews we read, yes? What is to be learned from them? I have an idea that the intention is something like this: these people love theatre to an extreme degree. If we could figure out how and why they got that way, maybe we could bottle it and give others a little sip." She looks at Advocate. "That could be wrong, I am only speculating, but I would like to run with it a little."

Advocate shrugs as if to say, *Be my guest*.

"These people are telling stories that are at once highly idiosyncratic and very much the same. They all had formative early-childhood experiences— outings with a beloved parent, opportunities to perform and get attention, the chance to do something distinctive that shed a positive light on their need to differentiate, making them quirky and interesting rather than just odd or unpopular. Each experience gave them a glimpse of something pleasurable, and they wanted more. So far, so good?"

Everyone nods.

"Now, think of something that is like this for you. It may be theatre—for Amateur, Acolyte, Artist, and Connoisseur, it almost certainly is, no? But it could be something else. Exec played football, perhaps he still loves it. For me, it is salsa, actually. I grew up dancing. My whole family loved it, and everyone I knew. A week without dancing is not a good week for me. By the end of the school day on Friday, I am craving it. My husband knows that if he does not take me out, it will not be a happy weekend.

"Okay, now imagine someone who is just as impassioned as you, but about something completely different, something you have absolutely no interest in: civil war re-enactments, Lindy dancing, dirt-bike racing, stamp collecting, Esperanto. There are millions of people who live for these activities, and all of them have some story of how they got started and why they continue. You have probably been seated next to one of them on a plane, wondering if you could pretend to be asleep, or whether the conversation would actually put you to sleep so you could avoid having to pretend."

Teacher lets them chuckle for a moment. "So, let us say they do this thing we are discussing: they capture the whole story of their passion, how it was ignited, what sustains it, why it feels important to them. And let us say that they share that with you. What would it take to influence you to take up the same passion? What would convince you to dive headfirst into Esperanto or stamp-collecting, if it held no interest for you until now?"

Teacher pauses, polishing her glasses, letting the silence gather.

"Is that a rhetorical question?" asks Amateur.

"No, no," says Teacher, smiling. "Please."

"Well, if their stories have anything in common with the interviews, I'd say someone has to be imprinted with the passion at a young age. It has to come at a critical time for personal development, either as a key pathway to intimacy—This is how my father and I bonded—or a strong attraction that shapes identity—This is my thing, the thing that makes me who I am and sets me apart from the crowd. I don't see any clues here as to how an adult who's already formed his or her own identity could be persuaded to shift course and make theatre a primary connection. When I try to imagine what would make me a stamp collector, I can only think I'd have to die and be reborn as one, because I can't imagine anything that'd pull me there instead of where I already choose to focus."

"Okay," says Teacher. "I will assume that no one sees it in a very different way—no one is thinking, 'Oh, absolutely, hearing the story of a stamp collector's passion would turn me into a stamp collector immediately.' So we have obtained some useful information for arts education advocates, which is that if you want adults to be involved, give them deeply satisfying personal experiences when they are young. But I do not think we have found the key to building audiences or support among already-existing adults."

Teacher counts off another finger. "Okay, my second point also has to do with support. Remember what Advocate said at the outset, that the old arguments no longer work?

"If they ever did," Advocate interjects.

"Yes," Teacher says. "Public and private funders do not agree to pour money into theatre because they believe it stimulates economic development or raises children's test scores, so Advocate and her colleagues are trying to look at what it really does. In the materials you sent us, you called it 'intrinsic impact,' right?"

"That's right," says Advocate.

"So now let us stipulate what has been said around the table." Teacher lifts her glasses on their chain and glances at a few notes on a scrap of paper. "We need stories to learn and face challenges. We need new ways of telling stories to open us to new realities and break out of habituated ways of seeing the world. We need to take part in creating stories with our own minds and bodies and feelings, and to experience them with that same immediacy, to develop our capacity for empathy. We need theatre as a form of spiritual practice, a way to remember who we are, a way to construct larger meanings that make sense out of our experiences, and connect us to the sublime. We need theatre as a human-scale lab for all this, one that doesn't require the massive resources of a Hollywood movie to get off the ground. And we need to be able to express all this in a way that grabs people and convinces them there are things theatre does that are unique and necessary." Teacher lets her glasses drop onto her soft green sweater.

"I believe these things too. Theater is not the center of my life, but I value it, and I am absolutely certain that the performances my kids have seen have greatly expanded their horizons. When I watch them encounter other worlds in the theatre—even when I watch them mingle with other theatregoers, when I see how the lobby is for them a kind of performance of a different world, and they are learning how to move between worlds—I know that they are getting something from coming to see live human beings perform in real time that could not be gotten from, say, watching a similar story on television. What they could never have gotten that way is the experience of being part of a San Francisco audience and feeling they belong, even though they are surrounded by people whose paths they might never cross otherwise."

Teacher pauses. "For me, this is very personal. I was the first in my family to do many things: go to college, teach school, have close friends from other worlds who did not share my cultural heritage. I remember how nervous I was anticipating each of these experiences, and how wonderful it was to come out feeling that sense they call agency, that awareness of expanded horizons and self-confidence. If it were up to me, I would make sure that every student has these experiences, many times each year.

"But here is my second question: these legislators and foundation people you want to give money, are these the things they care about? Are they going to want to pay for theatre as a path to empathy or mind-expansion or spiritual elevation or social inclusion for immigrant kids any more than they wanted to pay for it as economic development? I am not saying that I know the answer. I would like to think it is yes, but I have no way of knowing that. Remember, I am just teaching the controversy. And this is something that must be questioned if we are going to explore it without biasing the result towards our own preferences: the old way was not convincing to them, but will the new way do any better?

"Okay," says Teacher. "One more thing. And this is mainly for my friend Exec, because there is something I cannot understand in your argument, which is very similar to an argument I often hear in connection with education." Lifting the glasses, she looks down at her notes. "You said, 'If people don't want something, you can't make them pay for it.'"

Exec nods.

"But that is not true. Do you think if we took a referendum on how much voters want to spend on missile guidance systems, the Department of Defense budget would remain intact? Taxpayers are paying for all kinds of things they would not want to pay for if given a choice. Some of those things are what are called social goods, which, ideally we should all want for the common good. But the common good is not a very common goal right now, I think. Look at all the people who complain about paying for public education, simply because they do not have children in the schools.

"Most societies deal with that by requiring people to pay their taxes and giving elected officials the right to say where those taxes should go. But there are many things like that in the private sector too. We pay inflated prices for some things to cover the cost of advertising or research: look at the difference between what we pay for certain medications and what they cost in other countries. What we pay for fuel makes oil companies rich, but the only choice we are given is pay up or give up driving, so we pay. Even many of the products that supposedly represent the triumph of free markets get a boost from public policy. Look at corn, for instance, all the money that is spent growing corn nobody needs. There is a name for this, is there not? Corporate welfare.

"So it is not correct to portray things the way some people do: over here is the free market where everything is given its just value, and over there is the unfair system where people expect to be paid for doing nothing. What I see is, over here is the part of the system where people successfully lobby for advantage, and over there is the part where they don't have the money or the power to do that. Isn't that more accurate?

"A couple of the kids in a play I directed this year did a unit in social studies on how the arts are funded. One of them came into rehearsal with a statistic that made everyone loco: every single day, seven days a week, we are spending much more than two annual National Endowment for the Arts budgets on war. They had other figures comparing the prison budget with arts spending, things like that. Do you really think that this balance of expenditures reflects public choice? I am not able to offer proof, because I am not aware of polls on that precise question. But my kids would not have supported that notion of the public good. They were appalled by it. I am saying all this because I would like this conversation to be based on reality, and not the myth that the arts are the big welfare cheaters while the free market rules the day for everyone else. That just is not true.

"Remember what I said about teaching the controversy? I think it would be great to have a national conversation where we clear away the myths and look at what is left. Which things that do not earn their keep do we want to pay for? I would like to have a say in that. Personally, I would choose theatre and other such things—music and art and education and medical care and so on—over subsidies for agribusiness, banks, and oil companies. I have an idea that a majority of voters would agree. But even if that is wrong, if the outcome of the debate was based on letting the hot air out of all sides of the issue and giving our values a fair chance to contend, I think I would accept it. It would be a big relief to stop having those debates that ring so false, where we fling assertions at each other without fully believing them."

Teacher pauses for a second. "That is all."

"I bet you're a really strict grader," says Exec.

Teacher just grins, shaking her head.

"Oh, my God," says Advocate. "I'm just going to order dessert before I take my turn, okay? How many goat panna cottas with pomegranate granita, and how many chocolate pavés with fig and walnut conserve?" She goes to the door, confers with a waiter, and comes back.

ADVOCATE'S SPEECH

"In Plato's *Symposium*," Advocate tells them, "all the guests eventually leave or nod out except Socrates, who seems not to need sleep. Which is not the case with me, by the way. So, like I said, I won't talk your ears off till dawn, but I do want to add just a few things. And I'm going to stand," she says, rising and brushing her straight black hair behind her ears, "because I think better in a standing position."

"I'm really glad that Exec is here, because his challenges help us in two ways. First, to the extent that most of us arc advocates, we have to be able to respond to his questions. They are the ones so many people are asking, we can't ignore them. And second, as Teacher has pointed out, we have to surface and question the assumptions behind the questions.

"Exec asked us something that gives us that opportunity: 'What if there were no live theatre?' I get this as a kind of thought-experiment, like, 'What if there were no religion?' It feels like I've been in this conversation for a long time, and I keep noticing how often it gets deflected into questions which might sometimes be fun to argue about, but don't really move the needle in terms of our real challenge. 'No theatre' just isn't one of the actual options unless there is no world at all. People will go on acting out stories until the end of time, whether there is money for it or not. I want us to talk about the real questions. What impact will it have on our society if there is less theatre, especially less professionally staged theatre? That's a real question. Less theatre by people who don't have access to private wealth—okay, that's a real question too. Less theatre by people whose stories are not going to attract what the numbers tells us about the current mainstream theatre audience, mostly older white people. Those questions, I want to talk about: what does it cost us if the main criterion for the vast majority of the stories our culture disseminates is that they make money? In some sense, I think it costs us our soul, the idea that we're all in this together, the idea that we care about each other. To me, that really matters.

"It's easy to get cynical in this business. I know someone who's been watching the funding scene for a long time, and she says that even though the guidelines change, often with big fanfare—announcing a totally new funding program from Foundation X!—funders usually find a way to give the money to the same groups they were supporting before. She says they adopt new guidelines so they can have plausible reasons to say no, which they need to do almost constantly, since they reject at least a dozen applications for every one they accept. Cynical, or what?"

Artist shrugs. *What.*

"But, yeah, there's some truth to it too. So I could just say, okay, yes, there's no reason to think that proving that theatre has a positive impact on individuals is going to change that. I don't know. Sometimes I get totally lost in the gap between the way things should be and the way they are. Like maybe we will be able to quantify intrinsic impact: you know, 43 percent of the audience members were transported and felt more connected, more able to see things in a new light. But should we have to quantify everything? Maybe what we're saying about the importance of stories and empathy is hinting at a completely new way to value things, where we can stop having to reduce everything to numbers as if that were the only way to judge. Sometimes I actually fantasize that we're doing the last iteration of the numbers game before it's finally over and done."

Exec raises his eyebrows with eloquent skepticism.

Advocate takes a breath. "Or maybe we will have to go on spinning straw into gold forever, because the people calling the shots like it that way. But I'm choosing to think this is a worthy effort, for a few reasons. It means I don't have to mouth a bunch of crap anymore about the economic multiplier effect: you know, every theatre ticket generates expenditures on parking and dinner and so one arts dollar actually equals a dozen dollars into the economy. So what? One dollar spent on baseball has the same impact. One dollar spent on a strip club. It's been sort of exhausting to keep saying this stuff. I'd way rather talk about how theatre can generate intellectual stimulation or emotional resonance. At least it's true, which is easier on the spirit.

"I also want to give funders the benefit of the doubt, and not just succumb to a cynical view of them as these cardboard cutouts, you know? There are places that theatres get hung up in the current system. Like you have to demonstrate "artistic quality," which usually translates into getting good reviews. If you're in a town where the critics don't cover small houses, you can't get reviewed. So what if instead of reviews, a foundation would accept that a high percentage of the audience felt captivated, or experienced aesthetic enrichment? Would that level the playing field for people who are doing really good work on a shoestring? That seems worth finding out.

"And then there's just this sort of sappy truth, which is that for me, it's like the girl said in her interview." Advocates picks up her sheaf of papers and reads, 'When you see a movie, you're leaning back, and when you see theatre you're leaning forward.' I know exactly what she means. From the first time I went to the theatre, I was pulled into what I was seeing, into another world, and I can't help wanting everyone to experience that. Or what this man said about seeing *Journey's End*:

> Not one person in the audience applauds. Not one. Because
> of the emotional impact… The experience was stunning….
> That's what theatre can do for you. Because it's live; it's right
> in front of you. There's no distractions, you're just there.

"When I read these interviews, I had to think hard about my own ideas about taste, because a lot of the plays that had the most profound effects on these people are things that I tend to dismiss as more or less live-action versions of Hollywood. Like *Wicked*, which this 11-year-old has already seen umpteen times and knows by heart and loves madly. Because when you spend a lot of time in a professional arts field, you tend to pick up the ambient snobberies.

And there's a sour-grapes aspect to that, you know? Like 'I'm a totally cool artist, I'm smarter than you, and if you don't like or understand what I'm putting out, chalk that up to your inadequacies, not mine.' Sometimes feeling superior to the audience is the only consolation an artist has for not being supported, if you know what I mean.

"So that's another reason I'm willing to try out this strategy of measuring impact, because it puts the emphasis on the audience experience, and that could have a good effect on theatres, not just funders. Because really, a surprisingly large amount of the time, I don't see the audience coming into the equation until it's time to sell tickets. For a lot of theatres, they're not asking what issues are important to us right now and what stories need telling, like Artist said. It's what play would be an interesting challenge for the company, and what would show off our skills the best, or attract the best critical response? I guess you need both, but just like I think it would be good for funders to think more about the impact on the audience, it would be good for artistic directors to think about the same thing when they put their seasons together.

"At least in advocacy terms, that would change the conversation from artists pleading for their own funding because they're so great to being able to say they're having an impact, and that is why they're worthy of support." Advocate sighs and sits down.

DESSERT IS SERVED

Exec jumps in. "I agree," he says. "And I've heard some other things in what you've all said that might be at least the beginnings of a concept brand that has power.

"I agree, Teacher, that there's no way to turn adults into theatre fanatics if they're not already torqued that way. But that isn't necessarily the goal, is it? Success doesn't depend on converting absolute indifference into absolute passion. If you just persuaded more people to try it—to risk buying a ticket once in a while to something they might like—that would help. So the things you've all been saying about the importance of stories to our species' survival, to learning moral lessons, to feeling connected; and the way theatre can show people stories that don't get told on TV, or tell stories in ways Hollywood can't do it: those could be good arguments, if they're developed in the right way.

"In business right now," Exec says, "'creativity' is the big buzzword. Creativity and connectivity. So the idea is that the world is changing really fast, and preparation for success in that world can't just be memorizing information and applying it. You have to have imagination, think outside the box, understand how customers are feeling, all of that. I could see positioning theatre as one of the ways we learn that. Imagine this," Exec says, raising his hands as if miming a picture frame. "An ad in *Forbes*, a picture of a full theatre, and the headline: 'Creativity Lab' or something like that. Pitch theatre as a way for people in business to develop creative skills."

"Actually, that's happening," Amateur tells him. "Have you heard of applied drama? Or sometimes they say 'instrumental theatre'? These are ways of consciously using theatre to learn and teach. There's all this work going on now where theatre artists come into businesses and help them act out different challenges, using performance as a way to devise alternate strategies. They call it 'arts-based business learning.' Or Boal's Forum Theater, where the actor and spectator merge into 'spectators,' or Playback, which walks the line between theatre and psychodrama. I won't go into all the different types, but there are many kinds of interactive theatre, where the audience shapes the action, and something is learned from that. So, yes, people are doing that in many different ways. But that's not what the people in these interviews mean when they talk about theatre. It's certainly not the mainstream."

"But it's growing," says Connoisseur. "Also, theatre as part of political action, like Occupy or flash mobs, or the performance collectives that sprang up around HIV activism a few decades ago—as a matter of fact, that was the subject of my thesis, Larry Kramer and ACT UP. We have to complicate our idea of what theatre is to take in all the performative modes artists are working in. But as far as the people in the interviews are concerned, none of that is even happening. It's all utterly conventional, and I just don't know that conventional theatre can sustain these big claims that are being made around the table. I'll ask it again: does going to see *Wicked* twenty times make you a better person? Or even a different person?"

"You know what I was thinking?" asks Advocate. "Those ancient philosophers were interested in the ideal, like Plato's *Republic*. These are the kinds of questions that obsessed them: what is the good, what is the just, how can we create societies that embody those qualities? When I think about how different our questions are today, my heart sinks a little. Sometimes it seems like all we are trying to do is make things marginally better in a unjust society. Right now, I don't know anyone who's spending their energy designing the ideal government. I barely know anyone who believes that at least my idea of the good will actually prevail. And there's no chance unless we can at least conceive of it. I think theatre can be a space to imagine that."

"Maybe," says Teacher, "but in the *Republic*, Plato says music, poetry, and theatre are debilitating. He advocates rule by unelected philosopher-kings."

"Some commentators say that proves that the book is an exercise in irony, because it shows how certain high-minded ideals turn out to be dangerous in practice," Connoisseur tells them.

"Okay," says Artist. "Forget Plato. Forget philosopher-kings. Just think about it for a minute. It's really much simpler than it seems. Do you want to live in a world in which we support the people and work that makes it possible to have the kinds of experiences described in these interviews? Or a world in which these experiences are dismissed as unimportant?"

"That's what they call a no-brainer," says Acolyte. "I pick door number one. But I'm starting to question the idea that all the change needs to be on the part of the funders. Don't you think theatres could do something differently to reach more people?"

"Interesting point," says Advocate. "Because of my job, I get to hear about experiments along these lines. You know, some companies have tried to develop ongoing relationships with audience members, so people invest in the work as it's being created. They come to see sections of a play in progress, and some kind of connection with the evolving work happens. When it's ready to be mounted as a real show, there's already at least part of an audience dying to see it. Or you hear about doing theatre in bars and diners, forgetting about the whole proscenium stage, rows of seats idea, and just go where the audience is. Or co-creating work with people whose stories need to be shared, so theatre is a collaboration with non-artists, and the audience ends up being everyone connected to those people. Or companies creating partnerships with organizations that care about the same issues, and together finding the audience that really needs to see the work—it isn't 'the theatre audience,' it's the particular group of people that a particular work is created for, the people whose presence gives the work its power. There's just a lot of experimentation going on right now."

"And is that experimentation getting supported?" asks Teacher.

"Yeah," says Exec, "are they investing in R&D?"

"And if they're not, will they start investing in it if your new strategy shows that the work has 'intrinsic impact'?" asks Amateur.

There's a knock at the door. Advocate says, "That's dessert." She pokes her head outside, calling to the waiter, "Just a minute." She lifts her sheaf of papers and reads again from the interview transcripts:

> We all need to be taken out of ourselves sometimes. Because, you know, you live in yourself, really, except when you're engaged in something that takes you out of yourself. For me, theatre really takes me out of myself the whole time the show's going on. You inhabit the world of these people, and you get involved with what they want, and away from what you want. And then some moment comes in the show, towards the end, when suddenly you realize that the reason you've been so involved in this production is because what they want is really what you want. And this moment happens where it all comes together. There's this connection between you and them and some kind of...higher order of things, you know? And it all kind of comes together at that moment and just kind of explodes all around you, surrounds you, and you're not alone.

"Thank you," says Advocate to all, "for a most enlightening conversation."

Before anyone has time to utter a word, the dining-room door bursts open with a bang. Three waiters swoop in, balancing plates of dessert. They rush around the table, setting a plate before each person. All three are talking at the top of their voices, ignoring the diners, who watch open-mouthed.

"Socrates!" cries Alcibiades, the first waiter, a strikingly handsome young man. "Forget about Socrates!" He looks at the second water, Agathon. "I fancied that he was seriously enamored of my beauty, and I thought that I should therefore have a grand opportunity of hearing him tell what he knew, for I had a wonderful opinion of the attractions of my youth.

"In the prosecution of this design, when I next went to him, I sent away the attendant who usually accompanied me. Well, he and I were alone together, and I thought that when there was nobody with us, I should hear him speak the language which lovers use to their loves when they are by themselves, and I was delighted."

Alcibiades turns away. "Nothing of the sort; he conversed as usual, and spent the day with me and then went away."

"You're kidding!' exclaims Agathon, squinting suspiciously. "Tell me more."

"The next time," continues Alcibiades, "when the lamp was put out and the servants had gone away, I thought that I must be plain with him and have no more ambiguity. So I gave him a shake, and I said: 'Socrates, are you asleep?'"

"And I said 'No,'" declares the third waiter, an upright man somewhat older than the other two.

"'Do you know what I am meditating?' I asked him," says Alcibiades, pointedly ignoring Socrates.

Socrates shrugs. "So I said, 'No, What are you meditating?'"

Alcibiades responds. "'I think,' I replied, 'that of all the lovers whom I have ever had you are the only one who is worthy of me, and you appear to be too modest to speak. Now I feel that I should be a fool to refuse you this or any other favor, and therefore I come to lay at your feet all that I have and all that my friends have, in the hope that you will assist me in the way of virtue, which I desire above all things, and in which I believe that you can help me better than any one else.'"

Socrates sets down the last of his plates. He declaims: "Alcibiades, my friend, you have indeed an elevated aim if what you say is true, and if there really is in me any power by which you may become better; truly you must see in me some rare beauty of a kind infinitely higher than any which I see in you. And therefore, if you mean to share with me and to exchange beauty for beauty, you will have greatly the advantage of me; you will gain true beauty in return for appearance. But look again, sweet friend, and see whether you are not deceived in me."

Alcibiades shrugs: "Without waiting to hear more I got up, and throwing my coat about him crept under his threadbare cloak, as the time of year was winter, and there I lay during the whole night having this wonderful monster in my arms. And yet, notwithstanding all, he was so superior to my solicitations, so contemptuous and derisive and disdainful of my beauty—which really, as I fancied, had some attractions—nothing more happened, but in the morning when I awoke, I arose as from the couch of a father or an elder brother."

For the first time, Alcibiades seems to notice the diners. "This, friends, is my praise of Socrates. I have added my blame of him for his ill-treatment of me; and he has ill-treated not only me, but Charmides the son of Glaucon, and Euthydemus the son of Diocles, and many others in the same way—beginning as their lover he has ended by making them pay their addresses to him. Wherefore I say to you, Agathon, Be not deceived by him; learn from me and take warning, and do not be a fool and learn by experience, as the proverb says."

"You are sober, Alcibiades," says Socrates, "or you would never have gone so far about to hide the purpose of your satyr's praises, for all this long story is only an ingenious circumlocution, of which the point comes in by the way at the end; you want to get up a quarrel between me and Agathon, and your notion is that I ought to love you and nobody else, and that you and you only ought to love Agathon. But the plot of this Satyric or Silenic drama has been detected, and you must not allow him, Agathon, to set us at variance."

"I believe you are right," says Agathon, "and I am disposed to think that his intention in placing himself between you and me was only to divide us; but he shall gain nothing by that move."

"The usual way," says Alcibiades, looking resigned. "Where Socrates is, no one else has any chance with the fair." He makes his way out the door, with Agathon trailing behind.

Socrates starts to follow, but at the last minute, he turns and takes a bow. Alcibiades and Agathon reappear behind him, bowing too.

Connoisseur begins the applause, and everyone joins in.

After a few moments, Advocate taps her spoon against her glass, requesting silence. "*Symposium* by Plato," she says. "I also may have forgotten to mention that I chose this restaurant for a reason besides the name and the dessert menu: all the waiters are actors!"

"As opposed to every other hip restaurant in San Francisco?" asks Artist.

There's a little more applause, but it's interrupted by Amateur's loud laughter. Everyone turns to stare at him. Amateur struggles to regain his composure, sitting up straight and buttoning the top button of his blue sweater. He picks up the transcript Advocate had abandoned on the table. He reads:

> You inhabit the world of these people, and you get involved with what they want, and away from what you want. And then some moment comes in the show, towards the end, when suddenly you realize that the reason you've been so involved in this production is because what they want is really what you want.

"He nailed you!" exclaims Exec. "You're Alcibiades, trying to get Socrates to love you and to reject Agathon. Only you're the theatres and Socrates is the funders."

"Life imitates art," mumbles Connoisseur, his mouth full.

"You were right about the panna cotta," says Teacher to Advocate, licking her spoon. "But did you taste this chocolate pavé? Not even Socrates could resist this."

"Sublime," says Acolyte. "Truly sublime."

The Patrons Speak
How are artistic experiences imprinted in memory?

interviews by **Clayton Lord** and **Erin Gilley**

Taylor Greenthal

My name is Taylor Greenthal. I'm a teenager, so I like to be with my friends a lot. I like to eat a lot of good food. Until recently, I have not been a huge reader, but this summer, I really tried to read a lot more, especially plays. Because I figure, if I'm going to college, I want to kind of know what I'm talking about when I'm studying theatre. So I've done that and it's been really, really great. I've read all the plays I think I should read, and then some random ones that I've come across. So that's been really interesting. I've read some classic plays, like *Our Town* and *Who's Afraid of Virginia Woolf?* I also read *The Laramie Project*, which is a play that I really felt I should read; I felt like I was really missing out on something. And I read *Wit*. I read *Doubt*. I read *Metamorphoses* by Mary Zimmerman. Trying to figure out more of what I like and what I don't like.

And I thought it was really interesting, because I read plays that are really well-known, that a lot of people I respect really love, that I didn't find particularly touching to me, and then I read some plays that not a lot of people think are very great, that I really loved. So it was a really great experience. I got to read a lot, but I also got to learn about my taste and what I look for in a play, what I find interesting.

Up until recently, my only theatrical experiences were acting pretty much, because school plays and all of that. That's really the only theatre opportunity I've had. But a couple of months ago, I decided I wanted to direct a play. I really wanted to do a production of *The Vagina Monologues* at my school. It's done at a lot of high schools even though the content is very mature and fairly graphic.

So last year, when I was a junior, I brought it to the administration, and I had a couple teachers backing me up. And we waited a little bit, because our new school head was leaving and a younger person was coming in, and we thought maybe that was our chance. I did a lot of research about the show. I found a lot of supporters. I looked into the productions at the other high schools. But unfortunately, our school being a K-12 school, they felt uncomfortable putting their name on that production, which is really understandable. It's frustrating, but it makes a lot of sense.

But because of that, I was forced to find another play that...well, what mattered to me was really a play that was written by a woman, that was about women's issues, and a play that really was controversial and spoke to people. And I think that it really killed two birds with one stone at my school, because in our curriculum, there aren't a lot of pieces that are written by women. We don't study a lot of women's history. And we also have very little theatre at my school.

So I found *The Children's Hour* by Lillian Hellman. And because that was written in the 1930's, it's incredibly tasteful, but it's also such a timeless piece and so powerful. And I directed it with a friend for my senior project and she acted in it. It was an awesome experience, one of the most incredible experiences I've ever had. So many teachers came. And a lot of our student body came too, even though it wasn't directly connected to the school. And to put on a piece that I felt really made people think, and really brought issues that weren't talked about a lot into light or bring issues that were not discussed enough into the discussion, was really a great experience for me. And something that I really want to do for the rest of my life.

I started actually getting into theatre probably toward the end of middle school. I had been in *Little Red Riding Hood* in kindergarten and done some little things. But I was always really, really, really shy when I was younger. It wasn't something that I really gravitated towards. But then I started taking classes in middle school, and thought, "Oh, this is fun. I could do this more. It could be my thing." And so, I started doing a lot of summer programs, taking classes, being in as many shows as possible.

Arts education is so important, and it's missing, and that's bad for us. And we should talk about it. Because we're the people who are actually experiencing it. It's a really important time to talk about it and to share our stories, because once we're past it, we can remember what it was like, but living it and being part of it is what makes our stories all the more powerful.

At my school, there's definitely theatre, but it wasn't everything that I wanted to get out of my theatrical experience in high school. When I found Berkeley Rep and the Teen Council, I was able to get my theatre fix here and still do the plays at my school, but really go deeper into the art form here. It's what made me sure that this is something that I really want to be involved in as a director, as an actor, as a producer, as a teacher, really anything.

Ten years from now, I could be teaching, being a very active part of arts education, touching the students that I come across, and sharing my experience. Teaching them about the power of the arts. I could be teaching or I could be directing. I could be creating pieces that make people go, "Wow. I got something out of that that I haven't thought about or felt from anything else. Theatre is really powerful and I want to go see more theatre," or, "I should sign my kid up for an acting class because maybe they'll learn something." Or, creating theatre that travels to schools, to really reach people and show them that theatre is really powerful and it's important. It's not for everyone, but a lot of people find it really important and think it's really great.

Or, I could be working on the more political end of arts advocacy and be lobbying for new education policies, and making sure that arts are a part of that. And working on funding for regional theatres. And to make the arts as bustling a community as possible.

But I'll be involved in the arts, I know. Being at Berkeley Rep made me realize that theatre is an art form. It's fun to watch, but it's also a community that is really, really great to be a part of. There's so much to do and there's so much that needs to be done, and there's so much that I can contribute. That makes me really excited. It makes me feel like it's the place to belong. I feel like I can always give more, or I want to always give more. I feel like I have so much more potential here than anywhere else. I'm never satisfied with what I'm doing, which seems kind of depressing. I get constantly really frustrated. But it's a really cool thing.

A lot of my friends from high school don't do theatre and don't even have anything that they've found yet that they are really passionate about. I'm so lucky that I was able to find something that I was passionate about so early, because it really drove me and it gave me goals. It gave me direction for where I wanted to go in the future and what I wanted to be doing. It really gave me purpose. And I felt like was getting a lot out of life and what I was doing in high school, as opposed to a lot of other people felt. They didn't know; they're still figuring out what they wanted to do and what they were interested in.

I really believe that there's a lot more to life than test scores and there's a different kind of intelligence than just being able to do statistics. You can't just measure intelligence based off of how well someone does on the tests. That's what makes arts education so important. There are so many different kinds of learners and so many different kinds of people, and all they are exposed to right now is academics, which are incredibly important, but there is also a creative intelligence, an artistic intelligence that a lot of these students have that they are not able to develop or even discover.

And especially with the problems the world faces today...we have climate change and we have a gazillion wars going on. The solutions that we are looking for require a lot of creativity. They require a lot of collaboration and really thinking outside of the box. I think that students being able to take a class in improvisation or take a ceramics class: anything where they are able to think on their own, do something different and do something that's theirs. I think that teaches them about thinking outside of a box, which we need to really progress.

My parents and their parents and their parents—my entire family isn't really involved in the arts. They're all business people. They're not thrilled with the idea of me being an artist and studying theatre. They're definitely more excited about the marketing side of it, or the management side, as opposed to the performance side just because of financial stability, but they are very supportive of me and my choices. My choices, more than of "theatre," I guess.

And now I have two younger siblings and they both do a lot of shows. So my parents, who both have pretty terrible stage fright and aren't really into performing, have three kids that love being on stage, that's really what we're excited about, which is interesting.

I mean, I think they appreciate art; my parents took me to a couple shows when I was younger, not a lot. It wasn't a regular thing that we did. I saw my cousin in a couple musicals when she was younger. I remember that. The first musical I saw was *Lil Abner*, and I came home and I was like, "Mom, we need to buy the video," and I watched it a billion times. And I knew all the songs. And so, I saw art in that way...it was more to support my cousin than to enjoy and appreciate art as an art form, or theatre as an art form.

Coming to Berkeley Rep was the first time I was able to see plays that were really different from what I'd seen before. Because the shows that I'd seen before, it was like...I'd gone with my Girl Scout troop to go see *Wicked* or I'd seen *White Christmas* in San Francisco. And coming to Berkeley Rep and seeing shows... The shows that I saw here opened my eyes because theatre doesn't just have to be the lights and the glitz and the high kicks. And the theatre I found here, that's the theatre that I really, really fell in love with.

I found myself looking for more shows like that and trying to find shows on my own. But because my friends in high school weren't interested in theatre, it was really hard to get them to go with me and I don't ever think they really did. Of my core group through high school, I was the only one involved in theatre. That was what was really, actually sparked my interest in arts and obviously arts education, because I was like, "Why don't they care?" They don't have to

411

get up on stage and sing a song, but why don't they just want to come and see a show? I mean, it's $10, and it's going to be amazing.

It's like this inexplicable apathy. When you ask them, "Well, why don't you want to come?" they're like, "I don't know. I just don't really like theatre." It's, "Well, have you seen a lot of plays?" "No, not really." I think it was just because, in school and growing up, they were taught... Some kids, maybe the drama geeks, take a drama class after school. But whatever drama that they heard of, it's always secondary to school and to athletics and to everything else. So to them, it just wasn't something that they thought of as part of their life. It was part of somebody else's life, and it was an after school thing, and it was the elective that they chose not to take.

It was really interesting, and really sad, and it made me want to do something about it.

I think that if they had a little exposure when they were younger, like I did, they might understand why it mattered to me, because I think that's something that was difficult for them to understand. I think it would have made a huge difference. Not that they would have become actors, but just that they'd be like, "Yeah, I'd love to see a show," or seeing plays as something that they do. I think that's why theatres have such a difficult time getting young people to be part of their audiences. It's not because theatre isn't cool enough or the plays that they're doing aren't relevant enough. It's really that the young people don't...really, they don't really know it's there and they don't know why it's important, what it could do for them.

I think that goes all the way back to education and what they were taught. Which is really sad, because once they're older it's really hard to teach someone to appreciate something. That just doesn't make a whole lot of sense. "It's important just because it's important, and you should know that it's important." No, they need that exposure when they're younger to be able to figure that out on their own.

Two years ago, I saw this show *Girlfriend* here at Berkeley Rep. It was the most memorable show that I've ever seen. It was very simple and it was very real. It was about two teenage boys in love, set to the Matthew Sweet album *Girlfriend*, which was really fun, really lovely, sweet music. Just how real the characters seemed, and how real their connection was, was so memorable. It wasn't that the plot was super complicated or that something really dramatic happened, like somebody died, it was really just a sweet story, and it made me really giddy and happy. I loved the music and I loved everything about it.

Everyone I saw it with was super skipping down the street after the show, because we were all in such a great mood. It was really cool that this really simple story made everyone so excited. It just seemed so effortless, the whole way the production was done. It was so day-to-day and so normal. But it was a love story, and being a teenage girl I just melted, and I don't think I'll ever forget it.

I saw it on Teen Night, and I was with a bunch of people that I knew. What I like about Teen Council and Teen Nights is that I'm not with my closest friends, and so I really just get to see the pieces for me. I don't know why having my closest friends there changes it, but I think it's really my experience and my own thing. And I never really understood why people like seeing movies by themselves and do all that. But it really changes it when you're on your own and having this experience just to have this experience, rather than it being a social thing.

I mean, theatre's a great social opportunity. But there's something kind of cool about seeing it on your own and thinking about it. It's only what you think. It's kind of frustrating when you can't go just talk about it with everyone, but it's nice, and it's your own experience. You get to keep it. It's special and it's no one else's. That's the cool thing about theatre, is that everyone sees the same piece differently.

In the beginning of the show, both boys are pretty into each other, but they're both very shy and very quiet about it. They have these phone conversations that are kind of like, "Hi." "Hi." "Want to go out?" "Yeah." "OK, bye." "Bye."

They're very awkward, but they're so adorable. We've all been there, where you just can't talk to that person. It was so relatable, so fun to watch, but also kind of painful because, again, we all know what it feels like to have that. And afterward, you hang up the phone and you're like, "Why did I... Why didn't I say anything? Why did that go that way?"

The whole audience, everyone, was giggling and everyone had the same reaction. That was really cool, because it's like, "Oh, I felt that way." And hundreds of other people sitting in this room with me right now have felt that way too. Which was cool. Like we all shared that moment of, "Yeah, I've been there and, yeah, it's really uncomfortable." Which was cool.

I like theatre that reflects things that I've experienced, that's very real and relatable and like things I've done, and I also like theatre that reflects things I haven't experienced, that just blows my mind, where it's like, "What just happened? Where did that come from?"

413

I think even though the most memorable piece I've seen was a very simple one, a lot of the theatre that I've loved the most has been the theatre where it's just out of this world, and really insane and larger than life, and something that I feel like I could never do in a million years, and that I can just sit back and be amazed by or really confused by, or a piece where I feel like I really need to talk to a lot of people after it. Because that's something that I think is so great about theatre, that it creates a lot of discussion.

It's sometimes controversial, and it's not an experience where you can just sit there, watch the show, get up and leave, and go on with your day. For me, at least, that's not how it is. I can't just watch a show without talking to people about it. And of course, that doesn't really go with the thing I said about going by myself. But even when I go by myself, I usually find people who don't really care and just talk at them for a really long time about it and try to get them to get excited about it, which sometimes works and sometimes doesn't.

I really like theatre that's not in this world, that's really a different experience. And this will be really corny, but that's what's so magical about it, is that they can create these things and create these pictures, and create these ideas that you just don't see in day-to-day life, and you can totally get sucked out of your everyday life and put into this place for a few hours, and that's great, that's really, really cool. Everyone should experience that.

When you see a piece of theatre, you see all the work that went into it. You see how hard the actors are working in front of you, you see how the lighting designer, and the set designer, and the sound designer really had to work together to make it happen. It's there right in front of you; you're sitting in the same room. And because I have been in shows before, I think about the stage manager must be going crazy right now, and the director, that was a brilliant choice. And I think there's so much more to stimulate you at a theatre. There's a lot of spontaneity, and there's a lot of revelation, and that's really unique to theatre.

I think that the experience of going to theatre is much more interactive; there's some kind of saying that when you see a movie you're leaning back and when you see theatre you're leaning forward. To me, that says it right there. I don't like a really passive experience. I like to feel like I'm a part of it and feel like it's not something that can just happen over and over again. It's just you and the other people in the room getting this right now. It's not playing in a gazillion theatres across the country, it's not a billion people seeing this right now, and that makes it so much more special and unique and interesting.

It's such a no-brainer for me to see theatre as opposed to a movie. I think it is how special that experience feels and how unique it feels and how there's just a lot of depth in a theatre, in a show. There's just so much that goes into it. To be able to experience it that one time, that exact show is never going to happen again.

When I go to a show, I expect to feel something that I'm not expecting. I saw the Mike Daisey show about Apple. I really didn't know what to expect. I thought it would be like, "OK, this one guy is going to talk for a really, really, really long time. I hope he's engaging." But what happened instead was I felt like a part of this journey that he took us on, this clear transformation from the beginning of the show to the end of the show. Afterward, I was exhausted. I was like, "Whoa." I was really not expecting to feel everything that I felt and that's what made it, to me, such a great show.

It's coming out of the show feeling so much more than you'd expect. I don't think I've ever gone into a show being like, "Oh, I'm going to feel a lot going into the show." I expect to see something nice and entertaining. And usually, what I get out of it is just so much more. I don't know how it keeps happening, but it does. I'm always pleasantly surprised by how I feel after a show. I'm not really going to question it because it's really exciting.

Directing *The Children's Hour*, reading so much more into it than I had read into really any other story ever, and it being such a packed and very interesting and powerful story I think I really learned a lot about how we feel and how certain people interact. That show changed my life in that it made me really want to read deeper into things. It made me want to learn about more people and more relationships. With every good play I've seen or read, something has stayed with me and affected the way that I think about things and the way that I learn about things.

When I say that I'm passionate about the arts, I mean that I think it's really life-changing and I think that experiencing the arts is really important and I think it's an integral part of who I am and it's really shaped how I see the world and what I want to do with my life and how I interact with other people. It's become such a huge part of me that if I didn't have it I'd be losing such a huge part of me. Being able to see art, being able to participate in art and create art—it's what I do and it's so much of me. It's creepy to think of myself without it because I wouldn't be a whole person.

The arts offer escapes from the mundane and the day-to-day things that we experience in life. They provide the opportunities to learn about the world and learn about each other in ways that aren't always presented to us. They offer outlets for a lot of people who have so much fire, passion, so many ideas inside of them—so that they can express it in a really beautiful way that other people can appreciate. It makes culture and it makes our world so much more interesting with people expressing themselves creatively.

If we didn't have creative expression, I don't even know...if we didn't have creative expression, we would implode. I don't know what would happen, it just wouldn't be enjoyable.

I see that, a little, when I've seen something that really makes me see the world differently and my family and friends haven't. There's this disconnection and that kind of tension. I see the world in this way through this new lens, even if it's temporary, and when other people don't see it the same way...it goes back to that I have the experience of learning about this and now I get to see the world this way.

I always get mad at myself, because I feel like I should share what I've seen, but I can never do it justice and I don't know why. I don't know. I think there's just something about having that experience that a lot of other people don't have. It causes a disconnect, but it's not always a bad thing. I want to teach them what I've learned and they want to teach me why they disagree or why they like what I've told them. And I think that's great.

Barry Levine

My name is Barry Levine. I have been retired since April 2005. Now we're up to 2011, so I've been very happy in retirement. I don't miss work at all. Most of my working life, I was in something that would be called public finance. It was mostly as a credit analyst, Bank of America, a company called Capital Guarantee Insurance. We insured farms. I worked for Charles Schwab. I have a long experience in public finance.

Artistically…I don't know. Well, I played piano as a kid. I was forced to do it. I didn't want to do it, but like a lot of other kids, parents said, "You're going to take piano." Then I stopped when I got a little bit older. I got back to it about 20-some-odd years ago, and now I still have the same teacher. We've become good friends and we have a good time.

Right now, I'm playing a Chopin waltz, and I actually heard it yesterday on the radio. Of course, it was done a lot better than I could play them. It was beautiful, and I was thinking, "Boy, that's a lot different than my version." I'm about halfway through it, listening to it, and this piece is just beautiful. Technique... I'm just listening to it, the technique, the way it sounded, and I was listening to the timing. I've got to work on the timing, because I had a lesson on Friday, and we're working on this piece, and I have to get the timing correct. And listening to this piece, on the radio, you can hear him, Chopin. How he'd do it.

So I said, "Ah…," and when I go back to the piano to the Chopin, try to play it, I hear him.

There're so many beautiful pieces of music. I'm just happy to be able to play a few of them. There're just so many. But to me, it's just fun. I enjoy doing it. Probably, as a hands-on artistic expression, that's probably the closest I come to an artistic expression, playing the piano. But I don't think I really have an artistic, creative bent. So I'm not sure piano counts as an artistic expression.

I guess, in a way, my artistic expression comes from experiencing theatre. I think I get the artistic experience—I was going to say "second-hand," but it's not the right word, second-hand. You get it more…passively. But it's an artistic experience, all the same, because you can appreciate the artistic experience and the creativity of what goes into it. What I get, why I think it's artistic—I get the pleasure from seeing something well done, and sometimes extraordinarily well done. That gives me a great deal of pleasure.

And it's one of the great things about retirement, having the time. We have our "T" for travel and our "T" for theatre, and that's how we spend our time now, mostly. We do a lot of traveling. We've gotten it up to about 12 weeks a year of traveling. We go to New York once a year for a couple of weeks. Then we try to do two big trips, five weeks or thereabouts.

We do a lot of theatre, we do a lot of live performances. My wife and I have been married over 40 years. We've been going to the theatre forever. We do it together. Only once in a blue moon did we see something without the other. She was in New York once, she went to see a play and I wasn't with her. So when I went to New York a few weeks later on business, I went to see the same play.

Now, we do have some jealousy because one time I was in New York and I took my mother to see three plays that my wife never saw. So I always give her the needle about those plays. "I remember when I saw that." And she gets very angry because she wasn't there to see it, not because I was doing it on purpose. It just worked out that way.

It's a long time. It's a lot of plays. And we are just—we talk about it. We talk about plays.

We are, I guess you'd could call it, culture mavens, but most of it is theatre. We maybe see about 100 live things a year: opera, ballet, miscellaneous things. But mostly theatre. We subscribe to ACT, Aurora, Berkeley Rep, TheatreWorks, Magic, San Francisco Playhouse. And we also have a small subscription to the Opera, and to the Ballet and to the Philharmonia Baroque Orchestra. We do a lot, but still it comes down to theatre.

As I said, we go to New York once a year, so that's theatre, and family and friends. And then maybe once every other year, we go to London. Last time we went was last September, after a trip to Russia. We went to London for ten days and saw maybe 12 plays; that's kind of the thing we do.

So we really spend our life with theatre and culture, and travel. That takes up a lot of time. And otherwise, the piano, though there I've been doing the same thing for 20 years. You go like this and you wind up going nowhere, but I have a good time. And once in a while, I'll take a language because we're going to go traveling. We go to France, Italy or Spain, I do the language. I speak some Italian, some French, enough to get by in both countries and the same in Spanish. We just got back from South America a few weeks ago. Easter Island, Chile, Argentina and then we went to Rio for Carnival.

418

I've wanted to travel forever. Forever since I've been a kid. I got the bug from my parents. They had done some travel in the '50s, when not many people were traveling. They actually went to Europe, they went to South America. And I thought it was very exotic and very interesting, going to these places you could see on the map. I always loved to look at maps to track where they went. When I was a kid, I went to a travel camp. It wasn't very glamorous. We got into the back of a truck and we went around the country. And I saw a lot of the country through the truck. Travel started then, and both of my wife and I love travel, so we kind of feed off of each other.

I love the history. To see places that you've read about, it gives you a platform to relate to when you read something. You say, "I've been there. I actually stood there. These events occurred." I just find that a terrific feeling.

When you get into an airplane these days, in 12 hours, you're elsewhere on the Earth. It's pretty amazing that these people are over there, and they have a life that's different from your life, but somewhat similar. Your little patch of land is a little bit different from their little patch of land. It exposes you to a lot of things. And the food's good, if you go to Italy and France. So every place has got its charms.

We live for the theatre in England when we travel, though when we go other places, maybe we'll go to one opera, or a performance, but mostly to see the opera house or the particular building. We did go to a play, once, in Salzburg, Austria. It was this play, *The Comedian Harmonists*, small, like an off-Broadway theatre. We had to find the theatre, get tickets and it was all in German but it was mostly music. It was a great experience because we have a wonderful time listening to the music. We knew that we got the gist of the plot. The Comedian Harmonists were a well-known group in 1930's Germany— very, very popular singers. They did some funny side songs but they were also caught up in Hitler's anti-Semitic policies.

Here we were, surrounded by locals, and we were obviously the only non-German speakers there. It was a great experience. But generally, we just don't do that. We go to London, that's where we really do our cultural endeavors.

I think, if you travel and if you see enough theatre, which brings a variety of ideas to you and to the audience…the ideas that you can get from theatre, someone's play, someone who's got an *idea*, whether it's social, political or commentary on today's life—it gives you a thought. It makes you think. And a lot of people don't think. A lot of people don't really know about other things. And theatre, can do that. Theater can give you an idea. Sometimes it's just entertainment. But sometimes they have a point, maybe a point that strikes you as not your point of view.

It gives you a point of reference and a thing to think about. Which makes you, to use another word, less ignorant. The world is so full of ignorance, because people don't want to be exposed to ideas, or they have no need to be exposed to ideas. And they're myopic. And they've got shutters on, and theatre exposes you.

Travel, in the same way, exposes you. You go someplace different; you leave this place and you go 12 hours and you're over here. And life is different, or somewhat different, or very different, depending where you go. You go to India and it's vastly different from here.

And if you get the chance to talk to people, talk to them. Listen to them. You get a whole different perspective, and it reduces your ignorance of the world. It opens you up to ideas, it opens you up to tolerance. It opens you up to living a better life and having empathy for other people. It teaches you that there isn't one view. There are a lot of views. Travel can do that. Theater can do that.

I used to go to theatre with my father in the '50s. We would go... I was the oldest of three kids, and he and I would go together, which was a great memory. We used to go together. We went to Manhattan, drove in.

We had a ritual. Before the theatre, we went to the steam bath. There was a place. In those days, it was... Back in the '50s, there were still places that had steam baths and massage: steam bath, hot room, steam room, a pool, and everything else. We went there. That was our pre-theatre. We spent a couple of hours. My father loved that stuff, so we did that.

And then, afterwards, we would sleep little bit. We'd take a little bit of a nap at this bath, and then we'd go to lunch, and then we'd go to the theatre. And so I saw a lot of theatre. I really became addicted. My father took me to see ballet and opera, as well, but I wasn't as interested in that. But the theatre was great. I saw *The Most Happy Fella*—the original with Robert Weede. We saw a lot I can't remember. A lot of plays. Andy Griffith in *No Time for Sergeants*, when he'd just become popular. *Inherit the Wind*, the original. It was just wonderful.

I was a teenager. Junior high and high school. I have just great warm feelings about that. My brothers were jealous, though, because I was the one always going. It was a nice way to spend time with your dad. And we both enjoyed it. He would go pick plays that got good reviews, and we would go.

It's a wonderful memory.

And theatre was a vehicle for the two of us to get a little bit closer. The memory of that sticks with me, of going to the steam bath and having this kind of ritual. That's something that I'll never—it doesn't fade from my memory, and the plays along with it. And that was it, I caught the bug.

I remember when we went to this Shakespeare Festival, I think it's gone now, in Stratford, Connecticut. Not the famous one, in Ontario; this was in Connecticut. And it was one of the first plays I'd ever seen, and it was—what was it? It was a Shakespeare. *Henry...* It's the one where he gives that great speech in the field of—when they go to France and...is that *Henry V*? No, *Henry IV*. The St. Crispin Day speech. It was great. It was wonderful. The color, just the color of the Shakespeare, it was a great experience.

And then, after I got out of college, I continued going to plays. And once we got married... We're both theatre lovers and she's been going to plays since she was young. And so we just continued on.

A few years ago, I saw this play called *Journey's End*. *Journey's End* was a play that was written in the 1920's. It was written after World War I. So it's an antiwar play, but it's a little bit more complicated. It's very melodramatic. It takes place in the trenches in Belgium, I believe, and it's just about these guys living in these trenches, and eventually they're going to have to go over the top. And you get to know these people. There's an officer, there's some non-commissioned officers, there's just a couple of infantrymen. One guy is afraid and has to be told that he's got to go over the hill, over the top.

And you get to know these people. And they know that it's pointless. They're all going to get killed. Every one of them is going to get killed. They know that. That's what's going to happen. They're going to cross, they're going to go 100 yards, and they're going to be obliterated by German machine guns. But they're going to do it. And they're going to do it because they have a belief system that, despite the stupidity of the upper echelon, the generals and everything else, that they still have to do this for God, king and country.

So at the end of the play, the guys go over the top. The end of the play. And you hear some gunshots...and that's it. And after the end of the play, after this is all done...the play is over and then, all of a sudden, down from the proscenium arch, there's this big, grayish-white scrim. It comes down and it's got names on it, names of hundreds and hundreds of people who died, British.

In front of that are the members of the cast standing at attention. This thing comes down, they're standing at attention, it's a bright light—and not one

person in the audience applauds. Not one. Because of the emotional impact...
and I had tears in my eyes. Everybody had tears in their eyes. You could drop
a pin and there was no... You couldn't applaud because it was...so emotionally
wrenching—and you couldn't applaud because it would seem to be improper
that you would do that.

The experience was just amazing. The emotional impact of the stupidity,
particularly World War I, the stupidity of it... I mean, it's bringing tears to my
eyes right now. It was just an overwhelming experience. You would just walk
out of there like, "Wow." You got...*bam*. You got hit like that.

It's one of those things that, when you go to theatre, if something like that
happens—it doesn't happen all the time, but when it does happen, it's *live*. It's
there in front of you like that. It's just... You have to experience it. It's tough to
talk about it. But that's what it felt like. *Boom!* And I'll never forget it, ever.

That's what theatre can do for you. Because it's live; it's right in front of
you. There's no distractions, you're just there.

Another time, we went to see *Romeo and Juliet* in London. It was
performed by an Icelandic repertory company. It was around Christmas time,
and they had sold out. So we were there at Christmas time the year later, and
they'd brought it back. It's very unusual. They had the part that was done on
trapeze. And at the beginning this guy welcomes you, and it's all in Icelandic.
He's speaking *Icelandic*.

He's going on in Icelandic, and someone reminds him, one of the cast
reminds him, "Well, this audience, they don't speak Icelandic. They speak
English."

So he started to change to English. Then, all of a sudden, they're doing
Romeo and Juliet, half of which was in Icelandic and half of which was in
English. The great scene, the balcony scene, it's all done in Icelandic.

But you see it, and you *know* it. You know what they're saying and you feel
it, even though they're speaking Icelandic. You feel the emotion even though
you don't know the language. You feel it. You know the context, you've seen
the play before. I mean, you know *Romeo and Juliet*. And all of this stuff,
when it's in Icelandic, you know it and you understand it, and you feel it even
though it's a different language. The heart and soul was there, which was just
wonderful.

Theatre is talking about ideas. And ideas might change your thinking,
they might change your viewpoint. I think, just by virtue of getting ideas and
listening and seeing and different perspectives and things, I think that can

change your approach, your life, to some extent. But you don't know it. It's like when you read something. An idea sticks in your head and you change your view on something. It shifts your perspective.

I think it's because I was brought up with theatre. It becomes part of your life to attend theatre. For me, theatre became an addiction. That's what it is. It became an addiction. And it goes back to—I knew, at the theatre, you're seeing a performance, that's the only time that that performance is going to be given that way. Because it's not going to be given the same way in the evening performance after a matinee or the next night. Every one is different.

So what you see is unique. It's unique. It's by itself. It's live, it's in front of you. There are real people out there on stage. And they have to act. They really have to do something, and it's tangible, touchable. These people are doing stuff, are performing, they're being other people, creating themselves, and you fall into it. You *believe* it with these people.

It's just part of what we do. It's an addiction; it becomes a part of your life. I read every theatre review in *The New York Times*. Just in case it's something that we're interested in, if we go to New York. Or if it shows up out here. It's an addiction. Live theatre, to me, is just superior to any other form. I mean, I go to opera, which is very pleasant. But I don't feel the same thing. I can go to the opera. I just don't get emotionally involved there, but I can get emotionally involved with theatre.

There's something about the magic of someone being on stage and turning themselves into somebody else right in front of you. And having to do it without any replays—no "Stop and let's do it over again." They've got to be able to function and they've got to interact.

And of course, the greatest thing is when you get an ensemble together that everybody works in a play and works together as a group. The interaction, you watch the interaction. I'm talking to you. We're in the play, but there's a third person over here that is also reacting to this. And you can see that. Something is just all in all about that.

You have to be passionate. You have to believe in it. And I do. Theater's been around for how many thousands of years? It's important. It's *important*. Theater is an important way to disseminate people's thoughts. It's important because it gives you ideas. The playwright can put his or her ideas in people's mouths, through the actors to the audience.

Theater is more accessible. Music is... I like it or I don't like it. Theater, you can understand theatre. You can understand the creativity. You can understand the mechanics. You can understand the sets. You can understand the costuming. You can understand it. You can grasp it. You can get your arms around it.

Theater is…magic unto itself. It would be so sad if it disappeared. It's a sad thing for any art form. Art is a human expression. It's a way for people to express themselves to others through theatre, opera, movies. These things are always for people to express themselves. We need them. You need those kinds of vehicles.

There would be gaping hole for humanity. Can you imagine not having Shakespeare produced? That's theatre. You're not going to see Shakespeare. You're not going to see George Bernard Shaw. You're not going to see...not that I like Chekhov, but you're not going to see Chekhov.

It would just be, it would be sad. It would be just like someone made a gaping hole in your soul. Theater, other kinds of art as well

We're passionate. We go. We subscribe, because that helps the theatre survive. We want to help keep them alive. So we subscribe. We're also donors. Because we don't want to lose it. We don't want to lose it.

And you never know what's around the corner with something. The next play you go to see might be a knockout. And the enjoyment of watching it, and the acting—you never know what's around the corner. Sometimes you will see something. You go see a revival of a play you never heard of. And you say, "Wow. That was really good. How come...? Where was...?" And you say, "Wow!" But if there wasn't a little production company doing it...

You've got to make sure they survive because, if they don't survive, theatre's not going to survive because there's no one to put on the plays. The plays won't survive, and it'll just be a dustbin of history. That really shouldn't happen. It really shouldn't. It would be harmful. It's part of our heritage, part of our heritage. We have great playwrights, and that shouldn't be lost as a relic.

That's why we support the theatre and we're passionate about it—because we're always open to surprise. You just don't know what the next adventure might be. Sometimes there's nothing. But you never know. There might be that one that really sticks in your mind forever. That's what theatre is all about.

Sydni Taines and Sarah Taines

CL: Can you just tell me a little bit about yourself? What subjects do you like in school? What do you like to do when you're not in class, and things like that?

Sydni: My name is Sydni. I'm eleven, and I'm in the sixth grade. I like math and science, and I like to draw.

CL: Is that a new school you just started?

Sydni: Yeah.

CL: How is it?

Sydni: It's good.

CL: We were talking before and you said you did some stuff for theatre productions at school, right?

Sydni: Yeah.

CL: What do you do?

Sydni: I do tech crew for spotlights.

CL: Just following people around?

Sydni: Yeah.

CL: Do you like that?

Sydni: Yeah.

CL: How long have you been doing that?

Sydni: Well I started doing it in the fall.

CL: You think you'll keep doing it?

Sydni: Yeah.

CL: What about you Sarah? Can you tell me a little bit about yourself, and what you do, and what you enjoy doing, and how you define yourself?

Sarah: I'm a nurse. I work nightshift. And I'm Sydni's mom and I have another daughter who's 13. I spend a lot of time doing that. Being a nurse allows you the time off to be a mom as well. So that's a good deal. I go to her shows when she's working. I do a lot of sports. I'm athletic, and I like to be outdoors.

CL: When you're not at school, Sydni, what do you do when you're hanging out at home?

Sydni: Play with my iTouch.

CL: Yeah. What do you play?

Sydni: I just mainly play games.

CL: What's your favorite game?

Sydni: "Robot Unicorn Attack." It's a game where you try to get the unicorn. You have to keep it jumping, smashing into stars.

CL: OK. Do you hang out with friends?

Sydni: Mmhmm.

CL: What do you do then?

Sydni: We just mainly go downtown, and hangout here.

CL: Good. And what about you Sarah? What do you do? I know you probably don't have much downtime with two kids.

Sarah: Yeah. I don't know downtime, I mean I read and try and keep up with that. Kylie plays soccer, so I'm the manager of her soccer team. I'm always busy, and chasing her down, making sure she's not downtown.

Sydni: I'm not always.

Sarah: Yeah.

CL: Sydni, do you play any sports?

Sydni: Yeah. I do gymnastics.

CL: Oh, I used to do gymnastics. What events do you do? Do you do floor exercise? And cartwheels and stuff for balancing?

Sydni: I do everything.

Sarah: The school she goes to it's mostly, they run them all. You're not specific to one. They do everything.

CL: Sydni, when you want to express yourself artistically, do you draw, or paint, or listen to music, or play music? What do you do?

Sydni: I just mainly draw.

Sarah: And you paint too.

Sydni: And I paint. And I have a great art kit.

CL: And what types of things do you draw?

Sydni: Disney characters.

Sarah: She draws Disney a lot. But she draws these pretty amazing geometrical designs, and then colors them all in. The whole paper is covered in geometrical shapes. Pretty cool. She's pretty talented for...she's never taken a class.

Sydni: Except for cycle.

Sarah: Yeah.

Man1: Oh, what's that?

Sydni: It's like a rotation thing that happens every quarter. There's like art.

Sarah: It's sixth grade electives. So instead of choosing, they cycle them through four different things.

Sydni: My friend's mom says it's like a cheese platter.

Sarah: A cheese platter. It's true.

CL: And do you do art in school? What art do you do when you're at school?

Sydni: Just mainly the Disney characters.

CL: Is that like you've got a class where you can draw at school?

Sarah: Not right now. It was part of that cycle. But then next year she's signed up for art and woodshop I think. And computer stuff, too. So she's in computer graphics. Right?

Sydni: Mmhmm.

Sarah: So there will be lots of art next year. And then you're going to do tech crew again for the play?

Sydni: Yeah.

CL: Sarah, would you say that you express yourself artistically?

Sarah: I'm not so artistic. But I like to listen to music. Mostly just listen to music and that kind of thing.

CL: What kind of music do you listen to?

Sarah: Whatever my daughter is listening to—so I know what she's listening to.

CL: Well then, so, Sydni what kind of music do you listen to?

Sydni: A lot of stuff.

Sarah: Yeah. It's all varied, huh?

Sydni: Yeah.

CL: I guess that's how it goes now.

CL: Sarah, I know when you're listening to their music, it's probably not just for leisure. Do you pick different types of music to listen to, to relax?

Sarah: Depending on how energetic I'm feeling or how relaxed I'm feeling, different stuff. I think the drawing kind of helps Sydni just relax as well. If she's had a hard day, just to take a few minutes just to be by herself and get things sorted, you know? I think art's really important for that in many ways. Right?

Sydni: Mmhmm.

Sarah: Mmhmm.

CL: If you had to pick one thing that's not at school that you like best to do when you got time, what is your favorite thing to do other than being at school?

Sydni: Drawing. I just like drawing because it's fun.

CL: How do you pick the stuff that you're going to draw? I know you said Disney characters. How do you know which ones you're going to draw?

Sydni: Well I don't always draw Disney, but if I want to then I will, but I just draw random stuff, like an alien.

Sarah: Whatever comes to mind at that time.

Sydni: Yeah.

CL: And when you draw something like that, are you proud of the stuff that you draw?

Sydni: Yeah.

CL: Do you show it to other people?

Sydni: Sometimes.

CL: You were telling me about the trip you're planning to travel. Can you talk to me a little bit about the kind of travel experiences that you've had?

Sydni: We've been to many places. Most of them were fun.

Sarah: For an 11-year-old, she's quite well-travelled. We love to travel. We feel there's a bigger world than what's in this old neighborhood, and we need to make sure they are introduced to it. So they realize it's a bigger world, too. So she's quite well-travelled. Where did you go last? What did you do in spring break?

Sydni: We went to New York.

CL: What did you do in New York?

428

Sydni: We saw plays mainly. *Wicked, Mamma Mia!, Addams Family*, and *Sister Act*.

CL: What did you think of them?

Sydni: They were good. I really liked *Wicked* and *Addams Family*.

CL: What about them did you like?

Sydni: They were funny. The music.

CL: You told me earlier, but how many times have you seen *Wicked*?

Sydni: Eight times.

CL: How long ago was the first time you saw *Wicked*?

Sydni: I was probably four. It was really a long time ago. I saw some shows at the Orpheum in San Francisco. I saw most of them at the Orpheum. I think about five of them I saw at the Orpheum. Right?

CL: How many times did you see it New York? Twice, right?

Sydni: Yep.

CL: So you saw it six times at the Orpheum.

Sydni: Yeah.

CL: Can you tell me in your own words the story of "Wicked" a little bit?

Sydni: It's about things that happen before Dorothy. And so it kind of like gives explanation about the Tin Man and the Lion and the Scarecrow. And then it shows how the Wicked Witch of the West became wicked. And then it showed how Galinda and the Wicked Witch of the West were like friends but then…it just showed that. And then it showed how the monkey became flying. They were just regular monkeys, first. Yeah.

Sarah: So it kind of explained all of *The Wizard of Oz*.

Sydni: Yep.

CL: When you see *Wicked*, how does it make you feel?

Sydni: Happy.

CL: Do you have a particular moment in the show that's your favorite moment?

Sydni: In the second act, when Galinda and the Wicked Witch of the West are having a cat fight. My favorite lines are in there.

Sarah: What are the lines?

Sydni: "We can't all come and go by bubble".

CL: That's a good line. Why do you think you enjoyed *Wicked* so much?

Sydni: Because it's funny, and good music, it's really very cool. That's probably my favorite musical.

Sarah: Yeah?

Sydni: Yep.

Sarah: Okay.

Sydni: I have a picture, from *Wicked*. From when me and my best friend went together.

Sarah: And what's the picture? Who signed the picture?

Sydni: The original cast.

CL: Where'd you get that, Sydni?

Sydni: New York.

CL: That's really cool. See, *Wicked* is the new *Rent*.

Sarah: Yeah, yeah.

CL: When I was growing up, that was the thing that we all got obsessed about.

Sarah: For us it was Rogers and Hammerstein, right?

CL: Right. Sarah, did you grow up with a lot of theatre?

Sarah: Yes.

CL: Can you talk to me a little bit about growing up, and what theatre was in your life growing up? And maybe why it's part of their lives as well?

Sarah: Well, my parents were very into the arts, although they weren't artistic in any way, shape, or form. They loved the arts and they worked to make sure that theatre was part of growing up. Every year we went to *Christmas Carol*. We saw Lamplighters shows and all the Gilbert and Sullivan musicals and whatever. At least once a month we would go. Back then it wasn't as expensive, so it was much easier to get to it versus now where it's a little more complicated to go see a show, because at $80 a ticket, for four of us, that doesn't make it all that feasible. But it's important for them.

I think it's a big part of growing up, learning the arts, the whole concept of it. And I'm thrilled that Sydni wants to be in the tech crew so she knows the backstage and all that. A little shy to be on stage, but if she ever wants to do that certainly we will support her in doing that. It's important, I think, for her to know the arts and then to know that art is available, and good for the mind, and relaxing, and makes her happy. Takes her away and that kind of thing.

I guess the whole worldly view is what I want them to have. The whole worldly experience of life, to not feel that this is it right here, to understand that there's a whole world to explore not only through travel, but arts and travel. Crafts and different kinds of music, world music, as well as going to theatre and the arts, that helps expand their minds and makes them think outside the box and know that there's more to think about. My theme for them is to think outside the box and this one does a great job of that. Not going with the status quo, not just always doing what everybody else is doing. I think that's really important.

That leads to a very dynamic person and a very dynamic life and can lead to anything in the future. And it teaches her not be afraid of anything; to be anywhere, to go anywhere, to change—and if change happens, they learn that they can just roll with it and it will just be okay.

CL: How often do you guys go see theatre?

Sarah: Well, they just spent the week in New York. Then she went to the high school and saw the high school play, she was in the middle school play and last night she went and saw the elementary school play. I guess it's at least once a month we do something theatrelike.

Sydni: Yeah.

CL: Sydni, did you want to go see the high school and the elementary school plays? Did you decide that you wanted to do that?

Sydni: Yeah. But I just mainly wanted to see the one last night because it was at my elementary school, so it was like I have to go.

Sarah: She volunteered at one of the other elementary schools plays. They were looking for help, and so she sold concessions at intermission for them.

CL: Would you like to go see more theatre than you do?

Sydni: Yeah.

Sydni: I just really want to see *Wicked* again.

Sarah: And there's other things we want to see.

Sydni: Yeah.

Sarah: Yeah? Like what? What's coming?

Sydni: *Twilight.*

Sarah: *Twilight* is coming? What else is coming? Anything is coming that we're interested in?

431

Sydni: Not really.

Sarah: Not really?

Sydni: I don't think so, at least.

CL: Do you think you get to see most of the stuff you want to see or is there stuff that you just can't go to for whatever reason?

Sydni: I'm not really sure.

CL: What about you, Sarah? Would you like to be able to go to more, or do you go to the amount that you have time for?

Sarah: I go to the amount that I have time for. Would I like to do more? Yeah, but time doesn't always play on that side. Between their schedules and my schedule and my work schedule it doesn't always permit. But I see what I want to see, so that's OK.

CL: What else have you had a chance to see, Sarah?

Sarah: I remember we saw *Oliver*.

Sydni: And the Homer right?

Sarah: Oh, yeah. That's right. We saw *MacHomer*. Homer and Shakespeare, I think. We saw those through Free Night of Theater. I think it's a great opportunity. I think one time we went and looked and there wasn't anything datewise that worked, but I know we went and saw *Oliver* together, but that's about what I remember.

Sydni: Yep.

Sarah: When I look at the list, I try to look for things that work datewise and then try to find something that I think that they'd be interested in, in the area of which that makes it convenient to go to. So you have to narrow it down.

Sydni: Yep.

CL: You know, it's really impressive, with kids, to still hear that you go to as much theatre as you do. Are you prioritizing theatre over other things, or is it really you just keep thinking about it and when you've got a slot that's when—

Sarah: Yes, exactly. Yeah. Or if people are in town and they want to go or whatever we try to make it work. Around here, there's lots. There's the Education Fund of Orinda and that pays for all the theatre. Everybody in the schools makes a donation to the schools for the arts so there is that opportunity in the schools to be able to do it and that opens up quite a few doors for them to go see plays, as well.

CL: Sydni, I think I know what you're going to say when I ask you this question. Let's see if I'm right. I want you to close your eyes and to think about the coolest theatre experience you've ever had. You got it in your head?

Sydni: Mmhmm.

CL: Can you tell me about that theatre experience? Where it was and who was with you and what the show was and why it was so neat?

Sydni: It was *Wicked* and I got to go with my friend from Belgium because he was a friend. I got to sit with him even though I don't see him often because he lives in Belgium, so I thought that was one of my best...

Sarah: Theater experiences?

Sydni: Yeah.

CL: Why was that *Wicked* so much better that time than the other seven times you saw it?

Sydni: Well, because I was with my friend from Belgium.

Sarah: And he hadn't seen it.

Sydni: Yeah.

Sarah: So you were sharing your experiences with him, huh?

Sydni: Yeah.

CL: Sarah, do you have a similar experience? Something that really sticks out in your memory?

Sarah: We saw *Billy Elliott* in England and it was just such an amazing show. It was the first show I'd ever seen in London and it was just such an amazing performance and an amazing event, and they just loved it—even though at first she was fighting because she wanted to see *Wicked* and she didn't want to go see *Billy Elliott*, but once we got there and were seeing the show, the joy on their faces makes it all the worthwhile.

Then, when *Lion King* was here, we saw that. I don't know what it was about *Lion King*, but it just was...to me it was just an emotional thing. I don't know what it was. I don't know why. Of course, we've seen *Lion King* on video forever, but I just thought it was so amazing, those puppets and the way they moved. Even when we see *Aladdin* in Disneyland and they use the same kind of puppets, it's just that they do such a great job. I saw that with the girls and my mother-in-law.

CL: Sydni, can you tell me a little about what you remember from *Billy Elliott*?

Sydni: Well, I remember the song... I think right before intermission, there was amazing choreography. He was doing flips off a wall and there was just great choreography and I thought that was like...

Sarah: And the kids dancing, huh? The kids were amazing dancers, weren't they?

Sydni: Yeah.

CL: Sarah, you touched on it a little bit, but what do you find meaningful about going to see theatre, as opposed to taking them to see a movie?

Sarah: I think it's the live performance. It's there, it's now, versus a movie where they can refilm it over and over and over again, but this is real and almost reach-out-and-touch and almost be part of it by being in the theatre. Like I said, it just helps them escape the day-to-day and relax and enjoy. The same thing with a movie, but I think that it just seems a whole different experience. You have to go to the city and all that.

CL: When you go to see a show, do you arrange dinner beforehand?

Sarah: No, no. We just go. We just go. Yeah. It's already complicated. Sometimes. We went to *Shrek* and we had to pick up the tickets at willcall, so we were there early enough and we went out for a little dinner, but we don't have a big fancy dinner or anything.

CL: Sydni, do you like going to movies?

Sydni: Yeah.

CL: Yeah? Do you like going to theatre?

Sydni: Yeah.

CL: Yeah, you like going to theatre, too. Is there a difference? When you go see a theatre show, is it somehow different to you than seeing a movie?

Sydni: Yeah. Because in a movie there's special effects that they can't really do in a play and so the special effect could not be done in real life because they were tested by *Mythbusters*.

CL: So seeing something on stage that doesn't have the special effects is different?

Sydni: Yeah.

CL: Why is it different?

Sydni: Well it's because they, if there was a fire scene, they couldn't really do the fire. They would just do lights.

Sarah: Because otherwise they'd burn the theatre down.

Sydni: Yeah.

CL: When they just do the lights and you have to imagine the fire, that's different?

Sydni: Yeah.

CL: Do you like that?

Sydni: Yeah, yeah. It's OK.

Sarah: But you can do it? You can imagine it?

Sydni: Yeah.

CL: Sydni, have you ever gone to see a theatre show where someone in the play has made you think about something that you hadn't really thought about before? Like something new, where you'd learned something new in a show?

Sydni: I don't think so.

CL: In *Wicked* for example, do you like Elphaba or do you like Galinda better?

Sydni: I like them both the same.

CL: You like them both the same. That's very diplomatic.

Sarah: We're very diplomatic. Yeah.

CL: When you first saw Elphaba, you saw her with her green skin, what did you think?

Sydni: It's cool how she gets green skin.

CL: Sarah, when you were a kid is there a show from when you were younger, not necessarily theatre but some sort of art experience from when you were younger that you remember really clearly?

Sarah: No, not really, no I don't. I enjoyed it. I enjoyed going, but... I mean I remember seeing *Fiddler on the Roof* with... Who was the original Fiddler? Zero Mostel. I remember my parents, like, said, "We have to see it with him," and I'm like, "Who is he?" You're a kid. So for seeing someone like that I didn't know how great he was at that time. Like she knows—Sydni, who were the witches in *Wicked*?

Sydni: Idina Menzel and Kristen Chenoweth.

Sarah: See? She knows all about them, right? Very different from me.

CL: What do you hope when Sydni grows up, what do you hope that she's getting out of all of the theatre that she goes to?

Sarah: Just a worldly view, ability to think outside the box, and just to be able to do whatever she wants to do and just feel that this can always be a part of her life. The fact that she's part of theatre is always an opportunity for her to be always part of theatre. So, I like that.

CL: Before you go in to see a show, do you know about the show you're going to see, Sydni?

Sydni: If it's one I've seen before I know, but if it's one I haven't, I don't know.

CL: Are you excited whenever you go to see a show?

Sydni: Yeah.

CL: Do you have expectations going in to see a show? Like do you have specific types of theatre that you like to see, Sarah?

Sarah: I like more of the musicals and comedy musicals and like *Beach Blanket Babylon*, that kind of thing that's fun and contemporary. I also like more musicals. Plays I like, but I like to know what they're about first so it's a little easier for me to follow. And the musicals, they make you happy. In the moment.

CL: Sydni, can you talk to me about your sister? Do you and your sister have a good relationship?

Sydni: No.

CL: No. You're at that age, aren't you?

Sydni: Yeah.

Sarah: She's the pesky little sister.

CL: Do you guys go to theatre? You go as a family, right?

Sydni: Sometimes.

CL: Does she like theatre as much as you do?

Sydni: No.

CL: What does she like to do?

Sydni: Text.

Sarah: She plays soccer. She's very different, very social. Sydni's more shy.

CL: Sydni, you like the arts, right?

Sydni: Yeah.

CL: You like doing art and being an artist. Sarah, did you expect that Sydni would end up doing theatre as well as seeing theatre or was that kind of a surprise?

Sarah: In 5th grade, she worked on the tech crew and just had interest in being part of it. She's not on any team sport, so this is her way of being part of a team, and I think that it helps her be part of something and cooperate with people. I think it's a very good thing. Is it a surprise? No. But I'm glad. Very, very glad.

CL: Sydni, what do you want to be when you grow up?

Sydni: I want to work at Disneyland.

CL: And do what?

Sydni: Be a cast member.

CL: Do you have a particular cast member that you want to be?

Sydni: Not really.

CL: Do you like the princesses or is it more like the cartoon characters?

Sydni: I don't really want to be that, but I just want to be a ride operator or something.

CL: When you go with your family to see shows, do you have fun?

Sydni: Yeah.

CL: Is it a special night out for you?

Sydni: Mmhmm.

CL: Can you tell me a little bit about why it's special?

Sydni: I don't really know why, but it's fun to see a new play or whatever I see. I enjoy it.

CL: Do you talk about it with your parents afterwards?

Sydni: If it's one of those plays I don't get, I just talk to them about that. But if it's one I did get, I just say the parts I liked.

CL: Sarah, would you say that you are passionate about the arts?

Sarah: I appreciate what they are and why they're there. I really do. And I find that very important, but am I passionate? No, I'm not passionate, but like I said, I do appreciate the fact that it's very important in the world. It opens your mind to other things that are out there versus just being in your own little cocoon. I think without the artistic outlets, Sydni wouldn't have an outlet for herself, as far as the drawing is concerned, to express herself. Like I said, she's shy, so having the opportunity to be able to draw really does help express who she is and be who she is. So I think it would be a very sad world for her. I mean there's so many people who need those outlets, like in schools and such, but they don't have the funding for it so they don't get to do it. So those kids are labeled as dumb or whatever, but really their strengths are just somewhere else.

CL: Sydni, do you think that as you get older you'll still go to the theatre?

Sydni: Yeah.

CL: Do you think you'll still do theatre, too?

Sydni: Yeah. It's fun doing the spotlight because... It's just fun because you get to be behind the scenes and...

Sarah: And you get to be part of a team, huh?

Sydni: Yeah.

Sarah: Part of something, right?

Sydni: Yeah. Part of something.

Sean McKenna

My name's Sean McKenna. I was actually involved in theatre for an early part of my life, close to a third of my life, I was involved in the theatre. I started going to theatre when I was a young kid. My dad was the head of the drama department at San Francisco State back in the forties and fifties. He did a lot of theatre events, centennial productions of pageants and things like that. So I used to go see shows there some, and he also cast me as Wally in *Our Town*.

When I was in first grade or so my dad was directing *Twelfth Night*. He took the whole cast down to what's now called Montalvo, on a Saturday, and he brought me with him, and I watched them rehearse the show all day. I was so caught up in this process; I was so caught up in the rehearsal. I'm watching these people transform themselves from people I would chat with—and they were nice to me, obviously, I was the head of the department's kid—but, nonetheless, they'd come over and we'd chat. And they'd go up on stage and transform themselves into these other characters. That was just mind blowing to me at the time; I'm just a first grader. And part of it probably was that these college kids were paying attention to me. All these people, to me as a first grader, were like really older people, and they were paying attention to me.

I was telling my first grade teacher about it and she got interested in how excited I was about the show. And things evolved to the point where we put on our own little version of *Twelfth Night* in first grade. I'm not quite sure why she facilitated this activity, but somehow she did. And so the production happened in the first grade classroom and the parents came. About half the kids were involved in the show. The other half were in the audience, and then all these parents would come.

It was more of a high-level summary of the play, of course. We kind of took a plot summary and animated it a little bit and used mostly our own dialog. And the thing I remember the most from the production was that I was playing Sebastian, and in the fourth act or so, there's a sword fight with Sir Andrew Aguecheek—I think that's what happens—and we were using these swords that were actually early stands for lights from a photographer's studio. So, they were about the right length when they were collapsed, but then they had this thing on them that you could loosen and they would become long.

So, we were banging away with these things during the production and mine somehow got loose and, with each bang, it would get a little longer.

And the little girl playing Viola, who is supposed to come on and interrupt the fight, is in the wings, looking, watching the sword get longer and longer. And I started going, "Come on. You've got to come in. You've got to come in." Finally she came in and, anyway, it was kind of a...it was a moment for me. It was kind of embarrassing, but I remember it really well.

I got so much attention for doing that show. And it was such an unusual thing to happen. I mean, Shakespeare in the first grade? Come on.

I followed in my dad's footsteps and got a degree from San Francisco State in theatre and then began teaching and producing. And then, I got involved in computer programming. I became a designer and coder. And I really loved that. It was a part of my brain that hadn't been engaged as much, and I found it was refreshing not to have to deal with people. Because theatre, as you probably are aware, is a very volatile incubator of emotion and person-to-person interchange and stuff. Which I was pretty good at, but it was so refreshing to just be in my little space and controlling everything. So I did that the remainder of my life so far. I computer program, independent at first, and then I worked for a company downtown for a long time. And now I'm semiretired, I still have a little company where I do all the design and coding, but it's very minimal effort. And I think of myself, essentially now, as retired. I'm kind of at a stage where I have to be a little less active for different reasons. And the last year and a half have been pretty sedate, really. But my theatre attendance hasn't diminished at all. Still go a lot.

I think of myself as a computer programmer with a strong arts background. I like going to museums: paintings, historical museums. Music, not so much, dance, not so much. Things outside of the arts, not too much. I read a lot. I used to do some gardening, but now I have people to kind of do most of that. I used to play Bocce. I can't really do that anymore. My hands aren't working the way they should. Hopefully, that is going to improve but we'll see.

Believe it or not, computer programming is a fairly rewarding creative process if you have the right situation, meaning that you are doing something you want to do that you think is interesting or exciting and that it will help people. You put a program together and then you see it used. See people actually using it to run their business or improve their situation in some way. It's a very exciting thing. I know that is hard to believe, but you're making something out of thin air. I mean, there are the people and there's the support staff, but essentially the thing you're creating doesn't exist until you start working on it and bringing it to fruition. In computer programming, you've got an idea for something or someone has expressed a desire to have something that does this for them, that does that for them. So you think about it, and you prepare—like you do in the theatre. There's a preparation process. You don't just sit down and start typing away. Then you bring the pieces together and you polish them. You make it work, and it comes to life.

I just kind of stumbled into it, wanting to create programs to help us run the lighting which is, of course, common now. But in the late 60's, that was not common. I got so involved in the programming then I continued in that bent, and I kind of had a dual career for about four or five years. Then eventually I just let the theatre stuff go because I was involved in the programming business.

Our company has software that runs, as they say now, "in the cloud." We're in the cloud. Most of our customers are in the medical field, and it lets them coordinate their resources around equipment and people. A certain hospital needs something, and it gets rid of all the phone tag, the white board scheduling, and all that for them and lets them essentially run their business. It sounds kind of dry, and it sort of is, but some of the things that I've helped create for them are pretty exciting in that context, although it doesn't have the power to move me or the people that are using it the way a theatre piece might. That's my work, but what I love is going to the theatre. I mean the great moments of my life, when I think back on it, have almost always been in a theatre.

Just living day-to-day is not very rewarding. You know: eating, sleeping, walking the dog. They're all very nice and they're soothing. In my mind, in my experience, unless you're involved in doing something that engages you on an emotional, intellectual, and let's say on a creative level, life isn't very interesting. You could read books, but after a while you want to do something yourself. When you go to the theatre, that's the difference. When you go to the theatre, you are involved in creating something in a way that isn't true of most anything else.

You know how exciting it is to be involved in this of-the-moment thing that just disappears when it's gone but leaves an indelible—well, maybe not indelible…certainly not indelible all the time—an occasionally indelible memory that you can think back on.

And you have to engage with other people, at least every once in a while. I mean, Bocce ball, for example, is a kind of sport where that's a lot about chatting and interacting with other people. And just a little bit about the, you know, game. So, there's that. Because if you aren't engaged with other people you're not really living a life, in my opinion. To be isolated and unengaged and uninvolved. That's why I got into theatre to begin with, I think. When I was in high school, I acted a lot. I went to a Catholic boy's high school in San Francisco, and there were a lot of Catholic girl's high schools who needed male actors to do the shows that they picked. So, in a way, it was a great way to meet girls. But in another way it was an interesting experience to be wanted to be an actor.

I was never into sports particularly. I wasn't very social. I wouldn't say I was an outcast exactly, but I certainly wasn't one of the "in group" in high school or earlier. But in the theatre, I was definitely part of a group. And a group that was extremely tight.

Like we had a reunion of a college where I taught for a number of years recently. And most of the people that came to the reunion were involved in theatre. Not all, but, they were predominately the theatre people who were so excited to get back in touch with their friends and catch up with people that they'd lost track of. I set up a website for the reunion, and people would...some of the comments were interesting, especially post the event, where people said things like, "Well, mainly it was the theatre people who were there."

And I was like, "That makes sense."

When I was teaching, I used to go around and try to see everything. Not necessarily every professional production. But the more innovative and educational things. I'd go to a lot of those. Not so much now, but it used to be I felt like I could get anything out of any theatre performance. I didn't care if it was bad or amateurish or whatever. There was something about what was going on that I found very, very interesting, no matter what.

Now, I'm a little more apt to search out things that have a level of polish and professionalism and so forth. When I was teaching it was really hard to afford going. Especially raising a couple of kids and living in San Francisco at first, then moving here. It was kind of hard to afford to go to a lot of professional theatre. Now I can. And I do.

We get to something like 35 shows a year, something like that, in town, maybe every other week. Or some weeks, like this last weekend, we'll go to two things.

I go to some things with one of my daughters, typically the older one, but mostly I go with my wife. Often, I'd say about half the time, we have another couple that we'll attend with. Sometimes I'll go just by myself. That's pretty rare. Or I'll hook up with a friend in San Francisco who's also interested in the theatre.

We subscribe to Berkeley Rep and Aurora and Shotgun Players. So we see all of those. So, that's I'm not sure how much that would be. That's maybe seven plus five plus five. So, that's about 17. We see things at Cal Performances, ACT, the Magic, SF Playhouse. Once in a while we'll get down to TheatreWorks, but that's a little bit of a trek. San Jose Rep once in a while, too, and we go up to Ashland every year and see most of what they have to offer.

And when we go places, we'll often go to the theatre. We're going to Stockholm later this summer, and while we're there we're going to get to see the Drottningholm Court Theater. It's the oldest continuously operating theatre in the world. And they're going to do Mozart's version of the Don Juan story, *Don Giovanni*. We went to see *Blood Wedding* at the Colonial Theater in Guanajuato, stuff like that. Those are really special.

A lot of productions have really been moving to me. And the way I can tell that it's a moving production, usually occurs near the end, when something happens that just creates...it's kind of like there's a connection between an abstract view of the world and the immediacy of that physical situation. It just kind of makes a tingle run through your whole body as suddenly these strings come together at this moment. It doesn't happen always. It doesn't happen often even, I would have to say. But it happens often enough that I know it's going to happen again. I'm going to see something that makes that connection, makes that moment that just thrills you.

Now, every time you go to the theatre, it's pretty involving and engaging on a personal level, but it's only occasionally that this kind of thing happens.

There was this production that William Ball did in New York in the 60's. He had this little theatre on Second or so, on the third floor of a hotel building, I think. In the round, and he did a production of *Six Characters in Search of an Author*.

And towards the end of the play, there's this denouement, around the child drowning in the fountain. I was alone for this production, and this moment towards the end of the play, this drowning came out in a kind of a pantomime show. And I knew the play; it's not like I was surprised by the plot, what was happening. But I was blown away by the way it was presented and the overwhelming emotional experience of this coming together at the end of the play.

I'll just never forget that.

Every time you get that feeling, I assume, without any empirical evidence to back it up, that everyone else in the audience is feeling that same thing at the same moment. And usually that's validated by the response at the end of the show, where people really get excited.

At the end of a show you always clap and give an acknowledgment to the cast and so forth. But some shows people just go nuts after. Everybody stands up almost spontaneously. It's not like you look around and think to yourself, "Oh, everybody else is...," like at Ashland—what a friend of mine calls the "Obligatory Standing O." I'm talking about the kind of standing up where everybody just gets up spontaneously at the same time—it's hard to really describe specifically what that is. A lot of emotional connection in those moments. That's what good theatre's about.

The most important, the most meaningful thing about live theatre for me is that it is live. I like movies, sure, but even a movie that really is moving—and there are some that are—you still don't have that sense of visceral connection with what's going on the way you do with live theatre. It's something about being engaged with people even though you don't know these people necessarily who are on the stage. It's a spark of connection that you don't get in film or see in painting. You learn a lot looking at those things and it's a whole different kind of involvement. And I love paintings. I can sit in front of a painting for a long time and get a lot out of it on a lot of different levels. I love movies pretty well, too. And I've had experiences with paintings and movies that have moved me similarly to the way real live theatre does. Similarly, but never as intensely.

But in the theatre…there's audience around you. In a movie or museum, you're really alone.

I'm a big baseball fan; I love baseball. And theatre's like that. You don't know exactly what's going to happen because it's live. I mean sure, it's going to follow the script and the characters but it also varies. It varies night to night, how different things can be, and there are little things that shift that add up to make a huge difference between, say Friday night and Saturday night.

The situation changes minute by minute. The pitch count. How many balls. How many strikes. As that progresses, it changes the situation. There are men on base. Where are the outfielders playing in relationship to the capability of the hitter? All of these things come together, these different pieces, all at once. You don't know what's going to happen. And unlike other sports, for me, baseball engages me intellectually as well as emotionally. I have a stake in the outcome of the game.

And what it really is about, for me, is the way that moment-to-moment thing happens. Something happens, and something else happens, and something else happens. The moments build on each other, and then suddenly there's a moment that's very exciting out of something that wasn't exciting, and you're surprised.

With theatre, one thing happens. Another thing happens. It builds, it builds, it builds. You're not quite sure where it's going to go, and then suddenly something explosive happens.

When somebody hits a home run at a baseball park—you don't say," Oh, I guess I should get up, everybody else is getting up." Everybody just *gets up*, because it's so exciting. You're so involved. You've been waiting for something to happen and then *bam* it happens and you connect with it.

That's the way it felt to me at *Six Characters*. It was a small audience, but the enthusiasm and the response to it was like there was a large crowd. We were all there together, on our feet.

Without theatre, life would be kind of bleak, really. You'd kind of be on a—what suddenly came to mind was *Waiting for Godot*. You'd be out on that barren land with this dying tree, waiting for something to happen, and nothing's happening. Not to say that my family and my friends and stuff aren't important, but so much of those relationships have always involved shared art experiences, that it seems like it's part and parcel of it all.

During the Cold War, and even way earlier during the Stalinist era that preceded it, the arts in those Eastern Bloc countries were pretty severely constrained. Necessity to adhere to the party line and whatnot. But they didn't go away. The impulse to do art never went away. And in fact, before the thaw, there was this active effort to resist this draining, this destruction of what's vital about our existence on the earth, and they made art under the radar, despite the consequences.

So maybe the idea of a world without arts, maybe it just couldn't happen. Maybe it's not even a possibility. I mean, how far back in our history, prehistory, really, do we have to go to find a world without art? I don't think we've found one yet.

It's so important for people to connect with one another. You have to be taken out of the isolation of your point of view about the world. You have to experience other worlds, other people's experiences of life. And there are lots of ways for people to connect with one another, but when you get 100, 500, 700 people together and have them experiencing something together, that's a connection. Theater does that better than any art form. And that's a real important thing for people.

This country right now is going through this kind of isolationist, weird thing where we're disconnecting from our ability to relate positively and empathize. Empathize, that might be the word, with other people. One of my sisters is one of those isolated kind of people. I wish I could just kind of shake her, go "What are you doing? What are you thinking about?" I don't understand how that happens or why that's happening, but I do believe that art can ameliorate that tendency to a great extent, and put people in touch with things that might not have occurred to them, and can possibly change their lives. We were talking earlier about experiences that change your life. I would think that that might be a possibility, with theatre. And that's an amazing thing.

We all need to be taken out of ourselves sometimes. Because, you know, you live in yourself, really, except when you're engaged in something that takes you out of yourself. Like with baseball: time just kind of goes by when you're at the park, and you're not thinking about yourself.

For me, theatre really takes me out of myself the whole time the show's going on. You inhabit the world of these people, and you get involved with what *they* want, and away from what *you* want. And then some moment comes in the show, towards the end, when suddenly you realize that the reason you've been so involved in this production is because what they want is really what you want. And this moment happens where it all comes together.

There's this connection between you and them and some kind of…higher order of things, you know? And it all kind of comes together at that moment and just kind of explodes all around you, surrounds you, and you're not alone.

5 GLOSSARY

This glossary is not meant to be comprehensive. It's more the starting point of a larger and longer conversation about the terms we use, the meanings we give them and how we, as a field, can standardize our language about the true impact of art.

ACTIVE ARTS PARTICIPATION – This term most often means arts participation in which the participant is creating or performing. With the advent of intrinsic impact research, we may ultimately be able to also indicate the level to which presentational art creates an active arts participation experience on an intellectual and emotional level.

AESTHETIC ENRICHMENT – "The extent to which the audience member was exposed to a new style or type of art or a new artist (aesthetic growth), and also the extent to which the experience served to validate and celebrate art that is familiar (aesthetic validation)." Term coined by the research team at WolfBrown, more information available at www.intrinsicimpact.org.

ANTICIPATED MEMORIES – A phrase coined by Nobel laureate and behavioral researcher to describe the driving force behind future decision-making—we move through life making decisions about possible experiences based on previous memories of similar experiences. Arts organizations are, in a way, in the business of creating good memories in the hope that it will lead to repeated behavior.

ANTICIPATION – A construct of Readiness to Receive. An audience member's psychological state prior to the experience, especially the degree to which they are looking forward to the event. Term coined by the research team at WolfBrown, more information available at www.intrinsicimpact.org.

ARC OF INVOLVEMENT – The lifelong path that a patron has in terms of an art form, artist or producing organization—as a patron moves along the arc of involvement, their level of familiarity rises, which in turn increases their rates of anticipation for and captivation in the art. See also "Captivation" and "Artistic Lifecycle."

ARTISTIC LIFECYCLE - A series of artistic events over the course of a person's life that shape who that person is. See also "Making of Meaning, The" and "Wayfinding."

AUDIENCE DESIGN - filling out, shaping out, "finishing" the audience as an artistic gesture of the show. Saying, " Who is going to make the conversation that the play tees up more meaningful by their presence in the theatre?" Via Woolly Mammoth Theatre Company.

AUDIENCE FEEDBACK LOOP – a method of audience engagement in which staff is checking actual audience impact against the assumptions they made about what a particular piece of work would do. By engaging audiences in this way, a company can also enrich the audience's experience and make the memory of that experience stickier.

BLENDING – The ability to integrate disparate concepts. From the book *The Social Animal* by David Brooks (quote from TED Talk by Brooks).

CAPTIVATION – "The extent to which the audience member was absorbed in the performance or exhibition; captivation is the linchpin of impact – if you are captivated, other impacts are likely to happen, whereas if you are not captivated (or, worse, if you snooze through the program), other impacts are less likely to happen." Term coined by the research team at WolfBrown, more information available at www.intrinsicimpact.org. See also "Flow" and "Limerance."

CONNECTIVITY – Used by the staff at Woolly Mammoth Theatre Company to mean the amount that each artistic production is allowing people to connect from a personal place into conversations that sparked by the work and are happening in the community. The director of connectivity's job is to ensure that the right people are part of the audience to engender the conversation and activation each show is meant to engender.

CONTEXT – A construct of Readiness to Receive. The overall level of preparedness an audience member has for the experience, including prior knowledge of the art form and familiarity with the specific work(s) to be presented. Term coined by the research team at WolfBrown, more information available at www.intrinsicimpact.org.

CREATIVE DESTRUCTION – A term that emerged out of Marxist economic theory, used in this context to mean taking an active role in deciding which arts organizations will continue to produce work if/when the sector becomes too large to support itself, as opposed to letting other bodies (governments, foundations, populations, etc) do it for us. Used by Diane Ragsdale in her

450

writing on her ArtsJournal blog Jumper.

EMOTIONAL RESONANCE – "The extent to which the audience member experienced a heightened emotional state during or after the performance or exhibition." Term coined by the research team at WolfBrown, more information available at www.intrinsicimpact.org. See also "Empathy" and "Sympathy."

EMPATHY – The ability to experience events from another point of view.

EQUIPOISE - "The ability to have the serenity to read the biases and failures in your own mind." "Epistemological modesty." From the book *The Social Animal* by David Brooks (quote from TED Talk by Brooks).

EXPERIENCING SELF - A phrase coined by Nobel laureate and behavioral researcher Daniel Kahneman, in contrast to "Remembering Self." The experiencing self lives in the present and knows the present. It knows the past, but basically has only the present. The experiencing self is who the doctor approaches when he asks, "Does it hurt now when I touch you here?"

EXPLOSIVE ENGAGEMENT – A term from Woolly Mammoth Theatre Company's mission statement that is used to describe the dual efforts to engage communities in conversation while also challenging them to explore their boundaries through art.

FIRST-TIME ARTIST – Term used at Cornerstone Theatre Company to refer to the community participants that almost always play roles in their productions. As in "when working with a cast composed of a mixture of professional and first-time artists, it's important to…" This phrase serves to remind professionals that our craft is not an impenetrable mystery, but rather something that can be shared and taught.

FLOW – "The mental state of operation in which a person in an activity is fully immersed in a feeling of energized focus, full involvement, and success in the process of the activity. Proposed by Mihály Csíkszentmihályi." From Wikipedia. This concepts hews closely to WolfBrown's intrinsic impact construct "Captivation." See also "Limerance."

HAPPINESS – The level of satisfaction one has with one's life. Researcher George McKerron has found that artistic experiences make up four of the top six most happiness-inducing activities (behind sex and exercise). See also

"Social Bridging/Bonding," "Pleasure," and "Transformation."

INTELLECTUAL STIMULATION – "The degree to which the performance or exhibition triggered thinking about the art, issues or topics, or caused critical reflection." Term coined by the research team at WolfBrown, more information available at www.intrinsicimpact.org. See also "Blending."

INTRINSIC IMPACT - the core benefits that can accrue to individuals by virtue of experiencing an exhibition or live arts performance. There are five constructs of intrinsic impact: captivation, intellectual stimulation, emotional resonance, aesthetic enrichment and social bridging/bonding. This term was first used prolifically in *Gifts of the Muse*, a research report published by the RAND Corporation. It was subsequently refined by the research team at WolfBrown.

LEVITATING EFFECT, THE – A term used by Roadside Theater that they equate to being "in the zone." See also "Captivation," "Flow," and "Limerance."

LIMERANCE - A drive and a motivation to find those "moments of transcendence when the skull line disappears and we are lost in a challenge or a task." From the book *The Social Animal* by David Brooks (quote from TED Talk by Brooks). The original term was coined in 1977 by the psychologist Dorothy Tennov to mean an involuntary state of mind resulting from a strong attraction to another person. As Brooks uses the term, limerance sits very close to Alan Brown's term "Captivation," which is in turn very close to the term "Flow."

MAKING OF MEANING, THE – The ability of an artistic experience or series of artistic experiences to provide a frame of understanding around the chaos of life.

MINDSIGHT - "The ability to enter into other people's minds and learn what they have to offer." From the book *The Social Animal* by David Brooks (quote from TED Talk by Brooks). See also "Empathy."

MIRROR NEURONS/MIRRORING - Mirror neurons are a type of neuron primarily found in the ventral premotor area and intraparietal area of the primate brain, with possible existence in other areas. They fire both when a specific action is performed and when a person observes the same action performed by another —a process called mirroring. It is unclear whether the link demonstrated between action, perception, production and comprehension (i.e. a play and audience) is true, but recent research seems to indicate it might be.

MISSION FULFILLMENT – On a basic level, this means fulfilling the letter and spirit of an organization's mission statement. More abstractly, it means matching impact goals for each produced piece of art to actual audience outcomes. Mission fulfillment assessment is impact assessment.

MYTH – In the context of artistic impact, the ordering impulse in human existence—the stories we tell ourselves to make sense of the world. With the ascendance of science and rationalism, true "myth" has been supplanted by art, and is necessary to provide voice to the parts of the human experience that are harder (though not impossible) to quantify. This idea of myth was espoused by Karen Armstrong in her book *A Short History of Myth*.

PLEASURE – One of two primary drivers of artistic experiences—the engendering of pleasant feelings (either of accomplishment or joy or social connectedness, etc). As discussed in *Gifts of the Muse*.

RADICAL HOSPITALITY – Mixed Blood Theatre's effort to remove the financial barrier for attending theatre by allowing their patrons to attend every show for free. This effort goes hand-in-hand with Mixed Blood's mission to identify particular segments (often non-traditional theatregoing segments) of the community as the target population for each show.

READINESS TO RECEIVE – the preparedness of an individual audience member to be open to an artistic experience. Readiness to Receive has three constructs: Context, Relevance and Anticipation. A high Readiness to Receive is crucial to a high intrinsic impact score for an individual. Term coined by Alan Brown of WolfBrown, more information available at www.intrinsicimpact.org.

RELEVANCE – A construct of Readiness to Receive. The extent to which the arts activity in question is relevant to the participant; primarily to identify individuals who do not normally attend the arts (not investigated in this study, but included here for definitional purposes). Term coined by the research team at WolfBrown, more information available at www.intrinsicimpact.org.

REMEMBERING SELF - A phrase coined by Nobel laureate and behavioral researcher Daniel Kahneman, in contrast to "Experiencing Self." The remembering self is the one that keeps score and maintains the story of our life, and it's the one that the doctor approaches in asking the question, "How have you been feeling lately?" The remembering self is a storyteller and drives decision making.

SOCIAL BRIDGING/BONDING – "Connectedness with the rest of the audience, new insight on one's own culture or a culture outside of one's life experience, or new perspective on human relationships or social issues." Term coined by the research team at WolfBrown, more information available at www.intrinsicimpact.org.

STORY – A delineated portion of the total life narrative of an individual, which can often be crystallized during an arts experience.

SUBLIME – A greatness that can't be entirely captured by calculation or measurement. Something that puts us in touch with the awe that is our natural condition, what Abraham Joshua Heschel calls "radical amazement."

SUMMATIVE IMPACT – The overall intrinsic impact of a piece of art on an individual, characterized most closely by the likelihood that the experience will be memorable for a long period of time. Coined by the research team at WolfBrown. For more information, visit www.intrinsicimpact.org.

SYMPATHY - "The ability to work within groups." From the book *The Social Animal* by David Brooks (quote from TED Talk by Brooks). Or, from Wikipedia, "a social affinity in which one person stands with another person, closely understanding his or her feelings." See also "Empathy."

TRANSFORMATION – The core impact of art—the ability of a piece of art to fundamentally change an individual intellectually, emotionally or empathetically.

WAYFINDING – the science of using signage and directional indicators to help people navigate through a space. In the context of artistic impact, this term is used to describe the ability of a piece of art to crystallize decisions and alternatives, and to give glimpses into possible future paths.

Biographies of Contributing Authors

ALAN BROWN is a leading researcher and management consultant in the nonprofit arts industry. His work focuses on understanding consumer demand for cultural experiences and helping cultural institutions, foundations and agencies see new opportunities, make informed decisions and respond to changing conditions. His studies have introduced new vocabulary to the lexicon of cultural participation and propelled the field towards a clearer view of the rapidly changing cultural landscape. Alan serves in a volunteer capacity on the Research Advisory Council of the League of American Orchestras, and has served on the organizing committee of the National Arts Marketing Project annual conference since its inception. He speaks frequently at conferences in the U.S. and Canada, as well as the U.K., Australia and New Zealand. Prior to his consulting career, Alan served for five years as Executive Director of the Ann Arbor Summer Festival, where he presented Ella Fitzgerald, Sarah Vaughn and many other artists. He holds three degrees from the University of Michigan: a Master of Business Administration, a Master of Music in Arts Administration and a Bachelor of Musical Arts in vocal performance. Alan makes his home in San Francisco with a yellow Labrador Retriever named Golden Brown.

ARLENE GOLDBARD is a writer, speaker, consultant and cultural activist whose focus is the intersection of culture, politics and spirituality. Her blog and other writings may be downloaded from her Web site: www.arlenegoldbard. com. She was born in New York and grew up near San Francisco. Her most recent book, *New Creative Community: The Art of Cultural Development* was published by New Village Press in November 2006. She is also co-author of *Community, Culture and Globalization*, an international anthology published by the Rockefeller Foundation, *Crossroads: Reflections on the Politics of Culture*, and author of *Clarity*, a novel. Her essays have been published in *In Motion Magazine*, *Art in America*, *Theatre*, *Tikkun*, and many other journals. She has addressed many academic and community audiences in the U.S. and Europe, on topics ranging from the ethics of community arts practice to the development of integral organizations. She has provided advice and counsel to hundreds of community-based organizations, independent media groups, and public and private funders and policymakers including the Rockefeller Foundation, the Independent Television Service, Appalshop and dozens of others. She is currently writing a new book on art's public purpose. She serves as President of the Board of Directors of The Shalom Center.

REBECCA NOVICK is a theater director and arts consultant based in the San Francisco Bay Area. She is currently the director of the Triangle Lab, a

457

collaboration between Intersection for the Arts and the California Shakespeare Theater to change who participates in theater-making and how they participate. She recently served as the interim program officer for the arts at The San Francisco Foundation and the Bay Area project coordinator for the Wallace Foundation's cultural participation initiative. Rebecca was the founder of Crowded Fire Theater Company and served as its artistic director for ten years, growing the company from an all-volunteer group to one of San Francisco's most respected small theaters. She has directed and developed new plays for many theaters in the Bay Area and elsewhere and her directing work has been recognized with numerous awards including the Goldie for outstanding local artists. She has also held a number of arts management positions, most recently serving for five years as the director of development and strategic initiatives at Theatre Bay Area. Her writing on the arts sector has recently been seen in print in *20under40: Reinventing the Arts and Arts Education for the 21st Century*, the *GIA Reader*, and *Theatre Bay Area* magazine and online in various blogs. She holds a B.A. from the University of Michigan in Theater and Anthropology.

CLAYTON LORD is the director of communications & audience development at Theatre Bay Area, one of the country's largest regional arts service organizations, which is devoted to uniting, strengthening, promoting and advancing the theatre community of the San Francisco Bay Area. At Theatre Bay Area, he oversees communications, marketing, audience development, research and advertising. He is the project director for *Measuring the Intrinsic Impact of Live Theatre*, the national intrinsic impact study, and also runs Free Night of Theater, the Bay Area Arts & Culture Census and the Leveraging Social Media program with Beth Kanter. Along with in-house research, Theatre Bay Area's research program has commissioned work from Target Resource Group, Enertex Marketing and WolfBrown, among others. Clay was a founding member of Project Audience and currently sits on the conference planning committees for the National Arts Marketing Project and the Association of Performing Arts Service Organizations. He writes for *Theatre Bay Area* magazine and theatrebayarea.org, has contributed to *American Theatre*, *Stage Directions*, *InDance*, *ArtsJournal.com*, *ARTSblog, Art Works* and *ArtsMarketing.org*, and has presented at the TCG, NAMP, and APASO conferences, among others. He holds a B.A. from Georgetown University in English and Psychology. You can read his blog, *New Beans*, on new art for new audiences, at ArtsJournal.com and follow him on Twitter @claytonlord.

DIANE RAGSDALE is currently working at Erasmus University in Rotterdam (the Netherlands), where she is lecturing in the cultural economics program and pursuing a PhD. Her research concerns the impact of social and economic forces on US nonprofit resident theaters since the early 80's. For the six years prior to moving to Europe, Diane worked in the Performing Arts program at

The Andrew W. Mellon Foundation and had primary responsibility for theater and dance grants. Before joining the Foundation, Diane served as managing director of On the Boards, a contemporary performing arts center in Seattle, and as executive director of a destination music festival in a resort town in Idaho. Prior work also includes stints at several film and arts festivals and as a theater practitioner. She is a frequent panelist, provocateur or keynote speaker at arts conferences within and outside of the US. You can read her blog, *Jumper*, on ArtsJournal.com and follow her on Twitter @DERagsdale.

REBECCA RATZKIN joined WolfBrown's San Francisco office in 2008, bringing her unique outlook on arts and culture as it relates to economic and community development. Her interests and skills focus on bridging theory with practical and achievable solutions and seeing opportunity in the midst of the deepest challenges. With a background in arts administration and urban planning, Rebecca has applied her skills and experience to a variety of consulting projects, including feasibility studies, market research, and strategic and cultural planning. Her clients have ranged from small culturally-specific arts groups to children's museums and arts districts. She has authored several articles and papers focusing on the role of the arts in community development. Rebecca graduated with honors and Phi Beta Kappa from Oberlin College with a BA in art history, and completed a Master's degree in urban planning from UCLA School of Public Policy. She is the recipient of the Lewis Center for Regional Policy Studies Thesis Award and the California Planning Foundation Award. Rebecca has worked in various galleries and arts nonprofits, including Gemini G.E.L. in Los Angeles, and SOHO20 Chelsea in New York, and has been a member of Collage Ensemble, a Los Angeles artist collective. She also plays the clarinet, experiments in various art media, particularly photography, collage, and water color, and teaches yoga.

WOLFBROWN is a cross-disciplinary team of professional consultants with experience in fundraising, marketing, planning, research, evaluation, program design, arts education and other areas. Our consultants have had distinguished careers as practitioners prior to becoming consultants. In those roles and later in their roles as advisors they have counseled hundreds of organizations – large and small – in almost every state and in numerous countries. Their publications have had impact on a number of fields. They have developed new methodologies and bodies of work which benefit new clients. More information at www.wolfbrown.com.